Strange Talk

The publisher gratefully acknowledges the generous contribution to this book provided by The General Endowment Fund of the Associates of the University of California Press.

Strange Talk

*The Politics of Dialect Literature
in Gilded Age America*

Gavin Jones

WITHDRAWN

UNIVERSITY OF CALIFORNIA PRESS
Berkeley   Los Angeles   London

Chapter 4 contains material previously published in essay form in *Race Consciousness: African-American Studies for the New Century*, edited by Judith Jackson Fossett and Jeffrey A. Tucker. Reproduced by permission of New York University Press. Chapter 4 also contains material that appeared originally in an essay by the author, "Signifying Songs: The Double Meaning of Black Dialect in the Work of George Washington Cable," *American Literary History* vol. 9, no. 2: 244–67. Reproduced by permission of Oxford University Press.

University of California Press
Berkeley and Los Angeles, California

University of California Press, Ltd.
London, England

Library of Congress Cataloging-in-Publication Data

Jones, Gavin Roger, 1968–
    Strange talk :   the politics of dialect literature in Gilded Age
America / Gavin Jones.
        p.   cm.
    Includes bibliographical references and index.
    ISBN 0-520-21419-6.—ISBN 0-520-21421-8 (pbk.)
    1. Dialect literature, American—History and criticism.
    2. American literature—19th century—History and criticism.
    3. Politics and literature—United States—History—19th century.
    4. English language—Dialects—Political aspects—United States.
    5. Afro-Americans in literature.   6. Ethnic groups in literature.
    7. Black English in literature.   8. Regionalism in literature.
    9. Local color in literature.   10. Race in literature.   I. Title.
PS217.D53J66   1999
810.9'358—dc21   98-40628
                                                              CIP

Printed in the United States of America
9   8   7   6   5   4   3   2   1

For my mother and father

"Py dunder! te funniest ting is dese Americans don't all shpeak te language alike."

T. S. DENISON, *HANS VON SMASH: A FARCE* (1878)

CONTENTS

ACKNOWLEDGMENTS

I am grateful to the many people whose generosity helped me to write this book. *Strange Talk* began as a doctoral dissertation in the English Department of Princeton University. My advisors, Hans Aarsleff and Lee Mitchell, were crucial to its inception, and they have continued to offer advice, encouragement, and friendship. I also profited in Princeton from the wisdom and guidance of Mike Davis, Grant Farred, Judith Jackson Fossett, William Howarth, Tom Keenan, A. Walton Litz, Arnold Rampersad, Elaine Showalter, Cindy Snyder, and Susan Wolfson. Bruce Simon and Jeffrey Tucker have continued to take an active interest in my work. The comments of my readers for the University of California Press—Shelley Fisher Fishkin, Howard Horwitz, and Elsa Nettels—were important to my final revision of the manuscript. I thank fellow researchers at Harvard for their suggestions on various parts of this project: Jonathan Bobaljik, Jeffrey Dolven, Hugh McNeal, Judy Richardson, and Tamar Schapiro. I am especially indebted to Lisa Wolverton, who read the entire manuscript and gave me the benefit of her rare editorial and intellectual talents. Daniel Aaron, Paul Machlin, Wayne O'Neil, and Elaine Scarry allowed me to share in their expertise.

I will always remain grateful to my teachers Val Skinner and Nigel Smith, and to John Comerford, who fed me with American literature at an impressionable age. Paola Sica's endless advice and constant support have strengthened this book in many ways. Finally, I thank my family, especially my mother and father, who have made everything possible.

Introduction

Nothing is more striking, in fact, than the invasive part played by the element of dialect in the subject-matter of the American fiction of the day. Nothing like it, probably—nothing like any such predominance—exists in English, in French, in German works of the same order; the difference, therefore, clearly has its reasons and suggests its reflections.

HENRY JAMES, "THE NOVEL OF DIALECT" (1898)

Late-nineteenth-century America was crazy about dialect literature. Vernacular varieties of American English burst into print with such vigor that critics feared a virulent epidemic was contaminating the nation. Readers could not get enough of black dialect, Appalachian dialect, Pike County dialect, Maine dialect, New Yorkese dialect—every region was mined for its vernacular gold, and every predominant ethnic group was linguistically lampooned in popular poetry and prose. Writers undertook special missions to remote districts in an effort to learn and record the *lingua rustica*. New and often baffling systems of orthography were invented to capture spoken sounds, and authors waged battles over whose dialect was most correct. Ethnic dialect jokes began to dominate the vaudeville stage. Boston parents became anxious when their children broke out with deep southernisms at the breakfast table—evidence of a secret consumption of dialect stories late at night. A young Missouri boy named Huck Finn was banned from Concord Public Library for speaking profane dialect in a book. Mark Twain and William Dean Howells were reported to converse with their wives in a strange French-English dialect from Louisiana, learned from the writings of George Washington Cable. Reading tours by dialect humorists packed theaters and grossed tens of thousands of dollars. New literary genres developed: the dialect poem, the dialect story, the dialect novel. Dubbed "the cult of the vernacular," this new movement was judged to be the most significant literary event of its generation. Henry James felt its reverberations in England; he became concerned enough to write a letter to the magazine *Literature*, asking why this literary cult should have formed. The *Cambridge History of American Literature* (1918) repeated the question: Why was dialect "so sparingly used by American writers before the Civil War" only to become "so constituent a part of American fiction immediately after the Civil War"?[1]

Dialect literature constitutes a distinct but critically neglected movement in American letters, a movement more clearly definable than realism or naturalism and as worthy of study on its own terms. Dialect texts are easily identifiable by their techniques of representing the phonetics of unfamiliar speech. On a deeper level, dialect writing is defined by a strong thematic interest in the cultural and political issues surrounding questions of linguistic variety. To an unprecedented degree, the social and personal significance of dialect provides the very framework around which late-nineteenth-century literary works are structured. A novel like Harold Frederic's *The Damnation of Theron Ware* (1896), for example, might seem to have little explicit interest in representing spoken dialect, yet closer inspection reveals how the entire work turns on points of linguistic difference and diversity. *Theron Ware* concerns the growing intellectual and social divisions in post–Civil War America, which it presents chiefly in terms of mutually unintelligible cultural dialects that divide a supposedly common tongue. The novel's construction of character, its structure of plot, the very logic of its moral meanings, are all embodied in its depiction of "strange talk."[2] In this sense, *Theron Ware* is part of a large group of texts in Gilded Age literature that explore the cultural and aesthetic politics of dialect difference: regional stories that consider social aspects of rustic language; highbrow novels that react against the spoken idioms of mass culture; popular texts that experiment with humorous accents of ethnic interaction; southern romances that create racial hierarchies of speech; minority works that overturn linguistic hegemony; naturalist novels that depict the blasphemous degeneration of city talk; African-American songs and stories that exploit the signifying alternative of vernacular discourse.

Dialect is not unique to post–Civil War American literature. Recent inquiries into the role of vernacular variety in authors such as Hugh Henry Brackenridge and James Fenimore Cooper suggest that dialect was—in the words of David Simpson—an "important and highly contested ingredient of the American literary language well before Twain and his immediate precursors."[3] We need only think of blackface minstrelsy or of the antebellum southern humorists for earlier moments when dialect sounded loud in American culture. In 1895, an anonymous reviewer in *The Dial* noted the obvious point that dialect literature was not solely an American phenomenon. Burns's Scottish dialect poems, Scott's *Waverley*, the Provençal poems of France, Goldoni's Venetian comedies, and Reuter's Plattdeutsch tales from Germany were works that "simply could not have been done at all without the employment of dialect." Yet, continues this reviewer, "no one would venture to assert that the exploitation of a dialect was the prime motive that led to the composition" of these texts. This was, however, the defining characteristic of post–Civil War American dialect literature: it was "written for the sake of dialect." Rather than using dialect "for the sake of the story," the depiction of "grotesque orthography" had become the *raison d'être* of the composition. This assessment was confirmed by other critics, who commented that not even Walter Scott "ventured upon a novel that depended wholly upon unusual or extravagant modes of speech and sought no higher and more important claim for either popular or critical approval."[4] As both a representational technique and a cultural theme, dialect was absorbing the creative energies of literary minds.

The distinctiveness of late-nineteenth-century American literature lay largely in the generative role of dialect within it. Dialect also began to appear in new and unexpected ways, as is clear from the opening page of the most famous novel of the period:

EXPLANATORY

In this book a number of dialects are used, to wit: the Missouri negro dialect; the extremist form of the backwoods South-Western dialect; the ordinary "Pike County" dialect; and four modified varieties of this last. The shadings have not been done in a haphazard fashion, or by guess-work; but painstakingly, and with the trustworthy guidance and support of personal familiarity with these several forms of speech.

I make this explanation for the reason that without it many readers would suppose that all these characters were trying to talk alike and not succeeding.

THE AUTHOR.

The question of whether Mark Twain was serious in his "Explanatory" to *Adventures of Huckleberry Finn* (1884) has generated heated debate. Many critics maintain that Twain was merely joking, because the linguistic reality of *Huck Finn* falls short of such specific claims. Others have sought to take Twain at his word, either by suggesting that the real varieties of language in the novel are moral rather than purely linguistic, or, less evasively, by attempting to classify the novel's different speech-types on phonetic and morphological grounds.[5] Reducing the "Explanatory" to questions of accuracy, however, clouds the wider issues it evokes, which are more concerned with the literary tradition of dialect writing than with whether Twain realistically represents his seven types of speech. The "Explanatory" is not so much a comment on the techniques of *Huck Finn* as a burlesque of the assumptions upon which dialect writing had depended since the early 1870s. Twain's claim to depict a series of dialectal distinctions within a single county in Missouri is best understood as an allusion to the enormous diversity that literature was claiming for the linguistic situation of the United States.[6] And the accompanying claim to linguistic authenticity marks the other characteristic of Gilded Age dialect writing: the authorial profession of a profound ability to differentiate, in utter realism, between these many forms.

Twain's claim to depict accurately such a variety of dialects defined the aesthetic of American dialect writing. While British writers (to offer one example) also busily recorded popular speech in the nineteenth century, Norman Page has shown how their approach to dialect remained shallow: Scott's rendering of nonstandard pronunciation was intermittent, Dickens lacked a deep and instinctive feeling for colloquial forms, and Hardy's dialect was strictly a written medium without any real effort at phonology.[7] It was this superficiality that American dialect writers rejected. They endeavored to transcend an occasional inclusion of provincial terms, clipped words, and nonstandard grammar in their works. The new systems of writing they developed contradict the recent critical opinion that "one would be hard put to differentiate between the spoken dialog and the written exposition of most novels before the mid-twentieth century."[8] It was the very difference between these two levels of language that dialect writing emphasized; the search for more radical and thorough depictions of sound led to widespread orthographic innovation. George Washington Cable illustrates this technique in *The Creoles of Louisiana* (1884), giving us first the standard English version followed by its translation into the French-English dialect of his white Creoles:

"I am going to do my utmost to take my uncle there, but he is slightly paralyzed and I do not think he will feel like going."—He would say—

"I goin' do my possib' fedge ma hunc' yond', bud, 'owevva, 'e's a lit' bit pa'a*lyze* an' I thing 'e don' goin' fill *ligue.*" [319]

Echoing a new philological concentration on questions of pronunciation, Cable's French-English speech sought to encode the delivery conditions of vernacular discourse: its tonality and stress in addition to its grammar.[9] This supposedly "phonetic" spelling was the hallmark of dialect writing, and, quite often, the source of its strangeness. The language of American literature was forced to carry a remarkable amount of extra-lexical information.

Writers attempted to redact an astounding variety of cultural voices. One of the first new dialects to emerge after the Civil War was the rustic Hoosier speech recorded by Edward Eggleston in *The Hoosier School-Master* (1871):

"Bill," said Bud Means to his brother, "ax the master ef he'd like to hunt coons. I'd like to take the starch out the stuck-up feller."

"'Nough said," was Bill's reply.

"You durn't do it," said Bud.

"I don't take no sech a dare," returned Bill. [16]

Although this passage deviates only slightly from conventional spelling, the degree of attention paid to local idioms is far beyond previous norms.

In a later edition of *The Hoosier School-Master* (1892), for example, Eggleston accompanies this short passage with three footnotes, explaining potentially confusing points of Hoosier grammar, phonology, and phraseology. The close representation of rustic language was a favorite device of the many regional dialect writers who portrayed the speech of virtually every state of the Union in the decades following the Civil War.[10] While the New England dialect employed by Sarah Orne Jewett and Mary Wilkins Freeman contained only a shade of colloquialism, there were other forms—usually from the South—that seemed much stranger to the eye. Take, for example, the dialogue of Mary Murfree's Tennessee mountaineers:

> "I hain't got no grudge agin' 'Vander . . . nur 'Vander's friends, nuther. It air jes' that dad-burned idjit, 'Lijah, ez I *des*pise. Jane Elmiry, ain't that old Topknot ez I hear a-cacklin'? Waal, waal, sir, dad-burn that thar lazy, idle poultry! Air she a'stalkin' round the yard yit? Go, Jane Elmiry, an' see whar she be." [*In the Tennessee Mountains,* 45]

Although Murfree's fiction can be unsettling in its use of strange words (*dad-burned*), unfamiliar spellings (*waal* for "well"), and outmoded grammar (*whar she be*), the more extreme forms of dialect occurred when the local was supplemented by an ethnic or a racial element. This was especially true of the many varieties of African-American vernacular English that were depicted by white authors such as Joel Chandler Harris and Thomas Nelson Page, and by black authors such as Charles Chesnutt and Paul Laurence Dunbar. Among versions of black speech, the creole language Gullah was the most difficult to understand for mainstream readers, as is clear from Charles Colcock Jones's approximation of the creole in *Negro Myths from the Georgia Coast* (1888):

> Buh Alligatur yent hab time fuh mek answer. Eh yent crack ah teet to Buh Rabbit. Eh jis is bex wid um is eh kin be. Eh yeye red. Eh tail swinge. Eh gone fuh de ribber, an eh fall in head ober heel. De water cool um. Eh ketch eh bref. Den eh raise isself on de top er de water an eh holler back to Buh Rabbit: "Nummine, Boy, golong dis time. Me know who mek all dis trouble fur me. Ef me ebber ketch you close dis ribber, me guine larne you how ter come fool long me." [3]

Black dialect may have been the most popular target of postbellum authors, yet its depiction was only one of many similar efforts to render ethnic discourse. Ethnic dialect could provide writers with a voice for social commentary and political satire, as was the case with Charles G. Leland's German-English dialect:

> Vhen ash de var vas ober,
> Und Beace her shnow-wice vings,

Vas vafin o'er de coondry
(In shpods) like afery dings;
Und heroes vere revardtet,
De beople all pegan
To say 'tvas shame dat nodings
Vas done for Breitemann.

[*Hans Breitmann's Ballads*, 96]

The Chicago brogue of Finley Peter Dunne's Irish-Americans had a similar political purpose:

"I see," said Mr. Dooley, "that th' Prisidint is plannin' an attack on th' good old English custom iv wife-beatin'. He wants to inthrajooce th' other good old English instichoochion iv a whippin'-post. . . . Not, mind ye, that wife-beatin' is much practised in this counthry. Slug-ye'er-spouse is an internaytional spoort that has niver become pop'lar on our side iv' th' wather." [*Mr. Dooley on Ivrything and Ivrybody*, 233]

And Abraham Cahan's Yiddish-English dialect was part of a literary drive to portray the gritty realities of New York City's Lower East Side:

"Dzake, do me a faver; hask Mamie to gib dot feller a couple a dantzes . . . I hasked 'er myself, but se don' vonted. He's a beesness man, you 'destan', an' he kan a lot o' fellers an' I vonted make him satetzfiet." [*Yekl*, 37]

Attempts to represent ethnic speech seriously, however, were matched by humorous burlesques of "broken English." Dialect gags and caricatures formed a central part of mass entertainment forms like vaudeville, and little-known sketchers mocked minority discourse in newspapers and joke-books. Leland's early attempt at Chinese "Pidgin English," for example, offered little more than comic orientalism:

Last year my look-see plum-t*l*ee all
     flower all-same he snow,
T'his sp*l*ing much plenty snowflake
     all-same he plum-t*l*ee blow.
He snowflake fallee, meltee, he *l*ed leaf
     turnee b*l*own,
My makee first-chop sing-song how luck go
     uppy-down.

[*Pidgin-English Sing-Song*, 15]

These examples by no means exhaust the varieties of dialect writing in the decades after the Civil War. It seemed that every regional utterance had its recorder, that every ethnic dialect found an eager audience. For the apotheosis of this dialect tradition we might look again to Twain, who attempted to notate a vast chorus of different voices, ranging from Missouri slaves and Mississippi steamboat pilots to New Haven fruit vendors and Nevada silver miners. More striking in terms of sheer linguistic variety, however, is the work of George Washington Cable. His novel *Dr. Sevier* (1883) brings together a bewildering collection of ethnic idioms: French-American ("But daz de troub'—de room not goin' be vacate for t'ree mont'"), African-American ("Dess keep dish yeh road fo' 'bout half mile an' you strak 'pon the broad, main road"), German-American ("Toctor, uf you bleace, Toctor, you vill bleace ugscooce me"), Italian-American ("Not got-a no more; dass all . . . Oäl de rest gone"), Irish-American ("Ye're a Prodez'n preacher! I'll bet ye fifty dollars ye have a rich cherch!"), and Spanish-American ("When win' change, he goin' start. He dawn't start till win' change").[11]

Perhaps never before or since has the representation of dialect been so various and extreme, yet also an integral part of a mainstream literature. The "cult of the vernacular" included a refined readership. Books of dialect-driven "local color" stories were tremendously popular—seventeen editions of Murfree's *In the Tennessee Mountains* appeared in two years[12]—and, for four decades, highbrow literary magazines such as *The Century* and *Harper's* were awash with dialect sketches. This brand of dialect writing was not regional in the sense of something produced by and for communities peripheral to a central culture. It was often the work of outsiders, or, most typically, of upper-class writers who had what they thought was intimate contact with the dialect speakers of their locality.[13] Murfree's Appalachian idioms may have originated in the mouths of impoverished rustics, but they appealed to the ears of wealthy urbanites seeking the quaintness of colorful discourse. If the "contagion" of dialect "extended to those periodicals which we too fondly fancied to stand for the dignities, as opposed to the freaks, of literature"—wrote the anonymous critic from *The Dial* whom we encountered earlier—it also "had almost complete possession of the *bric-a-brac* popular magazine. . . . [I]t has been disseminated and vulgarized by the newspaper and the popular reciter."[14] Readers of dialect parts made fortunes in lectures designed for a middlebrow audience,[15] and vaudeville's vernacular comedians became idols of the urban masses. Minority writers, such as Abraham Cahan and Paul Laurence Dunbar, developed dialect voices of their own, voices that appealed to the white mainstream *and* to an ethnic or a black readership. Dialect satisfied a vast range of motivations; it had widespread appeal to all sections of the Gilded Age population.

The development of postbellum dialect literature is a crucial phenomenon in American letters, yet it has received limited scholarly attention. When critics have tackled this issue, they have tended to focus on the political relationship between author, literary subject, and audience. Early commentators such as William Dean Howells and Hamlin Garland saw dialect literature as part of a sincere, democratic interest in recording the speechways of subaltern cultural groups—a view supported by the *Cambridge History of American Literature* in 1918.[16] The consensus changed radically in the 1920s, mainly through the work of the linguist George Philip Krapp, who used the notion that no proper dialects existed in the United States to argue that dialect writing was a highbrow convention which employed exaggerated, humorous speech to camouflage a patronizing sentimentality and satire.[17] Despite occasional challenges, Krapp's views have remained dominant.[18] In *The Colloquial Style in America* (1966), Richard Bridgman echoed the idea—supported by Krapp and H. L. Mencken—that the United States lacks European-like degrees of regional dialect. Dismissing "the various first-generation immigrant dialects," and ignoring the tremendous increase in literary dialect after the Civil War, Bridgman argued that the late nineteenth century saw a "progressive flooding of the literary world with a common speech that for more and more readers [was] accepted as a literary norm"; America's narrative prose style moved toward a "colloquial center" based on middle-class speech.[19] The work of recent critics such as Alan Trachtenberg, Michael North, and Richard Brodhead has begun to overturn this neglect of dialect and its jarring political implications, but it has done so by returning to a thesis little different from Krapp's. Dialect literature, they suggest, was a means by which a social elite found cultural reassurance, either by creating a nostalgic elegy of pre-capitalist rural bliss, or by forging fictions of racial dominance that countered contemporary ethnic threats.[20]

Work on American dialect literature has remained trapped within the limits of single-author studies,[21] of single racial perspectives (especially concerning the African-American vernacular),[22] or of strictly regional settings.[23] And preoccupation with the "realistic" rendition of nonstandard voices has obscured the wider thematic and political scope of literary dialect, its link to questions about the coherence and quality of the supposedly standard language itself. The primary aim of *Strange Talk* is to bring together the many ways that dialect featured in literature, to look at how different uses of dialect intersected in texts. Admittedly, this was the era when regional fiction took root, with its apparently neat polarization of standard and nonstandard discourse. But it was also a time when these regional models of dialect were breaking down, exploded by a vast range of other linguistic forces based variously on class, ethnicity, race, gender, immigration, and urbanization. An effort to broaden the field of inquiry connects with another critical purpose of this book: to overturn the belief that dialect functioned chiefly to uphold the dominance of an elitist ideology,[24] that it acted solely as a reassuring means of regional nostalgia. Without doubt, dialect could function in literature as a way of controlling social, cultural, and ethnic threats to polite linguistic norms, as I demonstrate at various points. Yet we must understand further how this controlling effort interacted with other, conflicting functions and, moreover, how these attempts at linguistic dominance were themselves fraught with complex anxieties.

The Gilded Age was an intense and sustained period of linguistic reflection which qualifies James Crawford's belief that "Americans lack a tradition of language politics—that is to say, a history in which language predominated as a symbol, weapon, and stake of ethnic conflict."[25] America might lack the same institutionalized political concern with the national tongue that characterized, say, nineteenth-century France or Italy, yet this does not mean that it lacked an important *cultural* debate over language. Although linguistic contention has always been present in United States history, with obvious flashpoints like Noah Webster's agitation for a standard Federal English in the 1780s, discussion of language took on new prominence and new formations in the final decades of the nineteenth century. American English became the subject of political controversy over the quality of national culture in an age that saw a broad and well-recognized series of historical developments: the growth of large-scale industrial capitalism, with its vast inequalities of wealth and poverty; the formation of large urban centers; post-slavery race segregation; the enormous influx of new immigrants from eastern and southern Europe; the foundation of nationwide networks of communication; and, simultaneously, the heightened awareness of America as a heterogeneous society, divided along lines of ethnicity, race, and class. All of these issues were perceived to have a strong impact on the national tongue. The negotiation of linguistic questions took place in classrooms, magazine articles, self-help books, volumes of "verbal criticism," dictionary prefaces, and in the more elusive forum of public opinion. The literature of the period, moreover, reveals these deeper language ideologies in operation. And because, of course, language has a foundational role in literary texts, the stakes are doubled: narrative structures and techniques of representation become as politically charged as explicit topics or characters. Both medium and theme, the language of late-nineteenth-century American literature speaks volumes on the larger linguistic assumptions of its era. The rise of literary dialects registered the enormous political weight that was placed on questions of linguistic variety.

American dialect writing was, in part, a confirmation of cultural hegemony. The focus on "incorrect" dialects sanctioned belief in the pure, standard speech of a dominant elite. This Gramscian explanation of dialect literature, however, is not entirely adequate to the American situation.[26] For one thing, the United States has never had a clear sense of its hegemonic, high-prestige speech; the standard language has always been an unstable, ill-defined entity. Moreover, the linguistic map of America is not simply marked by well-established, subordinate regional dialects. There is also the constant influx of non–English speakers who maintain their national tongues alongside newly learned, transitional dialects of English heavily influenced by their own language patterns. During the late nineteenth century, these new Englishes began to seem an integral part of American culture. Rather than a definite hierarchy between standard and dialect, there was a strong sense that the dominant language was being influenced or threatened by the ethnic and social dialects that were supposed to reside beneath it. Thus, on his return in 1904, what Henry James feared was not that so many foreign languages were spoken in New York City, but the effect these languages would have on the nature of English itself. Debate over language in the Gilded Age was dominated by the concern that the meaning of national identity was culturally shifting, away from its familiar Anglo-Saxon traditions.

American nervousness about the stability and correctness of spoken standards stemmed from the deep fear of linguistic contamination, the fear that subaltern forms were radiating upward, affecting the language of the elite. This anxiety arose largely, though not exclusively, from situations of racial and ethnic contact. In the intimate meeting of different races, argues John Szwed, there is a tendency for the culture and, in particular, the language of the dominant group to be influenced by the behavior of the subordinate group. Paradoxically, while the high-status group may be denying the very existence of culture among the low, it is also becoming "mongrelized," "degenerate," and "polluted" by an absorption of these low-status traditions.[27] Recent theorists have used similar ideas of contamination to explore the complex ambivalence of colonial societies—the equivocal, vacillating power relation between Master and Other, in which the unity and authority of the dominant discourse becomes unsettled by the presence within it of subaltern significance.[28] These ideas have provided new ways of interpreting an ambiguous racial dynamic, present throughout American history, in which cultural institutions of whiteness are inextricably informed by the blackness they would seem to reject: hence recent explorations of the combined domination and desire in blackface minstrelsy, or recent inquiries into the importance of black creativity within mainstream American literature.[29]

The authorship of dialect was often a claim to authority, not just over the quality of another's speech but over the nature of a dominant reality. (In this sense, I treat "realism" as an ideological practice that goes on *in* a text, not as a generic category that contains the text in its entirety.)[30] The misrepresentation of African-American dialect, for example, was a popular means of encoding racist beliefs in black intellectual inferiority. Yet black language also encompassed the power of cultural contamination.[31] African-American dialect was a sign of black–white intermixture; it was a hybrid form with the force to infiltrate and adulterate the dominant language. This double function of black English relates to a wider ambiguity that defined the role of diverse dialects within Gilded Age literature. Dialect writing was not always a proof of hegemonic command. It could also register an anxious, constantly collapsing attempt to control the fragmentation and change that characterize any national tongue. And dialect could encode the possibility of resistance, not just by undermining the integrity of a dominant standard, but by recording the subversive voices in which alternative versions of reality were engendered.

The notion of dialect has become recently controversial in a number of ways. Some linguists avoid the term *dialect* because they see it as wrongly implying a natural hierarchy between the standard, correct language on the one hand and the nonstandard, incorrect dialect on the other. For Marc Shell, a focus on dialects of American English has masked the disappearance of non-English languages in the United States, thus deflecting attention away from the linguistic rights and significant cultural differences of the speakers of those languages.[32] *Strange Talk* refutes the opinion that discussion of dialect is necessarily ideologically repressive. The term *dialect* is employed throughout this study in an effort to preserve the political dynamic of subordination *and* resistance that defined linguistic conflict at the end of the nineteenth century. To recognize dialect is not simply to confirm the dominance or purity of standard discourse.[33] One of the main points of this book is that what many believed to be the standard language was deeply threatened and radically informed by supposedly inferior dialects. I focus on dialect and not on non-English languages to capture a crucial characteristic of the late nineteenth century. The main fear, at least for the caretakers of Anglo-American culture, was not that there were foreign-language speakers in the United States: this only emphasized English as the language of power. Instead, the most threatening notions were (1) that the disunification of American English itself was a sign of profound cultural fragmentation; and (2) that foreign-language users *were* speaking English—very "improperly" and with the effect of transforming Anglo-American linguistic traditions.

In late-nineteenth-century literature, black language was the most obvious victim of misrepresentation because it was the most powerful demonstration of cultural contamination. The complex literary treatment of black speech occupies a central part of this book. A major purpose of my work on dialect, however, is to supplement accounts of the black vernacular with forays into linguistic issues surrounding not only other ethnic and regional groups but also key manifestations of gender and social class. The same fear of infection that surrounded ethnic and racial dialect also informed reactions to the diseased degeneration of the nation's spokesmen of cultural authority, and to the blasphemous impropriety of the urban tongue. My approach is more thematic than author-based: it mixes both minor and major writers to investigate different ideas of dialect in Gilded Age literature and culture. A central structuring principle of *Strange Talk* is the exploration of the various ways in which *dialect* and *nonstandard language* were understood. As we proceed, the very meaning of dialect steadily shifts: it refers to regional speech divisions, to the neologisms of popular culture, to the distinctive speech of American women, to creole languages, to urban slang, and to the so-called broken English of recent immigrants.

Throughout these various definitions we return to the idea that literature was part of a crucial cultural debate in which ideological attempts to forge an ideal America—a nation conceived in linguistic unity—were constantly undermined by new and strange ways of talking. My concern is not with the question of whether national consciousness requires a single language, but with the factors that lie behind extreme anxieties over variety within a single tongue. I emphasize dialect, rather than individual languages, to highlight the pervasive phenomena of cultural contact and merger—not to reinscribe the dominance of Anglo-Americanism, but to explore the ways it was breaking down, the efforts it was making to preserve an often tenuous consistency and control in the face of constant threats of change from the impact of linguistic otherness. My argument is an attempt to investigate the dents and penetrations in the hegemonic armor of a dominant language, whose untroubled absoluteness is perhaps too easily assumed.

Chapters one and two examine philological and cultural debates over the nature and the national significance of American dialects, together with their political and aesthetic implications for Mark Twain's western narratives, and for lesser-known regional and realist writers such as James Russell Lowell, Edward Eggleston, and Mary Murfree. Chapter three explores the impact that psychological and gender-based aspects of social modernization were thought to have on the standards of American vocal culture—an impact felt in contemporary works by Herman Melville and Henry James. The fourth chapter tackles the popularity of black dialect among white writers, pointing to some crucial ethical differences between representations of the creole language Gullah and George Washington Cable's neglected literary manipulation of the creole French of Louisiana. Chapters five and six expand this racial dimension of dialect into a discussion of the new voices of America's increasingly multiethnic and apparently immoral cities, voices that became vital for naturalist novelists (Stephen Crane), for immigrant intellectuals (Abraham Cahan), and for ethnic performers on the vaudeville stage. The seventh and final chapter returns to the dialect that has had the strongest influence on twentieth-century American literature—black vernacular English—by examining one of its most subtle yet misunderstood exponents, Paul Laurence Dunbar.

This wide circle of topics surrounds a central point: the vernacular voice was an ambivalent power in late-nineteenth-century America. Dialect had a mixed heritage. It could seem rooted in Anglo-American culture while also registering the effects of ethnic intermixture; it could evoke the ideal stability of America's regional past while also signifying concern over an increasingly unfamiliar and fragmented society. To capture this ambivalence, the predominant rhythm underscoring *Strange Talk* is that of repeated vacillation: between celebrations of an American community of vernacular voices and fears that nonstandard language spelled national disunity; between attempts to establish an elite standard of usage and realizations that traditional models of linguistic propriety were culturally contaminated; between the construction of hegemonic hierarchies of language and the counterhegemonic power of vernacular resistance.

ONE

Contaminated Tongues:
American Philology and the Problem
of Dialect

When complimented on the unusual correctness of his English by an Englishman he meets in Europe, Mark Twain replies with a statement that marks the new national confidence of postbellum America: "I said I was obliged to him for his compliment, since I knew he meant it for one, but that I was not fairly entitled to it, for I didn't speak English at all,—I only spoke American." The idea that the peculiar nature and institutions of the United States would furnish Americans with a unique language had been around since the beginning of the republic. Twain's restatement of this belief, however, transforms the criteria upon which these nationalistic language theories had traditionally been based. No longer can our linguistic standards come from "the little corner called New England," says Twain, or from the unrepresentative pronunciations in Noah Webster's *Dictionary*. The "spread of our people far to the south and far to the west" has "made many alterations in our pronunciation, and [has] introduced new words among us and changed the meanings of many old ones." According to Twain, the American language could no longer be dictated by a social and linguistic elite: "a nation's language is a very large matter. It is not simply a manner of speech obtaining among the educated handful; the manner obtaining among the vast uneducated multitude must be considered also."[1]

These words of Twain, from his sketch "Concerning the American Language" (1888), reveal an explicit concern with linguistic ideas that has been similarly noted in authors such as William Dean Howells and Henry James. This preoccupation with issues of language was endemic among writers after the Civil War: the factors informing the rise of dialect literature derived from widespread debates over the nature and status of American English. Twain's sketch lies at the hub of these debates because

14

it raises two crucial and, at that time, highly political questions: how to define the borders of the American tongue, and how to preserve a stable, unified linguistic standard. As we shall see, Twain's regionally and socially inclusive definition of the American language, his conception that it should encompass the various dialects of the masses, was both the ideal and the problem of the age. The tension in Twain's linguistic pluralism—the faith in the oneness of a common tongue despite the move to include many different voices within it—was beginning to trouble students of the national speech. Alongside the new interest in American dialects, a profound fear was developing: a language that remains in touch with the nation's diverse cultural groups is a chaotic threat to the coherence of cultural authority. Debates over the American language were marked by ambiguity. Dialect could incite a sense of linguistic anarchy and social fragmentation as easily as it could suggest a national distinctiveness based on a popular vernacular.

The tendency to celebrate the supposedly democratic efforts of American writers to commit vernacular voices to the printed page has been superseded in recent years by an awareness of the conservative political subtext of much dialect literature.[2] A more complex politics of representation is revealed, however, when this literature is read in the context of philological and popular thought about language during the Gilded Age. Dialect writing was, I suggest, an ambivalent literary genre in which both radical and conservative motivations were confused. Dialect literature moved the masses into the mainstream while polarizing social division; it elevated refined discourse while depicting a national language that was multifarious and strange. This initial chapter traces the theoretical reasons behind this ambivalence; the next chapter explores the formal and ideological implications of its literary implementation.

Recent critical attention to language in the United States between the Revolution and the Civil War has focused on the intimate relationship between linguistic ideas and American nationhood.[3] Disagreements have arisen over the uniqueness of this relationship: whether America "encountered and confronted the cultural, political, and ontological problematics of language in a way which was quite new, certainly in the history of the western world," or whether these problematics derived directly from European and Classical antecedents.[4] Whatever the case, the historical importance and national self-consciousness of linguistic debate in America cannot be denied. Inevitably quoting the description of the United States as "a pure unadulterated LOGOCRACY or *government of words*" in Washington Irving's *Salmagundi* (1807), recent studies have stressed the political ramifications of these linguistic ideas.[5] Civic eloquence, we are informed, is of utmost importance in governing a civilized democracy; hence the American emphasis on language as the mechanism of political stability, and the American obsession with links between linguistic corruption and socio-cultural disorder.[6]

An overview of linguistic theories between the Revolution and the Civil War reveals what the *North American Review* in 1860 termed a strong "tendency to force uniformity upon the language."[7] This penchant for linguistic sameness was partly the correlative of a democratic ideology that called for equality of speech, and partly a response to fears that the mid-century prominence of the popular voice was destabilizing traditional standards.[8] There was a particular resistance to—one might almost say conspiracy against—the very existence of dialect in America, a resistance that took a series of increasingly subtle forms. Most explicitly, conservative grammarians excluded regional and lower-class speech from their hierarchical theories of refined discourse.[9] The call of radicals like Noah Webster for a common language, equally available to all, likewise spelled death to dialectal difference. Webster's idea that language was a democratical state presupposed that rustic dialects, as well as high-status forms of speech, would disappear into a hegemonic standard which obeyed the natural and rational laws of the national language.[10] Lastly, and most subtly of all, behind Ralph Waldo Emerson's avowed fascination with the "language of the street," and behind Walt Whitman's self-consciously democratic interest in the regenerative power of "native idiomatic words," lay a conservative, abstract view of language that basked in spirituality while avoiding the jarring social questions of linguistic difference.[11] Central to these Transcendentalist ideas of language was the power of assimilation. English was believed to contain a dominating, harmonizing force—rooted in a Saxon past—that would absorb into its flexible norms the various dialects of America's diverse communities. Thus, for the Whitman of "An American Primer," the establishment of a brawny, natural language of the American masses assumed the imminent disappearance of differences in pronunciation, accent, and inflection. "Language," wrote Whitman, "must cohere."[12]

In the new currents of linguistic thought that developed after the Civil War, there seem to be two main changes in direction. First, the idea of an *American* English came into its own. The earlier moves of nationalists like Webster and Whitman blossomed into a pervasive feeling that America had developed a special, recognizable idiom. "Nothing can mark more completely the change of feeling which has come over this country than the manner in which the subject of language is now discussed," wrote Thomas Lounsbury in 1880. Americanisms were no longer considered inherently improper, and American critics possessed a new authority over questions of language and literature.[13] Second, this recognition of a national language was accompanied by a new acceptance of dialect. The philological rationalization against linguistic difference was being replaced by a scientific acknowledgment of dialectal variety. This was partly a response to a wider preoccupation with the spoken voice in late-nineteenth-century European philology. In Britain, phonology became—in the words of Henry Sweet—the "indispensable foundation of all philology," and never before had linguistic science been so concerned with recording speech in all its regional and social varieties.[14] Special alphabets and systems of graphical phoneticism were developed to transcribe spoken words, thus equipping philologists with the tools to seek the primal laws of language on the tips of rustic tongues. In the United States, this interest in vernacular varieties of speech was even stronger, deeper, and longer-lasting than in Britain.[15] It gained significant theoretical weight from philological societies (the American Philological Association was founded in 1863, the Modern Language Association in 1883, and the American Dialect Society in 1889), which emphasized how "the natural, careless, unconscious, colloquial speech . . . furnishes the philologist with his best illustrative and explanatory material."[16] These new scientific opinions found their finest expression in the writings of the American philologist William Dwight Whitney. "[D]ialectic diversity seems to be the inseparable condition of linguistic life," argued Whitney in 1867; moving firmly in the direction of linguistic relativism, he broke down the traditional hierarchy between language and dialect. "The science of language has democratized our views on such points as these," wrote Whitney in *The Life and Growth of Language* (1875): "it has taught us that one man's speech is just as much a language as another man's; that even the most cultivated tongue that exists is only the dialect of a certain class in a certain locality."[17]

At first glance, the factors behind America's massive literary interest in dialect during the Gilded Age appear obvious: new ideas about language had sanctioned dialect as a respectable area of inquiry, thus preparing the ground for its literary exploration. Dialect was no longer seen as an inherently debased product of degenerate intellects, beyond the realm of literary representation, but as an important area of linguistic activity that was an essential part of any effort to understand the mind and culture of its speakers.[18] This was partly true, yet ideas about dialect, and about language in general, were much more complex during the decades after 1860. The new confidence in America's "own" language was undercut by fears for its contamination and fragmentation. And the apparently relativistic, philological interest in dialect was challenged, not just by different schools of linguistic thought, but by contrary notions in the minds of philologists themselves. Dialect literature, in other words, was growing in a fickle linguistic climate.

Linguistic debate became so crucial to literate Americans after the Civil War not because of any single issue within language, but because language was understood as the central agency in a whole range of social, political, and cultural issues. The science of language is invoked to "illuminate psychological problems," to "arbitrate in ethnologic controversies," and to illuminate "the whole field of our philosophic thinking," wrote Whitney in 1863.[19] Not only were academic societies founded to record officially this heightened interest; monthly magazines of the period also became major sites of unprecedented linguistic controversy. The most prominent and influential manifestation of this fascination with words, however, did not seek to delve into the dens of dialect: far from it. This was the age of "verbal criticism," a conservative movement that interrogated American speech in an effort to preserve the purity of its cultivated standards. Verbal critics like Richard Grant White, whose enormously popular *Words and Their Uses* (1870) went through seventeen editions in fifteen years, saw themselves as a type of "linguistic detective police" with the power to arrest decay by alerting speakers to the errors of their ways, errors that were usually judged according to the critics' own conservative canons of correctness.[20] These critics were not in the game of linguistic relativism; their standards were both absolute and essentialist. For White, "language belongs to race, not to place": "[T]o the race or the nation, [words] are growths, and are themselves the fruit and the sign of the growth of the race or the nation itself, and have, like its members, a history, and alliances, and rights of birth, and inherent powers which endure as long as they live, and which they can transmit, although somewhat modified, to their rightful successors."[21] Language was motivated by its connection to national and racial issues, thought White, so that the question of whether men and women were "rightful successors" to their national heritage depended on their use of words. In a radical sense, language conferred the virtues of proper citizenship, and words were institutionalized as the embodiment of the national essence. As William Mathews phrased it in *Words; Their Use and Abuse* (1876), language is not just an index to the mind and heart; words are mirrors of the nation's entire moral and intellectual makeup. Paraphrasing the American philologist George Perkins Marsh (who in turn traced his ideas to Walter Savage Landor's *Imaginary Conversations*), Mathews demonstrated how linguistic qualities, such as the supposed tendency toward hyperbole in the Italian "social dialect," have the power to signal the utter degradation of national character. Linguistic difference fed the prejudice of these amateur ethnographers. According to Mathews, French lacks a strict equivalent to the English word *listener*, a point that led him to some profound conclusions: "Is there any other explanation of this blank than the supposition that every Frenchman talks from the pure love of talking, and not to be heard?''[22] For Mathews, there was not.

The entire philosophy of a verbal critic like Mathews rested and turned on the belief that words were living, spiritual things; that language was the incarnation, not the dress, of thought. This logic had powerful moral significance: a person's essential nature was stamped into the language he or she used; speech was a "physiognomy" that unconsciously revealed disorders within.[23] These ideas, of course, were hardly novel. In previous decades, Romantic thinkers had emphasized how language was a living moral power, qualified "by all that makes American life—by the geographic and climatic conditions, by the ethnology of America, by her politics, sociology, manners, mentality."[24] Nor were these ideas exclusively American. Although broadly rooted in nineteenth-century European Romantic philology (for support, Mathews was quick to quote Max Müller on the inseparability of thought and language), the more immediate origins of hypermoralistic verbal criticism can be traced to an English source: Henry Alford's *A Plea for the Queen's English* (1864). Here, the link between language and national character, which became so important for American writers such as White and Mathews, was turned against America itself. In a famous passage, Alford directly compared the humor, reckless exaggeration and contempt for congruity in American English with "the character and history of the nation—its blunted sense of moral obligation and duty to man; its open disregard of conventional right where aggrandizement is to be obtained; and, I may now say, its reckless and fruitless maintenance of the most cruel and unprincipled war in the history of the world." Deducing civil war from the national tongue may seem ridiculous today; at the time it was part of a sincere belief in philology as a historical science that could dissect the intellectual spirit of nations and communities.[25]

If this type of nationalist linguistic logic was not exclusively American in nature, it was, however, unusually extensive in the American public forum. Alford was a direct cause of this intense interest, as American sympathizers like George Washington Moon flew to the defense of the American tongue by finding fault with Alford's own English.[26] The controversy between Moon and Alford has pervaded the American press, wrote William Mathews in 1876, thus awakening a deep public interest in questions of language and grammar—an interest, moreover, that Mathews thought particularly opportune in checking the "deluge of barbarisms, solecisms, and improprieties" which were supposedly threatening American speech. The impact of this verbal criticism on American culture was enormous. It went far beyond the many books these critics wrote, considers Kenneth Cmiel: "Teachers at all levels incorporated their ideas into the English

curriculum," and they were recycled in magazines, newspapers, handbooks of usage, and home encyclopedias.[27]

Cmiel's history of popular speech in nineteenth-century America shows
how the craze for verbal criticism represented an entry of linguistic politics
into public discourse. Verbal critics saw the informal, imprecise nature of
American English as a sign that the commercial, democratic forces of the
nation were leading it away from the "traditional civility of refined decorum," which they hoped to reinscribe with their prescriptive language
lessons. Above all, argues Cmiel, the verbal critics focused on minute questions of speech in an attempt to re-establish a cultural elite in a situation
where traditional class hierarchies were breaking down.[28] The following
excerpt from White's *Words and Their Uses* gets to the heart of the matter:

> [T]he wide diffusion of just so much instruction as enables men to read
> their newspapers, write their advertisements, and keep their accounts, and
> the utter lack of deference to anyone, or of doubt in themselves, which
> political equality and material prosperity beget in people having no more
> than such education, and no less, combine to produce a condition of society
> which brings their style of speech, as well as their manners, much more to
> the front, not to say to the top, than is the case in other countries.

The problem for White was dissolution: American political and economic
life was pushing uncultivated people into prominent positions, from
where their degenerate language attained massive powers of infection.
The standards of authority were under threat because people were han-
dling the symbols of elegance without care for their meaning, and language itself was losing its value as a medium of communication. The only
solution for the general culture of the "middling folk," thought White,
was their submission to the "minds of the highest class," whose inborn
rationality and purity of expression alone could prevent further deterioration in the nation's moral fabric.[29]

This obsession with the decay of cultivated standards distracted verbal
critics from explicit questions of dialect, which they never tackled in any
depth. The essentialistic moral logic underpinning verbal criticism treated
regional dialects as absolute signs of inferiority and barbarity, thus removing their immediate threat. Again echoing the Romantic philologist
George Perkins Marsh, who viewed regional pronunciations like "Missis-
sippŭh and Ohiŭh" as obvious signs of "moral obliquity," William Mathews thought that dialect and slang were the natural languages of iniq-
uity: to speak them would inevitably lower one's moral level.[30] In this
respect, verbal critics seem a long way from contemporaries like Whitney,
who elevated dialect to a primary level of importance, and who countered
facile moral discrimination by pointing out that standard languages were
themselves just the canonization of politically powerful dialects.[31] Recent

historians have tended to view such differences as part of a radical antagonism between verbal critics and scholarly philologists at the end of the
nineteenth century. Both schools of thought, however, shared the linguistic ideologies of the era.[32] This is not to deny that profound disagreements existed between, say, the critic William Mathews and the philologist
Thomas Lounsbury. Mathews stressed how words were the spiritual em-
bodiments of thought and how language was an independent organism
whose corruption was the *cause*, rather than simply the symptom, of the
moral and intellectual degeneration of man. Lounsbury, on the other
hand, emphasized how language was merely a receptacle for whatever
meaning or morality man puts into it, and how "corruptions" were just
inevitable, healthy changes that would one day become accepted usage.
Yet, sounding like the verbal critics he vehemently criticized, Lounsbury
was dismayed at "the slough of linguistic anarchy in which we are now
largely floundering," and he sought ways to preserve a cultivated linguistic
standard. Lounsbury did not in fact deviate from the morality of taste
propounded by verbal critics; his real objection was to a situation in which
armchair purists like White dictated this taste, rather than the instinct of
"the whole body of the cultivated users of speech." The real guardians
of the spoken voice are not the verbal critics but those "who strive to
realize for themselves the highest intellectual and moral development of
which their natures are capable."[33] The argument was not so much about
what language should be—a morally cultivated standard must be firmly
in place—as about who should control it.

Whitney's apparently relativistic take on dialect was also limited; at
times he seems intellectually close to his supposed opponents. "[C]ul-
tivated speech" may be merely a dialect, said Whitney, yet it is still the
cultivated tongue and differs essentially from the "inaccuracies," "mispronunciations," and "blunders of application" of the "vulgar." Whitney
may have helped to sanction dialect as a legitimate subject for philological
inquiry, but he was by no means a celebrant of dialectal diversity. Lam-
basting several famous literary figures of the time, Whitney rejected a linguistic usage based on "an average of Tom, Dick, and Harry, Tag, Rag,
and Bobtail, Birdofredom Sawin, Hans Breitmann, and Miles O'Reilly, a
pot-pourri of native and imported improprieties."[34] It was a natural tendency for language to move from unity to diversity, thought Whitney, but
this tendency must be checked if the standards of literary civilization are
to be preserved against the insurrectionary power of less cultivated, popular dialects. Unlike many verbal critics, Whitney saw language as a conventional institution with the sole purpose of effective communication; in
effect, he placed language *after* questions of self and nation by severing
any necessary and internal connection between language and the human
qualities of consciousness, morality, and spirituality.[35] Yet alongside this

influential restatement of conventionality, Whitney suggested much more intimate and reciprocal connections between linguistic and social unity, linguistic and social cultivation.[36] Philologists like Whitney and Lounsbury, while they usually saw language as subservient to questions of self and nation, did not cut the link altogether. Language could still be read to reveal qualities of personal and national character; the difference was that, for them, language did not cause these qualities in the first place. Nor was the role of language as an agent of causation always so unambiguously dismissed. For Whitney, language was one of the key "constituents of our culture."[37] Without a stable, unified, and sophisticated language, the enlightening benefits of civilization were impossible.

Whitney's unfriendliness toward dialect, especially in his early work, led him to some positive conclusions about the American scene. Despite his recognizing that locality had produced pronounced differences, especially where colloquial speech was concerned, Whitney emphasized how the democratic nature of America's institutions, the universality and unity of instruction among its people, and the "mixture and intimate intercourse of all ranks and of all regions" meant that there was never a case "in which so nearly the same language was spoken throughout the whole mass of so vast a population as is the English now in America." The "assimilating influence," thought Whitney, "has had unequalled freedom and range of action," creating an American language that only varies slightly from the universal "standard of correct speech." Whitney's argument is important in regard to race, not least because it reveals a common irony in much philological thought of the time. In *The Life and Growth of Language*, Whitney used America as key evidence against "the theory of a language as a race-characteristic" because there people from all over the world spoke "the same dialect, without other variety than comes of differences of locality and education, none showing a trace of any other 'mother-tongue' or 'native speech.'" Yet this breaking of the absolute link between language and race was also a means to resist the idea that powerful elements of ethnicity might be transforming American culture and its language. The factor of assimilation lay at the root of moves to forge the fiction of a univocal nation. In this sense, Whitney's thoughts paralleled those of other academics like Brander Matthews, who had a strong need to believe in the Anglo-Saxon power to absorb differences. In his 1901 essay "The Stock that Speaks the Language," for example, Matthews pays lip-service to the idea that the qualities of a race are not the result of an "inherent superiority" or "native predisposition," and he states his disbelief in "any special virtue in the purity of race." Yet his essay as a whole is concerned with the early formation of "strangely enduring"

Anglo-Saxon "race-characteristics" that were modified only slightly when the English came to America. Echoing Whitney, Matthews suggests that the foreign elements entering America "have but little modified the essential type; for just as the English nature wrought its steady will through the centuries, so the American characteristics have been imposed on all the welter of nationalities that swirl together in the United States." The language of King Alfred was thus the language of America, and literature was empowered with the mission of propagating the racial essence. Ideas of a racially based manifest linguistic destiny were very much alive at the end of the century because American English was a powerful solvent in an emerging melting-pot ideology.[38]

Whitney may have severed any causal connection between language and racial evolution, yet the cultural logic of his philology was still evolutionary: Whitney followed Darwin's observation of the curious analogy between the gradual formation of species and languages, and he had a clear sense of a hierarchy of races and tongues, ranging from the "barbarous" to the "cultivated."[39] Whitney's apparent linguistic conventionalism and relativism thus masked a natural linguistic taxonomy, a surreptitious belief that "language is determined by race, since each human being usually learns to speak from his parents and others of the same blood." Whitney believed that European languages were inherently superior instruments that would allow "the exceptionally-gifted Polynesian or African" access to "departments of mental action which had before been inaccessible to him." In effect, Whitney replaced psychological determinism with a cultural determinism which assumed that the degree of advance in the development of speech varies "in accordance with the different capacities of the several races of man, as favored or the contrary by all the influences, natural and historical, which promote or retard human progress."[40] Whitney was close here to what Hans Aarsleff has identified as the Eurocentric "linguistic absolutism" characterizing Romantic philologists like Wilhelm von Humboldt, who presupposed that Indo-European tongues were inherently superior because their highly sophisticated structure allowed a correspondingly sophisticated development of mental and cultural intelligence.[41] Whitney was also rather close to his supposed antagonists, the verbal critics, who would quote his evolutionary idea—that language reflects the "enrichment or impoverishment" of minds and cultures—as they developed their notions that "[e]very race has its own organic growth, its own characteristic ideas and opinions . . . and the expression of all these peculiarities is found in its speech."[42]

Whitney embodied the wider paradoxes and inconsistencies of his era. Many philologists disguised racial agendas behind an apparent relativism, while their professed belief that language had the power to look after itself was accompanied by attempts to control speech in an even more rigid fashion than the much-maligned verbal critics. Notable here is the support of philologists for the spelling reform movement. Though not a new idea, spelling reform became a prominent and influential element in late-nineteenth-century America: Richard Grant White lamented that the "solicitude to conform sound to letter has become a disease among us."[43] Philologists viewed their interest in spelling as a form of democratic social work. Traditional orthography was considered "aristocratic" because its unusual difficulty prevented many people from attaining full literacy, thereby fostering an intellectual and social elite. This exclusion from the ethical influence of literate culture was seen as a direct cause of criminality; the more extreme reformers believed English spelling to be conducive to a "mind-stunting" irrationality and blind following of authority that inevitably destroyed the capacity for thought.[44] Much more was at stake with spelling reform than a simple tightening of the relationship between sound and sign. Francis March believed that a new mode of spelling would substantially reduce the time and effort required to learn and use English, an important point in a nation that contained more and more non-English-speaking immigrants. According to one reformer of the era, phonetic spelling would produce "distinct articulation, the removal of foreign accent and of local and peculiar intonations," thereby reducing linguistic insecurity among immigrants by allowing their easier assimilation into American society.[45]

Debates over spelling reform were primarily political. By making the written letter truly represent its spoken counterpart, previously subaltern social groups would be able to attain the tools of literacy, ensuring their representation within the dominant intellectual group. The necessary formal revolution in written language was intended as an ethical revolution toward greater equalities of thought. Yet, like Webster's attempts to reform orthography in the early years of the republic, this type of "democratic" language did not tolerate difference: it aimed instead for the total destruction of nonstandard speech. Francis March emphasized this when he addressed arguments that "fonetic" writing would introduce dialectal pronunciation into literature and cause the written language to mutate constantly in its attempt to reflect changing pronunciation. "We take for granted there is a standard pronunciation," he stated, into which it is "wholly undesirable to admit . . . the ever varying glides and finishes and coloring of fashionable or vulgar articulation." Spelling reform embodied the desire for an ideal literary language in which, wrote Lounsbury, the "exact pronunciation would be imposed upon the word by its very form," a language that would erase vocal manifestations of cultural difference. In this sense, spelling reform exposed a wider political tension in the thought of linguistic scholars. For Whitney, the speakers of a language "constitute a republic, or rather, a democracy, in which authority is conferred only by general suffrage." This was what philologists usually meant by applying democracy to language: the idea that language was a vast consensus of popular usage. Yet such theories were inherently problematic. Lacking Romantic faith in the natural powers of language, late-nineteenth-century philologists felt that leveling meant degeneration, that the democratic was demotic. Thus, for Whitney, democracy did not mean pluralism: "To attain that thorough democracy which is the best life and vigour of language, to keep our English speech vivid with the thought and feeling of a whole people, we should not bring down the tone and style of the highest, nor average those of all classes; we should rather lift up the lower to the level of the higher."[46] Spelling reform admitted that the only acceptable democracy of speech was a hegemonic imposition.

An important question arises here, one that gets to the heart of the politics of talk in the Gilded Age. If philologists recognized the fundamental importance of dialect to language, and if they believed, moreover, that the United States was as free from dialectal difference as possible, then why did so many of them support—often fanatically—a reform movement that sought to eradicate nonstandard discourse by officially instituting the usage of the cultivated? Why was there so much effort to remove linguistic differences when the very weakness of these differences was held to be a distinctly American quality? In attempting to resolve this apparent paradox, we should first note that the observation of America's dialectal dearth, which can be found in a host of writers and linguists from the eighteenth century to the present day, was typically based on a rigid, localized idea. In this country there are, "properly speaking, no dialects," wrote Lounsbury in 1880, because the "peculiarities which distinguish either the pronunciation or the vocabulary of the dwellers in any part of the United States" are not "universal within the limits assigned" as they are in Britain.[47] Lounsbury was taking the argument a little far: there were recognizable regional characteristics of speech in the United States, as the rise of regional fiction after the Civil War suggests, and it was possible to find occasional acknowledgments of a radical miscommunication between provinces.[48] Edward Eggleston, for example, cited an instance from the Civil War when a South Carolina lieutenant was unable to understand a North Carolina soldier.[49] Even so, it could not be denied that these contrasts were far less regionally defined or various than the European paradigms against which they were usually compared. Yet, where dialect is concerned, asked C. A. Bristed in 1855, are the rules not somewhat different in the United States?

> The English provincialisms *keep their place;* they are confined to their own particular localities, and do not encroach on the metropolitan model. The American provincialisms are more equally distributed through all classes and

localities, and though some of them may not rise above a certain level of society, others are heard everywhere. The senate or the boudoir is no more sacred from their intrusions than the farm-house or the tavern.

Ironically, the social and geographical mobility that were usually cited as key reasons why these regional speech-types failed to crystalize in America also created the potentially more disruptive situation in which provincialisms could freely affect the supposedly standard speech of the "cultivated" social classes. Tony Crowley has shown how there developed in late-nineteenth-century Britain a standard literary language that was "beyond dispute," a standard accompanied by the formation of what A. J. Ellis termed "the theoretically received pronunciation of literary English."[50] In the United States, however, language would never seem so neatly polarized into standard and nonstandard forms. The speech of the lower and middle classes might not vary among regions to the same extent as in England, yet the supposedly standard speech remains strictly regional. Bristed's recognition of this fact became widespread after the Civil War: it was shared by verbal critics like White and by philologists such as Whitney and E. S. Sheldon, the first president of the American Dialect Society. "The so-called standard language is not a fixed and infallible standard," wrote Sheldon, "but is itself constantly changing with the course of time, and is different in the different places where it is spoken."[51]

The notion that American dialect was active at all levels of society became an important part of philological theory toward the end of the century. Whitney would never substantially alter his view that America lacked dialects in the European sense, yet his emphasis shifted in *The Life and Growth of Language* (1875) away from the celebration of linguistic unity toward a recognition of the possibilities for disunity and miscommunication within a single tongue:

> We must be careful not to overrate the uniformity of existing languages; it is far enough from being absolute. In a true and defensible sense, every individual speaks a language different from every other. The capacities and the opportunities of each have been such that he has acquired command of a part of English speech not precisely identical with any one else's: the peculiarity may be slight, but it is certainly there. Then, what is yet more obvious and yet more important, the form of each one's conceptions, represented by his use of words, is different from any other person's; all his individuality of character, of knowledge, education, feeling, enters into this difference. And yet again, few if any escape the taint of local and personal peculiarities of pronunciation and phraseology, peculiarities which, because more conspicuous than the others, are more often noticed by us and called dialectic. This last shades off into the more wide-spread and deeper differ-

ences of district and class; every separate part of a great country of one speech has its local form, more or less strongly marked—even where, as in America, there are no old inherited dialects, of long standing, such as prevail in Britain, in Germany, in France.

Rather than designating a distinct area of incorrect usage, Whitney described dialect as a pervasive force within language that prevents stability or unity. While reinforcing the popular belief in the importance of language to the overall quality of self (again, we see Whitney's closeness to verbal critics in his relation of speech to questions of character, knowledge, and feeling), Whitney emphasized how language has an inherent tendency to degenerate into variety and disorder, a tendency particularly true of "democratic" situations in which a cultivated standard is not the agent of control. In effect, Whitney unsettled myths of univocal nationhood by moving toward a theory of linguistic multiformity: the idea that any single language is really a composite of many, partially separate dialects which descend in scale from regional to local and finally personal levels. This protean idea was repeated by Sheldon in his attempt to explain the nature of dialect to readers of an early *Dialect Notes* (1896), suggesting that it became a widely held view of the time, especially among those who took a scientific interest in the spoken voice.[52]

Whitney may have been talking about language in general, yet his idea of the prevalence of "*quasi*-dialectic discordances existing within the limits of the same language in the same community" had a special application to the American situation. Whitney gave theoretical structure to the particularly American idea that the forces of miscommunication, usually associated with regional dialect, were operating in all sectors of society. Thus, his theory of dialectal ubiquity closely echoes the political thoughts of Alexis de Tocqueville a generation before. While Tocqueville's *Democracy in America* (1835) added to the recognition that the lack of fixed social positions and widespread communications meant that there were no dialects in the New World, this did not necessarily mean an end to miscommunication: quite the contrary, as the activities of the American literati reveal.

> Here, then, is a motley multitude with intellectual wants to be supplied. These new votaries of the pleasure of the mind have not all had the same education; they are not guided by the same lights, do not resemble their own fathers; and they themselves are changing every moment with changing place of residence, feelings, and fortune. So there are no traditions, or common habits, to forge links between their minds, and they have neither the power nor the wish nor the time to come to a common understanding. . . . [T]he continual restlessness of a democracy leads to endless change of language as of all else. In the general stir of intellectual competition a great many new ideas take shape; old ideas get lost or take new forms or are

perhaps subdivided with an infinite variety of nuances. . . . [T]he origin of
words is as much forgotten as that of men, and language is in as much
confusion as society.

The majority might lay down the law about language in a democracy, yet
this majority chooses from the prescribed common stock of speech "at
random" and without discrimination. By giving new meanings to old
words, democratic peoples make signification ambiguous, and the fact
that language must be loose enough to accommodate such wildly oscil-
lating thoughts means that abstraction, vagueness, and obscurity become
necessary, and to some extent gain a certain charm among democratic
writers. Tocqueville was not alone in recognizing the peculiar forces, operating within American democracy, that fragment a seemingly homogeneous speech community, bringing disorder to apparent oneness. In *The
American Democrat* (1838), James Fenimore Cooper also criticized America's hifalutin discourse, "ambiguity of expression," and "perversions of
significations," while in the following year the English traveler Frederick
Marryat scotched the idea that America was without indecipherable varieties of speech. One has only to look at this Yankee girl's reply to the
question of whether or not she has a sweetheart: "Well, now, can't exactly
say; I bees a sorter courted, and a sorter not; reckon more a sorter yes
than a sorter no." No English dialect, thought Marryat, was as unintelligible as this inherently ambiguous way of talking.[53]

Whitney gave the name *dialect* to America's many new and peculiar
types of speech, thus codifying cultural styles and linguistic aberrations
that had become publicly prominent in the middle of the century.[54] Following a predominant pattern within philological thought, this theoriza-
tion of difference did not necessarily mean a new, unbiased relativism. In
a largely favorable review of White's *Words and Their Uses*, Whitney echoed
the same anxiety of verbal critics that ungrammatical language was "ut-
tered by persons in good social positions" and seen in quality newspapers;
he offered as possible reasons the increase in America's foreign element
(a point to which we return shortly), the growth of its "shoddy" classes,
and an "increasing spirit of carelessness and want of reverence for all rule
and system." Whitney fed the politicized fear after the Civil War that dialect had become loosened from its regional moorings and was active as
a much less defined but much more subversive factor of chaos within every
strand of America's cultural fabric. Hence Whitney's consideration that a
"tendency to slang, to colloquial inelegancies, and even vulgarities" was
"the besetting sin against which we, as Americans, have especially to guard
and to struggle"—a statement that verbal critics were keen to quote.[55]
Whitney may not have been opposed to the leveling forces of democracy
in theory, as were many verbal critics; yet he still recognized the potentially

dangerous, destabilizing linguistic forces that a commercial democracy released.

The tendency to equate political and linguistic institutions, which marks Whitney's work, was widespread at the end of the century. For some, this equation was much more immediate: it was not so much that language was politicized as that politics was actually damaging language. The extension of suffrage to the "lowest" and "most ignorant" classes, noted Schele de Vere, "favored the admission of so many vulgar and cant terms that in politics, above all, the line between slang and solemn speech is not always perceptible."[56] Schele de Vere voiced explicitly the antidemocratic political logic, the fear of collapsing hierarchies, that underpinned verbal criticism and philology alike. For E. S. Sheldon, it was not politics but education that was the real force of destabilization: "children are carefully taught to avoid various forms of 'bad English' by persons not all of whom can correctly distinguish in every case between bad English and idiomatic colloquial English."[57] Whichever social force was held to blame, these observers were united in the fear that there were no strict boundaries between the nonstandard and the standard, however hard they might try to construct them. "The absence of sound criticism, and the little respect paid to the authority of good writers and sound teachers," sensed Schele de Vere, left the American language dangerously vulnerable to what he called the "contamination" from nonstandard forms like slang and neologism.[58]

Echoing Whitney's point that boundaries between languages, dialects, and idiolects are prone to dissolution, the key quality observed in American dialect was that of intermixture (or *contamination*, as it was more negatively figured). Just as imported British English dialects had originally mixed with one another in the seventeenth century, so too were the dialects of the late nineteenth century in a state of constant coalescence and flux.[59] Dialect was not absent from the United States, thought W. D. Howells; it was present "everywhere": a sign that "[w]e are an intensely decentered people in our letters as well as in our politics."[60] Those who believe that the common schools have obliterated dialects, wrote R. L. Dawson in 1890, "do not know human nature" and do not appreciate the "great undercurrents" that pick up particles of dialect in one place and drop them in another, creating a situation in which everyone we meet has "his own mannerism, and is a dialect speaker to some extent." For Sheldon, these processes of interaction were particularly important because they suggested that dialects were only just beginning to grow in the United States, an idea shared by other scholarly philologists of the era. The reason that Sheldon gives for this potential growth, moreover, captures the other critical point that distinguished the American from the English scene, and marked the new direction of linguistic fears after the

Civil War: "[W]e have the phenomena of dialect mixture to study here, and we can watch these as they take place, as the speakers of foreign languages (and, for that matter, of some forms of English, as Irish-English) who come as immigrants mix in varying proportions with the English speakers already here."[61] The tendency to dismiss the presence of American dialect from a regional perspective ignored the much more pervasive process in which dialects arose from the contact among speakers of different languages, a factor that was particularly strong, thought Sheldon, in French-speaking Louisiana, German-speaking Pennsylvania, and the Spanish-speaking Southwest. It was a factor, moreover, that increased exponentially with the so-called new immigration into American cities toward the end of the century.

American philologists like E. S. Sheldon were pioneering in their codification of these ethnic, urban linguistic phenomena as dialects, and more recent scholars have followed in their wake: J. L. Dillard, for example, believes that language contact "may have been the greatest single factor in the development of American English non-standard dialects."[62] For many nineteenth-century Americans, however, the distinct English of French, German, or Spanish speakers (to name but a few) represented merely forms of "broken English" that needed correction. Yet, whether they were considered dialects or not, the tremendous power of these ethnic forces to alter English could not be ignored. It was not retentions from East Anglia, thought one writer in 1890, but the "commingling of races" that had led to America's "curious and wonderful maze of English dialects."[63] The linguistic consequences of ethnic contact were especially audible in the West. An awareness of Chinese pidgin English was widespread there by the 1870s, and the consequences of "pidginization" were beginning to be recognized in literature and philology.[64] Fitzedward Hall noted in 1874 that English had formed a lingua franca among immigrants in Pennsylvania, who, presumably, spoke variant German dialects, suggesting that "[o]ur lingual hybridism is ineradicable"—a point made earlier by John Bartlett, editor of *The Dictionary of Americanisms* (1848), who believed that Pennsylvania German "will leave behind it an almost imperishable dialect as a memento of its existence." The wider implications of this hybridism were captured in the unidentified quotation that heads the chapter "Immigrants from Abroad" in Schele de Vere's *Americanisms: The English of the New World* (1872): "When a score of nations, each with its own dialect, unite to make up our population, some effect must be produced on our language; some peculiar threads will be found after a while interwoven with the national web."[65]

These ideas about the complex processes of quasi-creolization, in which foreign groups were losing their native tongues and acquiring English in ways that transformed English itself, were not unique to the Gilded Age; indeed, similar ideas tend to be inherent in all observations of linguistic contact and change. Such was the degree of ethnic influx and interaction in late-nineteenth-century America, however, that the impact of these dialectal forces was attracting unprecedented attention. Even in a British context in the early twentieth century, Robert Bridges pointed to America as the ultimate paradigm: "wherever our countrymen are settled abroad there are alongside of them communities of other-speaking races, who, maintaining among themselves their native speech, learn yet enough of ours to mutilate it, and establishing among themselves all kinds of blundering corruptions, through habitual intercourse infect therewith the neighbouring English." This situation was even more obnoxious, thought Bridges, when the "blind optimism" of American philology was simultaneously urging that "*the old Lady*"—meaning the English language—"*may be trusted to take care of herself.*"[66]

Bridges's purism was just one reaction to the transformative effect of these peculiar ethnic threads within American culture. The radical language reformer Elias Molee, for example, proposed in 1888 to make use of these processes of hybridism—or at least those that conformed to his ideal racial stock—by creating a tongue that merged English, Irish, German, and Scandinavian elements: it would be a "union spiek . . . for to agenferein al tutonish folka into ein spiek mitin feivte jiera."[67] Most commentators on language, however, reacted against the threat of linguistic transformation posed by ethnic presences. Some developed racially deterministic ideas that language was "always the same in variation and tone in the articulate sounds of any particular race—brogue in the Irishman, accent in the educated German, 'Pigeon Yankee' in the Chinaman, or gibberish—not to put too fine a point upon the word—in the native African."[68] As we saw earlier, others clung to the equally oppressive belief that Anglo-Saxon "race characteristics" were able to assimilate virtually all foreign elements that came into their path, thus maintaining ideas of Anglo-Saxon purity in a nation notable for its ethnic variety. Confidence in the power of English either to resist or assimilate all outside elements without assistance, however, was not shared by all. Ironically, Darwin's idea that the spread of a language like English was aided by its selection of the fittest words and constructions "from various conquering, or conquered, or immigrant races" fed pseudo-Darwinian fears that, as a highly "evolved" language, English needed increased protection from foreign contamination. For William Mathews, the fact that English was "so hospitable to alien words" ("bastardised," said Darwin) meant that it needed "more powerful securities against revolution than other languages of less heterogeneous composition." Similarly, the *North American Review* carried

the suggestion in 1889 that an American Academy of Language was necessary to abolish dialects, and thus to prevent the linguistic changes that
arise from the "varied foreign elements pouring into our country," the
"extent and variety of our territory," and the "habit of taking intellectual
pabulum from all nations and languages and tongues." A writer in *Godey's
Lady's Book* put it more succinctly: we should exclude undesirable words
as we should exclude immigrants who cannot show themselves to be useful
members of society. Even the usually optimistic Brander Matthews called
for linguistic intervention:

> Foreign words must always be allowed to land on our coasts without a pass-
> port; yet if any of them linger long enough to warrant a belief that they may
> take out their papers sooner or later, we must decide at last whether or not
> they are likely to be desirable residents of our dictionary; if we determine
> to naturalize them, we must fairly enough insist on their renouncing their
> foreign allegiance. They must cast in their lot with us absolutely, and be
> bound by our laws only.[69]

Rather like the recent immigrants who were expected to display patriotic
fervor on American national holidays, foreign languages were required to
assimilate fully to the Anglo-American identity. When it came to foreignness in America, the writing was clearly on the wall: words, just like immigrants, must give up their native ties and accept the dictates of the
dominant, anglophone culture. Non-English speakers, it was exhorted,
should leave no dialectal traces on the American tongue.

Fear of foreign contamination obsessed scholarly philologists; their relativistic theories of conventionalism were directly undercut by racialist beliefs. In this respect, close attention to George Perkins Marsh's *Lectures on
the English Language* (1859) is enlightening, as it helps to explain some of
the reasons behind patterns that remain fairly constant in later thinkers
such as Whitney. In a manner similar to Whitney, Marsh began to move
away from the idea of an absolute, organic relationship between language
and mind, language and national character. Again like Whitney (and in
language foreshadowing Whitney's so closely that it suggests direct influence), Marsh began to develop relativistic ideas whereby "every man has
a dialect of his own" because he "selects from the general stock his own
vocabulary, his favorite combinations of words, his own forms of syntax."
Yet, predicting Whitney's later ambivalence, Marsh immediately qualifies
his ideas. Language is not a conventional, external institution but an organic power that reveals the inner ethical life of men and the intellectual
heart of nations. And dialects, at first described as the inescapable possession of all, become much more iniquitous entities: they are "very serious obstacles to national progress, to the growth of a comprehensive
and enlightened patriotism, to the creation of a popular literature, and

to the diffusion of general culture." Similarly, in one breath Marsh admits the natural law of change in language, only to state in the next breath the need "to retard the decay of our tongue, and to prevent its dissipation into a multitude of independent dialects," thereby predicting Lounsbury's similarly ambivalent wish to freeze a language that he recognizes will always be developing.[70]

One way to understand these apparent contradictions in American philology is to see them in terms of a clash between scientific and cultural motivations. The logical outcome of scientific theory came into conflict with deep-seated cultural prejudices: hence, the contrast between Marsh's attempt to separate the language–nation equation and his less than enlightened opinions about Italian language and culture that we encountered earlier. Here Marsh gives us the key to the loudest ambivalence that resounds in late-nineteenth-century linguistic thought: the combination of the belief that America has an unprecedented oneness of speech with the almost paranoid fear that dialects will divide the American community "into so many disjointed fragments." Since Marsh's theory about language in America suggests nothing but regional sameness, why this anxiety? Again, the answer lies in the most powerful factor behind America's linguistic peculiarities: "the great influx of foreigners speaking different languages or dialects, . . . in adopting our speech, cannot fail to communicate to it some of the peculiarities of their own."[71] Such fear of foreign infiltration makes Marsh's anti-Italian outburst clearer still.

The various camps of linguistic thought after the Civil War believed the American language—a primary sign of the nation's cultural identity—to be under attack. The main weapons of this attack were foreign-language speakers, with their transformative impact, and the forces of democracy, which challenged any attempt to form an authoritative cultural center. Both were eroding the American standard from within. This double-edged challenge was nicely described by William Mathews: "Not only does political freedom make every man in America an inventor, alike of labor-saving machines and of labor-saving words, but the mixture of nationalities is constantly coining and exchanging new forms of speech, of which our busy Bartletts, in their lists of Americanisms, find it impossible to keep account." We need look no further to understand why supposed celebrants of vernacular unity were inventing spelling systems that would destroy dialect altogether. The observation of America's lack of distinct regional dialects was supplemented by recognitions of the "infinite number of fluctuating forces" in American English which were arising from an "endless variety" of new cultural elements.[72]

These reactions to American speech paralleled the larger problems of social authority that are typically associated with the Gilded Age.[73] James Russell Lowell's nativist fear that American democracy was being threatened by inassimilable foreigners who were contaminating the breath of public opinion with their malarious, unsanitary exhalations was part of an anxiety that the nation's own ideological machinery might be turned against it.[74] So often, the supposed strengths of America—its political system, universal education, social mobility—were perceived to be the very agents of linguistic and cultural disorder. This helps to explain why dialect was, for philologists like Marsh, a much more disruptive presence than foreign languages: "What we regard as distortions of our mother-tongue are more offensive to us than the widest diversities between it and unallied languages; and we regard a fellow-citizen who speaks a marked provincial English with a contempt and aversion, which we do not bestow upon the foreigner who speaks no English at all." The real threat was, in a sense, internal rather than external; it involved English, not foreign languages. The most terrifying thought was that the marrow of Anglo-American culture might be contaminated by otherness. Nowhere was this more evident than in an American speech that was—thought Brander Matthews—"freed from all control by a central authority and exposed to all sorts of alien influences."[75]

The alien influences that troubled Matthews were legion. In 1893, the president of the American Dialect Society E. S. Sheldon asked the question "What is a Dialect?" His answer: just about any form of cultural discourse, from national languages and regional variations, to slang, trade jargons, and the distinct vocal style of women. Not surprisingly, there were many who still adhered to the belief that regionalism was the clearest and most predominant characteristic of American dialect.[76] The drift of opinion, however, was away from regionalism toward a much wider appreciation of linguistic difference. Dialect was understood as a protean force that made communication difficult in a single tongue; it comprised all the powers that challenged the ideology of a dominant, unified national language. This new emphasis was more on attitudes toward language use than on questions of lexis or pronunciation. Hence the language of the West was defined by its attitude toward exaggeration and metaphor rather than by individual words or sounds; the speech of African Americans in the South was described as depending more "upon the manner, the form of expression, and the inflection, than upon the words employed";[77] the dialect of working-class Yankees was marked by its general spirit of ambiguity rather than by any solely linguistic factors; and ethnic dialect was defined not by stable grammatical or phonetic elements but by the mysterious and variable processes that inevitably occur when two linguistic systems meet. Ethnic dialect was just another wave in a vast spectrum of social speech types whose origins may not have been entirely clear but whose power to challenge a belief in linguistic oneness could not be ignored.

Dialect was understood generally as a way of talking: it could thus include judgments about the artificial, overly highbrow language of the cultivated, or the bombast of the political stump speaker, in addition to the provincialisms of Appalachia. Indeed, one of the most important distinctions of the era was not between the standard literary language and the nonstandard dialect but between the natural power of idiomatic, colloquial speech and the purportedly lackluster, over-redundant, and effete nature of artificial "book-talk."[78] The *North American Review* realized this as early as 1860: America is crying out for "that medium style of speech, that natural, plain, unstudied utterance, equally removed from pedantry and vulgarity, which is the charm of conversation. The talk of the educated abounds in bookish expressions and constructions, and in words of Latin derivation."[79] The "hybridism" that marked the speech of the multiethnic lower classes was also observed in the language of the educated: the infusion of Latinate constructions and French words into polite discourse was a constant cause for complaint.[80] Whitney's relativistic idea that literary English is itself a dialect was thus matched by observations of an American "proper" language contaminated by all the elements of error with which dialects were typically associated. The sense of linguistic collapse was total; nonstandard English was effectively everywhere.

The Gilded Age conflict between "scientific" and "armchair" philologists may have revealed basic differences in the understanding of whether language was a conventional institution or a spiritual organism, yet there was also a shared sense that language was not merely a register of deeper social forces but a primary factor in their being. This was why such immense weight was placed on the question of the language: for verbal critics it generated the national-racial essence; for philologists it founded the conditions for a cultivated civilization. This common emphasis, moreover, explains why intellectual distinctions in the period are so blurred, why Whitney considered White's *Words and Their Uses* to be "most praiseworthy in design, generally commendable in execution, and certain to be beneficial in result."[81] Ambivalence was endemic, nowhere more so than in considerations of nonstandard language. The most conservative thinkers, like Richard Grant White, could exalt the racy, pungent idioms of the ignorant and uneducated,[82] while supposed celebrants of the vernacular were fearful that dialectal difference spelled national disintegration, and saw dialects themselves as signs of "physical and intellectual stagnation."[83] Language became a fundamental weapon in the battle for American national identity, yet where dialect was concerned this weapon was two-edged. Dialect could embody notions of national stability by confirming the predominant patterns of Anglo-Saxon settlement, while also representing the fear that American culture was being transformed by foreign immigration; it could evoke a nostalgic sense of rural quaintness, while also illustrating the more menacing implications of mass urbanization. The panic over miscommunication among provincial dialects that drove the reformist ideas of Noah Webster may well have died down in the 1830s and '40s, yet new dialectal forces grew toward the end of the century that were every bit as subversive in their implications of fragmentation and contamination.[84]

The encounter between old ideas of regional dialect and new notions of social difference in speech helps to explain the remarkable coexistence of the belief that America was a model of linguistic homogeneity with the idea that a kind of dialectal discordance pervaded society. The simultaneous opinion that the nation was both unified and splintered into differences was related to much broader pairings of wholeness and fragmentation in Gilded Age culture. Concerning literature, this was the era of the standardized plots and the standardized characters of dime novels, but also the era when the nation's readership was—thought Henry James—beginning to seem "subdivided as a chessboard, with each little square confessing only to its own *kind* of accessibility." The age of machine-produced cultural sameness, or "Chromo-Civilization" as E. L. Godkin termed it, was also the age of vast infusions of ethnic and social difference that were perceived to arise from industrial culture and mass immigration.[85] An ideology of dominant Anglo-American nationalism coexisted with the growing recognition that national culture was defined by alien elements, antagonistic to American customs. The study of language after the Civil War was a crucial part of this complex cultural situation. Attempts to forge an authoritative linguistic identity based on ideal theories of a cultivated standard came into conflict with the idea—the fear—that traditions of linguistic propriety were being contaminated by new social conditions. Ideologies of dialectal indigence confronted new definitions of dialect that registered the transformative impact, not just of ethnic immigrants, but of a whole series of disturbing cultural developments. The creolized voices of emancipated Africans, the slang and neologism of popular culture, the feminized discourse of the American woman, the "broken English" of urban environments: these were the newly recognized dialects of America, just as they were the material of the newly popular dialect literature that sought to translate their implications.

TWO

The Cult of the Vernacular

Ever since John Adams wrote his "Humphrey Ploughjogger" letters to Boston newspapers in the 1760s, there has been an intimate connection in American literature between dialect and political criticism. Adams used the "speech and persona of the plain New England farmer," writes David Simpson, "to highlight the problems of the rural class in an expanding commercial economy." This use of dialect to represent plain, common-sense criticism of weighty political problems would persist, resurfacing in Finley Peter Dunne's Mr. Dooley sketches at the end of the nineteenth century, for example, and in Langston Hughes's Jesse B. Semple sketches in the middle of the twentieth. Dunne's comments on his use of Chicago-Irish brogue to criticize local and national politics in the 1890s reveal a key reason why dialect became so important to these writers: "while it might be dangerous to call an alderman a thief in English no one could sue if a comic Irishman denounced the statesman as a thief."[1] Dialect was much more than a humorous gimmick: it *enabled* certain types of political criticism, especially among those who were alienated from centers of power, by creating another level of discourse in which deep ethical convictions could be safely represented.

Between the 1830s and the Civil War, dialect entered American magazines and newspapers as the natural language of political satire. Fictional characters such as Sam Slick, Jack Downing, Sut Luvingood, and Petroleum V. Nasby spoke in broad regional vernaculars that served a range of agendas: they criticized corrupt political activities and discourses with the language of down-to-earth moral wisdom; they represented and appealed to growing populist sentiment; they encoded Whiggish disdain for the irrational, violent, and barbarous qualities that were perceived at the heart of Jacksonian society.[2] During the Civil War, dialect was a weapon wielded by opposing camps. In the mouth of George Washington Harris's Sut Luvingood, the violent vernacular of a belligerent South railed against the North, while in the writings of David Ross Locke, creator of Petroleum V. Nasby, a similar southern speech encoded a stinging satire of the racist South.[3] To some extent, these early exponents of the American vernacular revealed a type of ambivalence that increased after the Civil War. In the work of the southern humorist Augustus Baldwin Longstreet, for example, moral polarities of language seem always on the verge of collapsing into one another. Alongside attempts to restrain the degenerate dialect of democracy within an idealized discourse of gentlemanly propriety, we see a deep attraction to the vernacular qualities that were being lampooned, and a lampooning of the polite language to which such writers were meant to be attracted.[4]

From the perspective of the Gilded Age, however, these antebellum and Civil War writers were not seen as precursors of dialect literature but as models to react against. Although Longstreet maintained that he had depicted the actual dialect of backwoodsmen, and Mark Twain believed that George Washington Harris had represented the Tennessee dialect correctly,[5] the language of earlier dialect writers was mostly marked by puns, malapropisms, and outrageous misspellings—an orthographic buffoonery that inscribed the semiliterate status of the speaker or writer while forcing comedy from dressing conventional phrases in what one humorist called a "lingual garb so quaint, eccentric, fantastic, or extravagant."[6] This "misspelling bee," as Walter Blair calls it, reached immense proportions in the years surrounding the Civil War. Although the southern humorist Charles Henry Smith "reconstructed" his orthography as an act of political reconciliation immediately following the war, his later hostility to the disasters of Reconstruction politics reawakened extremely bad spelling.[7] Clearly, the deformed languages of Civil War satirists were generated by the need for grassroots spokesmen whose languages were belligerent and unconventional enough to voice violent political dissent. These dialects of political abuse, together with the humorous misspelling of words that assaulted linguistic propriety for its own sake, became less and less popular in the 1870s and '80s.[8] Many humorists took to the lecture platform in response. While their material was still political in tone, it became less sectarian and confrontational, and their voices became less regionally distinct as linguistic attention was turned to the burlesquing of hifalutin and sentimental styles rather than nonstandard dialects.[9] Sporadic earlier efforts to record the varieties of American English had seemingly degenerated into either political poison and bizarre misspelling, or malapropistic stage clowning. The ground was prepared for a reaction: the regional writing that came to dominate the late-nineteenth-century literary marketplace seized upon the supposed misuse of the American voice as the primary target for its new representational energies.

The postbellum "cult of the vernacular" differed from earlier manifestations of American dialect in several crucial ways: it was part of mainstream literature; it avowed realism, not humor; its political content sunk to a deeper, less overt level. We saw in the previous chapter how cultural and philological debate over dialect in the Gilded Age oscillated between celebrations of dialectal variety and fears over linguistic disunity, between attempts to establish a moral hierarchy of social languages and recognitions of the inescapable hybridity of the national tongue. The literary treatment of dialect echoed this pattern. While the burgeoning "local color" movement sought the soul of America in the rugged, racy vernaculars of a rustic past, there was a contrary sense in which dialect frustrated the ideology of national unity by demonstrating the growing distances and differences within English itself. And although much dialect writing seemed to uphold an elitist agenda by juxtaposing the "proper" language of the narrator and the "improper" language of the character, as recent critics have emphasized, dialect also had the power to antagonize the standard it appeared to presuppose.[10] The ambivalent political aesthetics of dialect writing was developed in James Russell Lowell's *The Biglow Papers* (1848, 1866), a pivotal text in the transition of literary dialect from its pre–Civil War glimmering to its post–Civil War blossoming. The defining characteristics of the subsequent craze for dialect literature illustrate the idea that dialect could embody the dissolution of the nation in addition to its essence. This is demonstrated in the vernacular cult's regional and social ideals, its technical efforts to make voices visible on the printed page, and—as we see in the second part of this chapter—in Twain's exploration of western dialect. Before turning to the many ways that dialect interacted with diverse questions of gender, race, and urbanization, we should first understand the aesthetic and political complexities within the quintessence of Gilded Age dialect writing: the movement to represent, realistically, the colorfulness of regional discourse.

REALISM, REGIONALISM, AND THE POLITICS OF REPRESENTATION

For writers of the 1870s and '80s, James Russell Lowell was a pioneer: Edward Eggleston described him in 1871 as "the only one of our most eminent authors and the only one of our most eminent scholars who has given careful attention to American dialects."[11] Eggleston was referring to Lowell's *The Biglow Papers*, a collection of poems published in two series, the first written in response to the Mexican War, the second in response to the Civil War. Lowell emphasized throughout the work that his dialect poetry was a direct product of political turmoil (43–44, 371). Like the many dialect-speaking commentators who erupted in the popular press during those same years, Lowell viewed his representation of Hosea Biglow's Yankee dialect as a "natural stronghold," a homespun political and satirical weapon that could make serious points "in a way that would tell" (155). Rather than merely using dialect as the medium of political protest, however, Lowell expanded the idea that pronunciation is inherently moral (the Yankee's avoidance of the rough *r* sound shows his "considerable ingenuity" while the failure to sound the final *g* in words bespeaks "self-denial") into an extensive meditation on the political valency of speech and of signs in general.[12] America's political problems, in other words, are figured linguistically—indeed, they seem to result directly from imperfections of language. The failure of the nation to protest against the Mexican War, for example, arises from "some malformation or defect of the vocal organs" that prevents our uttering the word *no*, or "gives it so thick a pronunciation as to be unintelligible" (63). Similarly, nationalistic phrases like "[o]ur country, right or wrong" are an "abuse of language" (68); the politically charged "big talk" of politicians is without intellectual content (67); Congress is a latter-day Babel of unintelligible meanings (87–88); and the "republic of letters," which arises from the epidemic of letter-writing before an election, is full of error and ambiguity (112–15). The second series of the *Papers* likewise juxtaposes philological questions with political questions of slavery and war, emphasizing how political crises originate from errors of pronouncing or interpreting words such as *disunion* and *abolition* (327).

The structure, themes, and final moral message of *The Biglow Papers* also center on questions of speech. The work brings together a series of linguistic levels: Hosea Biglow's rustic Yankee dialect; the pedantic, scholastic discourse of Homer Wilbur, the fictitious editor of the *Papers;* and the vernacular voice of Birdofredum Sawin, a Yankee soldier who becomes sympathetic to the southern cause. Biglow's dialect is largely presented as the natural voice of truth, pitched against the "foreign tongue" (26) of classical poetry and the standardized, school-mastered language that was spreading rapidly through mass education and popular journalism. The opposition between dialect and standard is thus more than a simple clash between the grammatical and the ungrammatical. Hosea's racy vernacular is presented as superior—both linguistically and morally—to the supposedly "high" discourses that surround it: namely, the over-redundant rhetoric of the press, the empty, corrupt language of politics, and—to a lesser extent—the weak, unsubtle poetry of the pretentious Homer Wilbur. The main opposition in the poem is between the under-grammatical but natural speaker and the over-grammatical, artificial speakers who devalue English with their rhetorical inflation. Yet the real point of *The Biglow Papers*' linguistic politics is that true moral sentiment is more subtle than this inversion of a "high"/"low" hierarchy. Wilbur's pedantic speech can also encode virtuous beliefs—Lowell makes clear in his introduction to the second series that Wilbur was meant as a complement to, not an opponent of, Biglow (156). Moreover, the "spellin'-book" is not always a negative factor that takes energy from English; rather, the education facilitated by the spelling-book is necessary to emancipate the minds of white Americans from racism (340). The vernacular of Birdofredum Sawin or the avowed plain-speaking of politicians just as easily portrays racism and prevarication as homely wisdom. *The Biglow Papers* points toward the deeper ethics, the spiritual substance, that can exist in both conventional and vernacular language. Lowell's work is a lesson in the morality of interpretation, in which natural and artificial, virtuous and corrupt levels of language are the real dialects that give inner power to outward forms.[13]

Lowell wrote a long introduction for the second series of the *Papers* (1866), explaining the roots and qualities of Biglow's Yankee speech in philological detail. The introduction reiterates many of the points implicit in Lowell's earlier poetry, especially the need for an energetic vernacular to remedy the artificial, redundant English of newspaper and classroom, and the emasculated rhetoric of the political system (158–59). Yet Lowell's celebration of the Yankee dialect also shows signs of tension and ambivalence, especially concerning questions of linguistic vulgarity. Worried that readers might think his spokesman trapped in a world of "mere *patois*," Lowell informs us that Hosea can speak "district-school English" when he wants to (155–56)—a point made by Hosea himself toward the end of the *Papers* (370)—but prefers the vivified common sense of the vernacular for its satirical effectiveness. Biglow thus reflects Lowell's idea of himself: the polite speaker who writes in dialect "as in a mother tongue" (208). Rather than sanctioning the merits of Yankee dialect without qualification, yet not wishing to relinquish the power of common speech, Lowell denies Yankee its status as dialect, suggesting instead that it lies somewhere between a *lingo* and a *patois*, whereby "certain archaisms, proverbial phrases, and modes of pronunciation" are maintained "among the uneducated side by side with the finished and universally accepted language" (165). Lowell can accept neither America's schoolmastered language—pedantic, artificial, and "foreign" to living thought (159)— nor a truly dialectal alternative where the nation is fragmented into languages of absolute cultural difference. Foreshadowing fears about nonstandard language that philologists and verbal critics would come to share, Lowell accepts dialect only as a realm of heightened poetic usage, from which the "polite" language can borrow energy without losing its quality of politeness. Lowell's ideal language was, in his own words, "the tongue of the people in the mouth of the scholar."[14]

The contorted negotiations of Lowell's introduction, especially his desire both to have and not to have dialect, reveal another political agenda beneath his vernacular attack on American rhetoric and politics. In a bout of postcolonial anxiety, Lowell wants to prevent Americans from using the English language like Scotsmen:

> not as if it belonged to us, but as if we wished to prove that we belonged to it, by showing our intimacy with its written rather than with its spoken dialect. And yet all the while our popular idiom is racy with life and vigor and originality, bucksome (as Milton used the word) to our new occasions, and proves no mere graft by sending up new suckers from the old root in spite of us. . . . No language after it has faded into *diction*, none that cannot suck up the feeding juices secreted for it in the rich mother-earth of common folk, can bring forth a sound and lusty book. True vigor and heartiness of phrase do not pass from page to page, but from man to man, where the brain is kindled and the lips suppled by downright living interests and by passion in its very throe. Language is the soil of thought, and our own especially is a rich leaf-mould, the slow deposit of ages, the shed foliage of feeling, fancy, and imagination. . . . There is death in the dictionary; and, where language is too strictly limited by convention, the ground for expression to grow in is limited also; and we get a *potted* literature, Chinese dwarfs instead of healthy trees. [158–59]

This seminal description of America's dialectal potential is suffused with the language and assumptions of Romantic nationalism. The call for authors to inject the vibrant speech of the folk into their literary language was a call to reestablish the Anglo-Saxon roots of American culture. According to Lowell, Biglow's Yankee speech is a pure and vigorous form of Anglo-Saxon that has an "antiquity and very respectable literary authority" (167), traceable to Donne, Dryden, Spenser, Chaucer, and virtually every major figure of English literature from Anglo-Saxon times onward. Lowell's "Chinese dwarfs," moreover, do not merely refer to horticulture: they hint at the racial basis of his argument. Lowell's celebration of folk language is a defense against the conspicuousness of other ethnic groups in the nation. Biglow's speech is a reminder of the language spoken in the "time when an Irish day-laborer was as rare as an American one now" (208), and an antidote to the "Orientalism" found in the exaggerated diction of the West (163). Lowell's introduction was thus part of a wider movement to keep culture "pure" by identifying non-English elements as foreign to the American essence.

There were, then, two separate political motives behind Lowell's use of dialect: on the one hand, Biglow's vernacular is a higher moral language that criticizes the rhetoric and politics of American expansionism, slavery, and racism; on the other hand, dialect has a deeper racial mission to authenticate the Anglo-Saxon roots of the nation's culture. Dialect as an ethical language confronts dialect as an ethnic language: the one seeks to overturn racial boundaries, the other to confirm them. The ambivalent attitude toward the vernacular described by Lowell, and the relevance of this ambivalence to questions of race and nationhood, would dominate the literary treatment of dialect throughout the last decades of the nineteenth century.

Lowell's work also marked the new seriousness with which American dialects were beginning to be treated after the Civil War. His long introduction threw the weight of academic scholarship behind the idea that a genuine vernacular was being recorded, and regionalists such as Eggleston identified Lowell as a protorealist. Writers had always reacted to the unreality of one another's dialect, and such criticism often had an obvious political subtext: Lowell objected to Thomas Chandler Haliburton's ("Sam Slick's") Yankee dialect, not least because of Haliburton's antidemocratic opinions, while the dialect in *The Biglow Papers* was criticized for inaccuracy by *The Spirit of the Times*, a magazine with a far more conservative outlook than Lowell's.[15] The opinions on dialect expressed by the regionalists of the Gilded Age, however, were broached not in the name of explicit political agendas but in the interests of accurate representation. Thus, William Dean Howells argued in the *Atlantic Monthly* (1867) that Hosea Biglow speaks a "genuine vernacular" embodying "the type of a civilization," whereas Petroleum Nasby is only "a moralized merryandrew."[16] The important point for Howells was not politics—he would have admired the political effect of both Biglow and Nasby—but verisimilitude.

Walter Blair has argued convincingly that regional writing had its origins in the earlier tradition of humorous political satire: Edward Eggleston published an early comment on politics in Hoosier dialect, and Uncle Remus was originally conceived as a commentator on current events.[17] Yet, according to regional writers themselves, their strong emphasis on dialect could not have been more different from that of the funny fellows who had gone before. Edward Eggleston felt that his *Hoosier School-Master* depicted dialect with a seriousness superior to the "coarse boisterousness" of the "primitive humorists" of the old Southwest, and with greater accuracy than earlier purveyors of regional literature like Bret Harte (Harte was often a benchmark against which writers claimed greater dialectal authenticity).[18] Similarly, it was the intention of Joel Chandler Harris to replace the stigma of comedy with the sincerity of ethnography, to work against the stereotype that led publishers to include *Uncle Remus: His Songs and Sayings* (1880) in "their catalogue of humorous publications." According to Harris, his dialect was wholly different from that of humorists such as "the Hon. Pompey Smash and his literary descendants," and from "the intolerable misrepresentations of the minstrel stage"; it was "at least phonetically genuine." At their most optimistic, the defenders and the writers of dialect saw their language as a realistic representation of speech. They believed that dialect writing was a "perfect illustration of the fitness between sound and sense," that "a close enunciation of the words as spelled will . . . bring out the dialect with wonderful precision," that these new "combinations of letters" could express "the actual sounds supposed to be made by the speakers." "Surely never before," wrote a reviewer of Cable's *Old Creole Days* in 1880, "were such novel and varied vocal effects represented by the twenty-six letters of the English alphabet and a few italics and apostrophes." Hamlin Garland considered Joseph Kirkland's literary dialect to be "phonetically exact."[19]

Echoing the moral assumptions that advocates of simplified spelling had exposed in the spoken–written relationship, these writers believed that their new methods were ethically sound because they could represent the voices of people previously beyond formal literature by expanding the techniques of writing to include the prosodic qualities which generally differentiate the spoken from the written word. Similarities were occasionally noted between spelling reformers and dialect writers, and the latter were quick to use the tenets of graphical phoneticism to validate their linguistic experiments.[20] Joel Chandler Harris assumed that phonemes could be depicted on the page in a new form of literary language capable of capturing the essence of an integral folk, and *Uncle Remus* was described by critics as "the first real book of American folk lore" *because* it provided "exactly the sounds of the negro dialect." Rejecting Thomas Hardy's belief that dialect disturbs the proper balance of representation by diverting attention from the speaker's meaning, these writers exploited the supposed intimacy of meaning and form. The use of dialect was a necessity, stated Armstrong Wauchope in the *North American Review* in 1894, because "[m]ental traits are often inseparably wedded to the linguistic medium," so that we cannot "differentiate this individual from his manner of thought, nor the thought from the medium of expression." Following a similar logic, Harris believed that by recording the sound of the spoken voice his language could embody the African American's poetic imagination, his quaint and homely humor, his picturesque sensitiveness, and his "curious exaltation of mind and temperament not to be defined by words."[21] At their most enthusiastic, dialect writers believed they could capture the extra-lexical expressive qualities of America's many different ways of talking. Words were described as going beyond the previous limits of language by embodying an entirely different level of meaning not previously approached by written representation.[22]

While recent critics have exposed the difficulties of establishing "any consistent definition of 'realism' (or of 'naturalism') as a specific kind of literary representation," writers of the post–Civil War period were certain that they had discovered, in dialect, the very secret of realistic portrayal. Fred Lewis Pattee noted in 1915 that realism could be defined by its new attention to talk, and more recent critics have supported the idea that the reduction of authorial omniscience by foregrounding the voices of characters was an essential factor in creating the realistic tradition in America.[23] According to Hamlin Garland, "[d]ialect is the life of language, precisely as the common people of the nation form the sustaining power of its social life and art," and it must be represented accurately in all its various forms if we are to create a "democratic" literature that truly reveals the national character. Similarly, Howells's wish to hear characters "speak true American, with all the varying Tennessean, Philadelphian, Bostonian, and New York accents," was part of his vision of realism as an implementation of "democracy in literature" that might replace the "aristocratic spirit . . . now seeking to shelter itself in aesthetics." For these writers, dialect was the sharp end of realism's penetrating power. It was a new formal and ethical language—"a style with a politics in view," wrote Leo Marx—that could depict neglected or misrepresented races, classes, and regions. Thus, dialect writers like Eggleston believed that their depictions of American voices would "always have a certain value as materials for the student of social history."[24] The overt politics of race, slavery, and sectionalism, which had infected the dialect of the Civil War years, was replaced by moves to heal old wounds with dialect as the balm of a new national unity and self-awareness. Dialect was now seen, wrote the *Cambridge History of American Literature,* as an "expression and a cause of the interstate knowledge and interstate sympathy that have linked the far separated sections of the United States into closer bonds of union and fellowship."[25]

Beneath its glowing ethical surface, however, much of this new dialect literature contained another level of linguistic politics. In a situation in which not even the most "refined" members of society spelled exactly as they spoke, the decision about whose speech should be subjected to phonetics was loaded with moral implications. As we saw in the Anglo-Saxon ideology contained in Lowell's celebration of Yankee speech, this linguistic politics was frequently racial, and it became more so in the 1880s with the popularity of white writers who specialized in black dialects and subjects. The idea that dialect was necessary to represent particular modes of thought was a mirror image of the attitude that intellectual capacity was strictly limited by nonstandard speech. Often against their stated intentions, the demeaning elements of rustic humor and backwoods primitivism that had marked earlier southwestern dialect writing resurfaced in the work of these postbellum writers. While appearing to represent a democratic desire to record America's multifarious speech-ways, much literary dialect attempted to reinscribe a qualitative hierarchy between standard and nonstandard speech. This was the ideological power of dialect literature: the assumption that dialect recorded the way minorities *really* spoke encoded deeper beliefs that this was how they processed and structured reality, that this language revealed their stream of consciousness, their worldview, their very stuff of self.[26] The extreme lengths to which writers like Thomas Nelson Page went in their efforts to redact the particularly elusive elements of black speech masked a racist logic of black difference and inferiority. Indeed, the *Century* magazine deferred for several years the publication of Page's story "Marse Chan," partly from fears that the "black" dialect was too difficult to read, partly from disapproval of Page's glorification of slavery.[27] Like Lowell's *Biglow Papers*, the dialectal form of this literature was charged, at its deepest level, with powerful political meanings.

Recent critics such as Michael North and Eric Sundquist have emphasized the racial significance of postbellum dialect literature. Sundquist's discussion of the African-American writer Charles Chesnutt is persuasive in arguing that the problems of representing dialect were particularly pronounced for the black vernacular, owing to the inherently musical element of African-American cultural tradition, its "tight fusion of aural and semantic qualities." Sundquist shows how, in his Uncle Julius tales, Chesnutt explores the black vernacular's political challenge to "the controlling discourse of white America" by revealing how literary dialect is inevitably an inadequate transcription because the standard language is unable to record the speaker's tonal meaning, the "implied phonetics lying outside the range of white cultural hearing."[28] To a great extent, however, Sundquist's observations go beyond a racial agenda to embody the fundamental formal problems of representing any nonstandard voice with the written word. Indeed, Sundquist's methodological paradigm for *To Wake the Nations*—Franz Boas's recognition that the anthropologist's records of phonetic variations in the speech of the ethnic subject are "in reality alternating apperceptions of one and the same sound" because the anthropologist lacks the cultural knowledge necessary to appreciate fully the sounds of another language—is related to a wider recognition, during the late nineteenth century, of the impossibility of quantifying and qualifying speech. The verbal critic Richard Grant White, for example, was quick to note "the variableness in the perceptions of sound, even among professed phonologists. They do not agree as to the speech of people generally; and not only so, they differ as to each other's speech, and are even unable to record their own with satisfactory accuracy."[29] While the very notion of dialect has been subsumed within a racialized critical discourse in recent years (North's work, for example, tends to assume that the "dialect movement" only concerned whites depicting blacks), dialect writing tended to raise fundamental issues of class difference. Chesnutt's skepticism over the possibilities of representing black speech was based on considerations of region, educational status, and historical period— black dialect is "English pronounced as an *ignorant old southern* Negro would be supposed to speak it"—rather than solely ones of race.[30] The formal difficulties of redacting dialect were beginning to worry many writers in the 1880s:[31] the key question for them was not just whether black voices could or should be depicted in literature, but whether America's "folk" was a valuable and integral cultural entity, or instead debased, outdated, and antagonistic to normative literary depiction.

White's emphasis on the inherent resistance of speech to faithful written representation was part of his reaction to the fear that spelling reform would tie language to the "anarchy" of popular speech rather than to "the usage of the most cultivated society." The more negative responses to American dialect literature similarly fused formal and social issues. George Philip Krapp's 1920s attack on America's craze for nonstandard speech, for example, juxtaposed the flawed technique of literary dialect— the fact that a genuine representation of the spoken voice would contain "an enormous amount of detail which would merely distract and often puzzle the literary reader"—with the counterfeit quality of dialect literature as a cultural form: it is not a "reflection and echo of an authentic folk interest in literary expression," but a realm of literary pretense designed for sophisticated readers who "stand superiorly aloof from popular life."[32] Recent literary historians such as Alan Trachtenberg and Richard Brodhead have expanded on Krapp's comments by showing how dialect literature was intended for highbrow readers of "quality" eastern periodicals rather than for the speakers of dialects themselves—hence Edward Eggleston's scornful response to the belief of certain readers that he had sprung from "the rustic class he has described." Dialect writing was not, as Hamlin Garland phrased it, simply "a literature from the plain people."[33] Brodhead's brilliant analysis of regional writing's dynamics of readership, moreover, has shown how this literature was not merely a "cultural elegy," an act of nostalgia—as Trachtenberg and others have argued— for bygone variety in an age when "regional cultural differences" were "washing away." It was, argues Brodhead, a means to suppress still existing regional cultures by condemning them to the past and, more importantly, a response to profound class anxieties aroused by the influx of foreign-speaking immigrants into late-nineteenth-century American society. The function of literary dialect in this situation was to produce "the foreign only to master it in imaginary terms . . . by substituting less 'different' native ethnicities for the truly foreign ones of contemporary reality."[34]

Yet there are limits to arguing, along with Brodhead, that literary dialects were thus simply a means of stabilization, a way for "culturally dominant groups" to deny the "radically heterogeneous" and thus bring diversity under their "normative sway."[35] Reactions to literary dialect, even to that representing rustic whiteness, could also evoke a worrying sense of linguistic and social disunity. Nowhere was an ability to antagonize cultural conventions more pronounced than in the peculiar effect that dialect writing had on the act of reading. The painstaking effort of authors to develop intricate and supposedly phonetic systems of spelling, while it made some readers believe they were actually accessing speech, created feelings of strangeness and alienation in others. At their most optimistic, critics believed that the more difficult forms of dialect could be mastered with an act of linguistic re-education: Cable's dialect, for example, was "new, and must be learned." Yet for other readers, Cable's "phonetic atrocities" would seem unreadable: "[o]ur eye simply balks at untangling the paragraphs." The extremity of other dialect types led some to the conclusion that they would become an "undecipherable jargon" in fifty years time.[36] These complaints were an inevitable result of interference with the cerebral conventions of reading. In this sense, the main argument behind that other late-nineteenth-century attempt to write phonetically, the simplified spelling movement, was the greatest obstacle to such representational schemes: the lack of correspondence between sound and letter that makes writing a type of hieroglyphic code intelligible only to the educated was, noted William James in *The Principles of Psychology* (1890), essential to the very speed and ease of reading. To emphasize single phonemes rather than the ideographic wholeness of words would work directly against reading's psychological mechanisms.[37] These arguments against spelling reform were explanations of the distinctive effect that dialect writing had on its audience: it disrupted the natural process of reading, making it seem difficult for people of supposed linguistic competence, slowing them down in an age when dime novels and pulp magazine fiction were making reading habits seem faster and more superficial. By forcing people to pronounce words by spelling them out, dialect writing had the power to alienate the "literary" reader within his or her own language.[38]

Written dialect thus harmonized two seemingly discordant effects on the act of reading: it relegated the nonstandard to the realm of inferiority while it transferred the difficulties of subliteracy onto "sophisticated" readers themselves; it was simultaneously an affirmation and a mutilation of the linguistic standard. The ability to disrupt the smoothness of reading by disrupting the apparent oneness of writing corresponded to the wider tendency of literary dialect to disrupt America's sense of national linguistic unity. Not only did dialect literature make reading difficult; it also presented the reader with a need to translate within his or her native tongue, a fact emphasized by extensive glossaries (some ran to hundreds of words) and constant footnotes explaining even the less extreme dialects such as Eggleston's Hoosier speech.[39] This literature led people to believe that the encouragement of dialect would produce a situation in which speakers "of the same race, and the same commonwealth . . . can communicate only through an interpreter"—a source of alarm and distress for the self-appointed gatekeepers of American culture like the philologist George Perkins Marsh. By illustrating "what strange things can happen to English without changing the language into something which is not English," wrote Krapp, by stretching the orthographic borders of the language, literary dialect demonstrates the linguistic variety and room for incomprehensibility that can exist within a single tongue.[40]

There were other, more subtle ways in which even the most politically conservative dialect literature undermined the hegemonic linguistic situation it would seem at first glance to uphold by verifying and presupposing a standard language. The flavor of Cable's dialect words could only be appreciated, thought one reviewer, if their letters were pronounced "as they naturally would be . . . by a fairly-well-educated person." Yet, as Eggleston demonstrated in his 1894 essay "Folk-Speech in America," the pronunciation of regional literary dialect was a more complex question:

> Our Southern dialect writers succeed in misleading all but Southern readers by using an *r* where none is sounded. All my friends say "Brer Rabbit," as Mr. Harris writes it, but as neither he nor any other Georgian, white or black, says it. It is "Bruh Rabbit," if one gives the common sound to the letters, but the Virginian and the Georgian regard a final *r* only as a modifier of the vowel.[41]

Eggleston illustrates how the idea—emphasized by philologists at the end of the century—that America had only local standards of pronunciation was crucial to the interpretation of much regional writing.[42] Echoing the example of *brer*, Harris leaves words such as *I* and *my* conventionally spelled in the mouth of Uncle Remus, rather than using *Ah* and *mah* as did many northern depicters of southern speech. This was not a concession to easy reading but an indication of regionalism within the speech of the writer: Harris himself, in other words, would have pronounced *I* and *my* in a manner similar to that of Uncle Remus, thus precluding the need for dialect transcription (the wider implications of racial intermixture inherent in this situation are discussed in chapter four). The many points where Remus's dialect is spelled in conventional English, indicating the pervasive lexical overlap between the speech of narrator and character, implicate the supposedly standard language within the author's regional criteria.[43]

Certainly, as Michael North suggests, dialect literature was "another way of managing the social pressures behind the standard language movement" by emphasizing the incorrect and subordinate nature of nonstandard language. We should not overemphasize dialect literature's iconoclastic qualities: James Whitcomb Riley pointed out in the early 1890s that much dialect writing was "simply a pretence—a wilful forgery, a rank abomination" in which authors "maim, cripple, and disfigure language." But to dismiss as a total fabrication the inherent irony of this literature— that the speakers within it were not necessarily the writers of it—is to miss an important dynamic of the dialect text: the collision between the real, represented dialect and the authorial language politics through which it is refracted.[44] Typically, the "low" speech of the character becomes trapped within the parodying forms of another linguistic intention. But this clash of languages also gives rise to the countertendency in which the literary language becomes unsettled and transformed by contact with the dialect it is attempting to control.[45] There was often a nagging awareness of an element within the target dialect that could not be fully translated. Rather than participating in a simple relationship of power, the literary language confronted that which was partly beyond its reach. Moreover, as much as it was a form of linguistic domination, dialect literature transformed belief in a pure, unified standard language by recognizing the diverse accents of otherness with which this standard was intimately connected. Close attention to writers like Harris, for example, reveals that this standard was itself regional in nature, thus complicating the integrity of the hegemonic language which these writers were supposedly supporting.

The peculiar double movement within much dialect writing—its ability to destandardize the standard at the same moment that it contains nonstandard language within its hierarchical structure—corresponds to a series of much wider literary paradoxes of the era. For recent critics, American literary realism has come to seem an "anxious and contradictory mode"; it is a genre defined by formal ambiguities that arise from attempts to represent a changing and increasingly unfamiliar social reality, or by ideological contradictions that stem from writers who saw themselves as (in the words of Howells) "theoretical socialists and practical aristocrats."[46] Because of its deep involvement with realism's representational and moral aims, the literary treatment of dialect illuminates the unevenness of this larger literary terrain. For example, Howells may have seen dialect writing as part of realism's rejection of the conventional literary language and traditional style that he considered "aristocratic."[47] Yet in another sense such writing represented an even more intricate and artificial form of stylization that made literature at times seem as challenging and inaccessible as any "aristocratic" creation. The type of interpretive obscurity seen as marking the collapse of literary realism at the end of the century was already present in realism itself, at least in the experimentation of American writers in depicting the spoken voice.[48] Because it was so difficult to read, dialect writing tended to undermine the assumptions of realistic access and phonetic reconstruction upon which it was based: efforts at naturalness only increased unintelligibility. This formal paradox, moreover, was directly related to the ethical mission of literary realists, their attempt to forge national unity from sectional difference. Howells's belief that the justification of dialect lay in its synecdochical capacity to capture the essence of the nation was countered by dialect's tendency to suggest a whole irresolvably divided into parts—an irony that Elsa Nettels considers pervasive in American literature of the period. *Harper's Magazine*, for example, repeatedly described its purpose as being to bring all sections of America "ever nearer the main currents of our national unity" and to create "a bond of sympathy and union among men of various climes and pursuits," yet for seventy years it printed "innumerable anecdotes and verses in dialect in which certain groups, especially Negroes, Hard-Shell Baptists, rural Yankees, and the Irish, are made comic by their speech." The assumption of Howellsian realism that dialect was a democratic, energetic, and native means of expression was undercut by another view of nonstandard speech as the humorous sign of cultural degeneration. Howells's call for American fiction to "speak the dialect, the language, that most Americans know" was an attempt to collapse two potentially antagonistic notions: dialect could suggest the fragmentation of the nation in addition to the unique and common qualities of its language.[49]

As much as it was a nostalgic palliative or an expression of common feeling, the new dialect literature after the Civil War was a sign of cultural dissolution, both in its questioning of sociolinguistic wholeness, and in its propagation of what many saw as vulgar, uncultivated tastes. Even Richard Watson Gilder, editor of the *Century* and "high priest" of the cult of the vernacular (as Hamlin Garland called him), had profound fears about the literary form he was helping to create. In a letter to Garland, Gilder confessed that a dialect story containing vulgarisms "should very strongly recommend itself before being sent out into almost every cultivated household in the United States! . . . People who are trying to bring up their children with refinement, and to keep their own and their children's language pure and clean, very naturally are jealous of the influence of a magazine." Fears over dialect as a source of moral disease were widespread, as we shall see in the following chapter. Writing in *Lippincott's*

Magazine in 1897, T. C. De Leon noted the dialect story's inherent "coarseness through every strife to hold its high morality. It has horn upon its palms, grime beneath its nails, and its clothing is smirched with the soil of drudgery, or worse." For the Harvard professor of rhetoric and oratory Adams Sherman Hill, the popularity of "local color" and local dialect was a sign of today's "jaded minds"; true literature should "speak a language so noble that while we read we forget our own vulgar and provincial modes of speech." In an era when philologists like William Dwight Whitney were voicing a wider belief that the very role of a national literature was to "check dialectic divergence and effect uniformity of language," this literature itself was obsessed with divergent dialectal voices and with the linguistic varieties of cultural difference.[50]

Popular dialect literature did not always reassure its readers, as recent critics suggest, by disguising ethnic with rustic regional speech. In the early 1880s, for example, reviewers of George Washington Cable's popular novels and stories of Louisiana noticed that Cable was at last providing a truly American literature in which—as one reviewer put it—characters were free from Cunard labels on their handbaggage, but that he was doing so by representing a community of "mongrel dialects" that characterized traditionally French-speaking New Orleans.[51] Forces of ethnic transformation were active in regional writing itself. Charles G. Leland's popular *Hans Breitmann's Ballads* (1884), to give another example, was written in a strange "German-American-English" dialect that required a glossary of over 500 words, mostly German with some English words transformed by their contact with German speakers (Leland assumed that the reader must be well acquainted with both English and German to understand his poems). In his introduction, Leland attempts to deny that Breitmann's "strange speech" is in fact a dialect, arguing that it is too irregular and regionally unfixed, and that its crude ways will inevitably be rejected by the natural intelligence of Germans. The philologist Maximilian Schele de Vere, however, had somewhat different opinions about its linguistic significance. *Breitmann's Ballads* "give an example of the process which, artificial in the poems, goes on naturally in the regions where Germans and the descendants of such come in contact with the superior English which is spoken throughout the United States," the result being a "jargon . . . shocking in its barbarous admixture of English terms, which it mutilates as savagely as its own"—a jargon, moreover, that Leland himself reports to be spoken by millions of mostly "uneducated" German Americans.[52] Another example of this predominant characteristic of American dialect, in which different languages coalesce to produce an ethnic way of speaking, was provided by Leland's *Pidgin-English Sing-Song, or Songs and Stories in the China-English Dialect* (1876). Again accompanied by an enormous glossary, and written in an extremely difficult hybrid language, these poems and stories were designed to illustrate the translation of English into what their author believed to be Chinese sounds and principles of grammar. Leland's description of this Chinese trade language as an inherently inferior equivalent to "negro minstrelsy or baby talk," however, only thinly masked a deep cultural fear. The "anticipated immigration of 'millions of the Mongolian race' is beginning to cause serious reflection in America," wrote Leland, and the use of this pidgin may become necessary for "those who expect to meet with Chinese, either in the East or California."[53] Leland's work reveals how dialect literature did not serve just to control nonstandard language; it also showed this language gaining power as an agent of ethnic contamination.

Fears of cultural difference resounded in traditional regional contexts. There was a sense that, by manifesting "a consciousness of the continental diversity of its forms of life," as Eggleston put it, America was acquiring a characteristic literature from voices and places that were strange and varied when compared with the nation's literary heritage.[54] The period's major works of regional fiction reveal the moral complexities that arose from this ambivalent sense that vernacular language could create yet disrupt national identity. Take, for example, Eggleston's *Hoosier School-Master* (1871), a work often credited—not least by the author himself—as the first proper dialect novel in American literature. Here was a writer who claimed to represent sympathetically a social class he scorned; who professed "provincial realism" yet fell back on the humorous stereotype and romanticism he eschewed; who bemoaned the influence of the "vandal school-master" in reducing "the vulgar tongue to the monotonous propriety of what we call good English" yet chose a proper-speaking and glowingly moral schoolmaster as the hero of his novel.[55] Eggleston's linguistic ambivalence is clear: he was—like his predecessor Lowell—trapped between a vulgar dialect and an implicitly faulty standard. The common people in his 1871 novel are described as savages and wild beasts (12), philistines "sick and dying of their own commonplace" (18). Yet the region's bastion of polite values, Squire Hawkins, is equally degenerate, as can be heard from his speech: a strange hybrid of Yankee idioms, southwestern pronunciation, and grotesquely grandiloquent rhetoric (39, 45–46). The larger linguistic issues of the novel are just as complex. The narrator berates English orthography for its crookedness (49), yet the ability to command this crookedness in a spelling-bee is the absolute sign of virtue and intelligence. The novel's common characters have internalized the idea that mastery of the literary language is equivalent to morality and eloquence (174); they are in love with the educational process that will destroy their cultural distinctiveness. Yet what will this regional dialect be replaced by when people are obsessed with spelling words of whose meaning and pronunciation they are ignorant (24–25), and when the cultivated characters in the novel are themselves miseducated (92)?[56]

For a novel that professes moral didacticism, *The Hoosier School-Master* has a linguistic message that is unusually confused: it hovers uncomfortably between a barbarous past dialect and a future degenerate standard. Such moral ambivalence was far from unusual, as can be seen in other regional classics such as Mary Murfree's "Electioneerin' on Big Injun Mounting," part of her immensely popular collection *In the Tennessee Mountains* (1884). This story explores the double-consciousness of Rufus Chadd, a Tennessee mountaineer turned high-flying lawyer and politician, who is torn between "the inherent inertia and conservatism of the mountaineer" and an untutored, alien intellectual power that bewilders him (174). This "harassing sense of doubleness" (174) also inhabits Chadd's voice: "he still possessed the tone and idiom of the mountaineer, but he had lost the characteristic pronunciation" (167). It is a doubleness, moreover, that explains the political power of his eloquence: Chadd's natural intelligence is supplemented by the plain, honest talk of the mountaineer, giving him a "magnetic earnestness" (163) that wins conviction in every word. The vocal politics of the story, however, runs deeper than this seemingly ideal mixture of the tongue of the people in the mouth of the scholar, as Lowell would have phrased it. Mountain dialect is not simply a rustic well of pure English. It is also brutal, "incorrect," and primitive; like the very faces of the mountaineers, it is stolid and without sharp "turns of expression" (161). In the opposite direction, educated legal language is not necessarily a realm of high morals: Chadd's "wordy dexterity" brings ethically dubious legal victories and an "arrogant *hauteur*" (164–65). Like Eggleston's novel, this story traps the reader in a collapsed moral polarity of speech. Admittedly, resolution comes in Murfree's story when Chadd reclaims the value of his intellect by making "a keen and subtle distinction in a high moral principle" (181), while the multitude overcomes ignorance by finding again its collective, resonant voice that sounds forth a sympathetic heart (180–81). Yet beneath this final compromise lies a profound anxiety. The unique values of dialect are inherently uncivilized; any polite discourse that loses its roots in this vernacular, however, becomes artificial, unemotional, and morally repressive.

If "Electioneerin' on Big Injun Mounting" combined issues of politics and dialect, it did so in ways vastly different from those of earlier dialect-speaking, amateur literary politicians like Sut Luvingood and Petroleum V. Nasby. Publicly debated questions such as slavery or manifest destiny disappeared: this was mainstream literature, not journalistic propaganda. Yet the self-conscious move away from the contemporary political

topics of previous dialect writing only reinscribed another type of linguistic politics at a deeper level. In this respect, Murfree's stories parallel those
of other regional works of the period, like Hamlin Garland's *Main-
Travelled Roads* (1891), which also contains a moral logic that rests on
questions of talk.[57] As in Murfree's story, Garland's dialect is a slippery
entity: it can embody the simple, direct, and honest moral qualities of
rural life, or its vulgarity, backwardness, and intellectual stagnation. Such
ambivalence was a direct echo of the wider oscillation between celebration
and condemnation that marked both scholarly and popular reactions to
vernacular language during the Gilded Age. It was an inevitable outcome
of an era that exploited the uniqueness and creativity of its vernacular
voices while simultaneously feeling anxious that dialectal diversity might
frustrate the ideal of a national language by contaminating society with
"uncivilized" elements.

MARK TWAIN'S WESTERN VOICES

Anxiety over the nation's vocal culture was focused sharply on problems
posed by westward expansion: the movement away from the settled quality
of New England's authoritative cultural center. (We should remember here
that even literature from Indiana like Eggleston's *Hoosier School-Master* was
considered western.) As we saw at the beginning of chapter one, Twain's
sketch "Concerning the American Language" (1888) encapsulated this
new need to expand the frontiers of language and literature beyond hegemonic regional arguments, like Noah Webster's for New England speech.
Garland and Howells also praised western writers for their ability to infuse
language and literature with a native spirit that transcended Britain's colonial legacy.[58] Yet alongside such optimistic celebrations of the self-reliant
democracy of America's western vistas were other voices more cautious
about manifest linguistic destiny. "As our countrymen are spreading westward across the continent"—warned William Chauncey Fowler's *English
Grammar* in 1868—"and are brought into contact with other races, and
adopt new modes of thought, there is some danger that, in the use of their
liberty, they may break loose from the laws of the English language, and
become marked not only by one, but by a thousand Shibboleths."[59] Dialects
were considered dangerous by philologists after the Civil War because they
combined the threat of ethnic transformation with the fear of political
instability. Fowler shows how this dual challenge was particularly pronounced in the West. In addition to the "border defects" that were noticed
in English when it came into contact with other-speaking races, the West
was described by philologists as an area where American democracy existed
in its purest form, an area where the potential for anarchy was great-

est.[60] While the liberties of the West energized English, too much of this liberty was believed to disrupt national order and coherence.

This paradox was captured in the most extensive consideration of the West's contemporary linguistic situation: Maximilian Schele de Vere's chapter "The Great West" in *Americanisms: The English of the New World* (1872). According to Schele de Vere, the West was, in one sense, the embodiment of the freedom and independence of the American nation:

> Speech, there, is free as the air of heaven, and moves with impulsive energy of independent youth, conscious of matchless strength, and acknowledging no master in word or deed. It is an intensified, strangely impulsive language, just as the life's blood of the whole West throbs with faster pulse, and courses with fuller vigor through all its veins. . . . Its slang, also, is as luxurious as the weeds among the rich grasses, but at least it is home-made, and smells of the breath of the prairie or the blood of the Indian, and is not imported from abroad or made in the bar-room and betting-ring.
>
> Hence the student of English finds in the West a rich harvest of new words, of old words made to answer new purposes, often in the most surprising way, and of phrases full of poetical feeling, such as could only arise amid scenes of great beauty, matchless energy, and sublime danger.

Western language was the vocal institutionalization of an ideology, the realization of America's wholesome, self-reliant power, in which even the blood of Indian slaughter feeds neologism and slangy grandeur. Yet Schele de Vere's Romantic vision was undercut by his more skeptical sense of what it meant for language to be a "fair representation of the Western world": the West's "vast extent, the boundless plains and gigantic rivers, and all the matchless features of Nature on the largest scale ever beheld by man, impress upon language also a certain freedom from restraint and a certain tendency to employ vast terms and large-sounding phrases, which give an air of unconscious grandiloquence and genuine slang even to ordinary conversation." This use of "high-sounding words of extensive meaning for comparatively small matters" was seen as partly the result of the enormity and sublimity of the landscape, and partly the result of a rampant libertarianism. The fact that the West lacked "severe critic[s]," courts, "polite society," and "classic writers" led to the type of ambiguity—the forcing of single words to "answer many purposes"—that Tocqueville had recognized as an inevitable condition of democracy. According to Schele de Vere, the westerner would often partake of high-flown expressions that sounded like "the height of extravagance and absurdity," especially to "the more economical son of the East." (Schele de Vere was fairly restrained in his criticism; others described the West as "one great, windy lunatic.")[61] Matching a characteristic that Stephen Fender has detected in a series of western discourses from the mid-nineteenth century, the language of the West was at once an escape from the dull repression of eastern culture and a sign that any such escape could easily lead in the direction of linguistic misrule and cultural collapse.[62]

The literary consequences of such ambivalent reactions to the western vernacular, and to American dialect as a whole, appear in a work published in the same year as Schele de Vere's *Americanisms—Roughing It* (1872), by Mark Twain. Anticipating his ideas in "Concerning the American Language," Twain's text is punctuated with the notion that the narrator's primary task is to challenge the hegemonic control of New England over the American language, associated with Webster's *American Dictionary of the English Language* (1828). This *Dictionary* features literally in Twain's text, in the "Unabridged Dictionary" that accompanies the characters on their overland trip to Nevada (after 1864, the term "Unabridged" became synonymous with Webster's *Dictionary*).[63] The appearance of this *Dictionary* suggests that Twain is consciously undermining a Websterian lexicon by confronting it with the linguistic realities of the American West. When we first meet the "Unabridged," this confrontation is physical. As the heavy dictionary flies around inside the unstable stagecoach during the bumpy journey west, "it 'barked' the Secretary's elbow; the next trip it hurt me in the stomach, and the third it tilted Bemis's nose up till he could look down his nostrils—he said" (19). The *Dictionary* is surrounded by the linguistic forces that question its authority: its activity produces a recent neologism—*to bark*, in the sense of "to scrape or rub off the skin," is recorded by the *Oxford English Dictionary* as first entering the written language in 1850—and provokes from Bemis the archetypal western slang phrase, metaphorically exuberant, bizarre, and picturesque. By participating in this physical confrontation, the "uneasy Dictionary" (18) has its authority eroded by providing the motivation for the innovative, extravagant western language that Webster had attempted to restrict.

The "Unabridged" is called upon at several other points in the work to describe particularly western experiences—for example a journey through an "alkali desert" (124–25)—but each time proves inadequate to the task. Webster's *Dictionary* does not represent a mobile fund of descriptive terms, but rather the limit of the eastern lexicon when confronted with western life. It is therefore a cumbersome presence both physically and linguistically. The logic of this *Dictionary*, that new national conditions produce new languages, is shown in *Roughing It* to undermine Webster's own attempt to establish the hegemony of New England usage. Journeying through Twain's pages, we encounter the language necessary to describe the "things new and strange" (30) of the western world: *pepper-box gun, sage brush,* and *alkali water* are but a few of the unusual terms the narrator takes time to define in detail (5, 13, 52). Twain feels a duty to talk about the western practice of "pocket mining" because it is "seldom referred to in print" (415), and the terms of western mining jargon are either defined contextually, as in chapter thirty-six, or given in the form of lengthy footnotes.[64] Some words, for example "*Slumgullion*" for a cheap, nasty beverage resembling tea (24), were perhaps initially committed to print by Twain.[65] We gain a sense of the peculiarly western development of words, for example how the mud-colored bricks, named *adobes* by the Spanish, have become " 'dobies" in the American tongue (21). The narrator is particularly concerned to ensure that the Eastern reader is aware of the correct pronunciation of western terms: we are told, for example, that *coyote* is pronounced "ky-*o*-te" (30).[66]

To some extent, *Roughing It* can be read as a celebration of the "western freshness and novelty" of "the vigorous new vernacular of the occidental plains and mountains" (25–26), and a critique of the defunct powers of eastern linguistic authority. The work questions an eastern literary style—writes Lee Mitchell—that "at its worst involved a mix of pseudo-elegant phrases, dead metaphors, and euphemistic terms all bound together in a more or less crippled syntax," and replaces it with a vision of the West as "a realm of revitalized language for all, not simply a physical outlet for the few."[67] Yet Twain does not leave his celebration of the western idiom unchallenged. An ambivalent attitude develops: celebration of the vernacular is countered by a movement in the direction of linguistic anarchy foreseen by Tocqueville.

> Now—let us remark in parenthesis—as all the people of the earth had representative adventures in the Silverland, and as each adventurer had brought the slang of his nation or his locality with him, the combination made the slang of Nevada the richest and most infinitely varied and copious that had ever existed anywhere in the world, perhaps, except in the mines of California in the "early days." Slang was the language of Nevada. It was hard to preach a sermon without it, and be understood. Such phrases as "You bet!" "Oh, no, I reckon not!" "No Irish need apply," and a hundred others, became so common as to fall from the lips of the speaker unconsciously— and very often when they did not touch the subject under discussion and consequently failed to mean anything. [308–9]

This description captures the multilayered understanding of dialect in America that would be expressed most prominently by Whitney in *The Life and Growth of Language*. Rather than an integral regional variety, the locality of speech is shown to be a melting pot of national, regional, and personal elements. It consists of "the slang of his *nation* or his locality," suggesting the idea that contact between different foreign languages was transforming—or "contaminating"—English. Moreover, Twain foreshadows Whitney's realization that "every individual speaks a language different from every other," by showing how dialect can become a composite of idiolects, and how vernacular words, taken out of their contexts, can become unmotivated signifiers disconnected from the experienced world.[68] The idea of a democratic language is taken to its extreme: the mutual intelligibility upon which a coherent nation depends is usurped by a language that represents too completely the arbitrariness and idio- syncracy of individual meaning.

Twain's celebration of the western vernacular was offset by his exploration of the decay of language in its western environment. In this respect, Twain matched other western writers, like Ambrose Bierce, who were far from unanimous concerning the virtues of the vernacular. Replying directly to Garland's western euphoria, Bierce saw dialect as valuable only to "the hardy philologer tracing backward the line of linguistic evolution to the grunt of the primeval pig," and he described the dialect poems of John Hay as "formless blobs of coarse, rank sentimentality in the speech of snuff-rubbers and clay-eaters."[69] *Roughing It* contains an equally skeptical reaction to western voices. The novel reproduces at various points Schele de Vere's criticism of the Westerner's love of sound for its own sake,[70] and the narrator is constantly concerned with criticizing what Schele de Vere (576) described as the Westerner's use of extravagant and absurd expres- sions, such as "propelling" for *walking,* neologisms like "*judgmatically,*" and bizarre phrases like "talk off the ears of a cast-iron dog." There are many illustrations of a type of linguistic inflation that destroys the econ- omy of meaning in the West. Take, for example, the "grim Sphinx" who accompanies the narrator early in his journey and who possesses a speech so free, fluid, and "decomposed" that it is effectively unintelligible (8– 9); or the silver miners who, on finding a moderately promising rock, "used strong adjectives and frothed at the mouth as if a very marvel in silver discoveries had transpired" (287); or the narrator's friend, Mr. Bal- lou, who uses "big words *for their own sakes,* and independent of any bear- ing they might have upon the thought he was purposing to convey" (181). Expression becomes synonymous with exaggeration; in the West, "[w]ords are cheap" (74). The most significant example of linguistic breakdown is the much-discussed dialogue between the Nevada "rough," Scotty Briggs, and the parson from an eastern theological seminary, concerning the forthcoming funeral of Briggs's friend, Buck Fanshaw—a dialogue given close scrutiny by Whitney, who saw it as an instructive example of "how far the phraseology of the mine and the card-table can be made to go in figurative substitution for ordinary speech."[71] This dialogue captures Twain's ambivalence most clearly. The clichéd, dull propriety of the "aris- tocratic" language of the East is confronted by a western vernacular that has become so democratically representative of individuality that it no longer really means anything: Buck Fanshaw's favorite phrase, "No Irish need apply," originally expressing hatred of Irish-Catholics, is inevitably taken out of context by Scotty Briggs when he uses it at the end of Fanshaw's funeral "without apparent relevancy" (316). The very comedy of the passage originates in the fact that Briggs replaces the parson's dead metaphors with ones so alive with idiosyncratic meaning that they are virtually unintelligible. Language is no longer a means of intellectual communion, but a repository for a seemingly infinite variety of dialects. Anarchy appears to rule because authority is nonexistent in this western context.[72]

Roughing It explores the paradoxical politics of a national language. The question of dialect—of distinctly different systems of meaning within a supposedly unified tongue—disrupts the concept of hegemonic control in the American language even as it undermines the effectiveness of any democratic alternative. The reader confronts the linguistic factors of the West that challenge the authority of eastern dictums of correctness and propriety, while encountering the linguistic factors that devalue the referential power of this vigorous new vernacular. Twain records the way in which names can be inspired acts, naturally fitting their subject by being "the voluntary offering of a whole nation" (422), while simultaneously recording the regional dialect communities that deviate from this national language, as well as the "corrupt" nature of language-users within these communities who treat words without consideration for their meaning. Twain's description of the West in the 1860s parallels the idea of the United States as a nation fundamentally uncertain over whether it was the exemplar of new linguistic powers, or whether it was pervaded by dialectal forces that unsettled national harmony.

In terms of overall narrative structure, *Roughing It* seems to have more to do with dialectics than dialect: its unapologetically digressive style oscillates between travelogue and tall tale, realistic detail and outrageous incident, sincerity and satire, representational confidence and the breakdown of language as the medium of meaning. Critics have been quick to identify Twain's aesthetics of inconsistency, tempted into decoding the formal principle of the novel by the potential paradigms of narrative method that Twain scatters in his text: Jim Blaine's digressive, incomplete tall tale of his grandfather's old ram (361), for example, or the "symmetrically crazy . . . artistically absurd" drunken narrative written by a dissolute stranger for the *Weekly Occidental* (342).[73] The disjointed quality of Twain's narrative voice inevitably derives from a series of sources, and we should be careful not to view an understanding of dialect as the single key to Twain's narrative mysteries. Yet in examining an age that placed such emphasis on speech as the primary agent of linguistic representation, it is difficult to ignore the correspondence between the philological ambivalence over nonstandard language discussed in the previous chapter, and the vacillation in Twain's text between standard and nonstandard voices, conventional and unconventional literary styles. Rather than wavering between the ethical vernacular of the West and the stuffy gentility of the East, or between a similar dialectic of "genteel" and "savage" values in the West itself, Twain's narrative inconsistencies are caught up in wider questions of representation, rooted in a fundamental uncertainty over whether American voices were spontaneous expressions of reality or signs of linguistic degeneration and social disintegration.[74]

Michael Davitt Bell notes how questions of vernacular speech have also been central to readings of *Adventures of Huckleberry Finn* (1884). As in *Roughing It*, the ethical and structural uncertainties of *Huck Finn* center on representations of the human voice. The most popular argument has been that Huck's vernacular is a natural, realistic moral alternative to the artificial linguistic codes that surround him: namely, Tom Sawyer's romantic discourse of adventure fiction, with its emphasis on the false authority of a written world of private codes and secret marks; Emmeline Grangerford's sentimental, macabre poetry; the duke's hyper-literary, pseudo-Shakespearean language; and the king's "humbug talky-talk" (221), which secures confidence through linguistic deceit.[75] Yet the world of vernacular value that Huck represents is countered throughout the novel by a sense that rustic dialect can also signify moral and cultural bankruptcy. This becomes most apparent in the "lazy town" episode in chapters twenty-one and twenty-two. The language of the unlettered is "lazy and drawly," repetitious and predictable in its obsession with "chaws" of tobacco: "What a body was hearing amongst them, all the time was—/'Gimme a chaw 'v tobacker, Hank.'/'Cain't—I hain't got but one chaw left. Ask Bill'" (181). This "chawing," moreover, is not just the subject of conversation but a style of discourse. Boggs "chaws up" (184) Colonel Sherburn with his drunken, bombastic speech that verbally abuses without being grounded in any realistic intention. Against this corrupt vernacular, Sherburn turns his measured and unregional voice (his speech is represented in conventional English and we are told that he has lived in both North and South). Unlike Boggs, Sherburn means what he says; he defeats a crowd by exposing how its talk about "big things" like lynching and southern honor is mere "jawing" and "blowing" (187–91).

In addition to the vigorously vernacular Huck, there are other linguistic heroes in *Huck Finn* who are studies in a powerfully refined, rather than a dialectal, discourse. The "iron-jawed" (216) Dr. Robinson directs his refined and truthful tongue (his speech is much less dialectal than that of those around him) against the fake English pronunciation and empty etymology of the king, and against the naivete of the rural community that takes the king's false language at face value. The book's ethical uncertainty over the merits of standard and nonstandard language, moreover, is also present within individual voices themselves: Huck's vernacular, for example, lies halfway between unlettered dialect and literate standard.[76] Similarly, Jim's dialect is partly the repository of virtuous character and partly the embodiment of an oral folklore of "natural" signs that is just as out of step with reality as Tom Sawyer's literature-based clichés. Nowhere are these mixed feelings more apparent than in the section on keelboat talk and manners that Twain moved from the manuscript of *Huck Finn* to *Life on the Mississippi* (1883). Twain's belief that these keelboatmen were coarse, foul-witted, and profane, yet trustworthy, faithful, and magnanimous, is revealed in their way of talking: picturesque, metaphorically exuberant, and humorous on the one hand; an insincere and bombastic mask for moral cowardice on the other.[77]

Much more could be said about the language of *Huck Finn*. My point here is to demonstrate how the dialectal issues in *Roughing It* reappear throughout Twain's work. As with his earlier account of Nevada, an ambivalent attitude toward dialect is related to wider ethical and stylistic inconsistencies that have forever worried students of *Huck Finn*. The usurpation of Huck's vernacular, and hence of the entire moral structure of the book, by the irresponsible romantic discourse of Tom Sawyer during the final Phelps farm episode, is part of a larger oscillation between moral registers of language, concentrated in the ambiguous treatment of rustic and polite dialects. Twain has been portrayed as the true champion of the folk voice, the creator of a literary mode that records the "homely wisdom" and "rugged honesty" of the American vernacular (Henry Nash Smith), while others have taken the view that such stylistic naturalness only thinly veils ingenious authorial artifice (Janet McKay), or that Twain's wider agenda was to explore the confusion and breakdown of popular speech and of language in general (David Sewell).[78] The solution to these divergent opinions, I suggest, is that both activities—the celebration and the questioning of popular speech—occur simultaneously in Twain's work. The fact that a debate exists over whether *Huck Finn* represents dialectal realism or authorial artifice, whether it embodies or rejects the vernacular values supposed to be at the heart of realist texts, shows what an accurate barometer of its literary climate this novel is.[79] Twain's ambivalence was characteristic of an age that sought a community of linguistic nationhood in dialect voices that also expressed cultural decay.

The burgeoning of literary dialect after the Civil War was not a response to any particular factor but an essential part of popular debates over the national significance of the nonstandard voice. We need only look at Whitney's interest in the Briggs–parson dialogue from Twain's *Roughing It* and Twain's reciprocal fascination with questions of philology.[80] Dialect writers became amateur philologists in an age when people were being urged to record the dialectal materials around them. As part of these wider linguistic debates, moreover, dialect writing shared their endemic controversies and contradictions. Hence the support of writers who thrived on the depiction of vernacular voices—Twain, Cable, Joel Chandler Harris—for a spelling reform movement that sought to eradicate dialect altogether.[81] The type of ambivalence that recent cultural theorists have discovered in white reactions to African-American voices, the simultaneous attraction to and debasement of black oral culture that marks blackface minstrelsy and "plantation" literature, was part of a much wider prevarication over whether subaltern cultural groups were to be considered fit subjects for art.[82] Concurring with a philological milieu that urged interest in dialect while fearing its socially and racially counterproductive effects, dialect literature fluctuated—often within individual texts—between a supposedly democratic interest in the energetic voice of the masses and a hegemonic need to forge fictions of cultural dominance by demeaning dialectal difference. Regional literature may have attempted to constrain the nonstandard voice within a hierarchical discourse of linguistic propriety. As will become even clearer in chapter three, however, this did not necessarily mean that dialect was rendered incapable of undermining the idea of a standard language against which it was usually judged.

THREE

Language, Gender, and Disease

The hero of Herman Melville's novella *Billy Budd* has a speech impediment: "under sudden provocation of strong heart-feeling his voice, otherwise singularly musical, as if expressive of the harmony within, was apt to develop an organic hesitancy, in fact more or less of a stutter or even worse."[1] In his defective speech, Billy Budd is not alone in American literature of the 1870s and '80s. We need only think of the silver miners in Mark Twain's *Roughing It* who froth at the mouth whenever a moderately promising rock is discovered, or of the faulty English pronunciation and ridiculous slips of the tongue that expose the king's confidence tricks in *Adventures of Huckleberry Finn*.[2] Whether concerning western speculation or eastern industrial expansion, Twain was always keen to satirize corrupt language as "at once a symptom and a cause of social decadence," as David Sewell has shown in his analysis of Twain's contributions to *The Gilded Age* (1873–74). In this respect, Twain was at the forefront of the unprecedented attention paid to the American voice and its disturbances in the post–Civil War years, an attention that typically saw faulty speech as the direct correlative of social and cultural disease. The quality of American voices came under the close scrutiny of psychologists and social critics, in addition to philologists, who used their findings to speculate on the nature and problems of the national psyche at a time of rapid social change and cultural disquietude. The very notion of dialect—understood as an implicitly improper form of speech—became intertwined with these debates over mental and social coherence. The humorist Melville D. Landon considered stories about stammerers to be "a species of dialect": dialect itself came to seem a type of speech impediment with detrimental implications for the mental health of its speaker and for the stability of society as a whole.[3]

While Melville might appear an alienated figure in the 1880s, his fiction sadly out of tune with the reading public, Billy's stutter connects directly to this American obsession with vocal health. The first part of this chapter, rather than offering a conventional reading of *Billy Budd*, interweaves Melville's tale with a series of contemporary philological and medical debates; analysis of *Billy Budd* allows entry into the late-nineteenth-century understanding of American vocal culture. In addition to metaphorical links between linguistic decay and cultural degeneration, improper forms of speech were understood as *actual* diseases—both physical and mental—that had the power to infect Gilded Age society. In particular, cultural authority was perceived to be collapsing because its agents were contaminated with the linguistic disorders of a new medical condition known as American Nervousness. Rather than a tale about reading, as Barbara Johnson has recently argued, *Billy Budd* is a tale about the politics of the spoken word. It is Melville's meditation on the links between psychological diseases of language and power relations in post–Civil War America.

Part two shows how Henry James's contemporary novels, *The Princess Casamassima* and *The Bostonians*, reflect a cultural and psychological understanding of language strikingly similar to Melville's in *Billy Budd*. While linguistic disease in *The Princess* reveals the class conflicts of its British context, *The Bostonians* suggests a more fundamental sense of social collapse in its examination of the peculiar and highly contagious dialect of women.[4] This skeptical view of American national health arose from a situation in which—as James explains in his turn-of-the-century essays on "female speech"—American women became guardians of cultural values *and* bearers of a nervous, diseased language that turned these values into chaos. The ambivalent narrative patterns of *The Bostonians* reflect this vocal irony. Moreover, in James's social and cultural investigations of language disorders lie the origins of the radical problems of communal meaning that mark his later fictional projects.

The juxtaposition of two dissimilar and seemingly unrelated writers illustrates the widespread links between linguistic disease and cultural/mental collapse in literature of the 1880s. A discussion of two authors so obviously distant from the postbellum "cult of the vernacular" shows how concern with the American voice ran deeper than the explicit depiction of dialect. Melville's and James's works responded to a strain of thought in the Gilded Age that viewed spoken language as crucial to a series of psychological and cultural questions, which in turn reflected a sharp anxiety that American society was being undermined, not just by nonstandard language, but by the crisis and decay of the standard itself.

LINGUISTIC NERVOUSNESS AND HERMAN MELVILLE'S *BILLY BUDD*

Billy Budd's "occasional liability to a vocal defect" (53) has received only sporadic treatment from recent critics. Alan Trachtenberg reads *Billy Budd* as a partial reflection on the social turmoil of Melville's times, yet he entirely neglects Billy's speech impediment. Michael Paul Rogin, who echoes Trachtenberg in understanding the tale as Melville's skeptical message about the repressive power and seductive authority of the state, pays slightly more attention to Billy's stutter: it underlies "the inadequacy of speech to present meaning on the *Bellipotent*," while perhaps illustrating Billy's unconscious, finally ineffectual hostility toward authority.[5] Barbara Johnson's deconstructive analysis views Billy's stutter as "the pivot on which the entire story turns," a discontinuity of knowledge that allows innocence and guilt to change place, a "deadly space" within language itself that makes interpretation of the tale so difficult. Johnson attempts to situate the linguistic drama of *Billy Budd* in a political context; the tale is an "exemplary context in which to analyze the interpretive and performative structures that make politics so problematic." Yet Johnson gives little hint of what the story's "social structures" and "historical context" might actually be.[6] While not wishing to reduce *Billy Budd* to a single interpretation (it is difficult to disagree with Johnson's idea that the tale renders problematic the act of interpretation itself), nor to see it solely as a contemplation on the era of its composition, we should not miss the central elements of Melville's tale that relate directly to wider cultural and medical debates over the American voice in the Gilded Age.[7] The linguistic politics of *Billy Budd* derives from this contemporary obsession with the social significance of defective speech.

Billy Budd is the story of a narrowly avoided mutiny at sea, a story of social unrest that has linguistic disease at its heart. Billy's stutter is just one of several language problems in the tale. John Claggart, the ship's head of police surveillance who accuses Billy of uttering "sundry contumelious epithets" (79) and who finally falls victim to Billy's deadly blow, is the embodiment of the linguistic corruption that he sees in others. Just as his sea title of *master-at-arms* may seem "equivocal" to landsmen (64), Claggart is himself double-voiced: he speaks in ironies while he reads subversion into the innocent events surrounding him. As the narrator of the tale makes clear, Claggart may in fact be the victim of extreme psychological illness, a dangerous, self-contained, sporadic lunacy in which, though "the man's even temper and discreet bearing would seem to intimate a mind peculiarly subject to the law of reason, not the less in heart he would seem to riot in complete exemption from that law" (76). Claggart's words to Billy Budd partake of this illness; seemingly complimentary on the outside, they mask a deep, psychotic antipathy. His is a diseased language, the Dansker reveals to a bemused Billy Budd, because of the deadly space between word and meaning.[8] Claggart's corruptive influence, moreover, arises from his dubious national and linguistic heritage: the "hint of something defective or abnormal in the constitution and blood" (64) is matched by "a bit of accent in his speech suggesting that possibly he was not [an Englishman] by birth, but through naturalization in early childhood" (65). On a ship of state where police discipline depends on the secret communications of ears and tongues (89), the very mechanisms of this discipline are linguistically and patriotically impure.

Claggart's nonstandard speech, which reflects his role as a disrupter of social order on the *Bellipotent*, has its parallel in the speech of "the people," the common sailors on the ship. We feel the vocal presence of the masses, during the time of Billy's execution, when they begin to make noises of rebellion. Their collective voice is a confused "murmur" (127), a "sound not easily to be verbally rendered"—beyond the limits of intelligibility and representation—and "being inarticulate, it was dubious in significance" (126). Theirs is an antilanguage which blends with the "inarticulate" scream of the large seafowl that flies to the scene of Billy's final burial-at-sea (127). It is threatening to authority on the ship, as represented by Captain Edward Fairfax Vere, not through its irony and ambiguity, but through its secrecy and apparent chaos. The fact that the voice of the masses remains unintelligible, a register beyond the hearing of the dominant culture, signals its ability to undermine social order and control.

Billy's stutter thus combines with a variety of vocal improprieties on board the *Bellipotent* to produce a general atmosphere of linguistic breakdown, which the narrative links to fears over foreign infiltration and mental illness (embodied in Claggart) and to the degenerate, inarticulate language of the masses. These notions of linguistic disease stemmed directly from a deep anxiety over vocal culture in the Gilded Age, which posited decayed, foreign, and inarticulate speech as radical threats to social authority.

Images of linguistic disease came to be used with some frequency as registers of, even explanations for, social corruption and cultural illness in post–Civil War America. Indeed, the presence of a stutter in Billy Budd, who at times seems the embodiment of a Romantic poet,[9] suggests that the Romantic conception of language as a natural, organic process—a view that dominated the Transcendentalist language theories of the previous generation—was severely questioned in the Gilded Age. As Billy's "organic hesitancy" (53) implies, organic conceptions of language could also accommodate tendencies toward disease and decay. The first English language textbook to be used at college level in the United States, for

example, William Chauncey Fowler's *English Grammar* (1868), contained
what Dennis Baron calls a "germ theory of language decay," which
warned against the dangers of abnormal linguistic growth.[10] The notion
of linguistic disease provided conservative social critics with a means to
conceptualize their belief in the degeneracy of modern society and in the
disastrous direction of cultural change.

Nowhere was this notion of language decay more analyzed than in the
writings of verbal critics, the self-styled linguistic detective police who saw
errors in speech as part of a deeper cultural sickness. Maximilian Schele
de Vere's *Americanisms* (1872) diagnosed some of the major symptoms of
this illness, including the slang of women, the "low-toned newspaper, written for the masses," the American love of extravagant sound and innovation, and the brevity of communication necessitated by the modern telegraph and cable—an obvious example of the disrupting effect of
economics on language.[11] These symptoms of linguistic disease were virtually identical to those catalogued by Richard Grant White in the archetypal work of verbal criticism, *Words and Their Uses* (1870). White placed
strong emphasis on the corrupting influence of mass culture and industrial society. He termed the faulty coinages of the popular press *words-no-
words:* the masses produced a type of "unmeaning jargon" indicative of
their deficient processes of thought. According to White, these words-no-
words were "usurpers, interlopers, or vulgar pretenders ... deformed
creatures ... oppressive, intolerable, useless ... living a precarious life on
the outskirts of society, uncertain of their position, and a cause of great
discomfort to all right thinking, straightforward people." White linked
speech to the wider factors threatening cultural order; he drew analogies
between words and the social misfits who were seen to arise from the
wasteland of industrial culture and from the influx of immigrants after
the Civil War. White's main concern was that peripheral, minority discourse had the power to affect the cultural center. Like a virus, this antilanguage was chaotic and beyond control, qualities that gave it still more
power to infect and corrupt mainstream language. White exemplifies the
tendency among late-nineteenth-century critics of language to see cultural
and linguistic degeneration as two sides of the same coin.[12] Whether
caused by the popular press, commercial advertising, social mobility, or
universal education, the decay of language and the decay of culture became reciprocal forces.

Academic philologists such as William Dwight Whitney and Thomas
Lounsbury criticized the application of organic metaphors to language.[13]
Instead, they sought to demonstrate that linguistic corruption was not a
form of disease but an inevitable and necessary process of change present
within every living tongue. Language might be a symptom of the disease,
in other words, but never the disease itself. This separation of speech from

disease, part of a wider attempt to separate language from psychology, was undercut by contemporary developments in psychology itself, which saw the link between language and disease as immediate and literal rather than simply an issue of metaphor.[14] Major studies of phonetics in this period, rather than viewing nonstandard words as an inevitable part of a self-governing linguistic system, tended to link dialectal accents with actual, medical speech disturbances. Thus, Alexander Melville Bell's *Principles of Speech and Dictionary of Sounds* offered advice to correct major blemishes like "clavicular and unhealthy respiration"—possible causes of consumption—*and* the "minor blemishes" of "Alphabetic Mispronunciations."[15] The combination of pathological and dialectal defects (common in pronouncing dictionaries from the late eighteenth century onward) also applied to the immigrant working class, and to homeless inhabitants of the burgeoning cities of late-nineteenth-century America.[16] Dennis Baron has shown how the metaphor of slang as disease was informed by fear of actual physical diseases that might arise from the social poverty of urban areas where nonstandard, often non-English speech was concentrated. For one verbal critic in 1903, slang, like chicken pox, was highly contagious and "severest, too, where the sanitary conditions are most favorable to its development."[17] The atmosphere of illness hovering around slang users and dialect speakers was believed to infiltrate their minds, leading to an essentially diseased condition of thought. Oliver Wendell Holmes, for example, considered the slang of the metropolis to be "at once a sign and a *cause* of mental atrophy."[18]

The intertwining of linguistic deviation and mental disease established and maintained class hierarchies. This worked particularly well in a British context, helping to cement already rigid class lines by providing an obvious physical badge of difference, indicative of innate mental incapacity.[19] The uncertain status of the standard language in America, however, meant that these linguistic differences were far from clear-cut. America's "middling folk," in the words of White, also "use language awkwardly, and as if they did not feel at home in their own mother tongue." Although various handbooks of usage were explicitly aimed at recent immigrants, many others were designed for American speakers in general. Frank H. Fenno's popular *Science and Art of Elocution* (1878) assumed that most Americans were ineffective readers and speakers; it emphasized the "correct utterance of the elementary sounds," which would allow everyone to command respect and to give thought "its highest mode of expression." The effect of such criticism was to implicate a wide area of American pronunciation in its definition of social and linguistic impediment. It was Richard Grant White's belief that America was the land of "phonetic decay," that the ear of the American public was uncultivated and depraved, and that American pronunciation lacked the consonants necessary to provide the articulation, strength, and clarity which endow speech with its distinct social value. Most Americans, thought White, "have a bad tone of voice, and very unpleasant inflections, in great variety of unpleasantness, according to the place of their birth and breeding." The sheer breadth of White's criticism is striking. American speech was inherently faulty; it suffered from a thoracic ineptitude and a nasality resulting from "constraint or interference with the free and natural action of the vocal organs." Intelligible, civilized speech was degenerating into vague animal noises, into snarls, whines, and grunts.[20] Quite simply, America was the land of speech impediments.

Dialect literature was also considered responsible for disseminating faulty linguistic forms among a wide audience. According to an 1894 sketch in the Boston literary magazine *The Writer*, the mounting feeling of the age toward its overflowing tide of dialect fiction was fear of contamination. This sketch depicts a dignified family of correct pronouncers who, following a surreptitious consumption of dialect stories before sleep, spontaneously and uncontrollably break out at the breakfast table into phrases like "befoh de wah" and "I b'lieve I'm feelin' po'ly this mornin'." Dialect enters this decorous community as a virus that attacks linguistic propriety.[21] Although the sketch was intended with some degree of humor, other writers of the period used the terminology and images of disease and decay to describe their negative reaction to the popular "cult of the vernacular." Writing more seriously in *Lippincott's Magazine*, T. C. De Leon placed himself in the role of literary physician:

> Had some such bitter, but more wholesome, quinine of comment been more freely and more boldly administered to the infancy of recent literature, the malarial influence of imitation had not outcropped so widely into the epidemic of dialect fiction. Drastic treatment had then been less indicated, and the application of many a fierce blister of criticism, the wearing process of rebuilding and recuperation, had been spared to many a feeble system.

The nauseating quality of dialect literature arose from the fact that it "disinclines, or unfits, the reader for segregation," thought De Leon: the voices of grimy, diseased people have the power to enter the most refined ears. For another critic in *The Dial*, the "epidemic" of dialect writing then raging with "unabated virulence" in America, was a contagious and corrupting influence that could destroy the education of the young mind.[22]

The threat to what Frank Fenno termed "vocal culture" (the cultural conditions and practices surrounding the production of the human voice) was so worrying because the logic applied to dialect speakers—that their defective speech signaled a defective mind—became equally applicable to the widest aspect of American civilization and its voices. Just as class distinctions were becoming harder to define in the Gilded Age, so too were differences of vocal value.[23] In effect, the idea of linguistic disease, rather than dividing speech into areas of good and bad usage, became a register of the threat to conservative values posed by improper language. Strange forces were at work in American culture. In addition to the disease of language rife among immigrants and the lower classes, there were curious strains of the virus operating *within* the dominant cultural group, undermining both its mental and its cultural health. Before returning to a more explicit consideration of this curious disease, let us see how three crucial elements of *Billy Budd*—stuttering, sanity, and spellbinding—relate directly to the vocal culture of which Melville was part.

One of the main points of *Billy Budd* seems to be that the linguistic corruption on board the *Bellipotent*, like the "contagious fever" (55) of mutiny that this corruption portends, will inevitably be defeated. Claggart, a key defective speaker in the tale, is thus the victim of Billy's fatal blow. In this respect, one vocal defect cancels another: Billy's inability to speak leads him to strike and kill the bearer of ambiguous, subversive language. And after this incident, Billy himself overcomes his stutter to become the eloquent spokesman of the people. The other linguistic threat on board the ship—the murmurous, mutinous voice of the masses—is also conquered at the end of the tale by the effective linguistic control of Captain Vere. Vere seems the embodiment of the ideal civic rhetoric propounded by the vociferous verbal critics of post–Civil War America.[24] His speech is free from jargon ("he never garnished unprofessional talk with nautical terms" [60]); he is a lover of literary language, a reader of writers "free from cant and convention," virtues he cannot find in "social converse" (62); he is honest and direct, yet his discourse never falls "into the jocosely familiar" (63). Vere embodies the very linguistic standards of correctness advocated by Richard Grant White and his fellow language police. Furthermore, Vere is able to apply this linguistic correctness to public matters. Vere's speech is a direct, powerful, and effective political rhetoric, not least because he is able to control the level of his discourse, enabling him to speak the dialect of other social classes. In this respect, Vere has the power to overcome a wider cultural disorder, whose symptom is a society fragmented into conflicting communities of speech.

The first application of this power is Vere's persuasion of the three officers of the summary court, each convinced of Billy's innocence, to execute the stutterer. He wonders how to talk to such "well-meaning men not intellectually mature" (109), and succeeds in securing their verdict in favor of immediate discipline. The second application is his control of the common sailors. Vere realizes his fundamental difference from the masses, owing to their inherent mental deficiency—indeed, their lack of

the "kind of intelligent responsiveness that might qualify them to comprehend and discriminate" is a reason for the quick execution of Billy
(112). Yet he is able to lower his discursive register to narrate events in
"clear terms and concise" (116), effectively disarming rebellion by creating a collective "dumbness" in the crew (117). Vere supplements this
dialectal flexibility with an active knowledge of the aural forms of the
"mechanism of discipline" (126). Thus, after the dumbness of the sailors
is replaced by a "confused murmur," Vere is able to break it up with the
"word" of order (117). Again, the "ominous low sound" that follows
Billy's burial is dissipated by Vere with whistles and drums, and with the
"official word of command" (126–27). In each case, language is the formal agent that controls social disorder. As Vere remarks, in a passage
added by Melville in the final penciled revision of the tale shortly before
his death in 1891: "With mankind, . . . forms, measured forms, are everything; and that is the import couched in the story of Orpheus with his
lyre spellbinding the wild denizens of the wood" (128).

The story of Orpheus has embodied, from Antiquity, a firm belief in
the power of speech to transform chaos into the forms of political civility,[25]
and Melville was surely aware of this general significance. Etymologically,
however, the above passage has a much more specific, resounding relevance to Gilded Age America. "The word *spellbinder* was coined in 1888,"
observes Kenneth Cmiel, "when two hundred Republican campaign ora-
tors attended a dinner in Delmonico's in New York and the city's press
termed it the Spellbinder's Dinner." A term coined just three years before
Melville's use of it in *Billy Budd*, spellbinding was a fervent type of American political speech concerned with actual results rather than the niceties
of form, with persuasive subject-matter rather than conventional style. It
was a speech with the sole aim of manipulation and intellectual control.
The spellbinder was in competition with the orator, argues Cmiel: whereas
the latter was "refined and well-read," his language "civil and well-
wrought," the spellbinder was "colloquial. He used slang. He flattered
his audience."[26] Vere represents this important development in American
political speechmaking—the public acceptance of a tough colloquial
style—yet his real strength is that he *combines* the roles of orator and spellbinder: he has the refinement of a verbal critic together with the colloquial and manipulative methods of the political speechifier. Vere
apparently embodies the conservative values of hegemonic vocal correctness, while having the rugged vernacular power necessary to suppress the
type of lower-class speech that poses a threat to those very values.

Debates over language and political rhetoric in post–Civil War America
reveal the nature of Captain Vere's spellbinding authority. The skepticism
that has been detected in *Billy Budd*'s representation of the authoritarian
state can also be traced to distinct elements in the vocal culture of the

Gilded Age. The skepticism, or at least the ambiguity, of the tale rests on the question of Captain Vere's sanity. It is the ship's surgeon who first notices, upon Vere's rapid decision to try Billy by a "drumhead" court rather than detaining the accused and referring the matter to the admiral, that the captain appears incoherent: his "excited exclamations, so at variance with his normal manner," make him seem "unhinged" (101–2). And again, Vere's "utterance," which commands the court to consider only the blow's consequence and not its probable causes, appears "to augment a mental disturbance previously evident enough" (108). The narrator leaves the matter of Vere's coherence for the reader to determine "for himself by such light as this narrative affords," stating that, in certain cases, it is virtually impossible to draw the line between sanity and insanity: "Who in the rainbow can draw the line where the violet tint ends and the orange tint begins? . . . So with sanity and insanity" (102). The possibility is left open that Vere's pronouncement on Billy's punishment, in addition to his effective political rhetoric both in front of the court and in front of the masses at the end of the tale, may well stem from a form of insanity. The voice of authority may itself be defective; the very mechanism of social control may itself be diseased.

Captain Vere is not alone in his potentially pathological condition. Claggart also possesses an ambiguous and corrupt form of speech which stems directly from an innate mental disturbance hidden behind a mask of reason. Here again, an agent of social control (Claggart being a kind of police chief on the ship) is shown to be inherently corrupt and incoherent. Billy Budd appears to be different. He is the bearer of pure, unambiguous language: "To deal in double meanings" is foreign to his nature (49). Billy is the spokesman for the masses and the inevitable peacemaker on the ship through his eloquent beguilement of the sailors into a benediction of Captain Vere shortly before his own execution. Yet beneath this virtuous linguistic surface, Billy is prone to radical linguistic breakdown and to actions beyond his control. Echoing contemporary beliefs that improper speech was inherently irrational, Billy's vocal impropriety signals his inability to reason. If Billy Budd suggests an absolute tie between language and thought, whereby the quality of voice reveals the "innermost man" (45), then it also illustrates the contrary condition: the degeneration of speech signals the collapse of cognition.[27] The tale emphasizes that Billy did not mean to kill Claggart, but struck him only because his impeded speech was inextricably linked to a mental gap that destroyed the possibility of intentional action: "I did not mean to kill him. Could I have used my tongue I would not have struck him" (106).[28] Melville takes pains to underline the psychological nature of Billy's disease in his description of Claggart approaching Billy, before the final blow, "[w]ith the measured step and calm collected air of an asylum physician approaching in the public hall some patient beginning to show indications of a coming paroxysm" (98).

At least one critic has noticed that Melville appeared to know something about the psychological implications of speech aberrations, for he had employed them previously in *Pierre* (1852).[29] Indeed, Melville's description of Billy's convulsed speech impediment—"the intent head and entire form straining forward in an agony of ineffectual eagerness to obey the injunction to speak and defend himself, gave an expression to the face like that of a condemned vestal priestess in the moment of being buried alive . . . The next instant, quick as the flame from a discharged cannon at night, his right arm shot out" (98–99)—closely echoes Alexander Melville Bell's description of the classic stammer which "gives rise to distortions of the mouth, lateral motion of the jaw, protrusion of the tongue, straining of the eyes, winking, rolling of the head . . . the Stammerer, not knowing what are the actions necessary to the desired utterance, yields to the embarrassing influence of difficulty and ignorance, and splutters on at random, with tongue, eyes, head, trunk, hands, feet, and the whole frame in effort." According to Bell, such stammering is "*the cause of nervousness*"; it has the capacity to "strike root into the muscular and nervous systems, and produce most pitiable objects in society."[30] That Billy can blame his stutter for his failure of mental presence and therefore his lapse of intentional action becomes more explicable in terms of Bell's medical discussion. Billy's speech impediment, I suggest, is connected to a state of nervousness that incapacitates his ability to reason.[31] This link between nervousness, defective speech, and mental breakdown connects *Billy Budd* still more integrally to a key element in the linguistic psychology of the Gilded Age. There were social and psychological factors at large that help to explain how the structures of vocal and cultural authority, represented by Captain Vere, could be diseased themselves.

Forces of urbanization, capitalism, and social mobility did not originate in the Gilded Age, yet never before had they been seen as such direct causes of remarkably prevalent types of psychological illness. The various symptoms of this reaction to modernization were grouped together in a new disease known as American Nervousness. Developed by the New York neurologist George M. Beard between the late 1860s and early 1880s, the theory of American Nervousness (or *neurasthenia*, as Beard technically termed it) presupposed that the particular demands of post–Civil War American civilization were robbing its citizens of their nervous energy, leaving them mentally and physically bankrupt. Recent historians have identified the cultural and economic implications of American Nervousness, its connection with the growth and the anxieties of a capitalist elite. This new disease was also related to a wider awareness of linguistic decay; it was part of a pervasive belief that the spoken language of social authority was in a state of nervous collapse.[32]

American Nervousness was an attempt to characterize, in its broadest aspect, the psychological and cultural uniqueness of Gilded Age society. According to Beard, the United States was "the nervous country by pre-eminence"; to solve this prevalent nervous exhaustion would be "to solve the problem of sociology itself." Beard's formulation of neurasthenia was an attempt to bring together the entire range of elements that formed a distinctive national character. In addition to social and environmental factors, Beard analyzed the nature of America's cultural products. For example, American Nervousness was responsible for the pervasiveness of American humor: the "excessive strain of mental and physical life" led to the need for abandonment among not merely the vulgar but the "disciplined, the intellectual, the finely organized man and woman of position, dignity, responsibility and genius." Beard's analysis of cultural products reveals the logic behind nervousness: it was, at least as originally conceived, a disease of the dominant social classes. According to Beard, American Nervousness was more particularly the disease of "brain-workers," the very few that "*make us what we are as a nation*," thereby explaining the apparent vulgarity of America's intelligentsia, their desire for humorists over more "instructive and dignified lecturers."[33] Neurasthenia justified dominant American culture: people were nervous because they were intelligent and successful, a fact that fitted neatly with the assumptions of social Darwinism and in some ways justified the American dream of social progress.[34] Yet nervousness acted simultaneously as a disease *within* the dominant group. In this way, neurasthenia was an integral part of what T. J. Jackson Lears has identified as the crisis in "Western civilization" at the end of the nineteenth century, a crisis that spawned the conservative and escapist movement that Lears calls "antimodernism." American Nervousness was part of the "psychic dimensions of the crisis of cultural authority. Internalized, private authority seemed threatened as gravely as external, public authority." According to F. G. Gosling, for the first time "the nation itself" was considered a possible "threat to mental health."[35]

Elaine Showalter has shown how the female malady of hysteria was understood in the nineteenth century as a private and silent entity beyond normalcy, unable to effect cultural change.[36] Neurasthenia, on the other hand, was not simply able to bring about cultural change—it became part of society's very understanding of culture. Neurasthenia had an especially strong impact on the American language. As Beard noticed, neurasthenia lacked an important symptom of hysteria: "the *globus hystericus,* or feeling as of a ball in the throat." Neurasthenia led not always to an interruption of speech, but quite often to a plentiful speech that was inherently faulty. Thus, while hysteria was associated with "unbalanced mental organization," neurasthenia "[m]ay occur in well-balanced, intellectual organizations."[37] Neurasthenia, when embodied in American speech, could act as a disease within the apparently normal atmosphere surrounding America's cultural guardians.

The five factors that Beard saw as distinguishing American culture from that of Greece or Rome, and therefore the five main causes of its new nervousness—"steam-power, the periodical press, the telegraph, the sciences, and the mental activity of women"—were all significant factors in America's understanding of its decaying speech.[38] According to Beard, American vocal degeneration was a direct result of neurasthenia. Of the many valuable treatises on and criticisms of Americanisms, thought Beard, "none of them would seem to give sufficient force to the study of the relation of language to nervousness, that is, to the effect of the nervous organization on our idioms, articulation, or lack or want of articulation." The deficiency of nervous energy leads to the clipping of words, to the distinctive fall of the voice at the end of sentences, to "compressed idioms, elisions, and the simple rapidity of utterance." The particular quality of the neurasthenic voice is a "softness, faintness, want of courage and clearness of tone" which "somewhat resembles the peculiar voice of the deaf." Concurring with numerous verbal critics of the time, Beard singled out the American woman as an important agent of this defective intonation. He explains the "phenomenally bad" elocution of Clara Morris, the foremost American actress of her day, in terms of her deficient nerve-force: Morris's ability to express strong emotion through her vowels uses up her nervous energy, forcing her to disregard her consonants, thereby making the task of understanding her extremely difficult.[39]

Beard's discussion of what might be termed "linguistic nervousness" shared the same mix of optimism and anxiety as other discussions of the American language. It assumed the need to preserve a cultural elite, and followed the logic that nonstandard dialect signified mental ineptitude. Yet Beard's understanding of the psychology of language did not place the threat to American speech outside the area of dominant usage. The threat was not from, say, the "broken English" of the immigrant but from forces of disease within the dominant group that were capable of disrupting both its mental health and its speech.[40] This diseased psychology of language disrupted the workings of society because it made people more difficult to understand, not just in their defective pronunciation or weak voice, but in their new inability to command meaning. Beard termed this curious effect *heterophemy,* which he explained as:

saying one thing and meaning another, saying oftentimes directly the opposite to what we meant to say; saying precisely what we wish to avoid; the
word we wish slips in ahead of the one that we would bring to the front.
Persons in health are frequently guilty of this very interesting blunder; but
in disease of the brain it becomes a very bad sometimes very amusing as well
as very annoying symptom. One of my old patients (the wife of a patient just
referred to), who has both brain exhaustion and spine exhaustion, sometimes is compelled to mention a number of different words before she strikes
the word she wishes. If, for example, she would have a book, perhaps she
would say chair or sofa. She was not troubled in this way until she became
neurasthenic, and since that time she has been troubled constantly.

Heterophemy was not simply a minor confusion between word and meaning; it was organically connected to a radical collapse of cognition, consistent with diseases of the brain. Stemming directly from nervousness,
heterophemy was again a peculiarly American disease: according to Beard
it was "probably more common in America than in Europe."[41]

If a coherent culture depended on the preservation of distinct vocal
values, as many critics of the American voice were suggesting at the time,
then this coherence must inevitably disintegrate in a situation where the
processes of signification were themselves diseased. In using the term *heterophemy* to describe this condition, Beard followed an essay by Richard
Grant White: "Heterophemy: The World's Blunder," published in *The
Galaxy* in 1875. According to White, heterophemy is "a positive psychological law" which has received little or no attention. It is "an example
of what physiological psychologists call unconscious cerebration; that is,
of an action of the brain which takes place without the volition of the
individual." It is the "daily mental aberration of the human race": "That
error consists in thinking one thing and speaking or writing another.
There is no inaccuracy of information, no confusion of thought, no for-
getting even for a moment. The speaker or writer has perfect knowledge,
thinks clearly, remembers exactly, and yet utters precisely what he does
not mean."[42] As the presence of linguistic disease within an apparently
normal subjectivity, heterophemy functioned in a similar manner to its
more famous relative, Sigmund Freud's notion of "slips of the tongue,"
part of his explication of the psychopathology of everyday life. Freud con-
curred with White in linking slips of speech to the operation of unconscious thoughts, and more importantly, he also identified these slips as a
threat to apparent normalcy.[43] Thus, the "slips of the tongue that we
observe in normal people give an impression of being the preliminary
stages of the so-called 'paraphasias' that appear under pathological conditions." Freud's essay helps to clarify what was thought to be at stake in
using language incorrectly. The "psychical contagiousness" of slips of
speech and their resulting contamination of language might have been

everyday forces, yet they had the potential to degenerate into profound psychological disease.[44]

Freud's idea of the contiguity of everyday and pathological speech disturbances agreed with that of another investigator of mental disease from the 1860s, the Englishman John Hughlings Jackson. Although Jackson's idea that certain speakers "have 'plentiful words,' but habitually use them wrongly" directly foreshadowed the observations of White and Beard,[45] the thought of the two Americans differed from purely psychoanalytical interpretations in that it linked speech disorders more explicitly to their wider cultural contexts. In other words, this way of looking at language in late-nineteenth-century America saw varieties of improper speech as signs of mental *and* social degeneration. Thus, White's words-no-words, the chaotic forces of minority discourse that threatened spoken standards, were both culturally defined—as the product of vulgar outsiders—and psychologically significant. Words-no-words had the power to contaminate the minds of all "right thinking" people with an element strikingly similar to more recent descriptions of jargon aphasia, in which the incoherence of thought "leads to disorder of syntax and grammar, choice of wrong words and errors in the phonetic structure of words, even the production of non-existent words."[46] The susceptibility of the dominant class to the forces of nervousness and to the neurasthenic voice or heterophemy that might result from this nervousness placed even the most decorous speakers within easy reach of a slippery slope that led to linguistic and/or psychological collapse.

While *Billy Budd* is much more than a simple meditation on language disorders, it is difficult to ignore the strong parallels between the tale and the psychological and cultural phenomena of linguistic nervousness. The most obvious parallel concerns the link between vocal breakdown and the individual's lack of intentional control over his or her acts of thought, a link that Alexander Melville Bell suggested in his description of speech impediments as "the galling fetters of spasmodic tyranny." Just as Billy's nervous stutter leads him to perform a murderous act entirely beyond his conscious intent, so too were neurasthenics described as losing this element of mental presence. According to Jackson Lears, the common effect of all neurasthenic symptoms was a loss of self-control, a "paralysis of the will" which echoes Melville's description of Billy, similarly paralyzed by Claggart's "mesmeristic glance" (98).[47] The question of criminality and conscious intent was highlighted in Melville's time by the trial of Charles Guiteau, who assassinated President James Garfield in 1881. This case hinged on whether Guiteau meant to perform the deed, which in turn depended on whether or not he was to be considered insane in a neurological sense. In fact, rather like Billy Budd, Guiteau was finally found guilty and executed because the possibility of neurological illness was dismissed by the court; Billy's mental aberration and resulting absence of intention are similarly discounted by Vere. Gosling has shown how the Guiteau case was related to developments in American psychology in the post–Civil War years, especially the questioning of definite lines between sanity and insanity—developments in which neurasthenia played a central part.[48] In the words of one doctor in 1885: "A great portion of our nervous patients are not insane, though they vibrate very close to insanity at times, and in paroxysms of high excitement bear a close resemblance to lunatics."[49] For the neurasthenic, the difference between sanity and insanity was merely one of degree. Relating directly to Captain Vere's ambivalent personality—who can "draw the exact line of demarcation" between his sanity and insanity, asks Melville (102)—the neurasthenic existed on an ambiguous border between normal and chaotic mental states.

The main similarity between *Billy Budd* and the neurasthenic climate in which it was written, therefore, concerns the belief that nervousness—unlike traditional states of mental imbalance—occurred in what Beard called "well-balanced, intellectual organizations," and could represent the seeds of madness within an apparently rational mind.[50] Such is the condition of John Claggart's "lunacy" (76), just as it is the possible condition of Captain Vere himself. Melville hints that Vere's words of command, his "mortal sentence pronounced at sea" (126), may in fact be part of a diseased discourse arising from a nervous mental instability: Vere's "utterance" and exclamations seem part of a "mental disturbance" (108) indicative not of eloquence but of insanity. Accordingly, the skepticism that critics have read in *Billy Budd*—the story is Melville's satire on the corrupt and repressive authority of the postbellum state—is directly related to the cultural and linguistic malaise of American Nervousness. Melville's skepticism accords with the neurasthenic notion that public and private modes of authority, while apparently normal, may actually be in a state of crisis and decay.

The other moments in the tale when speech and gesture occur without conscious intent also appertain to *heterophemy*, the disruption between utterance and meaning. When on board the *Rights-of-Man*, Billy foreshadows his deadly blow to Claggart by striking Red Whiskers although "he never *meant* to do quite so much as he did" (47; emphasis added). Again, it is not Billy's "intention" that his indecorous salutation to his former ship—"And good-bye to you, old *Rights-of-Man*"—should convey a satirical "sly slur at impressment in general" (49). Beyond these isolated examples, the entire tale seems to hinge on two distinct cases of nervous linguistic disease. First, Billy's nervous stutter leads him to say, in the language of gesture, something which he does not consciously mean when he strikes Claggart with his deadly blow. And second, just before his execution, Billy seems to project this nervous energy, forcing the masses themselves to heterophemize:[51] "Without volition, as it were, as if indeed the ship's populace were but the vehicles of some vocal current electric, with one voice alow and aloft came a resonant sympathetic echo: 'God bless Captain Vere!' And yet at that instant Billy alone must have been in their hearts, even as in their eyes" (123). Billy overcomes his stutter, but only by projecting his nervousness in the form of an electrical eloquence that usurps the vocal intention of his fellow sailors: their words are an "involuntary echoing of Billy's benediction." (Richard Grant White also compared eloquence to electricity: "In English, words are formed into sentences by the operation of an invisible power, which is like magnetism.")[52] Billy's linguistic affliction is contagious; the electricity upon which his nervousness depended spreads to the ship's populace, subverting their will and forcing them to utter words contrary to their meaning. In so acting, Billy plays directly into the hands of Captain Vere, the exponent of apparent vocal purity and political authority who, following the self-collapsing logic of neurasthenia, may himself be nervously infected. Both the voice of the masses, and the voice of authority that controls them, are potentially as defective as the very stutter that brings them into conflict. In this way, *Billy Budd* constructs the disturbing possibility that the forms of social power, in addition to subaltern forces of resistance, are contaminated by a single linguistic disease.

Billy Budd is not solely a reflection on the American 1880s, but it is strongly informed by contemporary concerns with the spoken voice and its nervous impediments. The tale joins Billy's explicit disease—a nervous stutter that disrupts his power to think reasonably—with a series of more subtle vocal defects, consistent with the notion that nervous mental imbalance could manifest itself in plentiful, though implicitly pathological and meaningless language. Melville describes an organic connection between this diseased type of nonstandard language and cultural disintegration, which he uses to explore the idea that American national health was being undermined from within by an epidemic of speech disorders. In the late 1880s, while apparently alienated from the American scene, Herman Melville crafted a tale in harmony with the nervous vocal culture of his age.

HENRY JAMES AND THE QUESTION OF SPEECH

His slow way of speech, sometimes mistaken for affectation . . . was really the partial victory over a stammer which in his boyhood had been thought incurable. The elaborate politeness and the involved phraseology that made off-hand intercourse with him so difficult to casual acquaintances probably sprang from the same defect. To have too much time to weigh each word before uttering it could not but lead, in the case of the alertest and most sensitive of minds, to self-consciousness and self-criticism; and this fact explains the hesitating manner that often passed for a mannerism.

EDITH WHARTON ON HENRY JAMES, QUOTED IN NOWELL-SMITH, ED., 37

Henry James's novels *The Princess Casamassima* and *The Bostonians* were both written at virtually the same time as *Billy Budd*, between 1884 and 1886. Although their styles appear wildly different, Melville and James shared a common exclusion from and distaste for the mainstream values of the Gilded Age: James's eventual exile in Europe can be compared to what Alan Trachtenberg describes as Melville's "internal exile" in New York City in the 1880s.[53] My reasons for drawing Melville and James together here, however, are less biographical than cultural. A powerful strain of thought in postbellum America linked notions of vocal defect to a sense of cultural degeneration. Strong parallels between two seemingly divergent writers—seen especially in the themes and structures of *The Bostonians* and *Billy Budd*—emphasize the era's fundamental concern with linguistic and social disease.

Like Billy Budd, Henry James was a stutterer, and like many of his contemporary compatriots, he was neurasthenic—two elements that have not gone unnoticed by students of James's prose.[54] In the above epigraph, for example, Edith Wharton follows Freud's idea that "in forming an appreciation of an author's style we are permitted and accustomed to apply the same elucidatory principle which we cannot dispense with in tracing the origins of individual mistakes in speech"; she explains the hesitating, involved, and self-conscious nature of James's spoken style in terms of his psychological aberration.[55] A similar type of psychological explanation for James's prose is equally appealing to Tom Lutz, who considers James to have a neurasthenic style, highly refined and civilized, enervated and hyperactive, in which "indecision is syntactically figured." According to Lutz, James's style is "as highly strung and finely organized as an ideal neurasthenic patient." Attempts to find a key to James's style in either his stammer or his nervousness are, to say the least, reductive: the most liberating of prose stylists is explained in terms of a single "defect."[56] It might not be the secret to his style, but James's speech impediment certainly relates to a network of ideas in his work, a thematizing of vocal culture that links defective utterance to individual psychology and to cultural identity.

The connection between defective utterance and cultural disease is apparent throughout James's fiction. His early novel *Watch and Ward* (1871), for example, describes the Pygmalion-like attempt of Roger Lawrence to create a potential wife with perfect pronunciation, culture, and manners.

This novel reveals the close association in James's mind between an explicitly American setting (at one stage James believed, optimistically, that *Watch and Ward* might be the "great American novel")[57] and cultural questions of speech. James confirmed the association some thirty years later in two essays written on his return to the United States after a long absence in Europe: *The Question of Our Speech*, initially delivered as a lecture to the graduating class of Bryn Mawr College in June 1905, and "The Speech of American Women," which was serialized in *Harper's Bazar* (1906–7). These essays suggest speech as the encoding of cultural value, the enabling force of human civilization. According to James, "the history of the voice" is "the history of the national character, almost the history of the people." All life comes back to the question of our speech, says James, because the spoken word facilitates the relational communication upon which civilization depends. "The imparting of a coherent culture is a matter of communication and response," which in turn requires a common, organized, and developed medium of expression. Urging his readers to resist the forces of decay within the "living organism" of language, James advocates a prescriptive practice of phonetic correctness which will preserve the forms and shades of speech:

> the innumerable differentiated, discriminated units of sound and sense that lend themselves to audible production, to enunciation, to intonation: those innumerable units that have, each, an identity, a quality, an outline, a shape, a clearness, a fineness, a sweetness, a richness, that have, in a word, a value, which it is open to us, as lovers of our admirable English tradition, or as cynical traitors to it, to preserve or to destroy.[58]

For James, the value of language resides in its fusion of ethics and aesthetics. A well-tuned language is not just a beautiful and efficient system of communication: it confers dignity and integrity to existence, lifting individuals above the gross mispronunciations of the multitude, while also grounding society in the authority of cultural tradition, in the authentic values of a "civilized" past.

These essays, rather than predicting structuralism, forecasting Roman Jakobson's idea of the social value of phonemes, as Lynda Boren describes them in her recent study of language and gender in James, seem simply a perpetuation of the "verbal criticism" so popular in late-nineteenth-century America.[59] This is particularly obvious in James's belief that an organic connection existed between coherent speech and national well-being, and in his corresponding equation of faulty language with a decaying culture. Thus, like the verbal critic Richard Grant White, James was especially concerned with the linguistic and social threats to America posed by the common school system, by the non-British immigrants dumping their "mountains of promiscuous material into the foundations of the

American," and by the popular newspapers whose dissonant shouts, shrieks, and yells reminded James of "a mighty maniac who has broken loose and who is running amuck through the spheres alike of sense and of sound." As with many of his contemporary language critics, James was not worried about the "instinctive and irreflective" dialect of, say, Georgia crackers; his real concern was with the "climatic, social, political, theological, moral, 'psychic'" forces of American life that had left its "tone-standard" in tatters.[60]

In "The Speech of American Women," James traces his ideas of language back to the early 1880s, just prior to his creation of *The Bostonians* (1886). If these ideas were formulated in an American environment, James's fictional exploration of vocal culture was not, however, restricted to the United States. Indeed, many elements of James's two essays in verbal criticism surface in a specifically British context, namely in *The Princess Casamassima* (1886), his study of class conflict in late-nineteenth-century London. James may have cited American literature's obsession with "[d]ialect, general or special—dialect with the literary rein loose on its agitated back and with its shambling power of traction" as the key reason why this literature had failed to affect his imagination, yet he was deeply concerned with dialectal issues of his own in the 1880s.[61] *The Princess Casamassima* reveals that James too was giving his ear to the public voice, scribbling down what he called the "phrases of the people" from the dark corners of London pubs—phrases like "he cuts it very fine," "that takes the gilt off, you know," and "'ere today, somewhere else tomorrow: that's *'is* motto."[62] While James would never attempt a thorough representation of anyone's phonetic peculiarity, *The Princess* pays careful attention not just to the "phrases of the people" but also to their distinctive pronunciation: "Miss Pynsent pronounced her name Enning" (54), "Mrs Bowerbank called it oppo*site*" (60), "she called it a *shime*" (163), "Mr Schinkel called it 'loaf'" (289), "she called it ''ouse'" (473), "as she had noticed before ... he pronounced 'weary' *weery*" (579).[63] *The Princess* is the closest James comes to the dialect tradition that he recognizes as popular yet dismisses so fervently in "The Novel of Dialect" (1898) and in his later essays in verbal criticism: the "attempt to represent [vocal laxity] by imitative signs is, besides being a waste of ingenuity, to impute to it a consistency which is really the last thing it owns."[64]

The Princess Casamassima is fundamentally concerned with questions of dialect: it explores what William Dwight Whitney described as the "personal peculiarities of pronunciation and phraseology" and the "widespread and deeper differences of district and class" which were then the concern of writers and philologists alike.[65] The novel's hero, Hyacinth Robinson, is torn apart by his conflicting allegiance to the cause of socialism and to the culture of the aristocracy (although raised in lower-middle-class London, Hyacinth is supposedly the illegitimate son of an English Lord and a French commoner). Hyacinth's psychological tension is pronounced when he encounters his childhood sweetheart and symbol of "the people," Millicent Henning, toward the end of the novel. It is a tension, moreover, with strong linguistic significance:

> [S]he could see he *was* in a fever; she hadn't noticed it at first, because he never had any more complexion than a cheese. Was it something he had caught in some of those backslums, where he went prying about with his wicked ideas? . . . Would his fine friends—a precious lot *they* were, that put it off on him to do the nasty part!—would they find the doctor, and the port wine, and the money, and all the rest, when he was laid up—perhaps for months—through their putting such rot into his head and his putting it into others that could carry it even less? . . . Suddenly she exclaimed, quitting the tone of exaggerated derision which she had used a moment before, "You little rascal, you've got something on your heart! Has your Princess given you the sack?"
>
> "My poor girl, your talk is a queer mixture," he resignedly sighed. "But it may well be. It's not queerer than my life."
>
> "Well, I'm glad you admit that!" the young woman cried, walking on with a flutter of her ribbons.
>
> "Your ideas about my ideas!" Hyacinth continued. "Yes, you should see me in the back slums. I'm a bigger Philistine than you, Miss Henning."
>
> "You've got more ridiculous names, if that's what you mean. I don't believe that half the time you know what you do mean, yourself. I don't believe that you even know, with all your thinking, what you do think. That's your disease."
>
> "It's astonishing how you sometimes put your finger on the place," Hyacinth rejoined. "I mean to think no more—I mean to give it up. Avoid it yourself, my dear Millicent—avoid it as you would a baleful vice. It confers no true happiness. Let us live in a world of irreflective contemplation—let us live in the present hour."
>
> "I don't care how I live, nor where I live," said Millicent, "so long as I can do as I like." [526]

Hyacinth and Millicent speak in different social dialects, and communication breaks down between them altogether—ironically, over the Arnoldian term *Philistine*[66]—at the very point where disease makes itself felt: "I don't believe that you even know, with all your thinking, what you do think. That's your disease." Millicent implies that Hyacinth's is a disease of language. The absence of a common tongue between the two characters signals not merely a diseased culture, but also a personal, mental disease in which Hyacinth's command of meaning has begun to "rot." Millicent's observation is not merely metaphorical. The fever that she notices in Hyacinth, although not picked up solely in the "back slums," is certainly a product of society. It is the fever of neurasthenia, produced in part by cultural conditions, and exacerbated by the aristocratic blood in Hyacinth's veins. Ironically, while Hyacinth's genetic lineage makes him in some ways an organ of vocal purity, freeing him from the most significant linguistic marker of working-class identity in nineteenth-century England (he had a "natural command" of the letter h from his earliest years [282]), it also makes him susceptible to the forces of nervous disease that undermine any claim to spoken correctness.[67]

To some extent, *The Princess* reenacts the same threats posed to cultural authority by "linguistic nervousness" that we encountered in Melville. Neurasthenia causes diseased discourse in the dominant class. Thus, Paul Muniment's firm working-class status results in an "inaccessibility to nervous agitation" (501) which makes him immune to stammering and to other defects of utterance (414). The main exemplar of defective speech among the upper classes is Lady Aurora Langrish, who possesses two spoken ticks considered typical of her class. "She sounded the letter r peculiarly" (134; in the 1908 "New York" edition of the novel, James changes this to "She sounded the letter r as a w"), a social signifier every bit as important as the dropping of the h; more significantly, she has a stammer that echoes James's own in giving an appearance of "overdone consideration" (138). The most common effect of this stammer, however, is not the appearance of consideration but incoherence. Although reluctant to represent Lady Aurora's speech impediments (only the mispronunciations of the masses are spelled out for the reader),[68] James is keen to describe her "nervous, hurried, almost incoherent speech, of which she had delivered herself pantingly, with strange intonations and grotesque movements of her neck" (222). Lady Aurora's nervousness leads to "ejaculations of which it was difficult to guess the meaning" (135), and to "inarticulate responses and embarrassed protests" (433). Her linguistic disease, moreover, is highly contagious, marking a general malaise of meaning throughout the aristocracy. Hence the Princess, in her conversation with the nearby Marchant family, professes "complete inability to understand the sense in which her visitor meant her thin remarks," owing to the fact that "the Marchant family produced a very peculiar, and at moments almost maddening, effect upon her nerves" (318). Similarly, Hyacinth's own neurasthenia (his failure, in Paris, to balance his accounts—an image typical of nervousness) leads to the "danger of becoming incoherent to himself," partly through a lack of "articulate words" (379–80).

Hyacinth finally commits suicide when he cannot carry out the revolutionary order to assassinate a member of the aristocracy. Yet his inevitable destruction arises not—like Billy Budd's—from a lack of words, but from a nervous tendency to talk too much. The quality of Hyacinth's speech first brings him to the attention of the aristocracy; it is through talk about the social conditions of the working class that Hyacinth gains momentary power over the Princess.[69] His prominent speech at the revolutionary socialist club, the "Sun and Moon,"—the turning-point in Hyacinth's life, halfway through the novel—defeats a tendency to blush and stammer before such political gatherings (286). Yet to overcome this stammer is not, ironically, to overcome his nervousness. At this gathering, Hyacinth becomes infected by the verbal "contagion of excited purpose" (291). His nervousness increases, until, amid the disorder and confusion at the end of the meeting, he is provoked to speak in response to the shrieked accusation that the people present are cowards (293–94). He eloquently pledges his life to the cause of socialism; he brings cohesion to the group, yet he "scarcely knew what happened" (294). In effect, Hyacinth's nervousness results in a classic case of *heterophemy:* his disrupted mental condition leads him "to speak without thinking" (286). Just as Hyacinth's favorite phrase, the "party of action," is criticized by Paul Muniment as "mere gibberish" (292), his speech of allegiance to this party—and his promise to commit a crime for it—is a type of nonsense: a senseless jargon arising from the nervous condition of his mind. Hyacinth loses command of his meaning; he says the opposite of what he intends by dedicating himself to a cause in which he does not fully believe. Hyacinth represents the type of neurasthenic speaker who, rather than stammering, utters plentiful though faulty and nonsensical language, the kind of speaker who produces what Richard Grant White called words-no-words.

The rhetorics of linguistic deviation and of mental and cultural disease are clearly intertwined in *The Princess Casamassima.* The fever that Millicent Henning notices in her young friend is physical, psychological, and linguistic. Hyacinth's nervous mental derangement, leading him to utter a corrupt speech of thoughtless words, contaminates the common language upon which—according to James's essays in verbal criticism—cultural value depends. Yet the treatment of British and European voices in *The Princess* only partly concurs with the contemporary American idea that linguistic nervousness was infecting the dominant culture. While aristocrats possess a proclivity to disordered language, they are also shown to have strong moments of vocal value. For example, the Princess herself has a "beautiful voice" (317) and specializes in "the cultivation, the facility, of talk" (482). An equal and similar attention is paid to the linguistic aberrations of the masses. In one sense, inadequate language signals poverty of thought: a worker's lexical limitation, his constant repetition of inane words, constitutes "the whole furniture of his mind" (280).[70] Yet, echoing ambivalence over elite discourse, suggestions that working-class speech is ignorant and imbecilic are countered by the beauty residing in folk expression: Paul Muniment's speech is fresh, original, racy, and frank (450); on occasion even Millicent Henning's "chaff" can be wholesome, spontaneous, and refreshing (524). Bad grammar coincides with individual good health, as in Millicent's case (340), while a fine ability to talk coexists with virulent illness, as it does for Paul Muniment's bedridden sister, Rose.

The incoherence of society represented in *The Princess* arises not solely from the disease of the dominant class, nor from the babble of the proletariat, but from a defining characteristic of Britishness itself: the conflict between classes.[71] In the novel, communication between different national languages takes place with some ease: Hyacinth understands his French-speaking mother despite their language difference (87), and he later picks up French "with the most extraordinary facility" (102). Yet communication within a common English tongue is inherently problematic. A series of incidents in the novel, corresponding to the conflict between Hyacinth and Millicent cited above, emphasizes how the separation of society into different class-based dialects is both symptom and cause of cultural chaos. This becomes obvious in Hyacinth's interaction with the upper as well as with the lower classes: when he initially meets the Princess, "her attitude made him feel how little *he*, in comparison, expressed himself like a person who had the habit of conversation; he seemed to himself to stammer and emit common sounds" (198). Hyacinth's stammer is, in this instance, emblematic of the type of speech defect that arises from the problematic interaction of people with vastly different psychologies of language. The upper classes have a unique method of pronunciation and punctuation that frequently leaves Hyacinth bewildered ("It must be added that he was far from understanding everything [the Princess] said" [250–51]).[72] Similarly, the sophisticated Mr. Vetch cannot be understood by the lower-middle-class world in which he lives because he speaks "a different language" (67); and Hyacinth's conversation with Millicent is punctuated by phrases that she proposes "to make use of . . . on some future occasion, but was quite unable to interpret" (163). There seems to be an absolute demarkation of conversational and cognitive boundaries. The novel's many moments of interclass communication breakdown are pivotal because they involve not just a failure of understanding but the disintegration of consciousness itself. When Hyacinth's parental guardian, Amanda Pynsent, fails to comprehend the complex vocabulary of her friend Mr. Vetch, for example, her very capacity for thought collapses.[73] In a novel that makes so many direct connections between "illness" and "the imperfect organisation of society" (121), the most infectious infirmity is the psychological crisis that stems from misunderstanding another social dialect.

Hyacinth is a nervous speaker who succumbs to a fatal moment of heterophemy. Yet his final self-destruction derives not from his partial membership in a diseased dominant class, but from the conflict within his "split" personality and the "mingled current in his blood" (165). *The Princess* makes several direct links between blood and language, and Hyacinth's divided heredity is figured by questions of speech.[74] He is intimately connected with a working class whose language disgusts and aggravates him,[75] while he desires entry into an aristocratic culture whose "words evoked all sorts of shadowy suggestions of things he was condemned not to know, touching him most when he had not the key to them" (251). Hyacinth is torn apart by ambivalent linguistic and class allegiances; he can neither be aristocrat nor worker, nor can he speak perfectly the language of either. Echoing James's wider view of late-Victorian society, Hyacinth becomes incoherent—his mind inevitably falls to pieces and his voice collapses into silence[76]—owing to the mutually unintelligible dialects of identity he embodies.

Hyacinth dies from the peculiarly British disease of class conflict. In James's contemporary account of the American scene in *The Bostonians* (1886), however, the configuration of language and society is significantly different. *The Bostonians* describes a more radical collapse in the modes of cultural authority, a collapse consistent with the neurasthenic society from which James's ideas of language seem to stem.

Predicting James's ideas in *The Question of Our Speech*, *The Bostonians* examines the linguistic forces that threaten the values of civilization. The spoken voice mediates the problems of the age in various ways.[77] The journalist Mr. Pardon (a character whose very name evokes miscommunication) talks in a flat tone with "words and even sentences, imperfectly formed" (116), just as the newspaper for which he writes is an agent of defective, mass language—the result of an abandonment of art for "publicity" (117). Selah Tarrant, a stage mesmerist, similarly embodies a sociolinguistic process of disease. His quack psychotherapy rests on a type of "talking cure" in which he speaks to his female patients "as if he didn't know what he was saying" (39). His production of a seemingly meaningless language corresponds with mesmerism itself as a symbol of the degenerate sensibilities of the era. And contemporary education is represented as a "gigantic farce" owing to its creation of "a lot of empty catchwords" (316). Confirming the link between coherent speech and cultural health, the linguistic defectiveness of these social institutions indicates a "rank civilization" (177), an age whose "public mind was in a muddle" (258). According to the novel's protagonist, Basil Ransom, it is a talkative, hysterical age, full of "unhealthy germs" and "dissipated habits," an age of false ideas in which degenerate language and thought are part of a general contamination of cultural values (181).

The main threat to national linguistic well-being in *The Bostonians*, how-

ever, derives from a source radically different than the class conflict of
The Princess Casamassima, as is evident from Ransom's pronouncement on
his surrounding cultural climate: "The whole generation is womanized;
the masculine tone is passing out of the world; it's a feminine, a nervous,
hysterical, chattering, canting age, an age of hollow phrases and false del-
icacy and exaggerated solicitudes and coddled sensibilities, which, if we
don't soon look out, will usher in the reign of mediocrity, of the feeblest
and flattest and the most pretentious that has ever been" (322). Positioned at the climax of James's avowed attempt to write a typically American novel, "a tale very characteristic of our social conditions,"[78] Ransom's
statement brings together a series of ideas central to the understanding
of American vocal culture in the 1880s. Echoing George Beard's identi-
fication of neurasthenia with both the language and the unusual social
position of American women, Ransom believes that "vociferating women"
are a direct threat to "civilization" (45) because feminine nervousness is
disrupting linguistic, mental, and social coherence. Feminine speech is
particularly disturbing for Ransom and, I argue, for James himself, because it exists as a force *within* the dominant cultural discourse, one that
challenges the basic principles of linguistic and social cultivation. Defective speech is not the sole possession of an inferior, uncivilized social class,
as James had argued in "The Novel of Dialect," but is present in the self-
proclaimed guardians of American culture.

The most remarkable element of *The Bostonians* and of James's essays
in verbal criticism is the identification of defective speech and cultural
disease as particularly feminine. In "The Speech of American Women,"
James considers the voices of American men to be beyond repair; they
are versed in the "yell of the stock-exchange or the football-field" to such
an extent that they are "incapable of knowing, that is, what sounds *are*,
what they may be, what they should or what they shouldn't be." It is left
solely to the American woman, therefore, to remedy the situation. James
acknowledges that the women of America are now in charge of its culture,
that the "whole of the social initiative" has been "abandoned to them
without a struggle." Accordingly, the disastrous condition of this culture
arises from the fact that the American woman also possesses an inherent
speech impediment, a decayed use of consonants which leads to "a mere
helpless slobber of disconnected vowel noises," keeping articulation "as
little distinct as possible from the grunting, the squealing, the barking or
the roaring of animals." In "The Speech of American Women," James
traces his realization of this idea to a confrontation with a group of vociferous girl pupils outside a fashionable Boston school in the early 1880s.
James is amazed at the degree to which they shriek and bawl to one another across the street, "all articulating as from sore mouths, all mumbling
and whining and vocally limping and shuffling, as it were, together." This

incident provides James with the key to the decrepitude of American speech. He sees that the mechanisms of cultural authority are themselves diseased: the teaching of a "tone-standard" is absent from the education of women, and their love of democratic independence is antithetical to the "oppressive obligation" of traditionally correct pronunciation. James concludes that the speech of women is an element within the "best society" of America which threatens physically to damage the shape of its spoken forms, and thereby its claim to cultural order and value. American vocal culture, in other words, is rotten at the core.[79]

James's essays reflect the ambiguous position of women, and of "the feminine" in general, in American society at the time. Kenneth Cmiel has shown how women's magazines of the period "called attention to the special role women had in maintaining the language," a view which presupposed that women's speech was better than men's, and how the maintenance of this purity depended on women "remaining shielded from the toughness of masculine public life." Thus, John Harvey Kellogg's *Ladies' Guide in Health and Disease* (1882) included "several pages on the 'moral disease' of verbal impurity." This focus on female speech coincided with what Alan Trachtenberg has described as a more radical "feminization of culture" in the Gilded Age: "The rise to power of culture was at once the rise of a powerful idea of the feminine, of woman's role: the dispensing of values nonmaterial, nonaggressive, nonexploitative. As culture came to seem the repository of elevating thoughts and cleansing emotions, it seemed all the more as if the rough world of masculine enterprise had called into being its redemptive opposite." Yet, just as intellectuals like William James were beginning to react against this "stifling, enervating, effeminate" middle-class culture, so too were the voices of women being challenged.[80] Rather than being indifferent to women, as Cmiel suggests, verbal critics of the time were increasingly skeptical over the voice of woman as a preserver of cultural quality.[81] George Beard regarded the female voice as being particularly prone to nervous incoherence. Similarly, Schele de Vere rebuked American women for "indulging to the utmost in unbridled license of expression, both in public and in private," while Richard Grant White noted that the constant "upward nasal inflection" of the female voice detracted from his ideal of "a simple, strong, and manly speech." William Dean Howells also joined in the criticism, accusing American women of twanging, whiffling, snuffling, and whining, of speaking English "as if they were reciting the Biglow Papers." According to White: "You shall see a lovely, bright creature, with all the external evidences of culture about her, a woman who will carry you captive so long as she is silent; but let her open her pretty lips, and she shall pierce your ear with a mean, thin, nasal, rasping tone, by which at once you are disenchanted."[82] As with nervousness itself, the corruption of cultural forms remained masked behind an apparently normal exterior.

James's opinions on female discourse were remarkably fervent. It is little wonder, then, that *The Bostonians*, based on what James considered "the most salient and peculiar point in our social life"—"the situation of women, the decline of the sentiment of sex, the agitation on their behalf"—should be such an extensive exploration of the linguistic chaos emanating from this very "point." *The Bostonians* is a testament to James's belief, developing in the 1880s, that his model of American speech as a bastion of innocence against the profligacy of European society—clearly visible in *The Europeans* (1878)—could no longer hold true.[83] Basil Ransom's idea of America's "nervous, hysterical, chattering, canting age" was part of an ambivalent cultural discourse that positioned women as preservers of, yet central agents of disease within, a fragile civilization.

According to Basil Ransom, the jargon of the women's rights movement in the Gilded Age is a "wordy, windy iteration of inanities" (227), devoid of reason and intellectual content, whose popularity only signals the crazy character of an age that demands such "fluent, pretty, third-rate palaver, conscious or unconscious, perfected humbug" (257, 308). Ransom is keen to ascribe Verena Tarrant's ability to address "cultivated and high-minded audiences" (51) not to the political and moral cause of the feminism she espouses, but to a brand of mesmerism symptomatic of devalued taste: "She didn't mean it, she didn't know what she meant, she had been stuffed with this trash by her father [Selah Tarrant]" (57). Ransom reads the meaning of Verena's voice, even at its most powerful and musical, as a "vague, thin, rambling . . . tissue of generalities," "so weak in argument, so inevitably verbose" (257–58). In effect, Ransom becomes a verbal critic of female heterophemy. His deconstruction of Mrs. Luna's slangy description of Olive Chancellor—"Isn't she a dear old thing?"—exposes a fracture between form and meaning in female discourse: "She was not old—she was sharply young; and it was inconceivable to him . . . that she should ever become any one's 'dear.' Least of all was she a 'thing'; she was intensely, fearfully, a person" (89). According to Ransom, the slang of women, rather like their public speech, suffers from diseased processes of signification: if it does actually mean anything, then this meaning is very different from the intention of the speaker.[84]

At one level it is possible to discern in *The Bostonians* a polarization of effective male discourse and defective female discourse—at least, this would be Basil Ransom's reading of the situation. Ransom's criticism of vociferating women, his failure to find meaning in their words, is counteracted by a supposedly male language, which James almost exhausts his supply of adjectives in an effort to describe: rough, derisive, articulate, cool, calm, severe, deliberate, accurate, explicit, distinct, mathematical, lucid.[85] The emotional battle between Ransom and Verena toward the end of the novel revolves around the question of whose language has the greatest claim to represent actual experience. Ransom charges Verena with "want of reality"; his manner, "so serene and explicit, as if he knew the thing to an absolute certainty," secures the predominance of his phrases over hers (326–27). His "effective and penetrating" words finally enter Verena's soul, forcing her "at last to believe them, and that was the alteration, the transformation" (370). This transformation results from an act of male linguistic aggression which culminates in the fulfill-ment of Ransom's desire to strike both Verena and Olive dumb. The novel initially appears, therefore, to validate Kathleen Jamieson's identi-fication of archetypal "manly" and "feminine" styles in language: the former organized, objective, and authoritative, the latter disorganized, subjective, and irrational.[86] *The Bostonians* seems to construct a fantasy of male linguistic domination, epitomized by Ransom's silencing of Ver-ena's public voice—a victory of male reason over the hollow catchwords of a nervous age.

Yet this polarization of masculine and feminine language is far from simple. Basil Ransom's "manly" discourse contains, ironically, a "femi-nine softness" (5).[87] Just as neurasthenia was figured as a feminine con-dition to which men were equally susceptible, Ransom's voice can only succeed by appropriating the forces of nervousness to which it is suppos-edly opposed. He is successful not through his victory over nervousness, but by becoming nervous himself: "Like his friends the Bostonians he was very nervous," the narrator tells us just before the novel's final confron-tation (390). The neurasthenia that was previously responsible for Ver-ena's "voluble, fluent, feverish behavior" (365), and for the "chattering" of the "canting age," is not relieved by Ransom but exacerbated in his attempt to win Verena for himself by preventing her from speaking in public. Thus, the speech impediment, viewed by Ransom as inherent in woman, finally becomes absolute: Verena is "too nervous to speak" (429), her voice becomes effectively paralyzed (431), and Olive's vehement fem-inism is reduced to a "low, inarticulate murmur of anguish" (396) and a bestial shriek (434). While Ransom gains a type of victory in *The Boston-ians* by silencing Verena's supposedly diseased discourse, it remains un-clear whether James himself condoned such a victory, as recent critics have argued.[88] Any victory in the novel seems ethically flawed because Ransom's apparent success depends on a replacement of one form of nervousness with another. Echoing George Beard's notion of American Nervousness as a disease of the dominant classes, *The Bostonians* is concerned with the seeds of corruption already present in the cultural elite, rather than with threats to cultural order posed by external forces. Women's discourse seems less a nervous sublanguage than a powerful antilanguage, capable not just of resisting patriarchal paradigms, but of contaminating them with its feminine difference.[89]

Ransom's nervousness is only one of several instances of a complex, self-undermining logic at work in the novel. Dividing *The Bostonians* into dominant male and subservient female discourse fails to recognize James's portrayal of the ambivalent position of women in society: while regarded as agents of corruption, women are also shown to possess a special moral, social, and personal condition in the United States (216). Olive Chancellor is the principal exponent of this point of view. Like Ransom, she criticizes the age's lack of "measures and standards," the demoralization caused by a lavishing of superlatives, which leads the narrator to suggest that "she looked to the influx of the great feminine element to make [the age] feel and speak more sharply" (119). Verena Tarrant's voice is a testament to the cultural value of feminine speech. It is musical, "so pure and rich, and yet so young, so natural" (253); it is capable of silencing the babble of the masses (430) and of bringing social unanimity by resolving audiences into a "single sentient personality" (253). Ransom's recognition of the corrupt nature of female language follows the logic of James's essays on the speech of American women: it recognizes disease within the only entity capable of maintaining the value and beauty of a coherent culture.

The novel's seemingly successful masculine discourse contains deeper improprieties. The narrator confesses, in the opening pages, that Basil Ransom is not himself a New Englander: "He came, in fact, from Mississippi, and he spoke very perceptively with the accent of that country. It is not in my power to reproduce by any combination of characters this charming dialect; but the initiated reader will have no difficulty in evoking the sound, which is to be associated in the present instance with nothing vulgar or vain" (2). Here James is playing with the "local color" tradition by evoking yet refusing to represent its most predominant characteristic: dialect.[90] This reluctance to redact Ransom's local accent might be read as James's displacement of regional difference. The conflicts within America—the strife between North and South recently fought out in the Civil War—have apparently been superseded by the tensions within a certain class: the conflict between male and female speech in the cultural elite. Yet Ransom's dialect has more radical significance; the narrator returns to its nonstandard features:

> And yet the reader who likes a complete image, who desires to read with the senses as well as with the reason, is entreated not to forget that he

prolonged his consonants and swallowed his vowels, that he was guilty of
elisions and interpolations which were equally unexpected, and that his discourse was pervaded by something sultry and vast, something almost African
in its rich basking tone, something that suggested the teeming expanse of
the cotton-field. [2–3]

James made his opinion of regional dialect more than clear to readers
of the magazine *Literature* in 1898: it is an "ignoble jargon," a "strange
outgrowth of expression," the "very riot of the abnormal." Especially
prevalent in the literary works of women, according to James, dialect is a
form of "vulgar linguistics" meant for the "lacerated ear." It is only concerned with "conditions primitive often to the limit of extreme barbarism—in which colloquial speech arrives at complete debasement."[91] Ransom's speech may not be represented "phonetically" on the printed page,
yet it partakes of James's notion of dialectal debasement in several ways.
Ransom tends to elide and chop his words, key traits of the nervous
speaker, and his interpolations suggest an erratic, disordered process of
thought. Moreover, there is a contaminating element in Ransom's voice
deeper than any nervous disorder, an *African* element that observers had
noted—controversially—in the southern American dialect throughout the
nineteenth century (the narrator of Charles Chesnutt's *House Behind the
Cedars* [1900] describes it as part "of the negro's unconscious revenge for
his own debasement").[92] Rather than displacing the importance of region,
The Bostonians implies that a regional, racial hybridity is present in the
novel's masculine discourse. The narrator's attitude toward this dialect is
clearly ambivalent. His refusal to represent it can be read as a deliberate
act of concealment that effectively corrects the "errors" of the dominant
language. Yet the early confession of Ransom's disordered, Africanized
speech undermines any effort at disguise. It warns readers that, even when
it seems most powerful, reasonable, and pure, Ransom's dialect is both
formally "lacerated" and substantially infected by the accents of racial
and regional difference.

Ransom's way of talking, rather than a force of purity challenging the
feminine disease of language, is both barbarously abnormal (to use
James's terminology) and ethically questionable. The "way he spoke" tells
Olive Chancellor "that it was no wonder he had fought on the Southern
side" in the Civil War (9). Ransom opposes the slangy features of his age
not just with a manly speech, but with a southern manly speech that embodies, in its very accent, a highly conservative social and moral code:
"He was a man who still, in a slangy age, could pronounce that word
[chivalry] with a perfectly serious face" (184).[93] Yet Ransom's conservative
opinions are implicitly undermined by the "black" accent in which they
are delivered. The defender of slavery is shown to be affected by the black
presence he would seek to segregate and control. Ransom's accent sug-

gests not the myths of a chivalric southern culture, but a racial interaction that has placed a blackness at the heart of the white voice.

Ransom's dialect is thus another manifestation of the neurasthenic notion that the traditions of American cultural authority are, at every level, inherently problematic. *The Bostonians* recognizes that it is no longer possible to segregate good male and bad female speech. The language of women, the only true agent of cultural value, is fundamentally diseased, while male speech, the aggressive victor in a war of words, is shot through with linguistic "corruption." The obvious lack of resolution in the last sentence of the novel—the narrator denies the possibility of a romantic male victory by suggesting that Ransom and Verena's match is "far from brilliant," and that Verena's present tears "were not the last she was destined to shed" (435)—is analogous to a lack of linguistic resolution at the center of the novel. The narrator's final ambiguous silence concerning the fate of his characters suggests both the abandonment of language that stems from a situation in which one form of defective speech is replaced by another and James's abandonment of an American cultural situation defined by the competition between diseased discourses. Rather than validating Ransom's conservative political values, as recent critics have suggested, *The Bostonians* seems a radical rejection of *all* American values, be they conservative or otherwise.

Although James and Melville must inevitably be considered outsiders to the dialect or "local color" tradition that would dominate American literature until the end of the century (indeed, Melville was an outcast from American literature itself by this time), their fictions of the 1880s were dominated by the intense concern with national vocal culture of which dialect writing was only one component. Both were in touch with the Gilded Age desire to place speech in its psychological and cultural contexts. For this reason, although Melville and James seem such different writers, there is much thematic common ground between the works discussed in this chapter. Hyacinth Robinson and Billy Budd, for example, are both destroyed by their nervous, defective speech: Hyacinth produces meaningless words that he is unable to perform, and Billy performs a meaningless act when he is unable to speak. Whereas Hyacinth collapses from empty eloquence into voiceless incoherence at the end of *The Princess Casamassima*, Billy progresses from voicelessness to an eloquent ventriloquism of heterophemy into the mouths of the listening masses—a progression that signals *Billy Budd*'s more radical sense of absolute cultural collapse. Melville's tale and *The Bostonians* are so similar because, while seeming to suggest the success of a masculine and repressive form of social control, both expose the contamination of cultural authority by nervous disease and vocal corruption. In an age obsessed with a type of dialect literature that created superficial divisions between standard and nonstandard speech, their works explore the underlying, undermining sense in which the standard forms of hegemonic culture were themselves degenerate.

Although James would never again come so close to engaging the explicit issue of working-class dialect as he did in *The Princess Casamassima*, his interest in talk did not cease. James's progression through the 1890s to his "late style" of the early 1900s can be seen as a direct development from his concern with vocal culture in *The Bostonians* and *The Princess*. *The Bostonians*, with its neurasthenic corruption of cultural authority, can be read as a dramatization of the reasons behind James's inevitable abandonment of the American scene as a source of fictional material.[94] Yet James's wholesale doubt about the public sphere, and about the vocal values at its heart, only reappeared in a European setting, fueled in part by the poor sales of his books and by his disastrous experiment with the theater in the early 1890s.[95] *The Tragic Muse* (1890), for example, questions the quality of the public voice in several ways: theatrical speech is criticized for being an impure, chaotic composite of "abominable dialects" (139); the public is described as stewing in the debased, deafening discourse of the age of "newspaperism" (375); and the language of politics is revealed to be "a lot of rot," a mere production of noise without intellectual content (74–75). Moreover, the novel as a whole is structured around the philosophical problems of making meaning public through language. The pivotal event of *The Tragic Muse* is Nick Dormer's decision to relinquish a career as a Member of Parliament for the artistic life of a portrait painter, a decision that embodies his growing skepticism over the existence of a common, cogent public discourse. The novel is punctuated by people speaking different, mutually unintelligible dialects, and by moments when conversation degenerates from direct communication into ambiguous, spiraling semantic contention.[96] The tragic muse herself, Miriam Rooth, is the classic example of this linguistic incoherence: she speaks a special, frequently incomprehensible language, defined by a bewildering multilingual variety and by an ironic technique of meaning the contrary of what she says (446, 437). Opposing this corrupt discourse is the silent, universally eloquent yet inevitably undefined "language of art" (497), together with a series of strange "brainwaves," "mysterious affinities," and "divinations of private congruity" that seem to exist without words between characters (293, 488), allowing communication despite "the absence of a common dialect" (369).[97] The novel leaves us feeling that any pure language, free from the debased world of spoken dialect, is so private that it eludes verbalization[98]—a solipsistic situation that generates a further set of questions: How can we ever know, with certainty, the stuff of

another consciousness, and how can the depths of character be represented in the linguistic space of a novel? These are problems that *The
Tragic Muse* never fully resolves.[99]

In James's work after *The Tragic Muse*, questions of speech seem related
less to the public problems of social and political identity than to the
radically private problems of individual consciousness. Sharon Cameron
detects situations in *The Golden Bowl* (1904) in which "speech is emptied
of significant implication" and the possibility of speaking meaningfully is
abandoned, a breakdown in communication she relates to James's larger
skepticism over objective knowledge of consciousness itself.[100] Without
doubt, James's late novels are conducive to poststructuralist interpretation, to the belief that James writes of a "verbal age" in which referen-
tiality has been abandoned and language becomes a self-enclosed world
that "creates the conditions under which perception is possible."[101] James
himself is partly responsible for such readings: the preface to *The Awkward
Age* (1899) records his desire for "really constructive dialogue, dialogue
organic and dramatic, speaking for itself, representing and embodying
substance and form." Yet we should not forget that James's late style coincided with his most outspoken remarks on "the question of our
speech," which place linguistic speculation firmly in a social and cultural
context. Toward the end of "The Speech of American Women," James
makes his understanding of language clear: "*there's no isolated question of
speech*. . . . The interest of tone is the interest of manners, and the interest
of manners is the interest of morals, and the interest of morals is the
interest of civilization."[102]

The social grounding of language that we find in *The Bostonians* and
The Princess Casamassima, I suggest, does not disappear in James's late fiction, but merely becomes more concentrated in its application. Although
James does not tie his interests so tightly to the class conflicts of London
or to the feminization of Boston, this only highlights his concern with the
problems of language in more "refined" forms of public culture. *The
Awkward Age*, with its contemplation of the infinite suggestions, ambiguous
metaphors, and euphemistic slang of London's drawing-room conversations, has been read as James's retreat into a nonreferential "autonomous
proliferation of language." It can also be interpreted as James's most explicit recognition that heterophemy—"saying one thing and meaning another," as George Beard defined it—had reached epidemic proportions.
Instead of representing nonstandard dialect, in late novels like *The Awkward Age* James turned his attention to the difficulties and divisions within
the supposedly standard language of the highest social classes.[103]

FOUR

White Writers, Creole Languages

Sounding remarkably like Mark Twain's claim to depict "four modified varieties" of the Pike County dialect in *Adventures of Huckleberry Finn* (1884), the 1918 *Cambridge History of American Literature* states that "[o]f the negro dialect in general as spoken in the United States today, there are four varieties": the dialect of Virginia, as represented by Thomas Nelson Page; the "dialect of the Sea Islands of the South Atlantic States," known as Gullah, which "can hardly be said to have found a place in literature"; the French dialect spoken by the "Creole negroes" of Louisiana, which is "best represented, though sparingly, in the works of George W. Cable"; and Joel Chandler Harris's "Uncle Remus dialect, or the dialect spoken by the negroes in the great inland sections of the South and South-west." The *Cambridge History* was describing the popular "plantation tradition" of post–Civil War dialect writing, in which white authors represented the black language and folklore of a slave past. These white attempts at black speech were often praised for their realism by readers—indeed, for the *Cambridge History* the distinction between spoken black dialect and its literary representation had disappeared altogether. The power of plantation literature to command belief is typically interpreted as embodying a racist ideology, a means for whites to segregate and demean black language and culture. Michael North argues that the political role of Joel Chandler Harris in defining the post-Reconstruction Jim Crow era expresses "the duplicity of the *whole* dialect movement."[1]

North's claim is difficult to sustain, however, in light of the fact that George Washington Cable—one of the most famous white dialect writers of the time—was simultaneously attacking the very politics of segregation to which North refers. The literary employment of black dialect was not a homogeneous act of repression but a complex collection of different ethical agendas. Just as the plantation tradition was divided into different regions, so too was it politically various. To stress this fact, the current chapter focuses on the two more marginal varieties of speech mentioned by the *Cambridge History:* the Gullah found in the Sea Islands of the South Atlantic states, and the creole French of Louisiana. Close analysis of these two language varieties reveals how the plantation tradition was not a uniform entity but the product of distinct vernacular situations that became implicated—quite differently—in the politics of language surrounding the "Negro Question" in the post–Civil War South.

Gullah and creole French failed to achieve the literary popularity of other black dialects, partly because they were not dialects at all but creole languages—formed from the contact between speakers of wholly different tongues—with their own grammatical structures and rhetorical modes. Beyond their inherent strangeness for a mainstream audience, the creole status of these languages had radical implications for the understanding of southern society and the role of African Americans within it. As I discuss in the first part of the chapter, the notion that Gullah exhibited the qualities of a creole language was doubly threatening to white culture. It implied that black speech had its own rhetorical techniques, perhaps based on African languages, that rendered it partially unintelligible to whites. Furthermore, it suggested an essentially *creolized* situation, in which black and white elements had amalgamated to form a new language and, implicitly, a new culture—a suggestion used by Henry James in *The Bostonians* to subvert the authority of Basil Ransom's southern dialect.[2] This understanding of creolization led to the disturbing idea that black language had generated many of the distinctive qualities of white language while still maintaining the power to undermine the white variety with a signifying difference. Writers repressed this recognition by creating linguistic myths and a type of dialect literature that treated Gullah as different not on account of its foreignness but because of its inferiority. Writers such as Ambrose Gonzales and Joel Chandler Harris described many of the realities of an African-influenced creole language, especially its ability to generate new and ambiguous meanings, even as they sought to reduce it to mere "humorous" linguistic ineptitude.

The idea of a dominant language threatened by contamination, discussed in the previous chapter, also informed the racial aspects of black–white speech interaction in the postbellum South. A belief that creole English was part of a fundamental intermixture between American and African elements (however varied and elusive the latter may have been), together with the idea that this intermixture may have helped to define southern culture, had upsetting implications for a racially segregated society.[3] This was particularly true in the context of Louisiana, discussed in the second part of this chapter, where there was a full-scale attempt after the Civil War to rescue the term *Creole*—as it applied to the white, former ruling class of the region—from implications of miscegenation. George Washington Cable's controversial suggestion of a racially mixed definition of *Creole*, I argue, was part of his wider development of a subversive literary mode, pioneered in his novel *The Grandissimes* (1880), which exploited the very elements resisted in the treatment of Gullah. In particular, the ambiguity of black language was shown by Cable to originate in an African-based satirical technique, one Cable himself employed in an allusive style that frustrated the racial fictions of the post-Reconstruction South. Instead of being repressed, the idea of creolization was developed by Cable into a political literature that uncovered how African-American linguistic creativity was transmitted to the white community of New Orleans—thereby contradicting claims to cultural purity and separateness—while it resisted white culture with satirical powers of double meaning. I agree, therefore, with Eric Sundquist that black dialect could be a "signifying alternative, another cultural language that has historically conditioned and transfigured white English while drawing force from its own liminality"—an argument based on the work of Charles Chesnutt.[4] Yet I would suggest that this view of black language as transformative *and* undermining is even more radical and fully developed in Cable's writing. Deriving his technique from a groundbreaking investigation of black artistic and linguistic creativity, Cable fashioned a new fictional style that unsettled the ideology of white culture to such an extent that he became the "most cordially hated little man in New Orleans" after the publication of *The Grandissimes* in 1880.[5]

By paying close attention to the literary and linguistic significance of Gullah, this chapter emphasizes the racial complexity in white reactions to black speech. My main aim, however, is to make a long overdue claim for Cable's revolutionary manipulation of the black vernacular. Melville Herskovits's belief that the modern scholar should take Cable's writings on African-American customs "into careful account" has gone unheeded even by critics who—like Eric Sundquist—give extensive accounts of racial ideas in nineteenth-century American literature.[6] As Shelley Fishkin's *Was Huck Black?* (1993) attests, scholars have instead focused much of their postbellum attention on Mark Twain. Cable's attacks on racism in the 1880s may not have been as "subtle" as Twain's, as Fishkin suggests, but his exploration of black rhetorical techniques in *The Grandissimes* was more subversive. It originated in a knowledge of African-American vocal culture that was far more detailed than can be claimed for Twain.[7] Without nuanced attention to Cable's work, any picture of racial and cultural interaction in the South, so crucial to the study of American and African-American literature, remains incomplete.

THE RACIAL POLITICS OF REPRESENTING GULLAH

Gullah first came to the attention of a largely white audience after the Civil War, most notably through William Francis Allen's introduction to the 1867 volume *Slave Songs of the United States*. A landmark in the formal recognition of the musical "creative power" (i) of African-American communities, this introduction established the fundamental tensions that would govern subsequent accounts of Gullah and of black creativity in general. The main paradox of Allen's introduction concerns the question of origins. Allen attempts to combine the notion that this music is "genuine" and "original in the best sense of the word" with the belief that it is "partly composed under the influence of association with the whites, partly actually imitated from their music" (vi). He entertains the idea that several of these songs "may very well be purely African in origin" (vii) while still considering them derivative of the white tradition.[8] In Allen's attempt to account for the "peculiar quality" of the spoken language in which these songs are delivered—the Gullah of St. Helena Island—this paradox becomes most extreme:

> A stranger, upon first hearing these people talk, especially if there is a group of them in animated conversation, can hardly understand them better than if they spoke a foreign language, and might, indeed, easily suppose this to be the case. The strange words and pronunciations, and frequent abbreviations, disguise the familiar features of one's native tongue, while the rhythmical modulations, so characteristic of certain European languages, give it an utterly un-English sound. After six months' residence among them, there were scholars in my school, among the most constant in attendance, whom I could not understand at all, unless they happened to speak very slowly. [xxiv]

Allen does not trace the essential alterity of Gullah to an African inheritance. In addition to "the familiar *buckra*" and a few proper names like Cuffy, Quash, and Cudjo, the only recorded "strange words"—by which Allen appears to mean "Africanisms"—are *churray* ("spill"), *oona* ("you," both singular and plural), and *aw* ("a kind of expletive, equivalent to 'to be sure'") (xxv). Instead, the uniqueness of this language is seen to arise from processes of "phonetic decay," "corruption in pronunciation," "extreme simplification of etymology and syntax," and other types of confusion and omission (xxv, xxxiii). The ambivalent notion that Gullah was original *and* derivative, that it behaved like a foreign language but was not actually foreign, facilitated the belief that it was an inherently debased dialect, distinct because of inferiority alone.[9]

It would be unfair to accuse Allen of ignoring or intentionally suppressing a recognition of Africanisms. Michael Montgomery has shown how difficult it was to claim any American word as an Africanism before the 1930s—quite simply, not enough was known in the United States about African languages.[10] Indeed, if we compare Allen's observations to the new understanding of Gullah that arose in the 1940s with the publication of Melville Herskovits's *The Myth of the Negro Past* (1941) and Lorenzo Turner's *Africanisms in the Gullah Dialect* (1949), we can appreciate the linguistic reality that lies beneath the surface of Allen's inadequate account: Gullah is a creole language with a substantial African component.[11] Turner's book, written to redress the assumption that the "peculiarities" of Gullah are traceable almost entirely to British dialects of the seventeenth and eighteenth centuries, or to a form of "baby talk" invented by whites to facilitate communication with blacks, unearthed thousands of West African words in Gullah:

> [B]esides many survivals in syntax, inflections, sounds, and intonation . . . I have recorded in Georgia a few songs the words of which are entirely African. In some songs both African and English words appear. This is true also of many folk-tales. There are many compound words one part of which is African and the other English. Sometimes whole African phrases appear in Gullah without change either of meaning or of pronunciation. Frequently African phrases have been translated into English. African given names are numerous.[12]

The strange modulations and rhythms in Gullah noticed by Allen are shown by Turner to follow the "characteristic intonation and rhythm" of West African tone languages;[13] what Allen noted as the "failure" of Gullah speakers to make distinctions in gender, case, number, verb tense, and voice are all qualities of creole grammar that have precedents in many West African tongues;[14] and the unusual proper names like "After-dark" mentioned by Allen are shown by Turner to be loan translations from West African naming practices.

The ability to describe but not recognize this African presence within creole language facilitated a similar acknowledgment and denial of the distinctive qualities of a black vernacular. An appreciation of Africanisms in Gullah would have offered a recognized substructure for an integral African-American way of talking, based on linguistic rules and vernacular practices—if not on actual vocabulary—essentially different from the English tradition. Allen presents a language variety with a tremendous capacity to signify in unique ways: for instance, he gives a long list of words whose meanings are "peculiarly" different from mainstream American English, such as *stan'* (signifying "look") and *talk* ("speak or mean").[15] Despite Allen's attempt to explain the entire Gullah language as a degeneration of English, certain usages lie beyond comprehension, "enigmatical words and expressions" which he leaves for the reader "to guess at the interpretation" (68). Allen lacks the appropriate tools to account for the alternative semantics of this enigmatic tongue, which leads to some of his more incredible suggestions: that African Americans enjoy the humor of "clearly nonsensical" phrases (ix) and, on many occasions, do not know the meaning of their own words (xix). The African-American linguistic quality of ambiguous signification, to which we will return throughout this chapter, is reduced by Allen to the realm of corruption and error.

Allen's observations on the fundamental foreignness of Gullah, both to mainstream American English and to "[o]rdinary negro talk, such as we find in books" (xxiv), were reiterated in subsequent discussions of the dialect.[16] John Bennett's two-part article "Gullah: A Negro Patois" (1908–9), for example, considers that even compared to the Louisiana variety of creole French, Gullah is "a hasty and foreign sounding patois" (1:336). Like Allen, Bennett observes the power of Gullah to disguise the "familiar features of one's native tongue" with its strange "rhythmical modulations and unfamiliar accents" (1:332). Yet Bennett's work differs from Allen's in allowing more explicitly for an African influence even as he insists that the dialectal peculiarities of Gullah are "still traceable to their remote spring in the shires of Britain" (1:339). Bennett admits that "the engaged grammar [is] a mystery"; that the folklore recorded in the language, and the intonation of the language itself, are African, the latter containing a "harshness" peculiar to the west coast from Sierra Leone south; that the African has added to Gullah by "deliberately" taking elements from it, or by using "nuances of sound covering a multitude of strange omissions" (1:337).

The paradox in Bennett's conclusion, that Gullah is "the most African" *and* the "most archaic" in its high level of survivals from older English dialects (2:52), makes more sense when we realize that—despite his apparent anglocentrism—Bennett's private notebooks and correspondence reveal "a long-term and very keen interest in tracing local words back to African languages." As Michael Montgomery shows, Bennett suppressed this material because politically it was "too explosive." In Bennett's words, these linguistic materials were "part of a great question already forced upon [observers] in too many ways to be welcome."[17] According to Montgomery, this "great question" concerned the extent of African-American influence on southern culture, an influence difficult to miss in music, dance, and religion, yet one denied with increasing vigor as it applied to the southern dialect of American English. The great fear was that African Americans may have had a fundamental influence on the language and culture of the South. As Bennett recognized, Gullah was a potential influence on the standard language: "It is true that, up to the age of four, approximately, the children of the best families, even in town, are apt to speak an almost unmodified *Gullah*, caught from brown playmates and country-bred nurses" (1:339). He makes more oblique reference to "throats which have been for life touched by childhood's enunciation" (2:44n), and recognizes that certain Gullah usages are also found in "cultivated" speech (1:347).[18] To admit an African presence in Gullah, therefore, was to admit an African thread in the cultural fabric of the white South. If Gullah was a creole language, merging African and English elements, then perhaps the South was a creolized culture, produced by the weaving together of two strands (broadly speaking, the Anglo-American and the African-American) into a new, hybrid mode. American English, in other words, might no longer be a sign of cultural affinity with England but a demonstration that racial intermixture typified the South.

Allen's and Bennett's views of Gullah show that discussions of spoken language had a strong racial agenda in the late nineteenth century. While neither of these writers employed the term *creole*, their accounts of Gullah at least recognized that it contained rhetorical and grammatical qualities unique to the African-American community. Bennett's work suggests, moreover, that behind demeaning treatments of Gullah's otherness lay the haunting idea that, while it remained partially unintelligible to whites, Gullah still had the ability to contaminate southern English with a possibly African component—the idea, in other words, that Gullah was both a creole language *and* reflective of a creolized cultural situation.

The apprehension that ethnic groups were transforming the American language, which stemmed from the vast influx of foreign immigrants after the Civil War, was hardly new. African-American speakers in particular were thought to have had a similar impact on the southern dialect of American English over the preceding two hundred years. Foreign visitors to the United States before the Civil War would often note that white southerners spoke like African Americans, or could switch into black dialect with ease. Although this idea of cross-racial linguistic intermixture became controversial during the turbulent years of Reconstruction, there were still recognitions that white speech had itself become black in a fundamental sense. Take, for example, James A. Harrison's 1884 essay, "Negro English": "It must be confessed, to the shame of the white population of the South, that they perpetuate many of these pronunciations in common with their Negro dependents; and that, in many places, if one happened to be talking to a native with one's eyes shut, it would be impossible to say whether a Negro or a white person were responding." Harrison believed—albeit regretfully—that African-American speech had transformed white speech, thus helping to produce the southern dialect of American English. This suggestion can be found elsewhere, for example in L. W. Payne's 1901 claim that, in east Alabama at least, "the speech of the white people, the dialect that I have spoken all my life . . . is more largely colored by the language of the negroes than by any other single influence"; or in William Cecil Elam's more class-conscious statement in 1895 that "the great body of the lingo commonly regarded as distinctively the negro's is equally the lingo of the wholly uneducated and socially degraded white."[19] Black English was recognized as "innovative rather than archaic," writes J. L. Dillard, in that it was more likely to have produced the differences between northern and southern white dialects than to have been originally identical with the latter.[20] White southerners, these writers implied, were using a language not entirely their own, a language that was partly the product of the black community.

Most remarkably, observations of a southern speech transformed by blackness were accompanied by the understanding that black speech nonetheless operated on a level of significance *beyond* white language. Thus, Payne's observation of the unity of black and white speech is accompanied by what he calls "a more or less distinct consciousness of the pure negroisms." Elam supplements his recognition of cross-racial dialectal sameness with an awareness that "there still remains a real negro lingo, having its peculiar and distinguishing characteristics. The principal of these cannot be shown by mere spelling or pronunciation. They exist in the tone of his voice, his manner of speech, his inarticulate interpolations and interjections. After these comes his frequent use of words in utterly unexpected senses." Harrison combines his certainty that a blind man could not tell blacks and whites apart with the belief that the African-American use of slang is "an ingrained part of his being as deep-dyed as his skin." The ability to use words in unexpected senses, noted by Elam, is expanded by Harrison into a celebration of the poetry and fecundity of black English, facilitated by "the ingenious distortion of words by which new and startling significance is given to common English words (eg. a *hant* in Negro means a *ghost*)." The numerous laws of language behavior recorded by Harrison yield twenty pages of partly untranslatable "Negroisms"—"[t]he English equivalents are far from conveying the pungent meaning of the Negro expressions"—together with a thorough explication of the different system of grammar upon which black speech depends. The African American's language is "not mere word-distortion" but "his verbal breath of life caught from his surrounding and wrought up by him into the wonderful figure-speech specimens."[21]

These observations formed part of an ambivalent white attitude toward the spoken black English of the American South. Late-nineteenth-century observers may not have explicitly traced black language to an African-influenced creole, yet there were strong implications of foreignness surrounding African-American English—a foreignness, moreover, partly responsible for the distinctive qualities of southern white speech. By fail-ing to divide black from white dialect completely, this version of the lan-guage history of the South suggested the subversive cultural intermingling of people from supposedly separate racial groups, even as it hinted at a private level of communication among people of African descent, a realm of meaning that drew the color line against the white community. Black language was doubly dangerous: it was understood to have helped pro-duce white southern speech while retaining the power to resist it.

White intellectuals in the South countered such notions by creating strict linguistic hierarchies. Allen's belief that Gullah was an alien variety owing to corruption, decay, and simplification entered the assumptions and terminology of much post–Civil War philology. In Schele de Vere's *Americanisms: The English of the New World* (1872), for example, black speech was described as subordinate to, and entirely without influence upon, the white variety; it was formed by "ignorance" and "carelessness," by "some difficulty both in their hearing and in their organs of speech."[22] Physical and psychological determinism combined to produce a linguistics of black subjugation. Instead of recognizing African retentions, or even an integral African-American way of talking, the emphasis fell on the presumed Anglo-Saxon ability to assimilate other cultures and races. Joel Chandler Harris thus claimed that the dialect of Uncle Remus was simply white English three hundred years out of date.[23] African-American language was forced into the anglophone tradition at the expense of its modernity and integrity: black speech was seen as archaic and imitative, the product of a backward and innately deficient mind. At best, it was the product of a geographical color line whereby the isolated nature of many black com-munities facilitated the retention of archaic dialectal forms from the Brit-ish Isles.

Because of the understood correlation between language and mind, dialect facilitated the founding of the color line in the post-Reconstruction South. White bidialectal tolerance of black English faded rapidly after the Civil War, amid new labor competition between blacks and poor whites and strengthening northern accusations of southern linguistic inferiority. Attempts to split southern speech apart were abetted by the formation of a racially segregated school system, explicitly designed, believes Ernest Dunn, to exorcise black influence on white speech and on other types of vernacular activity.[24] Another means of linguistic segregation was practiced by certain writers in the "plantation school" of dialect literature. William Cecil Elam discussed this type of dialect in his essay "Lingo in Literature" (1895):

> In actual life the negro talks more or less like the white persons he serves or comes most frequently in contact with; but when some of our accom-

plished literary artists attempt to delineate him, this likeness utterly disappears, and his "English as she is spoke" is exaggerated in all its features by elision and every literal device, while that of his white interlocutors is revised according to Noah Webster and Lindley Murray. The treatment accorded the two races in this murdering of the language is analogous to that dispensed to murderers under our old colonial laws, which allowed benefit of clergy to whites and denied it to negroes. This discrimination, however, is not only against the Reconstruction acts and the Civil Rights bill, but is forbidden by the Federal Constitution, as now amended; and it is to be said further, in behalf of printers and readers, that a fair and equal orthographical and syntactical dispensation would at once wipe out a large proportion of the lingual barbarisms attributed to the negro, while in many others he would appear to be no greater sinner than his former master and mistress. Yet it is greatly to be apprehended that the conventional negro and his conventional lingo are firmly fixed in our literature, albeit the real negroes would look upon him as an "outlander," and could not possibly comprehend the lingo if spoken as printed.

The construction of absolute racial differences, the exaggeration of rule-breaking in the African-American community, the establishment of the black man or woman as an "outlander" or perpetual alien: all were strategies employed in dialect writing and Jim Crow society alike. Elam demonstrated that dialect literature was part of a wider language politics. At its most extreme, this literature attempted to encode an essential blackness in the written representation of speech, making the lines of writing into color lines designed to segregate upon the printed page. What W. E. B. Du Bois called "the power of the cabalistic letters of the white man" was being used against the linguistic equality of races, and against the idea that the South may have gained distinctive qualities from the merging of two different, racially based cultures.[25] Dialect writing was often a reaction against, if not an attempt to correct, the presence of creolization in southern culture.

From the perspective of recent theory, Robert Young has discussed the type of creolized cultural intermixture observed in the American South throughout the nineteenth century.[26] In one sense, the coalescence of different racial traditions produces a new, hybrid language that tends to signify in two separate cultural realms. Its words are "double-voiced" as they belong simultaneously to two systems of belief[27]—an idea that echoes the double meanings recognized in "Negro English" in the late nineteenth century, the processes that Harrison termed *dimorphism*, "a principle according to which a word may appear in the course of time under two forms," and *hybridization*, in which existing words are compounded to form new meanings. Harrison's observations are related to wider inter-

pretations of black expression: the inherent ambiguity observed in English-based creoles of the West Indies, for example, whereby the creole
naturally lends itself to the remodeling of common symbolic forms "so
that they can mediate at least two sets of cultural identities and meanings"; or the African-American ritual of *signifying*, defined by Henry Louis
Gates as a double-voiced discourse that remotivates white language by informing it with the different rhetorical strategies of the black vernacular
tradition.[28] To acknowledge—with Harrison, Elam, and Payne—that black
English and white English were identical, yet black English operated in a
realm of signification beyond the white community, was thus to recognize
not a split between white and black speech but a division within black
language itself. Concurring with Du Bois's description of "double-
consciousness" in *The Souls of Black Folk* (1903), close observers described
African-American English as signifying in two different areas—white and
black—divided by a "veil." The effort by speakers of black English to
function in two cultural domains, however, did not lead to a DuBoisian
crisis of self-division; instead, it facilitated a "two-ness" of expression that
could mask exclusive racial meanings.[29]

Young also suggests that the duality of hybrid situations can accommodate political antagonism, whereby one language is set against and ultimately undermines the other. Applied by postcolonial theorists to colonial situations, such hybridity disrupts the generalizing authority of the
dominant language by confronting its center of power with supposedly
peripheral elements of cultural difference.[30] In the American South after
the Civil War, similar ideas prompted anxieties over a racially contaminated white speech. Black language was a powerfully disruptive force because its relation to white English was both generative and undermining.
Mixed with white language, black language had produced a distinctive,
hybrid southern accent yet had still retained the power of resistance in its
ambiguous, rhetorical rituals that lay partially beyond white comprehension. In the writing of George Washington Cable, this signifying activity
within black language became a means to disrupt the authority of the
dominant culture's political power, as we shall see in the second part of
the chapter. In the linguistic politics of representing Gullah, however,
literature supported ideological attempts to master the ambiguous otherness and influence of creole English by suggesting its familiarity and
difference simultaneously.

Since the appearance of the Gullah-speaking character Jupiter in Edgar
Allan Poe's story "The Gold Bug" (1843), the depiction of Gullah in
American literature has had a dubious history. What Toni Morrison calls
the stupidity of Poe's employment of misspelling—the use of "nose" to

represent Jupiter's *knows*, for example—epitomizes the parodic use of this variety of speech for shallow purposes of comedy. The earliest written comments on Gullah also point to its "humorous" qualities: "That 'spect, meaning *ex*pect, has sometimes a possible meaning of *su*spect, which would give the sentence in which it occurs a very humorous turn, and I always take the benefit of that interpretation."[31] This represents the archetypal incident in which a non-Gullah speaker—Frances Kemble—perceives the potential for ambiguity in the creole yet "takes the benefit" of reducing it to a benignly humorous level.

Not all were deaf to the satirical element in the humorous potential of black speech: N. S. Dodge's article "Negro Patois and Its Humor" (1870), for example, is prophetic in realizing that the "tendency toward the humorous in the very interchange of words the negro invariably makes" descends from an African rhetorical procedure in which "this quick sight for the ridiculous becomes, in argument, an effective weapon."[32] More often than not, however, postbellum notions of the foreignness of, and the subversive ambiguity within, black language were treated in ways that echo Poe and Kemble. Typical in this respect are Ambrose Gonzales's Gullah stories of the Carolina coast, which began to appear in *The State* magazine in the early 1890s. The foreword and glossary written for the 1922 volume *The Black Border* (a compilation of the 1892 stories and new stories published in 1918) provide access to the otherwise silent assumptions of a white record of Gullah at the end of the nineteenth century:

> Slovenly and careless of speech, these Gullahs seized upon the peasant English used by some of the early settlers and by the white servants of the wealthier Colonists, wrapped their clumsy tongues about it as well as they could, and, enriched with certain expressive African words, it issued through their flat noses and thick lips as so workable a form of speech that it was gradually adopted by the other slaves and became in time the accepted Negro speech of the lower districts of South Carolina and Georgia. With characteristic laziness, these Gullah Negroes took some short cuts to the ears of their auditors, using as few words as possible, sometimes making one gender serve for three, one tense for several, and totally disregarding singular and plural numbers. [10]

Despite the token recognition of a limited African vocabulary, this account combines the classic misinterpretation of the grammatical features of a creole language with a disturbing biological determinism and a belief in the mysterious disappearance of African linguistic features. Gonzales's opinion that the African "retained only a few words of his jungle-tongue, and even these few are by no means authenticated as part of the original scant baggage of the Negro slaves" (17), is remarkable given that the rest of his discussion catalogues the conditions recognized even then as necessary to the continuity of Africanisms on American soil, especially the belief that Gullahs represented a single African tribe whose language was adopted by other slaves.[33] Gonzales denied the retention of African linguistic habits, yet he could not ignore Gullah's uniquely African-American patterns of signification—the "transformation wrought upon a large body of borrowed English words" (18). This transformation required a glossary to record the reshaping of "our language by virtue of an unwritten but very definite and vigorous law of their tongue" (18), a law that creates "new and peculiar applications of words, twisted to meet its own needs, and making a single vocable serve the purpose of many" (279). Gonzales was astounded by the power of black English to create new significance and to employ words with multiple meanings: a vocabulary of 1700 words, published in his glossary, serves "the purpose and scope of at least 5,000 English words" (287).

The realities of a creolized black English are visible beneath the surface of Gonzales's otherwise racist and demeaning account. Among many examples, Lorenzo Turner reveals that beneath the phrase "*done fuh* fat," which Gonzales takes to mean "excessively fat" (on the assumption that "in the judgement of the Gullah Negro when a person is very fat he is done for," writes Turner), is a word from the Vai language of Liberia: *'dafa* (literally, "mouth full").[34] Many of Gonzales's sketches seem little more than excuses to record—and mock—the unique pronunciation and signifying alternative of creole speech. For example, the sketch "The Doctor Didn't 'Exceed'" is an extended pun on the fact that in Gullah—according to Gonzales—*exceed* means "succeed."[35] Similarly, "The Lady Couldn't 'Specify'" is an over-redundant play on the Gullah usage of *specify*, which, writes Gonzales in his glossary, contains a variety of meanings: "If a woman proves an unsuitable mate, she 'cyan' specify.' If trousers are frail, and 'de britchiz buss',' ''e yent specify.' . . . And even of a Bible text, the fulfilment of whose promise seems inadequate, the Gullah says: 'Buhrabbus' w'ud, him ent specify berry well'" (283). The repeated puns of Gonzales's prose are in fact reductive renderings of the capacity for multiple meaning inherent in creole speech. Gonzales depends for literary material on a language that he considers inferior and barbarous; he is deeply attracted to that which he disparages. Gonzales's sketches evoke the creative ambiguity of a creole language while limiting its subversive implications to the level of "incorrectness" and quaint "humor."

The ambivalence within white attitudes toward black language and folklore—the constant vacillation between recognition and reduction, appreciation and appropriation—is captured in Joel Chandler Harris's discussion of Gullah in the introduction to his *Nights with Uncle Remus* (1883). Harris's introduction is, to some extent, a radical acknowledgment of the "very curious parallels" between the "negro stories" (xxiv–xxv) in his volume and the folklore of the Kaffir and "Hottentot" peoples of south-

ern Africa, then being investigated by European ethnographers such as
G. M. Theal, whose *Kaffir Folk-Lore* appeared in 1882.[36] Yet the apparent
defense of cultural continuity between Africa and America has important
limitations for Harris, especially as applied to language:

> There is a plantation proverb current among the negroes which is very ex-
> pressive. Thus, when one accidently steps in mud or filth, he consoles him-
> self by saying "Good thing foot ain't got no nose." Among the Kaffirs there
> is a similar proverb,—"The foot has no nose,"—but Mr. Theal's educated
> natives have given it a queer meaning. It is thus interpreted: "This proverb
> is an exhortation to be hospitable. It is as if one said: Give food to the
> traveller, because when you are on a journey your foot will not be able to
> smell out a man whom you have turned from your door, but, to your shame,
> may carry you to his." It need not be said that this is rather ahead of even
> the educated Southern negroes. [xxiv]

At that same time that Harris implies a linguistic continuum between Africa and America, he qualifies it sharply in terms of the "Southern negro."
The ability of the African proverb to signify in a sophisticated, implicit,
ironic way—its "queer meaning"—is denied in the speech behavior of
African Americans. According to Harris, no southern black is so far
"ahead" as to be able to construct a sentence that means more than is
superficially apparent. Harris is more ready to admit that the words of the
phrase "Good thing foot ain't got no nose" may descend from Africa—
just as he accepts that wider aspects of black folklore may also originate
there—than to admit that a particularly African way of talking, one that
plays upon the ironic gap between signifier and signified, persists in African-American rhetoric. It was one thing for African-American folklore
to have an African heritage but quite another to suggest that black men
or women might mean more than they say, through the employment of
potentially African modes of discourse.

Harris's discussion of Gullah in his introduction to *Nights with Uncle
Remus,* and the inclusion in this volume of another of American literature's rare Gullah speakers—Daddy (or "African") Jack—maintains this
ambivalence:

> The dialect of Daddy Jack, which is that of the negroes on the Sea Islands
> and the rice plantations, though it may seem at first glance to be more
> difficult than that of Uncle Remus, is, in reality, simpler and more direct. It
> is the negro dialect in its most primitive state—the "Gullah" talk of some
> of the negroes on the Sea Islands, being merely a confused and untranslat-
> able mixture of English and African words. . . . The vocabulary is not an ex-
> tensive one—more depending upon the manner, the form of expression,
> and the inflection, than upon the words employed. It is thus an admirable
> vehicle for story-telling. . . . The dialect is laconic and yet rambling, full of
> repetitions, and abounding in curious elisions, that give an unexpected

> quaintness to the simplest statements. A glance at the following vocabulary
> will enable the reader to understand Daddy Jack's dialect perfectly, though
> allowance must be made for inversions and elisions. [xxxii–xxxiii]

Paradox pervades this passage. The dialect of Daddy Jack is more difficult
yet simpler; it is laconic yet rambling; it repeats yet elides. And Harris's
statement that this dialect contains "untranslatable" African words is difficult to reconcile with the forty-word vocabulary which purports to make
Daddy Jack's speech "perfectly" understandable. Harris's version of Gullah in the story "Cutta Cord-la!" (236–41) told by Daddy Jack—a story
to which Harris twice draws our attention in the introduction—records
the consequences of his ambivalence. In a time of famine, Brother Rabbit
has tricked Brother Wolf into killing his grandmother for food. Brother
Rabbit, however, has managed to hide his own grandmother safely in a
tree, where he feeds her by means of a basket lowered from the tree by
a cord. The plot follows Brother Wolf's attempt to mimic the voice of
Brother Rabbit in order to trick Brother Rabbit's grandmother into low-
ering the basket, allowing Brother Wolf at last to capture and devour her.
The story has metafictional value: it seems to be about the type of vocal
impersonation central to a "plantation tradition" that Michael North has
described as "almost exclusively a matter of white mimicry and role-
playing."[37] The fact that a story which appears to thematize its own conditions of production is also identified by Harris as a possible descendant
of a Kaffir tale from southern Africa (xxi) hints at a more radical recognition of African creative influence.[38] Furthermore, the tale clearly arises
out of Daddy Jack's discontent with Uncle Remus's twisted and presumably Americanized version of a similar tale, to which he reacts by mumbling to himself "in a lingo which might have been understood on the
Guinea coast, but which sounded out of place in Uncle Remus's Middle
Georgia cabin" (236).

Apparently matching this atmosphere of African retention, the tale
does contain a foreign word of "queer meaning": the word *jutta* in
Brother Rabbit's command to his grandmother to lower the cord, "Jutta
cord-la!" Brother Wolf's first attempt to pronounce this phrase—"Shoot-a
cord la!"—does not fool Brother Rabbit's grandmother, nor does Brother
Wolf's closer approximation of the sound after hearing his mispronunciation of *jutta* mocked by Brother Rabbit. Only after having his vocal
organs maimed by the insertion of a red-hot poker does Brother Wolf
correctly reproduce the sound. His success in devouring the grandmother,
however, is prevented by Brother Rabbit's timely intervention: he orders
his grandmother to "cutta cord-la," causing the basket—with Brother
Wolf in it—to fall fatally to the ground.

The story explores the tight link between language and identity: different selves command unique pronunciations. After the tale is told,

Daddy Jack and Uncle Remus continue to argue over whether the correct pronunciation of Brother Rabbit's command is *jutta cord-la* or *shucky-cordy* (249–50)—an argument that relates the question of linguistic difference to the larger issue of diasporic variants of African-derived folk tales. The distinction between Daddy Jack's *jutta* and Uncle Remus's *shucky* (possibly a version of *chuck*) seems to signify the vast cultural difference between the Africanized Daddy Jack and the Americanized Uncle Remus. To Harris's readers, *jutta* must have seemed a strange word, being neither English nor included in Harris's glossary of Gullah words. Was *jutta* intended to be understood as African? If so, then it would reflect Harris's belief that Gullah retained Africanisms and that these folk tales could be traced directly to Africa. Harris wanted to stage Daddy Jack's cultural strangeness, yet he finally altered the Afrocentric direction in which he was heading. Rather than an Africanism, *jutta* seems more likely to be the creole version of the French verb *jeter* ("to throw"). Curiously, the character Daddy Jack, whose speech—we are told—contains untranslatable Africanisms, in a story that—we are told—has clear parallels in southern African folklore, delivers a tale whose only word of "queer meaning" is French.

Although Harris leads the reader to expect an Africanism in "Cutta Cord-la!," his attitude toward African retentions remains ambivalent—indeed, the introduction to *Nights with Uncle Remus* suggests not only an African but a Caribbean origin for Daddy Jack's story. Linguistically, the tale pulls strongly in the direction of creole French, presumably of San Domingo or Martinique, from where Harris suggests the tale may have originated (xxxii). The presence of Daddy Jack highlights the essential foreignness of African-American language and folklore, yet it is a foreignness that—linguistically at least—does not derive from Africa. This displacement matched contemporary political attempts to establish the foreignness of the southern "Negro" without admitting an implicit Africanness. Just as Harris denies the existence of African ways of talking in the language of southern black folk, he ultimately defers the issue of black cultural otherness by placing its origins not in Africa but in the French-speaking Caribbean. Rather than linking Daddy Jack's creole to an African tongue, he merely links one creole to another, thus creating a circle of influence that never touches African shores.

In literature, Gullah highlighted the white writer's ambivalence toward black vernacular language. Representations of Gullah could serve a racist agenda by deforming African-American speech to confirm beliefs in black deficiency. The white writing of creole language was defined by mishearing and misrepresentation, but often the real difference of black signification shimmered behind racist prose. Ambrose Gonzales's literary creation of what he considered a barbarous tongue unconsciously represented, with at least some degree of accuracy, many aspects of creole English.[39] As Lawrence Levine has said of white representations of black dialect in the nineteenth century, the literature of Gullah was "a mélange of accuracy and fantasy, of sensitivity and stereotype, of empathy and racism."[40] Yet the very recognition of Gullah's linguistic uniqueness served deeper purposes, especially when its African heritage was explicitly denied. Gullah was employed to suggest—paradoxically—that black speech was essentially alien to mainstream white speech but was not foreign in a threatening sense. It was different, in other words, because it was inferior.

Despite a sporadic admittance of an Afrocentric presence, the white literature of Gullah attempted to deny creolization, to resist the idea that African tongues may have combined with English to form a new creole language. We saw in chapter two how similar efforts to segregate speech often registered an underlying phonetic similarity between black and white language—a formal irony that is explicitly illustrated in Charles Colcock Jones's *Negro Myths from the Georgia Coast* (1888). Rather than framing Gullah as dialogue within the "standard" language of the narrator, Jones made his mimicry of creole the language of narration itself. By collapsing the traditional distinction between "standard" and "nonstandard" discourse, Jones gave the white man a distinctly black voice: "Huccum you stop de wuk wuh me bin gen you fuh do?"[41] Whatever his intention, Jones's fiction emphasized the threatening notion that—without always realizing it—the white voices that spoke for blacks in the South were infiltrated by the very black elements they were attempting to repress. Jones's stories implicitly recreated a creolized cultural situation of racial intermixture that not even Gonzales could entirely ignore. In his foreword to *The Black Border*, Gonzales mentioned Edisto Island, which in old times was "noted for an unusual provincialism and for the habitual use of Gullah dialect by many of the planters' young sons. These were in constant association with their slaves on hunting and fishing parties, and unconsciously adopted the highly picturesque and expressive speech of their black servitors" (286).

Gullah was a minor element in nineteenth-century American literature, but one that suggested a series of unsettling ideas about the difference of blackness and the contamination of whiteness. Perhaps it is no coincidence that the burgeoning literary interest in Gullah among whites in the 1920s and '30s—witness the Gullah speakers in DuBose Heyward's *Porgy* (1925)—coincided with the full institution of a theory of black linguistic archaism that sought to deny the African heritage almost entirely, a theory of language that formed part of what Herskovits called the "myth of the Negro past." In the period immediately before Turner's and Herskovits's work became known, Gullah was considered a harmless, archaic, though still somewhat outlandish form of Anglo-derived English, well suited to quirky literary works. This dialect, a white myth of black language, substituted for a true understanding of the black vernacular and its impact on white language and culture in the South.

GEORGE WASHINGTON CABLE AND
THE CREOLE LANGUAGE OF LOUISIANA

Joel Chandler Harris may have evaded the subject of Africanisms in his story "Cutta Cord-la!" yet he did so by referring his readers to another creole language that was not without contentious implications. Harris's account of Gullah in his introduction to *Nights with Uncle Remus* ends by alluding to the Louisiana variety of black French that had gained the attention of philologists sooner and more thoroughly than its English counterpart. Whereas, in the understanding of Gullah, ideas of creolization tended to be repressed, in the description of creole French many of these aspects were explicitly debated, especially in the political controversy over what it meant for a person to *be* a Louisiana Creole. The Gumbo dialect, as creole French was derogatorily called, was part of a different vernacular situation that allowed for a very different literary reaction.

The earliest significant essay on Louisiana creole French is Alfred Mercier's *Étude sur la langue créole en Louisiane*, published in 1880.[42] Although Mercier believed that the slave forgot rapidly his native tongue, retaining only six or eight words of African origin in the "patois," his description of creole language, and of black–white linguistic interaction in general, overturned the logic of white linguistic superiority in several ways. Mercier described the impressive intellectual capabilities of Louisiana's black population, illustrated both in their high degree of bidialectalism—"there is not a little negro or a little negress, in the most retired roads, with whom it is not a point of honor, if you question them in French, to answer you in the language in which you speak"—and in the powers of invention and ingenuity required to fashion a new language with "all the parts of speech necessary to the expression of their thought." Much more than inaccurate "baby-talk," Mercier considered creole French to be a black creation that was both logically consistent and highly attractive to whites:

> All the white little ones of French origin, in Louisiana, have spoken this patois, concurrently with French; there are also among us those who have exclusively made use of the dialect of the negroes to the age of 10 or 12 years; I am one of those: I remember the reward presented to me on the day when I agreed with my parents not to speak to them in anything other than French in the future.

Mercier also observed that creole was still used as a domestic language among well-to-do white Creoles for a period after the Civil War. Rather than derivative or degenerate, creole was revealed to be an integral language which upper-class whites themselves used for extensive—and formative—periods of their lives.[43]

Many of Mercier's points were repeated in subsequent accounts of creole French. James A. Harrison's 1882 article "The Creole Patois of Louisiana," to which Harris referred in his introduction to *Nights with Uncle Remus,* brought many of Mercier's observations to readers of *The American Journal of Philology.* Although Harrison detracts from Mercier's relatively enlightened viewpoint in his description of "thick lips" and a black "aural myopia," he expands the notion of the transformative effect of the presence of African Americans upon the vernacular activities of Louisiana. Harrison points to the masses of Africans placed on Louisiana plantations who "soon produced important social, agrarian and linguistic changes in the speech, economy, life and civilization of the colony," a principle that he applies to the production of phonemes by "intelligent" white Creoles. By the age of ten or twelve, "their organs—larynx, speech-cords, pharynx, uvula—are so habituated to the drawling utterance of the kitchen and scullery that they chant rather than speak the cultivated French."[44] The creole language of Louisiana was noted for characteristics only grudgingly recognized in Gullah and in other forms of black English, perhaps because it was seen as less of a threat to white language as a whole. Creole French was seen as part of a larger creolization within southern society where the interaction of racial groups had produced a new and distinct culture.

The link between *creole* as a language and *creolization* as a wider cultural force was explicitly made in the Louisiana context. *Creole* referred to the "patois" of Louisiana, yet *Creole* could also refer to the French-speaking descendants of French and Spanish settlers in the region, *and* to the many inhabitants of Louisiana—the so-called quadroons and mulattoes—born of mixed racial heritage. During the post–Civil War years, the white Creoles of Louisiana became unnerved by this double meaning for the name of their racial group—the fact that, instead of signifying only a line of pure Latin descent, the word *Creole* had somehow come to signify a person of mixed blood.[45] It was even said that Washington ladies would faint when Louisiana politicians introduced themselves as Creoles, such was the degree of racial intermixture implied by the word. For white southerners increasingly intolerant of racial uncertainty, the need to reappropriate this term was paramount. Thus, according to the most prominent French-Creole historian of the day, Charles Gayarré, *Creole* meant "the issue of European parents in Spanish or French colonies"; it was a title of honor "which could only be the birthright of the superior white race." Eventually, argued Gayarré, this word was applied *by* the white Creoles to every-thing produced or manufactured in Louisiana, whether horses, corn, or "negroes."[46]

George Washington Cable entered this debate in his 1884 work *The Creoles of Louisiana*. Both Cable and Gayarré derive the word *creole* from the Spanish *Criollo* (a native of America or the West Indies), stemming from the Latin root *creare* (to create, to nurse, to instruct); the word thus has the etymological significance of a "created" being—a person whose nature has adapted to the specific environmental and cultural conditions of the New World.[47] However, according to James A. Harrison, Cable's authority on the subject, *Creole* is "a corrupt word *made by the negroes.*"[48] To this recognition of African-American creativity, Cable adds that "the term was *adopted by—not conceded to—*the natives of mixed blood, and is still so used among themselves."[49] These people of "mixed" African and European blood had undermined the hegemony of white language by appropriating, and remotivating, the term *Creole* as a badge of ethnic iden-tity. Cable recognized that if a Creole was by definition a creature of a new colonial culture, then such a person must manifest elements of the African-American creativity within that culture. By asserting that African Americans could both create and control language, Cable undermined what Joseph Tregle describes as the post–Civil War, white-Creole myth of cultural purity and separateness.[50]

Both as a language and as a term of ethnicity, *creole* implied racial in-termixture. And the post–Civil War controversy over the definition of *creole* shows how language became a weapon to fight intimations of hybridity, a tool to establish racial purity. Cable's intervention in this debate was no isolated incident. Matching wider philological interest in creole French, Cable made groundbreaking investigations into African-American linguis-tic and artistic practices. The knowledge he gained, moreover, was a direct influence on his literary technique. Cable developed a unique style of writing, designed to overturn not just white-Creole etymology but the ra-cial ideology this etymology attempted to uphold.

In *The Myth of the Negro Past* (1941), Melville Herskovits recognized the remarkable nature of Cable's fiction and ethnographic work:

> One of the richest stores of data pertaining to Negro custom is the writing of George Cable, whose articles on New Orleans life, and particularly whose novel describing this life in preslavery days, *The Grandissimes*, hold special significance for research into the ethnography of United States Negroes. Based on intimate knowledge of the locality and its history, it must be ac-cepted as a valid document if only on the basis of comparative findings. It is thus a real contribution to our knowledge of life in this area during the

time of slavery, and a book which investigations into present-day custom should take into careful account.[51]

Cable's articles on New Orleans life, "The Dance in Place Congo" and "Creole Slave Songs," published in *The Century Magazine* in 1886, were groundbreaking in their description of African-American musical instruments and techniques; their analysis of types and styles of dance and musical orchestration; their attempt to understand the vast array of African tribes represented in Louisiana; their description of the religious practices of the slaves; and their careful notation of music and lyrics. The most remarkable aspect, however, was Cable's interest in the verbal element of this vernacular activity, revealed in a thorough study of song lyrics and of the conditions involved in the development of what Cable calls the "African-Creole Dialect" ("Creole," 807). While aware of the studies in creole French by Mercier and Harrison, among others, Cable supplemented their findings with at least ten years of his own research into the vernacular art of African Americans in Louisiana—work that produced a complex and far-reaching Afrocentric argument.[52] According to Cable, creole is not "merely bad or broken French" but a "natural" result of the contact between black people and the French tongue ("Creole," 807).[53] By printing songs combining French and African words, together with phonetic renderings of songs solely in African tongues, Cable's essays work against the tendency, which Eric Sundquist has traced well into the twentieth century, for musicologists and philologists to belittle the degree of African retention, and of African-American creativity, within the black oral tradition.[54] Focusing on a geographical area considered by Gwendolyn Midlo Hall to be "the most significant source of Africanization of the entire culture of the United States," and on the private cultural activities of song and dance that necessarily lay beyond the reach of slave masters, Cable unearthed a whole underground network of African-influenced activity in Louisiana.[55]

Cable's essays go beyond recognizing African-American linguistic creativity: they chart its transmission to the white community. "The facile character of the French master-caste," observes Cable, "made more so by the languorous climate of the Gulf, easily tolerated and often condescended to use the new tongue" ("Creole," 807). While appearing to cement the notion of a linguistic hierarchy between races, this African-Creole dialect was instead transmitted to the master caste, forming a lingua franca that in turn affected the pronunciation and structure of the "standard" French of the colony. The idea that creole French had transformed the dominant language, mentioned by Mercier and Harrison, is applied by Cable to the wider cross-cultural transmission of the aesthetic products of African America.[56] Cable's work describes a white community eager to absorb African-American creativity: to speak its dialect, to sing its songs, and to employ its satirical techniques.[57] According to *The Creoles of Louisiana*, "for a century or more the melodious drollery and grotesqueness of the negro *patois* has made it the favorite vehicle of humorous song and satirical prose and verse" among the white population (318). In addition to being the medium of sorrow songs or spirituals, African-American dialect transmitted a satirical tradition that—in the words of Henry Edward Krehbiel, a fellow folklorist of Cable's in the 1870s—stems from an African "penchant for musical lampooning . . . more a survival of a primitive practice brought by their ancestors from Africa than a custom borrowed from their masters."[58] In *The Creoles of Louisiana*, Cable illustrates his contention that white Creoles used African-influenced cultural forms with a quotation from an 1874 copy of the Franco-Louisianian journal, *le Carillon*, satirizing—in the African-Creole dialect—the political tensions of Reconstruction (318). Even Alcée Fortier, a French Creole who advocated a complete separation of white from black speech, and who directly refuted Cable's suggestion that the Creoles of the past were not "men of energy" who "spoke, as a rule, very good French," made a similar admission: white journalists used the "Creole patois" extensively to satirize "most bitterly and wittily the radical administration of MR. KELLOGG," the Republican governor of Louisiana in the mid-1870s.[59] Cable makes clear that the "grossly personal satirical ballad[s]" of black Louisianians were not oppressed but "winked at" by white Creoles, who often "added stanzas of their own invention" ("Dance," 527–28). The song of the Calinda dance, a key vehicle of this satire, may have been suppressed in New Orleans in 1843, but the music survived by its transmission to the white Creoles—among whom, Cable tells us, "it has long been a vehicle for the white Creole's satire; for generations the man of municipal politics was fortunate who escaped entirely a lampooning set to its air" ("Dance," 527).[60] According to Cable, from the late eighteenth century until after the Civil War, the white community of New Orleans took the music and dialect of African-American song and transformed them into the vehicle of its own satirical attacks.

Recalling the subversive idea, discussed in the first part of this chapter, that black speech had produced the distinctive qualities of southern American English while remaining intact beyond white language, Cable's essays explore both the influence and the resistance of creole French. Cable undermined white-Creole claims to cultural separateness and purity by revealing the white Creoles employing, consciously or not, African-Creole lyric products. Yet Cable also questioned this appropriation by exposing the difficulties inherent in the transmission of black creativity. "The Dance in Place Congo" and "Creole Slave Songs" reveal the problems of translating African-American language, the first of which was the retention of African vocabulary, never entirely lost in the New World, for the purpose of secret communication. Cable printed the hunting song "Dé Zab" accompanied by the translation of his black interlocutors, with "their own assurance that the translation is correct" ("Creole," 823), but he was not so fortunate in his philological assistance with other African-language songs he sought to record. Notated according to French phonetic principles ("Annoqué, Annobia, Biataia, Querequé, Nalléoua . . ."), their words remain beyond our comprehension, testaments to a private significance.[61] The second problem of translation lay in what Cable believed to be the African-American use of "nonsense rhymes" as a verbal decoy, a mask that allowed derisive satire to pass unchallenged.[62] Such disguise was often found in songs commemorating events in the white community, over which "the fate of the whole land . . . hung in agonies of suspense," that were delivered with a "clownish flippancy . . . almost within the whisk of the public jailer's lash" ("Creole," 815). The most intricate problem of translation lay in deciding when these "self-abasing confessions of the buffoon" ("Creole," 815) encoded bitter satire. The difficulty was to decode what William Piersen has identified as a subtle "satire by allusion" at work in both African and African-American societies, or what Marcyliena Morgan has called a black "counterlanguage" that seeks to represent "an alternative reality through a communication system based on ambiguity, irony and satire."[63]

In his reading of slave songs, Cable is ambiguously positioned between the ability to translate and the inability to penetrate black meaning.[64] Cable hears only "nonsense" in a song with a relatively obvious satirical sense (its last line translates as "White man cannot walk without money in his pocket, it is to steal girls" ["Creole," 824]). When he concludes that a Bamboula dance takes place "all to that one nonsense line meaning only 'When that 'tater's cooked don't you eat it up!'," we are left wondering what sexual, political, or cultural significance *'tater* (presumably "potato") held for the audience of the song, meanings beyond Cable's interpretive power ("Dance," 523). Yet Cable's sometime deafness to black signification was frequently accompanied by a remarkable ability to decode the subtle African-American use of satirical double meaning, evident in his interpretation of a song in creole French:

> Milatraisse courri dans bal,
> Cocodrie po'té fanal, Trouloulou!
> C'est pas zaffaire à tou,
> C'est pas zaffaire à tou, Trouloulou!
> ["Creole," 808]

Cable translates "Milatraisse" as "mulâtresse," the "freed or free-born quadroon or mulatto woman," and "Cocodrie" ("Spanish, *cocodrilla*, the

crocodile or alligator") as "the nickname for the unmixed black man."
Thus, the first two lines translate as "Quadroon woman goes [runs] to
the ball, Black man carries the lantern." Cable translates "Trouloulou"
(from the French *tourlourou*) as "fiddler crab" ("Creole," 807), which
"was applied to the free male quadroon, who could find admittance to
the quadroon balls only in the capacity, in those days distinctly menial, of
musician—fiddler" ("Creole," 808). With Cable's help we comprehend
that there "is an affluence of bitter meaning hidden under these apparently nonsensical lines. It mocks the helpless lot of three types of human
life in old Louisiana whose fate was truly deplorable" ("Creole," 808).
Beneath the apparent animal imagery is an alternative level of significance
that tells of the free man of color who must watch in silence as the women
of his caste are seduced by the white men of the city.

Similarly, Cable's translation of the name *Calalou* (originally a term for
a West Indian ragout) as a "derisive nickname" for the quadroon women
who swarmed into New Orleans in the early nineteenth century ("Creole," 811), turns a song that had been interpreted by Lafcadio Hearn as
simply one of lamentation into a pertinent exposé of the condition of the
quadroon caste in New Orleans:[65] condemned to be "neither slave nor
enlightened, neither white nor black, neither slave nor truly free" ("Creole," 811). These examples resemble an earlier one given by Cable in
"The Dance in Place Congo": the song "Miché Bainjo," which Cable
reprints from Allen's *Slave Songs of the United States* (113). This song centers
on the "saucy double meaning" of the word *mulet*, signifying both "mule"
and "mulatto" in French ("Dance," 525). The song's refrain, which
translates as "Look at that *mulet* there, Mr Banjo, isn't he insolent!" shows
slave society exposing the contemptuous subtext of white naming practices, while it satirizes the ambiguous condition of the free man of color,
trapped between a pretension to whiteness and an inability to be fully
accepted by the black community. It is fitting that these songs, described
by Cable as the hybrid creation of an interaction between races, should
focus their satirical energies on that other supposedly hybrid form—the
"mulatto"—and the tragic consequences of what Joseph Tregle has called
"a racial morality which condones miscegenation yet penalizes those
whom it produces."[66] The only recourse for this free man of color, Cable
tells us, was to "let his black half-brother celebrate," in Congo Square,
"the mingled humor and outrage of it in satirical songs of double meaning" ("Creole," 808).

The potential for double meaning in black expression was beginning
to be studied in the nineteenth century, most notably in the speech of
the West Indies. J. J. Thomas's *The Theory and Practice of Creole Grammar*
(1869) recorded the ability of the French creole language of Trinidad to
deflect, contract, or divert French words "to totally different applica-

tions," one of his examples being *decapiter* ("to cut off the head"), which signifies "to slander" in creole.[67] Similar signifying usages were occasionally detected by whites in African-American English, yet nowhere to the extent of Cable's detailed exploration of black vernacular practices in Louisiana. Africanisms, creole grammatical and phonetic features, ambiguous rhetorical techniques, linguistic intermixture between racial groups—these shadowy elements in descriptions of Gullah were the focus of Cable's ethnographic essays. More importantly, the linguistic material contained in these essays provides the context necessary to understand the shocking literature developed by Cable in the late 1870s and early '80s. The predominant ploy of white writers of Gullah, in which the creole's capacity for resignification and multiple meaning became reduced to a realm of superficial punning, was transfigured by Cable into a literature that thrived on processes of creolization, one that engaged the satire, not the "mistakes"—the ambiguity, not the "nonsense"—of black expression. Even the resistance to comprehension that Cable encountered in creole French would prove useful in his political deployment of African-American cultural material.

Cable's *The Grandissimes* (1880) produced a "peculiar impression" on its early readers, many of whom found it difficult to say with certainty what the novel was about. Despite its conventional romantic plot, its "local color" atmosphere, and its idyllic treatment of the aristocratic French-Creole family of the title, the final effect of *The Grandissimes* was perplexing: it was, commented reviewers, too "full of allusions which are hard to trace," leaving the reader "like one guessing out a half-told riddle."[68] Another peculiarity concerned the novel's strange historical parallelism: clearly set at the time of the Louisiana purchase in 1803, it also spoke to the post-Reconstruction South, especially in the central section dealing with the brutal treatment of the rebellious slave Bras-Coupé. Early readers were intrigued by the apparent confusion of New Orleans society, manifested in a profusion of "mongrel dialects"[69] and in a chaotic racial situation that produced two Honoré Grandissimes: the first a "dazzling contradiction of the notion that a Creole is a person of mixed blood" (*Grandissimes*, 38), the second a free man of color and wealthy property owner cursed by a racial prejudice that belies his appearance. The plot of *The Grandissimes* revolves around this sense of racial ambiguity: Cable recreates the confusion felt by an outsider—the American protagonist, Joseph Frowenfeld—confronted by a society based on an elusive notion of "blood." Both reader and character are trapped, throughout much of the novel, in what the narrator describes as "an atmosphere of hints, allusions, faint unspoken admissions, ill-concealed antipathies, unfinished speeches, mistaken identities and whisperings of hidden strife" (96). *The Grandis-simes* was such a radical work not simply because it predicted the exposure of ironic racial boundaries in later works like Mark Twain's *Pudd'nhead Wilson* (1894) and Charles Chesnutt's *The House Behind the Cedars* (1900). Cable's allusive, enigmatic style was considered his most dangerous political weapon. It was a style largely dependent on the satirical ambiguity of black expression, a style in which the subversive potential of black dialect was fundamental.

The technique of manipulating language to imply cultural hybridity, which Cable's *Creoles of Louisiana* described in the "colored" appropriation of the word *Creole*, reemerged as an accusation against Cable in contemporary reactions to his writing. Alexander Nicolas De Menil recorded in *The Literature of the Louisiana Territory* (1904) that the white Creoles of New Orleans denounced Cable for having "maliciously caricatured . . . and satirized" their traditions by conveying to eastern readers, "while not so stating in plain language," the idea that Creoles have a strain of "negro blood." Similarly, in his 1886 lecture "The Creoles of History and the Creoles of Romance," Charles Gayarré argued that Cable's writing contained a "secret intention to produce the impression in his readers in his own sly and covert ways that the Creoles are instinctively attracted, by a sort of magnetic influence, to everything that is low, base and impure, as a natural effect of that Gallic recklessness which, since the foundation of the colony, was the cause of their ignoble descent from the ill specimens of three races—Indian, African and French prostitutes."[70] The main fear was that Cable had manipulated some surreptitious linguistic technique that satirized white-Creole beliefs in racial purity. In his article on New Orleans in the ninth edition of the *Encyclopaedia Britannica* (1884), Cable indeed stated that the early French Creoles took "such wives as could be gathered haphazard from the ranks of Indian allies, African slave cargoes, and the inmates of French houses of correction,"[71] while *The Grandissimes* affirmed that the "pilgrim fathers of the Mississippi Delta" took "wives and moot-wives from the ill specimens of three races" (22). It is otherwise difficult to find such explicit statements elsewhere in Cable's writing. The real threat came from *ambiguous* allusions to cultural and racial intermixture, like the unfinished sentence in *The Grandissimes* declaring that "the main Grandissime stock . . . has kept itself lily-white ever since France has loved lilies—as to marriage, that is; as to less responsible entanglements, why, of course——" (22).[72]

Cable's double meanings enraged the white Creoles of Louisiana. The implicit was feared more than the explicit in his work because it neglected to limit clearly the extent of intermixture. Cable's ambiguous allusions powerfully suggested the pervasiveness of hybrid modes—whether genealogical, linguistic, or musical—throughout white Louisiana culture. One of Cable's most surreptitious techniques was his representation of French-English dialect, the dialect that arose when native French speakers learned English. *The Grandissimes* explores the cultural and linguistic consequences of the influx of English-speaking Americans into Louisiana following its purchase by the United States in 1803, together with the corresponding cultural impact of black on white. According to Gayarré, Cable strayed onto the side of perversion and depravity by making the white Creoles in his novel speak "the broken, mutilated africanized English of the black man . . . [the] broken English of the negroes of Virginia, the Carolinas, Georgia, etc."[73] In his representation of French-English grammar and phonology—especially the loss of final consonants, the disappearance of the preconsonantal *r*, and the absence of the copula[74]—Cable was believed to be replicating the peculiarities of black English. As Cable remarks in *The Creoles of Louisiana*, the white Creole is "probably seldom aware that his English sparkles with the same pretty corruptions" as can be observed in the "African-Creole dialect" of French (318). Elsewhere, Cable is eager to record how "'Dey got' is a vulgarism of Louisiana Creoles, *white and colored*, for 'There is'" ("Creole," 823; emphasis added). Although Cable takes some care in *The Grandissimes* to differentiate between the French-English of white Creoles and the black English of slaves, a glance at these two language varieties reveals an extensive area of shared linguistic forms, such as "w'at," "de," "wid," "dat," "yo'," "nigga," "kyah," and "worl'." Just as there are characters in Cable's novel whose linguistic competence belies their supposed racial inferiority, the Creole-English dialect also undermines the hierarchical assumptions of caste.

Cable's depiction of dialect thus gets to the heart of the cultural hybridity that, for him, characterized New Orleans society. Cable removed many dialect spellings from the English speech of educated Creoles, such as Honoré Grandissime, in an 1883 revision of *The Grandissimes*—more a concession to easy reading than to his political opponents.[75] When Honoré Grandissime addresses the emotional issue of Louisiana's racial situation, however, his dialect returns: *our* becomes "ow," *most* becomes "mos'," and *never* becomes "nevva" (156). When discussing the impact of the African American on Louisiana culture, in the form of the "shadow of the Ethiopian" whose length and blackness pervade the moral, political, and commercial aspects of "ow whole civilization" (156), the linguistic legacy of this very impact—an African-American way of speaking English—surfaces in his speech. Cable's white Creoles employ linguistic forms similar to those of their African-American neighbors; Creole English is a pervasive dialect of ethnic intermixture.

There is occasional confusion over whether, by "Creole dialect," Cable intends the English of his white Creoles or the creole French of his African Americans—a confusion that suggests further uncertainties in racial definition.[76] Like the white Creoles' English, the creole French of African-American characters in *The Grandissimes* is another agent of transmission between black and white cultures. Creole French is established as the language of cultural hybridity during the *bal masque* at the beginning of the novel, when Agricola Fusilier, the fierce defender of French-Creole superiority, is confronted by the masked representation of his ancestral mixed blood, in the form of his great-grandmother, an "Indian Queen." Appropriately, she addresses him in the "familiarity" of the "slave dialect" (2). White Creoles in the novel switch into "negro French" (82, 321) or "plantation French" (71) when addressing members of the slave caste—a bidialectal ability that was angrily rejected by Cable's white Creole readers, who wished to be thought of as speaking only "pure" French.[77] When the story of the rebellious slave Bras-Coupé is initially told to the Frowenfeld family on their journey to New Orleans, it is delivered "in a *patois* difficult, but not impossible, to understand" (10). White Creoles apparently switch automatically into black French as if it were the only language of artistic creativity. Radically, Cable suggests that white Creoles use creole French in normal conversation among themselves: when addressing her daughter, Aurora Nancanou employs the creole verb *courri* (in the sense of "go"), before resuming in "better French" (218).[78] By concentrating on the conflict of French and English in *The Grandissimes*, it is easy to miss the tensions present within French itself. Between "unprovincial" French on the one hand (2), and "negro French" on the other, Cable situates the "dialect of old Louisiana" (4), a supposedly "corrupt" (60) variety of French clearly affected by its creole cousin.

In addition to being a register of what Lafcadio Hearn called "linguistic miscegenation,"[79] dialect is indisputably the language of satire in *The Grandissimes*. Black satirical ballads, delivered in the ambiguous creole French that Cable detailed in his ethnographic essays, provide the novel with a background of social commentary. Moreover, the Calinda dance, with its "well-known song of derision, in whose ever multiplying stanzas the helpless satire of a feeble race still continues to celebrate the personal failings of each newly prominent figure among the dominant caste" (*Grandissimes*, 95), is not a secret, masked activity within the slave community, but one that reverberates throughout New Orleans. Joseph Frowenfeld "suddenly became aware that the weird, drowsy throb of the African song and dance had been swinging drowsily in his brain for an unknown lapse of time" (96). The Calinda subverts the white mind by entering unawares. It represents a surreptitious transmission of African-American culture, which echoes the white adaptation of African-American satire as an artistic genre. This is the central irony in Cable's representation of black-white interaction. While the white-Creole community of New Orleans was interpreting Cable's depiction of its "africanized" speech as a satire upon its cultural separateness, Cable was describing a process in which this same community was, if not consciously adopting the spoken forms of African-American satire, then unwittingly absorbing the linguistic and artistic qualities of blackness that surrounded it.

This irony can also be observed in pamphlets published at the time in reaction to *The Grandissimes*. For example, Adrien Emmanuel Rouquette's *Critical Dialogue Between Aboo and Caboo on a New Book*, published under a pseudonym in New Orleans in 1880, accuses Cable of having "slanderously misrepresented" white-Creole customs, habits, and manners: Cable is "a scoffer, a banterer, a ridiculer" who must in turn be punished by ridicule. Yet the calumnious satirical poem with which this pamphlet ends, accusing Cable of taking part in voodoo ceremonies and in acts of miscegenation, is written in the African-Creole dialect.[80] Rather than extricating the author, and implicitly the white-Creole population of New Orleans, from the "crimes" attributed to Cable—namely, a familiarity with and a participation in African-American culture—this poem suggests both the knowledge of and the willingness to adopt black creative forms.

The Grandissimes is a case study in the ambivalence surrounding the presence of African-American creativity within the white community of nineteenth-century New Orleans. This ambivalence, whereby black satire is partly comprehended by whites, partly beyond their comprehension, is embodied in the character Clemence, a slave woman and vendor of cakes. Clemence is a "thinker" whose "mental activity was evinced not more in the cunning aptness of her songs than in the droll wisdom of her sayings[,] . . . the often audacious, epigrammatic philosophy of her tongue" (249). She is the major exponent of the African-American gift of satirical song. In the tradition of the African griot, Clemence studies her social conditions, records the history of her people, and derides the events of the dominant culture in lampooning lyrics.[81] She mimics the linguistic formulas of the white community—phrases like "de happies' people in de God's worl'" (249)—remotivating them in acts of seditious signifying. The dialect of her songs and sayings becomes the formal marker of a different level of signification whereby Clemence ridicules the white community's systems of belief. Yet for all her satirical powers, Clemence makes a mistake: she presumes too much on her *insignificance*. "She little thought," the narrator tells us, "that others . . . were silently and for her most unluckily, charging their memories with her knowing speeches; and that of every one of those speeches she would ultimately have to give account" (249). Clemence fails to realize that her dialectal, satirical songs gain—to borrow phrases from Eric Lott—a type of "currency" within the white community: they mark an "exchange of energies" between two sup-posedly separate, self-enclosed cultural realms.[82] Clemence fails to realize that her songs not only signify on the white community, but also, to a certain extent, within it.

Yet this white comprehension of black meaning is not absolute: Clem-ence's satirical message remains partly beyond the interpretation of whites. Her songs in the African-Creole dialect exploit their ambiguity, their resistance to comprehension, creating for her white listeners the unnerving experience of facing cultural forms with masked meanings. The key example is the song beginning "Dé 'tit zozos," which Clemence trans-lates into black English for the benefit of her American auditor: "[T]wo lill birds; dey was sittin' on de fence an' gabblin, togeddah, you know, lak you see two young gals sometime', an' you can't mek out w'at dey sayin', even ef dey know demself? H-ya! Chicken-hawk come 'long dat road an' jes' set down an' munch 'em, an' nobody can't no mo' hea' deir lill gab-blin' on de fence, you know" (104). This song might refer to the white romantic plot of the novel (which focuses on the two "ladies Nancanou"), or to the doublings involved in its racial plot (which features the "two Honoré Grandissimes"). On a deeper level of significance, however, the song seems to be about the existence of African-American cultural forms within white society. By exploiting its unknown referent, the song adver-tises the ultimate privacy of its meaning; it remains, even when translated from its "strange tongue," another "torn fragment" in Joseph Frowen-feld's "newly found book, the Community of New Orleans" (103). Like the two birds sitting on the fence, audible yet unintelligible, African-American song depended upon its jargonistic ability to mask meaning within an initiated group; indeed, the archaic meaning of *jargon* as a "twit-tering of birds" remains implicit in Clemence's song. The fact that Clem-ence is murdered at the end of the novel by the Creoles who uncover her insurrectionist plans demonstrates that her forms of resistance were par-tially appreciated by whites. It also, more importantly, illustrates how African-American cultural forms, like the "two lill birds" in Clemence's song, were often suppressed without being fully comprehended.

At several other points, rather than simply recoiling from untranslata-ble African-American songs, Cable inserts them into his novel without explanation, creating an interpretive dilemma for his readers by confront-ing them with the raw signs of an alien culture. Take for instance the only songs included with their accompanying musical notation, songs that show white Creoles performing African retentions—"*Counou ouaïe ouaïe ouaïe, momza*" (168)—approximating the sounds of African words without knowledge of their significance.[83] The inability of white Louisianians to translate African-Creole lyrics has profound political consequences. The most significant example is the wedding song of Bras-Coupé, the mythical runaway slave whose tragic rebellion against slavery is key to understanding *The Grandissimes*:

En haut la montagne, zami,   [High in the mountain, darling]
Mo pé coupé canne, zami   [I cut sugar-cane, darling]
Pou' fé i'a'zen' zami   [To make money darling]
Pou' mo baille Palmyre.   [For my beautiful Palmyre.]
Ah! Palmyre, Palmyre mo c'ere,   [Ah! Palmyre, Palmyre my dear,]
Mo l'aimé'ou'—Mo l'aimé'ou' . . .   [I love you, I love you . . .]
Ah! Palmyre, Palmyre, mo' piti zozo,   [Ah! Palmyre, Palmyre, my little
bird,]
Mo l'aimé'ou'—mo l'aimé, l'aimé'ou'.   [I love you, my love, I love you.]
[178–79]

The mountains of this song, an anomaly in the Louisiana landscape, are interpreted in the novel as the mountains of Bras-Coupé's native Africa (179). Yet this interpretation is at odds with Cable's reading of the original version of this song, in which he tells us that a "Louisiana slave would hardly have thought it possible to earn money for himself in the sugarcane fields. The mention of mountains points back to San Domingo" ("Creole," 809). Bras-Coupé's song is not therefore a love song but an assertion of black independence, which invokes San Domingo and its slave revolution of 1791—a revolution that depended on the possession of mountainous regions by insurgent maroons.[84]

The theme of slave insurrection dominates the Bras-Coupé episode of the novel. Palmyre Philosophe, we are told, "had heard of San Domingo," and she wishes to teach Bras-Coupé its lesson of "insurrection" (184). When Bras-Coupé strikes his Spanish master, the white-Creole wedding guests are "smitten stiff with the instant expectation of insurrection" (181), calling to mind the widespread slave unrest in Louisiana that reached its peak in 1795–96, the very period of Bras-Coupé's own rebellion.[85] As Barbara Ladd has shown, Cable's narrative of Bras-Coupé shares features with a whole web of stories about rebellious slaves from both Louisiana and the West Indies, including the story of the great eighteenth-century San Domingan rebel leader, François Macandal, who—like Bras-Coupé—had voodoo powers and was finally captured when drunk at a Calinda dance.[86]

Cable clearly recognized that African-Creole songs could function as forms of insurrection: in "Creole Slave Songs" he prints a runaway slave's song of defiance to the high sheriff, dating from the mid-eighteenth century (823). Accordingly, Cable's two ethnographic essays demonstrate his awareness of the subtle ways that this rebellious message might be encoded. The white community in the novel, however, fails to heed the double level of significance in Bras-Coupé's wedding-song and thereby fails to foresee the insurrection of which it warns. Even Bras-Coupé's name (in English, "Arm-cut-off") is implicitly derisive of the white community: it satirizes the fact that "all Slavery is maiming," yet remains sufficiently ambiguous to mask its satirical intent—if preferred, the name could signify that Bras-Coupé's African tribe, "in losing him, had lost its strong right arm" (171). Rather than rejecting his French name and maintaining his African one, a common form of resistance practiced by Louisiana slaves, Bras-Coupé uses French for satire; in effect, he turns their own language against his supposed masters.[87] His use of the verb "coupé" in his wedding-song also masks seditious meaning: as the characters in *The Grandissimes* come to realize, "coupé" is not simply a reference to cutting sugarcane but is Bras-Coupé's threat to cut down his white persecutors. Compare this to another song in "Creole Slave Songs," "The Dirge of St. Malo," in which a "famous negro insurrectionist" is accused of making a plot "Pou' *coupé* cou à tout ye blancs" (814–15; emphasis added)—that is, to cut the throats of all the whites. Or again, only moments after singing his wedding song, Bras-Coupé makes an explicit comparison of his white master's wife to sugarcane, commenting that her "voice is sweet, but the words are very strong; from the same sugar-cane comes *sirop* and *tafia* [rum]" (179). Ironically, the white characters miss the strong meaning behind Bras-Coupé's own sweet words, and they mistranslate a whole network of ambiguous signs foreshadowing insurrection. Cable confronted his contemporary readers with similarly obscure meanings: by interpreting the mountains of Bras-Coupé's wedding song as African rather than San Domingan, they would have remained oblivious to the song's implicit insurgent context, its dialectal encoding of revolutionary intent.

The "voudou malediction" with which Bras-Coupé carries out his rebellion is given "in wrathful words of his [African] mother tongue" (181), and even when delivered in creole French, Bras-Coupé's lyric is notable for its equivocation.[88] Yet it is clear from *The Grandissimes* that Cable is using black ambiguity rather than simply being bemused by it. An initial version of the Bras-Coupé story, called "Bibi," was rejected by publishers in the early 1870s owing to its "unmitigatedly distressful effect" and "terrible suggestion."[89] Cable was forced to avoid explicit reference to the threat of black insurrection that had dominated Louisiana society since colonial times—a censorship that continued throughout his career. A draft version of "Creole Slave Songs" shows Cable replacing a reference to "low white creoles—not milk white or lily white or even probably white, but just white enough to be ten thousand times better than a negro"[90] with the more benign "many a Creole—white as well as other tints" ("Creole," 820). From the original version of Bras-Coupé's wedding-song that appeared in "Creole Slave Songs," Cable omitted the lines: "Mo courri dans bois, zamie, Pou' toué zozo, zamie, Pou' fé l'a'zent, chère amie, Pou' mo baille Suzette'' (''I go into the forest, darling, To kill birds, darling, To make money, dear love, For my beautiful Suzette'') (824–25). In connection with Clemence's song ''Dé 'tit zozos,'' these lines suggest that killing birds was viewed as code for insurgent ideas, one so common that Cable may have considered it too explicit for inclusion.

It was in this climate of repression that Cable perfected his surreptitious linguistic technique of ''hints, allusions . . . [and] unfinished sentences'' (*Grandissimes*, 96) that so infuriated the white-Creole community. The name *Bras-Coupé* epitomizes this technique. It alludes to the dismembering effects of slavery, to the *coup* d'état feared by whites in the novel, and more specifically to the 1795 slave rebellion at Pointe *Coupee* (''Cut-off Point'')—a violent, multiracial abolitionist plot that reverberated throughout nineteenth-century Louisiana.[91] Like the secret significance of creole song and the ambiguity of dialect as a sign of racial identity, the multivalence of *Bras-Coupé* was another subtle means by which Cable taunted white supremacist southern readers, confronting them with the central fears of intermixture and insurgence they sought to repress.

''Mr. Cable has written under some constraint,'' remarked a contemporary reviewer concerning the absence of references in *The Grandissimes* to the Civil War and to the progress of the ''colored race'' thereafter.[92] It was a constraint that led Cable to replicate rhetorical strategies similar to those developed by African Americans during slavery, strategies that satirized the dominant culture from behind a mask of allusion. In some ways, this was not so unusual in post–Civil War Louisiana. Politically conservative French Creoles themselves employed the African-Creole dialect of French in their newspapers to attack the ''carpetbagger'' regime. Because unintelligible to most English speakers, this dialect allowed Creoles to disguise their satire and therefore escape censorship and prosecution.[93] Yet Cable used the black vernacular for different reasons and toward different ends. Rather than exploiting it as a convenient verbal mask, Cable transformed the subtle strategies of allusion and ambiguity that define the black vernacular into a new literary style, one that satirized not just Yankee intervention in the South but the roots of white southern culture, grown in hybrid soil.

Cable was repudiated both by Franco-Creoles and by Anglo-Americans because he used the earlier racial tensions of Creole society to satirize the contemporary conflicts of American race segregation. ''To-day almost all the savagery that can justly be charged against Louisiana must—strange to say—be laid at the door of the *Américain*'' (329). This is just one of several points in *The Grandissimes* where Cable specifies that the novel must be read as an implicit criticism of American society at the time of its composition.[94] In his essay "My Politics" (1888–89), Cable emphasizes still more pointedly that *The Grandissimes* was meant as "truly a political work": "It was impossible that a novel written by me then should escape being a study of the fierce struggle going on around me, regarded in the light of that past history—those beginnings—which had so differentiated the Louisiana civilization from the American scheme of public society."[95] The "beginnings" to which Cable refers were the elements of miscegenation and insurrection that the white-Creole population of Louisiana in particular, and the white population of the South in general, were attempting to deny after the Civil War.

Cable occasionally used examples of racial hybridity to undermine the popular belief in race instinct.[96] The resulting accusation that he was a "miscegenationist" prompted Cable to repeated denials that his advocacy of civil equality would inevitably lead to "a confusion of the races in private society, followed by intellectual and moral debasement and by mongrel posterity." Although "The Silent South" (1885) ends with the resounding call for a "national unity without hybridity," the idea of racial intermixture is by no means absent from Cable's political essays. It remains implicit, for instance, in discussions of the decline of southern literature and literacy. "When the whole intellectual energy of the Southern states flew to the defense of that one institution which made us the South, we broke with human progress," argues Cable in "Literature in the Southern States" (1882): "We cannot suppose that our community could hold a servile race in domestic subjection for a century and a half without producing a more lasting effect on the master race than a few subsequent years of partial change could dissipate." Again, in "The Freedman's Case in Equity" (1885), Cable states that the racist system of the South "blunts the sensibilities of the ruling class," leading to an intense sectionalism, an amateurism and provinciality in the arts, and an illiteracy not caused by but "so largely shared by the blacks." Here was a cultural hybridity of the most negative type: the white community places the responsibility for artistic creativity in the hands and voices of its black neighbors; the "intellectual degradation" of slavery contaminates the dominant culture. To counter this effect, Cable looked to the artistic regeneration of the South through the creation of a literature that would focus on the local yet achieve national acclaim. This literature must succeed through subversion: it should not "be expected to practice certain amiable and cowardly oversights and silences in order to smooth the frowns of sections and parties and pacify the autocratic voice of ruling classes and established ideas."[97]

Cable's own work had in part provided the model for this literature of political agitation. Many of the radical ideas of Cable's political essays appear in *The Grandissimes.* In the words of Joseph Frowenfeld, the Muses reside in the slave quarters because the white community has sold its creative soul for the "double bondage" of the "slavery of caste," which "compels a community, in order to preserve its established tyrannies, to walk behind the rest of the intelligent world," condemning it to become deficient in "art-effort," and "comparatively illiterate" (142–43).[98] Cable's novel depicts a society attempting to maintain the color line in what the narrator describes as a "hybrid city" (12), a city where people of mixed blood contradict the notion of race instinct, where spoken language counters the idea of cultural segregation, and where culture as a whole resists polarization into plain black and white. Reminding us of Benito Cereno's final words in Herman Melville's tale of 1855, Joseph Frowenfeld describes how the color line itself becomes the "shadow of the Ethiopian" (156). This shadow has a double function: it contaminates white civilization with the barbarism of slavery and racism, while it informs white culture with an African-American creativity that has the power to remain an inassimilable, mysterious, shadowy presence.

The Grandissimes shows dialect to be the vehicle of black cultural transmission *and* secrecy. Like the "weird, drowsy throb of the African song and dance" that surreptitiously enters Frowenfeld's consciousness (96), the African-Creole lyric is simultaneously transferred to the white community while it remains a nonsensical, subversive element within it. White Creoles sing African-Creole songs that encode the very forces of black rebellion the whites are attempting to repress. Just as Clemence makes the mistake of assuming that her dialectal satire is insignificant, that its meanings cannot carry to the white community, this same white community wrongly assumes that black meaning is entirely intelligible at its surface level. African-American linguistic creativity finally has a double meaning in Cable's work. It undermines the notion that the color line can be drawn in the culture of the South, while it satirizes white society by revealing its inability to comprehend the real significance of the cultural forms it is so eager to adopt. The Grandissimes confused its early reviewers and infuriated the white Creoles whose past it chronicled, with a revolutionary literary style that employed "mongrel dialects," ambiguous allusions, and black vernacular techniques to frustrate the racial fictions upon which white society depended.

White literary representations of Gullah and creole French were attempts to translate the racial implications of two creolized cultural situations that had radical implications for southern society as a whole. The question of the foreignness of these marginal languages was of central importance to a political era instituting civil distinctions that were designed to make African Americans outcasts and strangers in their own land, as Du Bois noted in *The Souls of Black Folk*.[99] The writings discussed in this chapter demonstrate how literary representation was involved in a politics of language that manipulated ideas about black speech to strengthen *or* attack the case for racial separateness and inequality. The literature of Gullah denied processes of creolization by exploiting the paradox that African-American culture was derivative of white culture yet different enough from it to be alien and inferior. In his literary depiction of Louisiana, Cable countered this paradox by delicately balancing a recognition of the foreign, implicitly African origins of black culture with a critique of the social alienation in which the post–Civil War black population was held. His works suggested that the interaction of blackness and whiteness had produced a southern language that still existed as an ambiguous discourse with the power to undermine the dominant culture's claim to command meaning. In an era when Louisiana newspapers stated that French was "the language of civilization" in order to prove that Creoles were not "hybrid creatures,"[100] Cable was exploiting linguistic techniques that emphasized hybridity as central to the foundation of southern white culture. Scholars are right to suggest that the dialect of the "plantation tradition" was often the vehicle of repression. Cable's work, however, demonstrates what a powerful tool of counterhegemonic subversion dialect could be.

FIVE

"Accents of Menace Alien to Our Air": Language and Literature in Turn-of-the-Century New York City

While searching New York City for a place to live, Basil March—the hero of William Dean Howells's novel *A Hazard of New Fortunes* (1890)—is confronted by a sight emphasizing the difference between New York and his home city of Boston: a decently dressed man picks up a cracker from the street and crams it into his mouth as if he were famished. March approaches the man to offer what assistance he can, but discovers that the well-dressed tramp cannot speak English. March is shocked by the encounter; after asking some questions in French, he leaves the tramp to lapse back into "the mystery of misery out of which he had emerged."[1] March's sudden awareness of the harsh realities of New York "low life" marked a moment of cultural anxiety for native-born guardians of Anglo-American values.[2] "Increasing ethnic diversity and the making of a new industrial working class constituted a single process," writes Alan Trachtenberg, "introducing cultural difference into American life on an unprecedented scale."[3] Class conflict and urban poverty developed alongside a vast influx of foreign immigrants—increasingly from southern and eastern Europe—who settled in remarkably diverse and seemingly impenetrable ethnic neighborhoods.[4] There was felt to be something un-American about the large, industrial cities of late-nineteenth-century America.

These newly prominent social forces provoked manifold literary reactions. Like many journalists of the era, Basil March turns his urban experience into anecdotal sketches designed to arouse moral consciences by making comfortable people understand how the "other half" lives.[5] In the tradition of evangelical Christian tracts, moralizing continued over the sinful world of urban poverty.[6] The 1880s saw the emergence of a school of tenement fiction, and by the end of the century a genre of the immigrant novel was established; both involved educated, middle-class writers airing their sentimental, often condescending opinions of the urban poor and the ethnic immigrant.[7] A more sympathetic perspective developed in the 1890s. Epitomized by Lincoln Steffens's New York *Commercial Advertiser*, this new journalism tried to see ethnic groups on their own terms, to understand how America might benefit from immigrant culture.[8] And toward the end of the century, minority groups pioneered powerful literary and journalistic voices of their own, voices that sought to educate mainstream Americans in the subtleties of ethnic life. These diverse literary phenomena shared a common aim: the depiction of an authentic, inside view of urban and ethnic realities.[9]

Central to these new perspectives on city life was the question of vocal culture. Thomas Bailey Aldrich's poem "Unguarded Gates" (1892), for example, used the theme of language to reflect nativist fears concerning the influx into America of "Malayan, Scythian, Teuton, Kelt, and Slav": "In street and alley what strange tongues are loud, / Accents of menace alien to our air, / Voices that once the Tower of Babel knew!" New York as a modern-day Babel was a common image of the age because it combined anxieties over urban growth with fears of linguistic confusion. The variety of non-English-speaking communities in the city posed an obvious barrier for those journalists—like Hutchins Hapgood—who sought access to ethnic culture. Hapgood remained trapped outside the Yiddish world of the Jewish ghetto; for him Yiddish was not an expression of ethnic identity but a "poor" dialect, an "inadequate vehicle of thought."[10] Similar problems of interpretation have been detected recently in realist novelists like William Dean Howells. How were they to construct a common language to represent a coherent social consensus when both the reality depicted and the audience addressed were increasingly unfamiliar, fragmented along lines of class and ethnicity?[11] Observers of the city scene were confronted by the jarring accents of social antagonism and by the ethnic dialects that arose from the fusion of different national tongues. How was the linguistic confusion of New York's growing ghettoes to be translated for America's magazine- and novel-reading public? It was a difficulty suggested in *A Hazard of New Fortunes:* how could the "jargon" of the Neapolitan's "unintelligible dialect," and the "inarticulate lamentation" of a drunken, middle-aged American woman, be made appreciable to those middle-class readers interested in "the future economy of our heterogeneous commonwealth"?[12] For the many "local color" writers of the 1880s, American dialect speakers tended to inhabit provincial, rustic spaces of an idealized antebellum past. The new voices of the 1890s, however, were increasingly urban and shockingly contemporary.

The vocal environment of New York City became the special concern of two young writers who turned to "low life" in the 1890s: Stephen Crane and Abraham Cahan. Howells noticed this parallel in his twin review of two novels that appeared in 1896: Cahan's *Yekl: A Tale of the New York Ghetto*, and Crane's *Maggie: A Girl of the Streets* (published by Appleton's in 1896, after an unsuccessful private printing in 1893).

> The student of dialect ought to be interested in the parlance of the class Mr. Crane draws upon for his characters. They are almost inarticulate; not merely the grammar but the language itself, decays in their speech. The Theta sound, so characteristic of English, disappears altogether, and the vowels tend to lose themselves in the obscure note heard in *fur* and *stir*. What will be the final language spoken by the New Yorker? We shall always write and print a sort of literary English, I suppose, but with the mixture of races the spoken tongue may be a thing composite and strange by our present knowledge. Mr. Abraham Cahan's "Yekl, a Story [*sic*] of the New York Ghetto" (Appleton's), is full of indirect suggestion upon this point. Perhaps we shall have a New York speech which shall be to English what the native Yiddish of his characters is to Hebrew, and it will be interlarded with Russian, Polish and German words, as their present jargon is with English vocables and with American slang.[13]

The literary parallels between Crane and Cahan have been recently underscored: both writers sought to undermine the romantic, condescending conventions by which "low life" had traditionally entered mainstream American fiction.[14] It was their manipulation of the new vocal culture of New York City, I suggest in this chapter, that made Crane's and Cahan's fiction so unconventional, while also marking crucial differences in literary method and outlook. Crane was interested in inarticulate, decayed speech—noted Howells—whereas Cahan, writing from a Jewish, immigrant perspective, was concerned with the linguistic hybridity of ethnic interaction. Crane turned to the swearing and blasphemy of city life, Cahan to its melting pot of dialects. An exploration of these contrasting literary interpretations of urban experience demonstrates that Crane's and Cahan's mutual reevaluation of "New Yorkese" dialect was a fundamental aspect of their groundbreaking literary techniques. With dialect Crane assaulted the naive, patronizing values that sanctioned dominant interpretations of how the "other half" lived, while Cahan represented the complex ambivalence of ethnic assimilation.

THE NEW YORKESE DIALECT

The urban and ethnic phenomena presented by lower Manhattan Island received special attention in the 1880s and '90s, most famously in Jacob Riis's analysis of slum life, *How the Other Half Lives* (1890). While Riis discussed the social and economic forces of New York's tenement houses that touched family life "with deadly moral contagion," his main concern was with the impact of foreign immigrants on the wider urban environment: "One may find for the asking an Italian, a German, a French, African, Spanish, Bohemian, Russian, Scandinavian, Jewish, and Chinese colony. . . . The one thing you shall vainly ask for in the chief city of America is a distinctively American community. . . . In [its] place has come this queer conglomerate mass of heterogeneous elements, ever striving and working like whiskey and water in one glass, and with the like result: final union and a prevailing taint of whiskey."[15] Some observers responded to this "reverse colonization" with guarded optimism: they clung to the notion that an Anglo-Saxon "race nucleus" remained predominant in the formation of the national character,[16] or they emphasized how successfully—through the medium of language—American ideals were being instilled in foreign peoples.[17] Others took a more alarmist tone. Instead of sending missionaries to the "barbarians" of "'Darkest Africa,'" wrote one journalist in 1892, we need only think of "the 'white savages' in 'Darkest New York.'" Many observers feared that these new ethnics were inassimilable. The maintenance of Old World cultures among diverse national groups fed the anxiety that New York was no longer an integral city but a collection of separate, mutually unintelligible colonies, each with the power to contaminate America with its foreignness. For one writer in 1897, the opinion that the squalor, poverty, and vice of the Lower East Side had disappeared was the "superficial view of those who think that deep-rooted racial traits can be overcome in a lifetime, or of those who do not know their New York."[18]

For Jacob Riis, the most threatening aspect of urban life—threatening both to the "colonial" group and to the health of the nation at large—was the fragmentation of the city into many national tongues. Riis described how the Italian "not only knows no word of English, but he does not know enough to learn. . . . Even his boy, born here, often speaks his native tongue indifferently," thereby exposing him to unscrupulous middle-men who act as linguistic and financial go-betweens. Similarly, the complete isolation and economic slavery of the Bohemian were seen to be caused mainly by "his singularly harsh and unattractive language, which he can neither easily himself unlearn nor impart to others," even after a lifetime in the United States. This multilingual situation created areas of the city that were utterly antagonistic to the notion of a homogeneous America, as was clearly the case in "Jewtown": "Pushing, struggling, babbling, and shouting in foreign tongues, a veritable Babel of confusion. An English word falls upon the ear almost with a sense of shock, as something unexpected and strange." Echoing Howells's description of the large number of Chinese in Chinatown, rendering "not them, but what was foreign to them, strange there," many Americans were beginning to feel culturally foreign in their native land.[19] The fact that New York contained areas where English was "practically an unknown tongue" was seen by Riis as a direct cause of poverty, crime, immorality, anarchy, insanity, and disease. It also signaled differences within the nation detrimental to its cultural vitality: "They must be taught the language of the country they have chosen as their home, as the first and most necessary step. Whatever may follow, that is essential, absolutely vital. That done, it may well be that the case in its new aspect will not be nearly so hard to deal with."[20]

The fear that New York City was becoming a modern-day Babel was part of the wider concern about the degeneration of the urban tongue. Despite some serious philological interest in the phenomena of urban dialect, most observers thought that newspaper English, commercial advertisements, and the slang of city life were powerful agents of cultural disease.[21] For the verbal critic Richard Grant White, newspapers were so dangerous linguistically because they catered to "the heterogeneous public of the large cities of a country in which every other Irish hackman and hodman keeps . . . his editor."[22] Urban language had begun to seem alien to polite, middle-class ears: already in the 1860s, Horatio Alger had implied that urban slang constituted a "peculiar way of speaking," partially unintelligible to the uninitiated.[23] Myths of rural value pervaded the study of popular speech in the 1890s, making urban dialect seem foreign to ideal conceptions of folk language. Even attempts to justify the existence of slang, by showing it to be "the source from which the decaying energies of speech are constantly refreshed," made an important qualification: "the slang of the metropolis," wrote Brander Matthews, "is nearly always stupid. . . . this use of slang is far more frequent in cities, where people often talk without having anything to say, than in the country, where speech flows slowly." While the language of the West was energetic and motivated, the language of the city comprised fleeting words, "doubtful in meaning and obscure in origin." Matthews gave the example of *growler* (a can used to transport beer from a bar to a private house) as a typically bastardized word without etymological pedigree. Just as the life of New York's urban poor was a mystery to many Americans, so too was the language of urbanization confusing and strange. The most mysterious New York expression—"Cheese it!"—was, disturbingly, its commonest.[24]

Contemporary, urban, and lower class, slang was seen as "coarse" and "foolish"—the degenerate language of America's "age of retrogression."[25] The rise to prominence of "low life" values made the spoken culture of the city as a whole seem every day more foreign to genteel traditions. For a writer in *The Critic* in 1897, "slanguage" was a major force to be reckoned with: it "has attained to such a luxurious completeness that it warrants serious treatment. So copious and comprehensive has it become that there is hardly a human want, feeling, or emotion of the heart, that cannot be translated into this vernacular of the bootblack. . . .

Not only does the slanguist find ordinary English tame, but he ends in
not being able to find any English at all."[26] No longer an occasional
phrase inserted into an otherwise "correct" speech—as Horatio Alger's
novels had described it[27]—city slang replaced conventional English fundamentally; it was imagined (most often by those wishing to emphasize
fears of national fragmentation) as a language of absolute cultural otherness that remained virtually inarticulate to the "proper" speaker. Swearing and blasphemy were the most powerful and controversial elements of
slang, signaling its total antagonism to polite notions of national character. According to evangelical tracts of the era, an urban culture of swearing thrived; blasphemy punctuated virtually every phrase of city speech:

> There is to-day in all our land no more prevalent custom, and no more God-
> defying abomination, than profane swearing. You can hardly walk our streets
> five minutes without having your ears stung and your sensibilities shocked.
> The drayman swearing at his horse; the tinman at his solder; the sewing-girl
> imprecating her tangled thread; the bricklayer cursing at his trowel; the
> carpenter at his plane; the sailor at the tackling; the merchant at the cus-
> tomer; the customer at the merchant; the printer at the miserable proof-
> sheet; the accountant at the troublesome line of figures;—swearing in the
> cellar and in the loft, before the counter and behind the counter, in the
> shop and on the street, in low saloon and fashionable bar-room.[28]

There were, then, two different sides to the new language developing
in New York. The native, working-class population was speaking a slangy,
blasphemous dialect that seemed radically separate from traditional English. And the alien quality of this tongue was exacerbated by the immigrant impact on the city. Ironically, the very process anticipated by Jacob
Riis, in which the foreign immigrant would become Americanized
through the acquisition of the English language, was inherently disruptive
to dominant cultural values. Americanization was not simply a progression
into a well-defined and fixed culture, nor was the learning of English
dictated by an otherwise "pure" language of the native inhabitants of the
city. Instead, the Americanization of the immigrant altered the very notion
of Americanness, and the acquisition of the American language became
a register of the effect that different ethnic groups were having on English
itself. The spoken language of New York revealed the cultural fusion of a
melting-pot situation—a fusion that became a disruptive reality when the
ingredients entering the pot were, it seemed, increasingly "more foreign."[29]

The prominent chronicler of New York life Julian Ralph wrote an article entitled "Language of the Tenement-folk" (1897): "The present
interest in our tenement population cannot bring to general knowledge
anything about the city's masses that is more unlike what is found else-

where than the language that has grown up among these people, and is now learned, *as if it were English,* by the new-comers from every quarter of the globe." The various ethnic groups of the city, through the process in which they acquired English, played an integral part in the creation of a unique city dialect spoken by the vast working-class population of the tenements, a dialect that was not quite English but only spoken "as if it were." If labor was beginning to seem a foreign culture in the Gilded Age, then the spoken language of these urban laborers also borrowed heavily from the city's international communities. According to Ralph, "[o]ur people of the streets are seldom so erudite as to nickname their neighbors with words taken from the tongues those people speak": hence "Sheeny" for Jew and "Dago" for Italian.[30]

The merging of foreign and native elements was creating what Ralph called a New Yorkese dialect that reached "the dignity of an accomplishment if not of a language" and was used by "such distinguished exponents as Senators and city officials." It was a "fluent East-side New Yorkese" that had become an even more evolved and "wonderful tongue" by the time Henry James visited the city in 1904, and wrote of his experiences in *The American Scene* (1907).[31] For James, the question of what the new public would be, in a city defined by "such a prodigious amalgam, such a hotch-potch of racial ingredients," was especially pertinent to "our language as literature has hitherto known it." The destruction of "the linguistic tradition" led James to consider east-side cafés as "torture-rooms of the living idiom":

> the piteous gasp of which at the portent of lacerations to come could reach me in any drop of the surrounding Accent of the Future. The accent of the very ultimate future, in the States, may be destined to become the most beautiful on the globe and the very music of humanity (here the "ethnic" synthesis shrouds itself thicker than ever); but whatever we shall know it for, certainly, we shall not know it for English—in any sense of which there is an existing literary measure.

James was concerned with the communication breakdown that arose from this multilingual condition: he was met with staring silence by the Italian diggers he encountered on the New Jersey shore, and he could find no language to communicate with a wandering Armenian in the New Hampshire hills. Yet James's main interest was not in conflict but amalgamation. The written culture of the city had already begun to register the presence of the newcomer: in an effort to attract immigrants away from a thriving foreign-language press, the daily newspaper had simplified its vocabulary, making itself more intelligible to the least-instructed reader.[32] James analyzed the spoken manifestations of this process in which immigrant groups helped to effect total transformations in the modes of American culture. The ethnic synthesis of "that babel of tongues"—thought James—was producing changes beyond the bounds of ghetto life. The city's language of wider communication was a fusion of national tongues that would eventually make it unrecognizable according to English norms. Echoing Howells's comments on the "composite and strange" language of New York City—potentially as different from English as Yiddish is from Hebrew—James saw the developing urban tongue as an integral and complete language variety, radically foreign to contemporary standards.[33]

For commentators on the New York scene at the end of the nineteenth century, the English language was an important agent of American values, but also the clearest illustration of the nation's social transformation and cultural contamination. The vocal culture of New York City was becoming alien to linguistic traditions in two interrelated ways: through the supposed moral degeneration of industrial life, and through the hybridity of ethnic contact. The New Yorkese dialect may have been a worry to critics of urbanization; for Stephen Crane and Abraham Cahan, however, this new dialect became a tool of literary experimentation, a crucial means of structuring urban experience.

"WHAT DEH HELL?": STEPHEN CRANE'S BAD LANGUAGE

Then, too, you give too complete a picture of the vulgar and profane talk of your characters; much less of this would be more effective and less offensive. The finest art in the writing of fiction is suggestion. It seems to me, for example, that you have overworked the expression, "What deh Hell?" I find it hard to believe that it would be used at all in several of the situations in which your characters have used it. But, of course, I may be all wrong about this.

JOHN BARRY TO STEPHEN CRANE, 22 MARCH 1893, QUOTED IN WERTHEIM, ED., 3

In a favorable early review, Hamlin Garland argued that Stephen Crane's *Maggie: A Girl of the Streets* offered an inside view of the linguistic reality of the New York slums. *Maggie* "is not written by a *dilettante;* it is written by one who has lived the life. The young author, Stephen Crane, is a native of the city, and has grown up in the very scenes he describes. His book . . . has no conventional phrases. It gives the dialect of the slums as I have never before seen it written—crisp, direct, terse. It is another locality finding a voice."[34] Recent critics have supported this idea. Frank Bergon argues that Crane managed "to present for the first time this lower class of society from a seriously rendered, insider's point of view."[35] Alan Trachtenberg reads Crane's 1894 newspaper sketches for the *New York Press*—"An Experiment in Misery" and "The Men in the Storm"—as rejections of the picturesque perspective and sentimentality that marked attempts to access "low life" by moral philanthropists like Jacob Riis. Instead, Crane approaches "a true exchange of point of view with the 'other half'"; he transcends traditional east-side inquiries by revealing to us the subjective reality, the "inner structure of feeling" of the slums.[36]

"An Experiment in Misery" records a young man's attempt to discover the "point of view or something near it" (31) of the urban poor by entering the underworld disguised as a tramp. Just as Garland linked urban realism to issues of voice, this experiment is a particularly vocal experience. The young man is rapidly incorporated into the linguistic environment of the city. He falls into a state of profound dejection when "he was so completely plastered with yells of 'bum' and 'hobo,' and with various unholy epithets that small boys had applied to him at intervals" (31). Thus labeled by the slang of the city, the young man penetrates further into New York: he is "swallowed" by the swinging doors, "snapping to and fro like ravenous lips," of a saloon that advertises free hot soup on a "delectable sign" (32–33). As he travels deeper into this world, acquiring "bum" dialect as he goes, the young man finally enters a cheap lodging-house—filled with the "exhalations from a hundred pairs of reeking lips" (35)—where he hears the "long wails that went almost like yells from a hound," emerging from a dreaming man "oppressed by some frightful calamity" (37). The young man strives to give symbolic significance to the "shrieks" and "melancholy moans" of this animalistic utterance (37). It gains the eloquence of another language— the voice of "a whole section, a class, a people" (37)—marking the young man's entrance into another "country" in his descent to trampdom (32), and matching the contemporary idea that the New Yorkese dialect behaved like a foreign tongue. Although his encounter with the "impersonal eloquence" (37) of this wailing enables the young man to construct "biographies for these men from his meager experience" (38), the final point of "An Experiment in Misery" is not that the young man enters the inner life of the slums. As he confesses at the end of the sketch, the young man is finally unable to exchange perspectives with the tramp.[37] His culminating vision is of the urban poor as a foreign entity within the nation—virtually an ethnic group in their own right—powerless to interpret the city's "confusion of strange tongues, babbling heedlessly" (42).[38] If city language appears alien to tramps, bum dialect seems equally inarticulate to outsiders. The sketch might promise to translate "low life" language, yet the final impression is that the urban poor speak in yells, wails, moans, and shrieks.

Crane's novel *Maggie* also stresses this inarticulate quality of slum talk, as Howells realized in his 1896 discussion of "New York Low Life in Fiction." Although *Maggie* was praised for its realistic rendition of Bowery language, the blasphemy and obscenity within this urban dialect troubled many of Crane's earliest readers.[39] *Maggie* was repeatedly refused publication because of the profane discourse of its characters, not because of candid physical details concerning drunkenness, prostitution, or urban squalor. Richard Watson Gilder offered Crane's language as his excuse for not publishing *Maggie* in its 1893 form, forcing Crane to print the novel privately in the same year. Howells's fear that *Maggie* was doomed likewise arose from his belief that such profane parlance would offend cultured ears: "All its conscience and all its art could not save it, and it will probably remain unknown, but it embodied perhaps the best tough dialect which has yet found its way into print." Other critics commented that *Maggie* included dialect too brutal to "find acceptance among the better and purer classes of the reading world."[40] *Maggie* fell victim to what Robert Stallman calls the "aesthetic malady" of the 1890s: the "obsession with the idea that art aims to inspire, please, and enlighten by tender and uplifting sentiments."[41] In its presentation of the new dialect of the city—a dialect entirely foreign to literary ideals—*Maggie* was revolutionary. When the characters in the novel said "What d' hell?" the gatekeepers of literary propriety trembled.

Howells felt there was an absolute difference between the speech of Crane's characters and the speech meant for "cultured ears": the "*language itself*" was decayed, not just elements within it.[42] Crane's language, clearly dissimilar to that of realists such as James or Howells himself, likewise differed from other more conventional attempts to fictionalize the "low life" of New York City at the time, for example Edward W. Townsend's popular *Chimmie Fadden* stories. These stories concern the interaction of a Bowery "tough," Chimmie Fadden, with the politer society of New York, and are full of supposed comedy arising from the conflict between two linguistic registers:

> "'Yer dead on,' says I.
> "'Wot t'ell?' 'e says, turning to 'is daughter. 'Wot does de young man say?' 'e says.
> "Den the loidy she kinder smiled—say, yer otter seed 'er smile. Say, it's outter sight. Dat's right. Well, she says: 'I tink I understan' Chimmie's langwudge,' she says. "E means 'e is de kid yuse lookin' fer. 'E's der very mug.' . . .
> "Naw, not dem words, but dat's wat dey means. Say, a felley can't allus be 'memberin' just de words dose folks use. But dat's wot dey means."[43]

Designed for the polite readers of New York's literary magazines, Chimmie Fadden is the lovable rogue with a heart of gold, who punches people in the nose only when so instructed by his wealthy employers. These stories demystify "low life"; they make New York's "dangerous classes" seem sentimental, romantic, and therefore harmless to the social elite. Further-more, by making Chimmie Fadden the speaking narrator of his own sto-ries, these tales exploit a degree of vernacular eloquence—they were noted for "vivid language" which "infected the nation."[44] Although the notion of native New Yorkers speaking different idioms was threatening to the ideal of national homogeneity, the profane blasphemy of Chim-mie's speech remained uncensored because it was represented in a dia-lectal "langwudge," separate from the refined language of the reader: the obvious example is the transformation of Chimmie's *the hell* into "t'ell." By exploiting this "low life" language as eloquent yet other, Townsend created a romantic fiction of working-class speech that was palatable to America's sensitive reading public.

Maggie's tough speech rejects this dialect tradition; Crane replaces un-conventional eloquence with inarticulation, humor with blasphemy. The difference between two linguistic worlds, which dialect writers had typi-cally exploited, becomes a source of violent conflict rather than gentle comedy. Take, for example, the scene in which the beggar-woman who lives in Maggie's tenement, and who later shields Maggie from the hy-pocritical moral righteousness of her family, is arrested for stealing a purse dropped in the street by a "lady":

> When she was arrested she had cursed the lady into a partial swoon, and with her aged limbs, twisted from rheumatism, had almost kicked the stom-ach out of a huge policeman whose conduct upon that occasion she referred to when she said, "The police, damn 'em." [16]

Here, dialectal difference initiates brutal social antagonism. Slum dialect seems a physical force with the power to assault the higher social classes. It is a blasphemous register of resistance, used against the social authority of the police. The narrator himself also participates in the inflated, de-valued phrases of the tenements whereby "low" people talk in oaths that promise cataclysmic physical events. The phrase "kicked the stomach out of," in its graphic, violent exaggeration, is reminiscent of vernacular phrases like "I'll stamp yer damn brains under me feet" (39) employed by characters in the novel.[45] Not only does Crane exploit the contrast between the bathetic colloquial language of his characters and the ele-vated literary language of the narrator, as critics of *Maggie* have noted; there are also clear examples of a linguistic overlap between character and narrator, where the violent nature of narrative description comes di-rectly from slum talk.[46] We are a long way from *Chimmie Fadden*.

According to his critics, Crane's profane dialect was an antiliterary lan-guage: it was not suitable for America's reading public because it rejected the moral conventions of the literary establishment, and the genteel hu-mor of the dialect tradition.[47] Indeed, one problem detected by editors and reviewers of the 1893 *Maggie* was that Crane's slum speech was frequently not dialectal enough. Whereas Townsend disguised blasphemy as the dialectal "t'ell," Crane insisted on leaving *hell* in its conventional spelling. Significantly, the only piece of obvious blasphemy allowed to remain uncensored in the 1896 *Maggie* is from the fat German who owns the collar and cuff factory where Maggie works: his *by damn* is left in the dialect version of "py tamn," and *in hell* as "een hale" (52). In one sense, dialect was an alternative, non-threatening register. Spelling bad language as dialect reduced it to a separate and lower level, of no ethical danger to polite readers: it was clearly a language spoken only by others. As a tool of propriety, dialect spelling was a register that Crane refused to exploit.

Criticism of the depiction of speech in the 1893 *Maggie* greatly affected Crane's literary language. The new version published by Appleton's in 1896 presented *Maggie* in what Crane admitted to be "quite a new aspect." As Crane confessed to an editor at Appleton's, he had "dispensed with a goodly number of damns," and had "carefully plugged at the words which hurt."[48] In the 1896 version people tend to "storm" and "brag" rather than "swear" and "curse," signaling a general decrease in spoken profanity. The 1896 *Maggie* was a much politer text. Crane was also forced to remove the derogatory term "micks" (7), replacing it with "mugs," and he deleted references to the larger ethnic tensions of the Bowery: for example, the fact that the music-hall crowd who sing the "Star-Spangled Banner" are mostly of "foreign birth" (32–33). The most significant alteration, however, was the removal of explicitly blasphemous language from *Maggie*'s "mouths of sin" (52). Over seventy references to hell, more than fifty uses of *damn*, and around twenty direct invocations of God were edited out of the 1896 text—an enormous change for such a short novel.[49] The characters simultaneously became less profane, less repetitive, and more articulate, chiefly because they were compelled to replace "hells" and "damns" with a variety of other colloquial comments.

Crane's altered representation of speech meant that the dictates of moral propriety in the 1890s had beaten a writer untroubled by many of the niceties of literary convention (his spelling, for example, often left much to be desired).[50] There are, however, key moments of resistance to this general cleaning-up of language: Crane occasionally retains *hell* and *damn* in their censored forms, "h—ll" and "d—n." This is crucial to the thematic purpose of Crane's profane dialect, which is to emphasize a world in which orthodox moral and religious values have become meaningless. Thus, when Pete says, "Ah, what d' h—ll!" his voice is "burdened with disdain for the inevitable and contempt for anything that fate might compel him to endure" (26). His speech emphasizes his hatred of Christians and his belief in nothing.[51] And when the narrator inserts an anonymous "What d' h—ll?" into the text, it is to emphasize a nihilistic point—"in this world, souls did not insist upon being able to smile" (65). The final scene of the novel, in which the women of Maggie's tenement forgive her in a "vocabulary . . . derived from mission churches" (75), ironically emphasizes the insignificance of orthodox religious sentiment, a triviality underscored earlier when Maggie seeks the "Grace of God" from a clergyman but is rejected with a "convulsive movement" that "saved his respectability by a vigorous sidestep" (67). Although Crane was allowed to leave uncensored the references to "D' Lord" in the final scene of the novel, these phrases only stress the brutal hypocrisy of a religious sentiment based on superficial respectability and the perfunctory nature of its linguistic codes. Attention to the textual politics of *Maggie* reveals much more than Crane's resistance to the reassuring atmosphere of the dialect tradition: it demonstrates his profound assault upon conventional morality and upon the significance of religious discourse.

To a large degree, Gilded Age debates over both urban and literary language sought to polarize speech into opposite moral registers. The polite, public, virtuous discourse of conventional moral values was seen as the antithesis of the vulgar, blasphemous, degenerate dialect of the slums. Crane grew up in an environment of religious fundamentalism (his parents were "hard-preaching" Methodist ministers from New Jersey), and he was undoubtedly aware of the vocal politics of evangelical tracts such as Talmage's *The Abominations of Modern Society* (1872), which lambasted the nation's sinful urban dialect of "wild shriek[s]" and "agonizing wail[s]" of despair.[52] This brand of religious work, with its harsh linguistic moralizing, was of fundamental importance to the themes and to the narrative structure of *Maggie*. This is clear in the strange scene in which Maggie's brother, Jimmie, visits a local mission church:

> He clad his soul in armor by means of happening hilariously in at a mission church where a man composed his sermons of "you's." Once a philosopher asked this man why he did not say "we" instead of "you." The man replied, "What?"
> While they got warm at the stove, he told his hearers just where he calculated they stood with the Lord. Many of the sinners were impatient over the pictured depths of their degradation. They were waiting for soup-tickets.
> A reader of words of wind-demons might have been able to see the portions of dialogue pass to and fro between the exhorter and his hearers.
> "You are damned," said the preacher. And the reader of sounds might have seen the reply go forth from the ragged people: "Where's our soup?" [20]

The horrified reply "What?" to the suggestion that there might be no distinction between the righteous and the sinful foreshadowed the reaction of the literary establishment to Crane's urban realism. Reviewers would be similarly horrified that the sacred realms of literature were infiltrated by moral reprobates, just as they would be shocked that literary language was so contaminated with blasphemy. Crane further develops the conflict between ethical languages in his reference to two types of reader: the "reader of words of wind-demons" and the "reader of sounds." The first is a self-righteous reader, concerned to observe the words of the city's "demons"—malignant spirits—and thereby judge that they are damned. Yet the wails and blasphemies of New York are also presented for the "reader of sounds" who is concerned with the objective presence of words rather than their conventional value: the reader interested in perceiving the "other half" of this class dialogue with an ear to what the masses say rather than how their language stands in terms of traditional religious morality. It is a reader who sees that the reality of the situation concerns soup and not the words of the Lord.

If *Maggie* challenges the ethical codes of the "reader of words of wind-demons," however, it also reveals to the "reader of sounds" the emptiness of subaltern speech. *Maggie* might collapse the hierarchy of conventional dialect writing by revealing the moral bankruptcy of genteel discourse, but this does not mean that Crane accordingly elevates the rugged reality of the vernacular over the corrupt language of polite society. At the center of *Maggie* are the environmental conditions that create a cacophonous, anarchic verbal culture. It is a world of shouting, "repellent dialogue," and "noise," as early reviewers of the novel noted. To read *Maggie*, thought one London critic, "is to put one's ears into the bell of a cornet blown by giant lungs. It leaves one limp, exhausted, mistreated."[53] Howells perceptively realized that the New York of "inarticulate or blasphemous life" was the source of Crane's inspiration.[54] Crane maintains enough blasphemous language (albeit in a bowdlerized form) in the 1896 *Maggie* to emphasize the fact that Maggie's mother and father "damned each other's souls with frequence" (13), that their home is a "reg'lar livin' hell" (17), and that Maggie is damned and sent to hell by her family before she even sins (41). The novel's first scene—the conflict between the youths of Rum Alley and Devil's Row—sets the tone for the work as a whole: the reader is accosted by a dissonant world of wrathful howls, "great crimson oaths," barbaric swearing, "roaring curses," "blasphemous chatter," savage songs, and lurid swearing (7–10). In *Maggie* people communicate with howls (13), roaring (16), hoarse shouting (16), feeble moaning (16), bass muttering (16), volcanic bursts (17), wailings (23), hooting (36), irrelevant remarks (37), wrathful snorting (39), cursing trebles (39), jeering cat-calls (39), shrieks (40), screeching (40), hoarse whispering (48), low hisses (48), gibbering (48), loud railing (63), and screams like wounded animals (64). The narrator employs an extensive vocabulary to describe the very absence of coherent vocabulary in his characters.

If there is poetry in Crane's Bowery dialect, as critics have claimed, then it is one of inarticulation and blasphemy, an antipoetry in which repetition does not bind and unify—as Richard Bridgman says of the colloquial style—but signals an inability to express or comprehend the situation.[55] Crane attempted to follow Howells's exhortation to depict the community rather than the fragmentation of working-class life in *Maggie*'s sequel, *George's Mother* (1896).[56] Yet the momentary ability of a group of male friends to speak thoughts "without fear of being misunderstood" turns out to be a drunken, valueless expression that disappears with the next day's hangover—it was "the whiskey talking" (129, 128). Or when Crane dwells on the violent power of cursing, as he does in his sketch "The Men in the Storm," he stresses the pointlessness of breaking norms, the desperate meaninglessness of impotent rage (27). Drunken speech typifies Crane's view of "low life" language as a whole; it is repetitious, blasphemous, clichéd, incoherent, and inane: "Yehs knows, damn it, yehs kin have all I got, 'cause I'm stuck on yehs, Nell, damn 't, I—I'm stuck on yehs, Nell—buy drinksh—damn 't—we're havin' heluva time—w'en anyone trea's me ri'—I—damn 't, Nell—we're havin' heluva—time" (*Maggie*, 74). Crane's drunken speech demonstrates not "psychological nuances"—as Bridgman suggests—so much as psychological and communicative collapse.[57]

Next to Chimmie Fadden's vernacular, Crane's dialect seems a degenerate antilanguage. His tenement talk is in constant rebellion against religious and moral codes that ironically embody hypocrisy and insincerity. We saw in earlier chapters how regional writers of the 1870s and '80s were ambivalent about vernacular language: Mark Twain's *Roughing It* (1872), for example, simultaneously exalts and censures the colloquial West. In *Maggie*, however, this ambivalence is replaced by an absolute skepticism that condemns both the vernacular and the standard without any hint of celebration. When Pete has a violent encounter with an upper-class "chump," the reader is trapped between two equally contemptible discourses: the chump's arrogant, effete accusation that Pete is an insolent ruffian, and Pete's inane reply: "'Oh, gee,' I says, 'oh, gee, go t' hell an' git off d'eart'!' I says, like dat. See? 'Go t' hell an' git off d'eart',' like dat" (27). A similar collapse of opposing moral languages is found in the novel's juxtaposition of the meaningless speech of characters and the romantic, over-literary language of the narrator, which describes slum life with inappropriate and clichéd metaphors: "Under the trees of her dream-gardens," the narrator says of Maggie, "there had always walked a lover" (26). The narrator's language has become contaminated by the characters' inappropriately romantic conceptions of themselves. Both languages, the colloquial and the literary, represent a falsified worldview based on worn-out conventions.[58]

Critical commentary on *Maggie*'s stylistic self-consciousness, in which "the reader is obliged to wonder which, if any, of the book's rival languages, the language of the narrator or the language of the street, is authorized by the author," has called into question the belief that Crane wrote typical naturalist fiction.[59] Naturalist texts traditionally suggest environmental determinism, yet Crane emphasizes how characters fall victim to their own pretensions: they are deluded by inappropriate, outworn, and misunderstood modes of interpreting reality.[60] James Nagel, for example, dismisses the naturalistic determinism of *Maggie* by focusing on the visuality of the novel: he argues that Crane's fiction is predominantly impressionistic rather than naturalistic because it focuses on personal self-delusion and distorted perception.[61] Such claims about visuality, however, miss the fact that Crane's characters are members of a community of degenerate *vocal* expression that precludes the act of thought, rendering them powerless to assign meaning to their world. Characters are not completely stupid in *Maggie*, but at key moments in the novel cognition collapses because the linguistic tools of thought become incoherent. Jimmie tries but fails to formulate thoughts about Maggie's downfall, breaking instead into meaningless swearing and violent action (43–44). Maggie's bewilderment when she loses her lover, Pete, is a direct result of an instance in which she "could not find speech" (67)—indeed, the reason she loses Pete to the "woman of brilliance and audacity" in the first place is her inability "to formulate an intelligent sentence" upon the conversation (58). Maggie is increasingly baffled by surrounding forces: her moral dilemma can only be expressed by the sudden, solipsistic question "Who?" which remains meaningless and comical to those around her (67). Paralleling the ending of Crane's "An Experiment in Misery," Maggie's final alienation and death are marked by her total exclusion from a world of language—she is shut out of the city by the closed "grim lips" of buildings, while the "sounds of life" are impossibly distant (70). The determinism of *Maggie* derives from the linguistic deficiencies of its characters: their inarticulate failure to command language renders them victims of incomprehensible situations.

In naturalist works such as Frank Norris's *Vandover and the Brute* (written 1894–95) and *McTeague* (1899), and Theodore Dreiser's *Sister Carrie* (1900), the forces of the modern city again render characters either slangy or inarticulate. Carrie's near voicelessness (when she does speak, in the play at the end of the novel, she barely knows what her words and actions mean) corresponds to the narrator's repeated skepticism over the efficacy of spoken language: "How true it is that words are but the vague shadows of the volumes we mean. Little audible links, they are, chaining together great inaudible feelings and purposes." Although Norris's McTeague has difficulty constructing coherent sentences, Vandover becomes completely inarticulate: his degeneration into brutishness leads him to snarl and bark like a dog. In these more explicitly naturalistic works, however, spoken language collapses when it is superseded by universal forces beyond the control of individuals. In *Sister Carrie*, words are unimportant because characters' feelings are dictated by strange chemo-electrical forces that pervade and determine the universe, and in *Vandover and the Brute* language breaks down because the self is crushed by "the great, mysterious force that spun the wheels of Nature and that sent it onward like some enormous engine, resistless, relentless."[62] Language, that is, falls victim to a determining yet meaningless materialism. In *Maggie*, however, the opposite holds: characters are victims of a deficient language. Their powerlessness to control life stems from their membership in a degenerate culture that lacks the ability to communicate or—at times—to think.[63] The world is meaningless because dominated not by incoherent materialistic forces, but by a blasphemous doom, an "unceasing babble of tongues" (*Maggie*, 64), a cacophony of animalistic shrieks and wailings. The determinism of *Maggie* arises not from chaotic and universal forces, but from a society in which the only alternative to an incoherent, inarticulate working class is a culture of supposed moral authority whose words are equally bankrupt.[64]

The more sympathetic of Crane's early reviewers noticed that the young novelist was not simply attempting to shock with crude speech, but that the spoken voice was of fundamental importance to his art, the very inspiration of his literary style.[65] Although many critics considered his New Yorkese to be dangerously realistic, Crane's primary purpose was not the authenticity of inside perspective.[66] Instead, Crane manipulated the dialect of his characters, and the theme of vocal culture in general, to assault romantic and morally condescending depictions of New York "low life"— depictions that naively presupposed genuine access to the reality of the slums. Rather than appropriating the urban poor, Crane emphasized their increasing alienation from the nation's cultural traditions by representing their strange, inarticulate tongue. He exploited the collapse of working-class speech, moreover, to stress a wider incoherence in established values. By combining decayed slum talk with the representation of an equally corrupt elite discourse, Crane echoed the most troubling element within linguistic investigations of New York City at the end of the nineteenth century: the idea that forces of degeneration were not just present in minority speech but were contaminating the conventional forms of mainstream language.

THE AMBIVALENCE OF ABRAHAM CAHAN

Abraham Cahan arrived in New York City from Russia in 1882 with little English and a deep knowledge of Yiddish culture and Russian literature. His subsequent immersion in American culture and in the Jewish ghetto of New York's Lower East Side produced a series of literary works in the English language: a short novel, *Yekl: A Tale of the New York Ghetto* (1896); a collection of short stories, *The Imported Bridegroom* (1898); and a long novel, *The Rise of David Levinsky* (1917)—a work that looks back to the last decades of the nineteenth century.[67] It was Cahan's status as an ethnic immigrant that intrigued his early readers. Although Howells was disturbed by Crane's "dreadful" and "hopeless" urban picture, he enjoyed the vitality of humor and imagination in *Yekl.* That vitality stemmed, in part, from Cahan's ability to allow the reader access to the new, multicultural world of New York City: "He is already thoroughly naturalized to our point of view; he sees things with American eyes, and he brings in aid of his vision the far and rich perceptions of the Hebrew race."[68] Alarmist reactions to the foreign contamination of American culture were common, as we saw in discussions of New Yorkese. It is more difficult to find accounts of how these impacts were felt in the opposite direction: how Yiddish was transformed by contact with English, for example, and how the languages and cultures of ethnic others were transformed by their contact with America. Cahan's English prose translated the Yiddish-speaking world of the eastern European Jewish immigrant, both for mainstream readers like Howells and for a Jewish audience comprised largely of American-born Jews—predominantly of German origin—who looked upon the new influx of their co-religionists with interest and some trepidation.[69]

The fact that Cahan *needed* to explain the inner life of the New York ghetto to a wider American readership presented difficulties of its own. The purported speech of African Americans and Irish Americans may have entered literature in a clichéd, oftentimes racist way after the Civil War, yet the existence of these stereotypes gave minority writers a tradition within which to represent alternative versions of ethnic life. Yiddish, however, was a foreign language to most American readers, and the developing Yiddish-influenced English dialects of the ghetto were not nearly as easily recognized or as acceptable as an Irish brogue.[70] Cahan's first novel, *Yekl,* is necessarily a delicate foray into uncharted cultural and linguistic terrain. To explain Yekl's Yiddish pronunciation, Cahan borrows from the better-known perspective: "his r's could do credit to the thickest Irish brogue" (3). Rather than exploiting the "mispronounced" English of the Yiddish speaker for comic effect, Cahan reverses the equation by revealing the inner humor of the Jewish community—a humor typically arising from linguistic contact. *Yekl* presents jokes based on the juxtaposition of American customs and Hebrew writing practices;[71] on the puns that arise from ironic similarities between English and Yiddish words (the fact that English *dinner* is Yiddish *thinner*, for example [80]); and on the process by which the immigrant assimilates the American language ("'America for a country and *'dod'll do'* [that'll do] for a language!' observed one of the young men of the group, indulging one of the stereotype jokes of the Ghetto" [44–45]). Outsiders often found easy comedy in the linguistic insecurity of ethnic groups. Cahan disarms such superficial interpretation by describing the humor within the immigrant experience itself.

Cahan's concern to show the linguistic basis of ethnic humor is part of a wider exploration of the links between language, culture, and self—links realized by the narrator of *The Rise of David Levinsky*. He finds it impossible to understand his English teacher's explanation of the differences between the perfect and imperfect tenses:

> The trouble with him [the teacher] was that he pictured the working of a foreigner's mind, with regard to English, as that of his own. It did not occur to him that people born to speak another language were guided by another language logic, so to say, and that in order to reach my understanding he would have to impart his ideas in terms of my own linguistic psychology. [134][72]

Throughout his fiction, Cahan used questions of language to translate the psychological and cultural transformations of the ethnic self. In his journalistic prose for Lincoln Steffens's *Commercial Advertiser*, Cahan forged "authenticity and power" by combining the diverse tongues of the city;[73] the language of characters in his fiction, however, gives a more jarring account of cultural interaction and merger. Rather than either authenticity or power, the speech of Cahan's ghetto dwellers often reveals conflict, corruption, and insecurity, as we shall see later in the chapter. This less positive side of Cahan's rendition of immigrant language has provoked the criticism that he perpetuates demeaning stereotypes, thus compromising his own attempts at ethnic representation.[74] I suggest, however, that the negative elements in Cahan's depiction of immigrant vocal culture stem not from artistic limitation but from a commitment to explore the ambiguity and tension in situations of acculturation.

Cahan's representation of the spoken voice embodies the larger social forces surrounding the Americanizing immigrant. Nowhere is this clearer than in his rendition of the Yiddish spoken by Yekl (or to use his American name, "Jake"):

"When I was in Boston," [Jake] went on, with a contemptuous mien intended for the American metropolis, "I knew a *feller*, so he was a *preticly*
friend of John Shullivan's. He is a Christian, that feller is, and yet the two
of us lived like brothers. May I be unable to move from this spot if we did
not. How, then, would you have it? Like here, in New York, where the Jews
are a *lot* of *greenhornsh* and can not speak a word of English? Over there
every Jew speaks English like a stream." [3]

The attempt to translate Yiddish rhythms and metaphors into English was
a common device, reaching its comic apotheosis in Montague Glass's
"Potash and Perlmutter" stories, early in the twentieth century.[75] Cahan's
main interest, however, lies with linguistic fusion: the incorporation of
English words into Yiddish, a result of the "omnivorous Jewish jargon"
(*Yekl*, 81) devouring the linguistic material of its new American environment. Throughout *Yekl* and his early stories, Cahan translates the Yiddish
of characters into "correct" (albeit ornate) English while leaving incorporated English words in their misspelled, italicized forms: *feller* ("fellow"), for example, or *preticly* (perhaps "particular"). Speech thus represents the cultural intermixture arising from contact between the
immigrant and American society, an intermixture captured in remarkably
hybrid sentences—"Don't you always say you like to *dansh* with me *becush*
I am a good *dansher*?" (*Yekl*, 41)—and even in individual words like *oyshgreen:* "A verb coined from the Yiddish *oys*, out, and the English *green*, and
signifying to cease being green" (95n).

This narrative technique also represents a reversal of perspective,
whereby English becomes the contaminating element within another language. The Americanization of Yiddish is given from a Yiddish perspective.
English words are thrown back—*rulesh* ("rules"), *deshepoitn* ("disap-
point"), *saresfied* ("satisfied")—transformed and defamiliarized by their
inclusion in another linguistic system. Just as Yiddish becomes Americanized in *Yekl*, American English becomes Yiddishized: transformative linguistic contact is shown as a two-way process. English is the "official language" of the Jewish dancing academy that Jake attends, an institution
essential to the Americanization of the immigrant. Yet this English remains "broken and mispronounced in as many different ways as there
were Yiddish dialects represented in that institution" (36). Real contact
between Yiddish speakers and New York's English-speaking population is
shown to be rare (51). Without access to a unified prestige speech, immigrant English remains a standardless conglomeration of various language-contact situations. The "official" immigrant language is therefore
inherently unstable.[76]

Jacob Riis had described east-side New York as a "queer conglomerate
mass of heterogeneous elements."[77] Cahan's literary dialect shows how

this variety also characterized the inner workings of a single immigrant group. Whether it concerns the difference between Boston and New York Yiddish, the different standards of English employed by men and women, or the radical difference between the dialect of the Polish-American Jew and the greenhorn Russian Jew, the ghetto is an exceptionally heterogeneous place.[78] "You find there . . . people with all sorts of antecedents, tastes, habits, inclinations, and speaking all sorts of subdialects of the same jargon, thrown pellmell into one social caldron—a human hodgepodge with its component parts changed but not yet fused into one homogeneous whole" (*Yekl*, 29–30). Just as cultural diversity in the United States was thought to be modifying American English after the Civil War, Cahan shows that similar processes operated in the Jewish community itself. A variety of Yiddish dialects were being transformed in complex ways: Jake's lover, Mamie, for example, speaks "the dialect of the Polish Jews," which is both "affectedly Germanized and profusely interspersed with English" (105). Without a firm linguistic standard in place, aspects of these Yiddish peculiarities determine the developing dialects of immigrant English. Both in Yiddish and in English, the ghetto is a confused area of intra-ethnic diversity.

From this chaotic situation, however, a pattern develops. Just as Jake-Yekl is disgusted by his recently arrived wife's greenhorn appearance and un-American Yiddish but is unable to enter fully into American culture himself (94), so too is his language divided between two worlds. Both immigrant English and American Yiddish are described as "jargons" by the narrator (41); both are the product of a cultural intermixture that creates essentially new languages, ones that remain partly unintelligible both to American-born English speakers and to the Yiddish speakers of the Old World. Americanization is revealed to be an ambiguous process in which the immigrant simultaneously occupies two cultural worlds, neither of which is strictly either American or foreign, and simultaneously speaks two different languages, neither of which corresponds fully to American English or to European Yiddish.[79]

Cahan's immigrants have ambivalent linguistic psychologies. In "The Imported Bridegroom," to offer another example, characters speak an American Yiddish that seems also English, and an immigrant English that seems also Yiddish.[80] Cahan explores the linguistic situations of his characters in an effort to complicate previous representations of the alienated Jew dangling between two worlds—formulaic representations that tended to assume a discrete, coherent set of Old World and New World values.[81] "The Imported Bridegroom" reveals how Old World Jewish vocal culture was similarly divided. Asriel, the Russian-born American Jew who brings a young Talmudic scholar to the United States, is already partly alienated from his own culture in Russia. He does not understand the holy Hebrew words he so adores; his world is split between sound and sense (6, 11).[82] And in the New World these divisions persist. Shaya—the young scholar— considers himself very Americanized, but he complains that the American librarians in the Astor Library are unable to understand his English, to which his fiancée replies: "*I* can understand everything you say when you speak English. You're all right" (79). Clearly there are two levels of English in the tale, the language of America and the "broken English" (55) that new arrivals are expected to acquire. While critics object to Cahan's describing immigrant English as "mutilated . . . gibberish" (*Yekl*, 3, 40), Cahan's main purpose was not to demean but to demonstrate the factors that make it so difficult for immigrants to learn—immediately—a "proper" English tongue. Yiddish is an impediment to assimilation, yet even when Jewish immigrants learn the English of the ghetto it remains alien to mainstream American English, and thus equally debilitating.

The Rise of David Levinsky is the success story of a Russian-Jewish immigrant in the New York garment industry at the turn of the century. The novel contains less explicit representation of ghetto dialects than Cahan's earlier stories, yet the theme of vocal culture is more developed, especially as it applies to the immigrant's double alienation. Levinsky's attempt at Americanization is equally the story of his effort to learn a fluent, nonaccented American English. The novel dwells on the many obstacles to complete acculturation. The first concerns possibilities of access to native English speakers. Even when Levinsky moves to a gentile neighborhood to learn better English, he is so alienated racially that he hears only a few words a week from his landlady, when he pays the rent (164). Much of the novel traces Levinsky's desperate search—whether at public lectures or among prostitutes—for this "real American" tongue (175–76).

When Levinsky encounters parvenu Yiddish society on holiday in a Catskill resort, this lack of access to the discourse of native-born Americans is all too apparent: "There was a hubbub of broken English, the gibberish being mostly spoken with self-confidence and ease. Indeed, many of these people had some difficulty in speaking their native tongue. Bad English replete with literal translations from untranslatable Yiddish idioms had become their natural speech" (426). Henry James's idea of an essentially foreign New Yorkese dialect is actualized in the more prosperous environment of a summer resort hotel. Like the speakers of immigrant English in *Yekl* and the diverse group of immigrant anarchists at the end of "The Imported Bridegroom," for whom "broken English" becomes a lingua franca virtually unintelligible to native-born Americans (120), these wealthy Jews have no anxiety—indeed, no choice—in perpetuating an implicitly "incorrect" form of speech. The English language has fallen victim to a rapid but problematic Americanization—a notion exemplified in *Yekl*, in the immigrant joke about "'*dod'll do*' [that'll do]" as a language (44). The "literal translations from untranslatable Yiddish idioms" in parvenu Jewish speech demonstrate what Marc Shell has identified as "an ineradicable tension" in American culture, between the assimilation of the foreign language into English and the fact that certain elements cannot be assimilated because they embody a set of values peculiar to another national culture.[83] This process, combined with the corresponding pattern of Americanization described in *Yekl*—where Yiddish is likewise "corrupted" by its contact with English—creates a situation in which immigrants are partially alienated from "good" English *and* from their native Yiddish tongue.

David Levinsky reveals a deeper problem in the Jewish immigrant's attempt at acquiring a second language: a preestablished "linguistic psychology" (134) makes it difficult to learn English grammatical structures and pronunciations (especially the English *th* sound).[84] Levinsky observes the effects of this predicament in a long section describing the tensions within a typical immigrant family when the American-born daughter begins to be educated in American culture. This child acts in positive ways on the mother by teaching her the American language and American codes of behavior, which in turn creates a "spiritual" relationship of mutual linguistic progression between them (276). Yet advancement alternates with moments of insecurity, jealousy, and violence as the mother is unable to keep pace with her child's rapid Americanization: the daughter is gradually becoming "like a little foreigner in the house" (288). The mother's uncertainty toward her daughter—the relationship oscillates between extreme love and a violent desire to punish the child for the mother's own ignorance—leads to an estrangement between husband and wife. She is too Americanized to respect her husband's immigrant culture, yet is too ethnic to participate fully in the American life she desires. Once more, the assimilating immigrant is trapped—ambivalently—between linguistic and cultural worlds.

Levinsky feels similarly divided. He dislikes the language of his own ethnic group, not only the Yiddish-English of Jewish parvenus but also the unintelligible "jargon of nicknames, catch-phrases, and allusions that was apparently peculiar to the East Side Bohème" (456)—in essence, a socialist dialect foreign to Levinsky's capitalist discourse. Levinsky believes that the native English speaker has an innate racial superiority (139), and considers aspects of Yiddish to be "disgustingly coarse" (154): it is "merely a German dialect" rather than an integral language (299). Yet Levinsky is unable to suppress the sing-song of his Jewish voice or his Talmudic gesticulations (28, 327). Despite his attempt to learn the jargon of the business world by clipping unintelligible sentences and paragraphs from the financial column of the newspaper and carrying them in his pocket until he can find an interpreter, Levinsky fails to penetrate fully this jargonistic element of the American language. Americans are so quick to discern and adopt business jargon that "it seemed as if they were born with a special slang sense which I, poor foreigner that I was, lacked. That I was not born in America was something like a physical defect that as-serted itself in many disagreeable ways—a physical defect which, alas! no surgeon in the world was capable of removing" (291). Levinsky feels fi-nally "insignificant" because he finds his own ethnic group partially "re-volting" (515–16) but is unable fully to join mainstream America. He remains too attached to his Old World past; the novel ends with Levinsky's nostalgic vision of his young Talmudic self (530).

Levinsky's entrapment, however, is more complex than this inability to enter an American English world. Levinsky admits at the end of the novel that his past and present "do not comport well" (530), but it is not merely his Russian-Jewish and American-Jewish selves that do not mesh. Levinsky's Old World identity is also divided: he feels his Talmudic, Hebrew voice to be "the voice of some other fellow" (38). And his reaction to the new American world is equally mixed. Levinsky worships the words of faulty speakers: he is obsessed with learning a language that he partially hates.[85] His English teacher (a third-generation Jew) has a slight lisp and a Yankee twang, qualities that, in combination with Levinsky's perception of the difficult English *th* sound as itself a "full-grown lisp," make him view American English as "the language of a people afflicted with defective organs of speech" (130), or at least with a perverse desire to distort basic sounds.[86] Levinsky is trapped between his own ethnic "defects" and the "defective" speech of America. The idea of a special American "slang sense" also has negative implications: it indicates the degeneracy of the vocal culture into which the immigrant wishes to assimilate.[87]

Levinsky's criticisms of the impure American idiom are akin to those of conservative verbal critics like Richard Grant White, who saw the com-mercialism of the city as a threat to vocal value in its encouragement of linguistic anarchy. Levinsky lambastes the degenerate urban forces that reward the "imbecile vitality" of a peddlar who "would make the street ring with deafening shrieks, working his arms and head, sputtering and foaming at the mouth like a madman" (107). He disparages the vocal environment in which prosperity depends merely on the force of one's lungs, and in which the new American businessman is uncouth, "[c]rassly illiterate" (179), and surrounded by the inflated, meaningless jargon of salesmen (321). Vocal value does not matter in a land where "money talks" (181). Echoing the debates that surrounded Stephen Crane's slum talk, Levinsky detests the oaths, blasphemy, and "revolting improprieties"

(123) of urban language. Inevitably, Levinsky is trapped between two equally degenerate vocal cultures. Not only is he horrified by the blunders of immigrant discourse; he becomes a spokesman for the fear that American ideals of language and culture are being disrupted by the modern world. Ironically, an immigrant espouses linguistic values that immigration itself was believed to threaten.

While the Americanization of the immigrant was an ideal of the late nineteenth century, Cahan's novel reveals this very process to be the source of the moral degeneration of the ethnic community.[88] The pattern established in Levinsky's attitude toward American English widens into an "odd confusion of ideas" that dominates his mind: "On the one hand, I had a notion that to 'become an American' was the only tangible form of becoming a man of culture (for did not I regard the most refined and learned European as a 'greenhorn'?); on the other hand, the impression was deep in me that American education was a cheap machine-made product" (167). *David Levinsky* further questions the respective values of "American" and "ethnic" cultures by revealing how it is these immigrants—"[f]oreigners ourselves, and mostly *unable to speak English*"—who have "*Americanized* the system of providing clothes for the American woman of moderate or humble means" (443; emphases added). If the immigrant self is ambiguously positioned between ethnic and American worlds, then America itself is equally divided: the very Americanness of the nation comes from native *and* immigrant sources. Levinsky gives the examples of Jewish businessmen, architects, doctors, and artists—among them Irving Berlin, whose compositions "are sung in almost every *English-speaking* house in the world" (529; emphasis added)—who are all at the heart of American national life. *David Levinsky* qualifies the destructive irony of accounts like Jacob Riis's, in which the demand for the assimilation of the immigrant was accompanied by belief in the absolute racial qualities of certain groups. Rather than resisting or "de-Americanizing" the country, Cahan shows how Jewish immigrants—whether speaking Yiddish or English—embody the very essence of national values.[89]

Cahan's fiction exhibits a strong—perhaps surprising—similarity to Henry James's description of New York City in *The American Scene* (1907). Both James and Cahan explore the New Yorkese dialect in order to formulate a shared understanding of an ambiguous national culture. For James, the alien may strike the outside observer *as* an alien, but the alien is in no sense antagonistic to the "singleness of impression" produced by the city because "the alien himself fairly *makes* the singleness of impression"; the "queer sauce" that pervades New York is "essentially *his* sauce" and "we" only feed from the alien's greasy ladle (453). Echoing Cahan, James describes the difficulty of assigning meaning to the "'American' character" in a land where the very distinction between "native" and "alien" has broken down: "which is *not* the alien, over a large part of the country at least, and where does one put a finger on the dividing line, or, for that matter, 'spot' and identify any particular phase of the conversion?" (459). Yet the visions of Cahan and James ultimately part along a line that marks the linguistic and cultural divisions of the ghetto. James is only able to see the "assimilative organism" as producing a *loss* of the "positive properties" of the home country, an emptying out of the immigrant self (James uses the metaphor of washing a "bright-hued" piece of clothing in a hot tub) into a "tolerably neutral and colorless image" (461–62). Recalling the linguistic alienation of Hutchins Hapgood, James was excluded from participation in the culture of the Jewish theater, and of the Jewish ghetto as a whole, by a language that he describes as "only definable as not in *intention* Yiddish—not otherwise definable" (524), by which he appears to mean a language so vague of idiom as to be neither Yiddish nor American, nor—according to James—really anything. Cahan counters this interpretive breakdown with his exploration of what James himself calls the "'ethnic' outlook" (463). Cahan reveals the impact of Americanization on American Yiddish in addition to the effects of immigrants on English: he defines both sides of the ambiguity of ethnic contact. He is able to show that—to expand on James's image—America is colored by the immigrant while the supposedly "colorless" ethnic self is partially dyed in an American hue. Thus, the "*il*legible word . . . belonging to no known language" (456) that signifies James's bewildered view of the future American character is shown by Cahan to be a hybrid word like the "*oyshgreen*" of *Yekl*—the product of an amalgamated cultural situation.

The cultural assimilation that enabled many first-generation immigrants to write an English-language novel, as David Fine has demonstrated, meant the adoption of American attitudes that frequently distorted the depiction of the ethnic group.[90] Rather than allowing language to limit vision, Cahan uses linguistic variety to render psychological complexity. His representation of vocal culture shows Jewish immigrants to be ambivalent both about their ethnic group and about mainstream America. In *The Rise of David Levinsky*, Cahan reveals how this ambivalence is continuous with an ambiguity in American culture as a whole. Echoing descriptions of the New Yorkese dialect, Cahan illustrates that Americanization is a double force, affecting dominant and minority cultures equally. In a situation in which the American absorbs the "energy" (445) of immigrant culture while the immigrant assimilates the ways of the American, the very terms "American" and "ethnic" break down, just as spoken languages—as Howells noted in his comments on *Yekl*—collapse into one another. It is dialect, in Cahan's work, that captures this new sense of ethnic inter-action. American English affects the language of the immigrant while the immigrant language transforms American English—a complex process that showed turn-of-the-century readers how American culture was deeply informed, if not actually defined, by a multitude of ethnic voices.[91]

Crane and Cahan counteracted the dialect-driven tradition of "local color" writing, of which readers were beginning to tire by the 1890s.[92] The new depiction within their works of an American English that had either broken down morally or become ethnically transformed in its urban context marked a shift in the literary treatment of the American language. For writers of the previous decades who had sought to conserve in dialect an Anglo-American essence, the linguistic choices presented by Crane and Cahan must have seemed equally grim.

Howells was right, in his essay "New York Low Life in Fiction," to stress important differences between Crane's and Cahan's representations of dialect. Crane's concern with inarticulate, decayed language was part of an assault on condescending romanticizations of vernacular speakers, on naively "realistic" attempts to appropriate subaltern society, and on sim-plistic celebrations of a coherent American character. Cahan likewise at-tacked stereotypical depictions of urban experience, yet his interest in linguistic intermixture, and in the attempts of the foreign other to be-come articulate in the dominant tongue, demonstrated not the collapse of culture but its movement toward a multivalent, multicultural mode. Despite these contrasts, Crane and Cahan returned to a common concep-tion of New Yorkese speech: in the new urban environment at the end of the century, traditionally antagonistic dialects—the blasphemous and the moral, the vernacular and the genteel, the immigrant and the American—were mutually contaminated.

SIX

Vaudeville Dialectics

When we Americans are through with the English language, it will look as if it had been run over by a musical comedy.
FINLEY PETER DUNNE, QUOTED IN RISCHIN, XVIII–XIX

Debates over New Yorkese dialect show that by the end of the nineteenth century American English had become an important register of multiethnic diversity, beyond regional models and bipolar divisions into black or white. Aspects of this hybrid, urban dialect were used by ethnic writers such as Abraham Cahan to represent immigrant psychology. The audience of Cahan's English-language novel *Yekl* may have included a number of acculturating immigrants, people like Cahan himself. Yekl's own attempt at Americanization, however, would probably have taken him to the same vaudeville show attended by Maggie and Pete in Crane's *Maggie*, a show that closes with the "assemblage of the masses, most of them of foreign birth," cheerfully singing "The Star-Spangled Banner."[1] I have argued throughout this book that the language of American literature in the Gilded Age felt the impact of a range of social, cultural, and ethnic developments. For readers and writers of highbrow novels, dialect performed important functions: it became a means to illustrate and understand, if not control, larger social changes, even as it embodied deeper cultural fears. Lowbrow theatrical entertainment revealed similar sociolinguistic concerns, as it satisfied the needs of its urban and increasingly ethnic audience. An area of recreative contact between diverse social groups— immigrant and native, ethnic and mainstream, black and white—vaudeville had the depiction of dialect at its heart.

Issues of dialect found a mass market in many ways during the last decades of the nineteenth century, through the dialect-speaking caricatures that populated cartoon periodicals, newspapers, joke books, and songs. Accounts of New York's ethnic, foreign-language theater from the 1890s reveal that many of its productions combined Yiddish or Italian with "the English of the Bowery,"[2] and recent analysis has shown how

Yiddish playlets mirrored the complexity of the immigrant's cultural situation in their exploration of multiple levels of language, ranging from various standards of American Yiddish to different dialects of German and English.[3] Foreign-language theater was an important but nevertheless peripheral part of city culture: this chapter maintains my focus on the impact of ethnic groups upon American English, rather than on the separate foreign languages of these groups, through an analysis of mainstream vaudeville performance. Vaudeville warrants attention because it became the most popular form of national entertainment between the 1870s and 1920s: it was an explicit, self-conscious attempt to forge a universal standard of taste. The managers of vaudeville theaters saw their mission as the creation of stage shows that would appeal to the largest possible number of people, bringing together in a single space an assortment of social, ethnic, and racial groups. Vaudeville may not have appealed to all newcomers "fresh off the boat," but its audience contained a high proportion of acculturating immigrants and second-generation ethnics, in addition to the more established working and middle classes, and to a lesser extent African Americans who were also drawn to the parallel tradition of black musical theater.[4] The stars of vaudeville were often the ethnic offspring of immigrants, if not immigrants themselves.[5] Vaudeville performances registered the multifarious tensions and transitions that came from the incorporation of minority cultures into the mainstream.

While vaudeville featured a range of acts—from juggling to Shakespearean burlesques—the representation of ethnic caricature was the central source of comic material, and dialect impersonation was the primary means of depicting ethnic identity. Vaudeville was dominated by so-called racial comics, whose humorous personae depended fundamentally on the puns, malapropisms, and other bizarre linguistic deformities that punctuated their fictionalized varieties of broken English. The popular Irish-dialect comedian George Fuller Golden, for example, did not don costume to convey his supposed identity: his Irish brogue alone carried the act.[6] Instead of putting on blackface, white performers needed only to "put on" black dialect to portray African Americans after the Civil War.[7] Spoken dialect was so critical to the performance of ethnicity that silent film comedy of the early twentieth century inhibited the comedic portrayal of ethnic difference, condemning it to a relatively insignificant role.[8] So great was the fascination with the inherent humor of ethnic dialect that a single line, "Vas you effer in Zinzinatti?," achieved national fame.[9]

Antebellum blackface minstrelsy, argues Eric Lott, was an "emergent social semantic figure" that both registered and created the emotional demands and racial politics of its audience.[10] This chapter supplements recent attention to the politics of popular entertainment by focusing on the various uses of dialect in a select number of vaudeville performances, together with developments in the linguistic performance of blackness— by both whites and blacks—at the turn of the century. The scope of my analysis might be narrower than Lott's, yet I hope to suggest some of the ways that stage language embodied wider cultural, racial, and psychological phenomena of the era. The appeal of American vaudeville, I argue, partly depended on new types of comic dialect that had the power to mediate difference by sustaining multiple interpretations and staging ethnic hybrids. As a transition from an account of the multiethnic linguistic fusions of New York City to an exploration of black vernacular English in the work of Paul Laurence Dunbar, this chapter is intended to throw light on a pressing question of my study: how did the bipolar, black-and-white understanding of American language, which dominated blackface performance, interact with the more fractured and diverse situation of ethnic dialect difference on the late-nineteenth-century vaudeville stage?

Stanley Brandes has argued that the tradition of Jewish-American dialect humor supplies "an ethnography of speaking": the type of jokes told by Jews in America, as compared to Europe, "recount a specifically linguistic story; they both reflect and demonstrate preoccupation with changing speech patterns over several generations in the New World," thus providing modern acculturated Jews with a sociology of the linguistic struggles of their ancestors.[11] Vaudeville's ethnic humor shares this linguistic preoccupation. Clowning with language is, of course, a universal aspect of comedy; it is not difficult to find other situations where dialect-driven ethnic jokes provide an important source of amusement. Vaudeville's linguistic humor is no more or less unique than the context in which it thrived: the large American cities at the turn of the century, where a wide variety of foreign groups gradually acquired—and transformed—American English and American ways, while simultaneously maintaining their ethnic cultures and languages. Analysis of vaudeville humor reveals a sociolinguistics of ethnic contact and cultural struggle remarkable for its diversity and complexity.

Racial comics of the 1880s and '90s became experts in what the Jewish comedian Joe Welch described as the inherent humor and "intensely human" qualities that could be found in the urban immigrant's "peculiarities of inflection and . . . foreign idioms."[12] Many American-born comics claimed to copy down immigrant speech word for word to use in their acts. The acts themselves were often generated by the impersonation of ethnic dialect and character. The famous "Dutch" dialect comedian, Sam Bernard, for example, found the inspiration for his act in New York City's German-American community of the late 1870s and early '80s:

Riding on a car one day, squeezed into an obscure corner, I saw a man snatch a German's watch and hop off the car. The chain hung down straight. I waited leisurely for the climax of the drama. The German emerged slowly from his usual somnolence. He emitted various gutteral [*sic*] sounds, half-finished sentences, clipped words in an effort to articulate his feelings. Obviously his mind was functioning. Anger and explanations were incumbent, but no one could understand what he was saying. Finally, he looked sadly at the chain and said: "Dis ist der zecondt vatch!"

That night in the joke factory I gave an imitation of this perplexed German, inarticulate, yet outraged. With variations, I have been doing the same ever since.[13]

Just as the German's watch is repeatedly stolen, so is his cultural property: the stressful struggle to articulate his situation, the deep psychological trauma arising from linguistic isolation, becomes the source of Bernard's vaudeville act. Bernard's dialect comedy appealed to his diverse audience in different ways because it already contained a complex attitude toward ethnic culture. To some extent, Bernard shows empathy for the German's frustration and alienation, which arise from an inability to verbalize his predicament in adequate English. Yet beneath Bernard's sympathy lies the implication that the German's English is broken not because he is linguistically uneducated but because he is mentally slow. It is difficult to know whether the German's lack of English leads to the appearance of confusion, or whether his inherent slowness causes an inability to articulate clear thoughts. Bernard's account of his encounter with dialect is ethnographically significant because it reveals the psychological ambivalence in mainstream reactions to minority cultures: sympathy coexists with an implicit attitude of superiority.

Not all dialect impersonation would have registered even the ambivalence exhibited by Bernard: much of vaudeville made little attempt to understand ethnic groups or to represent them with subtlety. For one humorist, writing "The Philosophy of Wit and Humor" in 1890, ethnic dialects were funny not in what they suggested about an ethnic group but in their purely superficial linguistic deformity. Whether Chinese, Irish, or German did not matter: simply reading a joke in distorted speech was enough to bring down the house.[14] Dialect caricature also had a deeper, more pernicious function. Analysis of works such as *Choice Dialect and Vaudeville Stage Jokes* (1902)—one of many vaudeville joke and sketch books that appeared at the turn of the century—reveals as typical the situation in which the outlandishness of an immigrant dialect cements a demeaning stereotype, thus confirming ethnic otherness and inferiority. For example, the nonsense words and mock eloquence of a black debating society severely limit the idea that African Americans are having an "intellectual" discussion (58–63). Similarly, an Irish immigrant's failure to

understand the conventions of standard written English confirms his ignorance and cultural ineptitude (12). The representation of spoken language is also used to debase the virtues attributed to foreign cultures.
Thus, the wisdom of a Chinese proverb is delivered in English so broken
as to make it unintelligible (99), and the beauty of the Italian language
is diminished when an Italian woman is made to recite an English poem
in her monstrously Italianate dialect (105).

The use of dialect to depict racist stereotype, common in antebellum
blackface performance, persisted after the Civil War. The craze for "Coon
Songs" during the two decades after 1890 propagated offensive images
of blacks as chicken-loving simpletons or razor-toting dandies who were
vicious and in need of control, and the use of heavy dialect helped to
suggest this vision of violent otherness: "De Niggers dey wer' slashin', /
Steel dey wer' a clashin' / Coons were scrapin' all aroun de floor."[15] This
racist linguistic logic was applied to various immigrant groups after the
Civil War. Douglas Gilbert has argued that joking about Irish, Germans,
and blacks "was but to thrust at a minority which generally took the jibes
good-naturedly." But much of this racial comedy was deliberately offensive. And there was the tendency, observed by Lott in antebellum minstrelsy, for certain audiences to take these damaging ethnic stereotypes
for realities.[16]

Further analysis of *Choice Dialect and Vaudeville Stage Jokes*, however, reveals that more reconciling uses of dialect developed alongside demeaning depictions. The comedy that ensues when an Irish-American servant
mishears the New England provincialism of *pail* (bucket) as *peal* (both are
understood to have the same sound in an Irish immigrant dialect) is employed to represent, and to some extent placate, the tensions of a situation
in which older, native regionalisms were threatened by new ethnic cultures (53–54). Such regional conflicts were supplemented by much newer
ones—not between "alien" and "native" English but between "alien"
dialects themselves. Out of more than fifty sketches in *Choice Dialect and
Vaudeville Stage Jokes*, only two are in traditional, regional American dialect;
the rest employ various forms of English supposedly spoken by Chinese,
Irish, German, Jewish, and Italian immigrants, as well as African Americans. Many of the sketches, presumably written at the time of the Chinese
Exclusion Act (1882), treat the Chinese question by pitting one minority,
say an Irish American or Jewish American, against a usually mysterious
Chinese immigrant. Much of the humor seems to lie in the complaints of
one minority about the other's English, in an equally broad dialect. Typically, no standard language is present in these confrontations: both
groups "haf such vay of shpeaking nefer heard" (22), and each assumes
that the linguistic ineptitude of the other signifies their stupidity and gul-
libility. This differs significantly from earlier depictions of dialect in lit-

erature or onstage, in which a dialect speaker was strongly contrasted with a speaker of standard English.[17] There seems to have been a shift, beginning sometime in the 1880s, away from a binary understanding of America's ethnic situation—in which conventional English was juxtaposed with, say, "Irish" or "African-American" speech—toward a more diverse inclusion of many different ethnicities and dialects.

The many dialects on the vaudeville stage expressed different sides of a multifaceted situation. Much depended on the ethnic makeup of the audience, on the ethnic background of the performer, or on a combination of both. Propelled by the desire of vaudeville managers like B. F. Keith to appeal to the widest audience, strict censorship was imposed on offensive ethnic caricature and racial epithets, especially in the early 1900s when ethnic groups such as the Irish and the Germans dominated the mainstream audience.[18] During earlier decades, however, ethnic caricature coexisted—mainly unchallenged—with the passage of ethnic Americans into the vaudeville audience and, more importantly, onto the stage.[19] As in Sam Bernard's attitude toward the German immigrant, an important reason for this tolerance was that stereotypes often had an ambivalent rather than a purely negative function. To some extent, stereotypes presented ethnics as clowns and jesters, "symbolic figures of loneliness and alienation"; they introduced minorities to the mainstream culture and to each other.[20] As James Dormon has argued, ethnic stereotype could suggest that Jews, say, were unthreatening because inassimilable, thus cementing difference, while at the same time making it easier for Jews to Americanize by undermining active resistance to them.[21]

Complicated issues also surrounded the performance of ethnic caricature by minorities themselves. Jewish performers transformed linguistic stereotypes into signifiers of ethnic community by highlighting Yiddish elements of speech before predominantly Jewish audiences in the Bowery.[22] The many Irish Americans who played stage Irish would often wield their dialects with political purpose. In the plays of the Irish-American writer Edward Harrigan, for example, the dialect of Irish characters was strong enough to suggest ethnic community but was weaker than that of his German and African-American characters, thus suggesting the Irishman's more natural membership in the nation. In the words of one of Harrigan's Irish politicians: "My district is the town of Babel, and the Irish flag floats from the top."[23] Yet it was not uncommon for Irish-American performers to run into trouble with Hibernian societies who accused them of exploiting the "devil of dialectism" to demean sections of the Irish community. Rabbis likewise complained to Jewish performers about the self-deprecating nature of their lampoons.[24] The key point about the 1880s and '90s, however, is that Jews acting stereotypical Jewishness, or Irish Americans playing clichéd Irishness, were popular among members

of these same communities—an appropriation of mockery that was celebrated, perhaps, for its deflection of hostility, away from persecuting outsiders.[25] Although it is not easy to gauge the psychological effects of such
stereotypes on their observers, ethnic groups within large theater audiences must have actively laughed at greenhorn stage types as a means to
establish their own status in mainstream society.

Vaudeville shows had protean, ever-shifting formats, and the representation of ethnicity was similarly variable.[26] To some extent, vaudeville dissolved differences by absorbing minorities in an American melting pot.
Yet the prejudice found in blackface minstrelsy also expanded on the
vaudeville stage, as the dialects and characters of Irish, Germans, Italians,
and Jews were represented in as deviant a manner as the "black" voices
before them. By the end of the century the power of dialect to divide and
demean had hardly disappeared, but it became significantly more nuanced as vaudevillians developed aesthetic techniques to deal with their
fragmented audience, especially its growing contingent of partially Americanized immigrants and their American-born sons and daughters,
perched between ethnic and mainstream cultures. (African Americans
and other non-white groups, as we shall see at the end of this chapter,
were never fully drawn into the picture.) Echoing the earlier tradition of
blackface minstrelsy, masking was at the heart of these new techniques.
Rather than forming racial binaries, however, it was a more flexible masquerade that fused a range of ethnic differences. It was, above all, a *linguistic* masquerade that caricatured aspects of ethnic discourse in an attempt to reach speakers of remarkably diverse dialects.

In 1926, *Life* magazine carried a review of the vaudeville act of Joe Weber
and Lew Fields, a dialect comedy and slapstick duo who performed under
the names of Mike and Meyer. The reviewer, Robert Benchley, imagines
that he is writing thirty years earlier, at the height of Weber and Fields's
fame in the 1890s. He admires the duo not for their comic popularity
but for their purported philosophical significance. These comedians are
Jamesian pragmatists; they have learned from Francis Bacon "the denial
of Truth as a substantive"; they are providing a "new philosophy of the
subconscious"; and their dialogue is "pure dialectics." Take the following:

MEYER: Vot are you doing?
MIKE: Voiking in a nut factory.
MEYER: Doing vot?
MIKE: Nutting.
MEYER: Sure—but vot are you doing?
MIKE: Nutting.

MEYER: I know, but vot voik are you doing?
MIKE: Nutting, I tole you.
MEYER (POKING HIS FINGER IN MIKE'S EYE): Ou-u-u-u, how I lofe you!

In such comedy, the reviewer continues, "a consciousness of national so-cial satire" is being born. "Here, in these words, lies America. The America of to-day, with its flaring gas lights, its thundering cable cars, the clatter of its hansoms, and the deafening whistle of its peanut stands. The young, vibrant spirit of America, locked in the message of two clowns!"[27]

The review is in one sense deeply satirical, with its juxtaposition of philosophical discourse and ridiculous comic dialogue. If this is "philos-ophy," then it seems to announce the bankruptcy of an American soul, or at least the emptiness of its mainstream entertainment industry. Yet the review also has less ironic implications. Theater historians have observed how vaudeville did indeed express a national state of "consciousness" at the turn of the century by responding pragmatically to the psychological needs of its diverse audiences.[28] Moreover, there is substance to the claim that the "words" and "message" of Weber and Fields, the very language of their performance, were reactions to the social noise and confusion of late-nineteenth-century America. What the *Life* reviewer calls, equivocally, the "dialectics" of Weber and Fields's routine—the dialect-laden speech and the dialectic situation in which two ethnic speakers misunderstand one another through the internal contradictions of a supposedly common language—were key elements in vaudeville performance. And these dia-lectics were crucial because they echoed the multifarious linguistic con-flicts and transitions that were beginning to sound in contemporary Amer-ica's increasingly multiethnic society.

Weber and Fields's nut factory sketch immediately presents ethnic syn-thesis: here are two Lower East Side Jews performing in a "Dutch," or German-English, dialect. Jewish performers would often appear in vaude-ville as "Dutch" characters, using the similar sounds of Yiddish-inflected and German-inflected English as a means of entry to the stage.[29] Jews, that is, would mask themselves in another ethnic identity—if not German then usually Irish—more familiar to an American-born audience. This parodic act, however, did not necessarily provide a unified front behind which to hide ethnic insecurity, since it was precisely the disorientation of their German personae that Weber and Fields emphasized. We saw in the pre-vious section how comedy was created from what many considered a dan-ger of urban life: the confusing, unstable situation in which different for-eign speakers attempted to communicate in an English-based lingua franca that was not fully understood or commanded. What Charles Musser has argued for the comedy of the Marx Brothers holds true for vaudeville: the confusion, wordplay, and sudden shifts in pronunciation and accent that arose from the "ethnic interfacings" of the Lower East Side became the foundation of its discourse-based humor.[30] In a Weber and Fields sketch, however, we do not laugh at the misunderstanding between *different* ethnicities: the language of the individual ethnic group has become incomprehensible to its very members. Weber and Fields spoke a "double Dutch" that was internally divided.

In their most famous act, Weber and Fields explored the immigrant's attempt to learn the language and rules of the American game of pool. The humor of the pool room sketch is largely grammatical. The inversions and twistings of linguistic structures reveal a wider unfamiliarity with social rules: "'Remember, you got to break der balls before as you bust dem.' . . . 'I got to bust dem before I break dem?'"[31] Battle with the structural difficulties of American English represents a burlesque struggle with the subtle grammar of New World behavior. In vaudeville as a whole, this grammar-based comedy was subservient to a phonetic element. Many puns and double entendres were humorous equivalents of language-contact phenomena, as English became filtered through the phonetic peculiarities of another tongue: hence the *nutting/nothing* pun. Weber and Fields were experts in exploiting the comic potential of this aural/verbal medium:

MIKE: I receivedidid a letter from mein goil, but I don't know how to writteninin her back.

MEYER: Writteninin her back! Such an edumuncation you got it? Writteninin her back! You mean rotteninin her back. How can you answer her ven you don't know how to write?

MIKE: Dot makes no nefer mind. She don't know how to read.

MEYER: If you luf her, vy don't you send her some poultry?

MIKE: She don't need no poultry; her father is a butcher.

MEYER: I mean luf voids like Romeo und Chuliet talks:

If you luf you like I luf me,
No knife can cut us togedder.

MIKE: I don't like dot.

MEYER: Vell, vot do you vant to say to her?

MIKE: I don't vant you to know vat I'm saying to her. All I vant you to do is to tell me vot to put in her letter.

MEYER: Such a foolishness you are! If I don't tell you vot to say, how vill you know vot to write if she don't know how to read?

MIKE: I don't vant nobody to know vot I'm writteninin to her.

MEYER: You don't vant anyone to know vot you are rotteninin?

MIKE: No.

MEYER: Then send her a postal card.

MIKE: Send her a postal card? If I do she'll think I don't care two cendts for her.

MEYER: Are you going to marry her?

MIKE: In two days I vill be a murdered man.

MEYER: A vot?

MIKE: I mean a married man.

MEYER: I hope you vill always look back upon der presendt moment as der habbiest moment uff your life.

MIKE: But I aind't married yet.

MEYER: I know it, und furdermore, upon dis suspicious occasion, I also vish to express to you—charges collect—my uppermost depreciation of der dishonor you haf informed upon me in making me your bridesmaid.

MIKE: Der insuldt is all mein.

MEYER: As you standt before me now, soo young, soo innocent, soo obnoxious, there is only one void dat can express mein pleasure, mein dissatisfaction——

MIKE: Yes, yes?

MEYER: Und I can't tink of der void.[32]

Weber and Fields's fictional, exaggerated discourse makes light of illiteracy and linguistic insecurity. Mike and Meyer are trapped at the level of sound: the phonetic substitutions in their conversation—"suspicious" for *auspicious,* "depreciation" for *appreciation*—reveal the homophonic potential of language to yield unintentional, baffling meanings. The incomplete assimilation of linguistic rules, and the psychological stress that comes from assimilation itself, allow familiar English to degenerate easily into obscurity and confusion. Yet many of Weber and Fields's substitutions are not accidental: they generate antithetical meanings that express the ambivalent relationship of this immigrant pair. Meyer's cry of "how I lofe you!" was usually accompanied by his violent abuse of Mike: love and hate, honor and dishonor, appreciation and depreciation are combined in their friendship because ethnic community is undercut—as in Abraham Cahan's fiction—by negative reactions to incomplete Americanization. This seemingly controlled manipulation of meaning, however, is accompanied by a more chaotic process in which language is cut free from rigid rules. Mike and Meyer are victims of a language not entirely within their control—an idea developed in the pool room sketch, where language controls reality by constantly remolding the rules of play. Their mistakes lead to communicative breakdown as often as to double meaning. Although correct meanings are occasionally realized by the speakers themselves (as in the case of *poultry*), for most of the dialogue there is no consistent standard against which to appeal. The resulting situation is one of profound linguistic instability, in which Mike and Meyer seem unintelligible both to each other and, more worryingly, to themselves. Typically, mistakes are corrected with different mistakes—*rotteninin* for *writteninin*—and command over individual meaning is lost. Whether or not the pun is intended, words become "voids": empty spaces without fixed significance.

The humor of the Jewish dialect jokes discussed by Stanley Brandes also depends largely on miscomprehension within a supposedly unitary speech type. Speakers lose control over their "own" language, for example by failing to realize that their Yiddishized dialect gives away ethnic identity. At other times, jokes emphasize linguistic differences within the Jewish community itself, especially concerning a varying knowledge of religious practices. Brandes argues that these dialect jokes express an ambivalence within the Jewish community—indeed, to tell them well requires bidialectal competence in both American English and ethnic dialect. This type of humor divides native Jews from greenhorns, while also acting as a source of anxious unity in the face of an absorption into mainstream culture. Vaudeville shares the capacity of this dialect humor to suggest that, for the acculturating immigrant group, there is no unified, uncomplicated essence of identity. The Weber and Fields letter-writing sketch challenges unitary language with its semantic confusions, thus representing ethnicity as a fusion of differences—a point underscored by a hybrid dialect that Albert McLean describes as owing "something to the German, something to the Yiddish, and something to the English language."[33]

The communicative differences between Mike and Meyer echoed the internal differences of their stage personae: two Jews were representing two Germans trying to speak English. This ethnic masking developed from vaudeville's uniting of diverse representations of ethnicity within single productions. Vaudeville managers recognized that the multifarious structure of the vaudeville show could appeal to a diverse audience by presenting them with—among other attractions—a series of different ethnic caricatures.[34] Similarly, Edward Harrigan's popular plays combined Irish, German, and black characters; his early sketches also dabbled in Italian and Chinese types. It was not uncommon to see sketches uniting, say, Irish, Dutch, Italian, and blackface dialect comedians.[35] This seems a continuation of the polyethnic themes that Werner Sollors detects in the antebellum burlesques of John Brougham, which united their mixed urban audiences by allowing them to "laugh alternately at Irish, at German, at Anglo-Italian, at haughty French as well as at Indian and black motifs." In vaudeville, this diversity of comic types was part of many individual acts. Early in their career, Weber and Fields impersonated a range of ethnic groups, appearing in blackface or singing Irish nationalistic songs containing Gaelic words which they did not understand. Other acts specialized in multiple, often vastly different types: the Jewish performer Eddie Cantor could appear in blackface or as a Polish servant, and Lee Barth, another comedian, advertised himself as "the man with many dialects / I please all nationalities and cater to originality." The Jewish comedienne Belle Baker typically impersonated a range of ethnic caricatures in her act, claiming that "[w]hen I sing an Italian or Irish or Yiddish song, I have a definite character in mind that I've known for years. I present the character from that point of view—not the outsider's." Baker attempted to interpret Bowery life for the audience by positioning herself centrally in social diversity, claiming a special skill and versatile knowledge—both of stage performance and of the streets.[36]

Dialect was pivotal to this kaleidoscopic switching of identity. What Henry Jenkins calls vaudeville's aesthetic of "affective immediacy," its attempt to give busy urban audiences rapid, intense, and various stimulation, required an emblematic "system of typage" that would allow regional and ethnic personae to be instantly recognized.[37] Dialect was the most adaptable and immediate element in this coding of types. A few over-redundant linguistic markers conveyed instant ethnicity. In addition to the already widely recognized signs of "black" speech like *gwine*, one could find *py gollies* (German), *begorra* (Irish), *just-a lak-a dat* (Italian), and *me likee, velly good* (Chinese)—key words and phrases that let the audience understand immediately which ethnic type was intended. Such rigid linguistic coding did not favor subtle depictions of character: according to the vaudeville critic of the Pittsburgh *Post* in 1900, the Hebrew character was *always* played in "the same stereotyped makeup, the same dialect, the same mannerisms." It did, however, allow for some unusual contrasts and fusions: as Brett Page recorded in his guidebook, *Writing for Vaudeville* (1915), the establishment of limited ethnic stereotypes did not leave "much chance for a new character, you will say—but have you thought about the different combinations you can make?" Transcending confrontation between separate caricatures, there was a more radical process in which individual performers staged different ethnicities simultaneously. In Weber and Fields's case, Germanness and Jewishness existed together, and their impersonations of other minorities did not seek to disguise the element of masking. One night in the Bowery, for example, they put their hands over their noses and sang "Here we are, an Irish pair," thus playing stereotyped Irishmen while reminding the audience of a clichéd element of their Jewish identity. Two ethnicities were simultaneously present, but neither was "real": both were presented as stereotypes in an overt act of masking that foregrounded what it pretended to hide.[38]

This playing, in a single persona, with a layering of minority selves and dialects was common in vaudeville acts. Early Jewish comedians performed parodies of Irish songs with bits of Yiddish and Jewish dialect inserted; the Irish excelled as "Dutch" comedians, occasionally including Scottish highland flings in their acts; Weber and Fields wrote burlesque parts for German characters who spoke in Irish brogue. It was not too difficult, at that time, to find Italian organ grinders from Cork, or song writers who specialized in the language of "Ethiopian Hibernicism"![39] Popular sketches, like T. S. Denison's *Patsy O'Wang: An Irish Farce with a Chinese Mix-*

Up (1895), were explicit and sustained explorations of ethnic intermixture. As the title suggests, Denison's central character is half Chinese and half Irish (although, predictably, he prefers his Irish to his Chinese side): a hybridity demonstrated by a dialect that alternates between "[v]elly much glad see Missee Fluke" and "aint I good enough Irish for New York or Chicago or Cork ayther."[40]

One of the most striking examples of this ethnic fusion was a play staged by the Weber and Fields Company in the mid-1890s, called *The Geezer*. A burlesque of a more serious work—*The Geisha*—Weber and Fields's production was about a Chinese viceroy visiting America to find a bride for his emperor. The Chinese parts, however, were played not by regular actors but by "Irish" and "German" comedians—that is, by Americans who specialized in Irish and German roles. According to the playwright, Joseph Herbert, in the notes to the play:

> Two-Hi was played by a German Comedian [Sam Bernard], who made up like a Chinaman and put on a chin piece, such as a Dutchman would wear. As the parts were specially written for this special company under my stage direction, I suggested that the part be played as a composite character; a Dutch Chinaman.
> Li Hung Chang was played by an Irish Comedian [John T. Kelley] who made up exactly like Li Hung Chang, but spoke in Irish dialect.[41]

Thus, the play presented an American playing an Irish immigrant playing a Chinese, and an American playing a German immigrant playing a Chinese. The character of Two-Hi, moreover, was an even more radical composite than the Irish-speaking Chinese, Li Hung Chang, as shown in his dialect: a strange English-German-Chinese hybrid containing phrases like "Velly good, py gollies" and "One piecee beer mit pretzels."[42] *The Geezer* reveals the extent to which ethnic identity could be compressed into streamlined dialects: the markers of *velly* (Chinese) and *py* (German) would have been enough to communicate the intended stereotypes—and their combination—to the audience. Such compression made different ethnicities seem simultaneous: hybrid characters were represented in double- and triple-voiced sentences.

To some extent, this linguistic play can be explained by the personality-dominated star system of vaudeville. Henry Jenkins points out that vaudevillians exploited the contrast between the stock character being portrayed and the "real" ethnicity of the performer: "the very Jewish Fanny Brice, for example, appeared as an Indian squaw, a French courtesan, or a black housewife, lapsing into occasional Yiddish phrases to underscore the effect." Brett Page's advice on writing in dialect confirms this reason for ethnic fusion: "[M]erely suggest the broken English here and there. . . . Remember that the actor who will be engaged to play the part has studied the expression of that particular type all his life. His method of conveying what you intend is likely to be different from your method."⁴³ The dialect of many performers clearly came as much from their own stage personalities as from any role they were assigned to play: hence the strange fusions that occurred when German and Irish dialect comedians like Bernard and Kelley played other ethnic roles.

The multiethnic polyphony of individual sentences had a deeper significance. The hybrid nature of vaudeville speech reflected the street meeting of cultures that was producing the composite urban dialect encountered in the previous chapter—a dialect described by the popular playwright of New York, Edward Harrigan:

> The "argot" of the rougher class has changed. "Say, sis! Git up an' dance wid me," is now formulated into "It's me gurl! Please being so kind if youse will to chuck a speil at her!" The latter idiom is the result of the struggle by the foreigners of the Latin races, who came to America and settled in the northern cities immediately after the Civil War, to master the English language. The commingling of the children of these people with the children of the English, Irish and native born has developed a jargon that twists our language into a dialect only matched by that spoken by the costermonger of London.⁴⁴

So confusing were the multiethnic fusions of city speech—both for immigrants and for American natives—that they required the simplifying exaggerations of vaudeville to render them intelligible. Echoing the fiction of ethnic writers such as Abraham Cahan, stage dialect was—in part—a sensitive register of minority discourse. Weber and Fields's slapstick parody of the unstable dialectic within ethnic speech shows how vaudeville played upon the linguistic situation of much of its audience and many of its performers. The burlesque intermixture of words like *gesproken* (German-English past tense of *to speak*) suggested the ambivalence of ethnic groups positioned between American and foreign cultures.⁴⁵ In the mouths of vaudeville's "racial comics," the ethnic interfusions of urban dialect described by Harrigan were turned into humorous composites of difference: "velly good, py gollies."

The dialects of vaudeville were not always appreciated by their audiences as objectifications of ethnic heteroglossia. Many dialects were pure nonsense. *The Geezer*, for example, fuses English with bizarre representations of Chinese ("Chinny chinny hoplick / Yokahama chop stick") and Irish Gaelic ("Druman drugalie thaush ashin gomisk"), and other vaudeville shows featured grotesque hybrids like the following German-English dialect song: "Give a listen to the Mocking Bird . . . / Die Mocking bird ein grosser macher ist. / Vas macht die mocking bird? . . . / Es mox nix ous vas macht die mocking bird."⁴⁶ This dialect could have been interpreted as an exaggerated staging of Anglo-German fusion, yet more likely it would have appealed as verbal slapstick, laughable for its sheer ridiculousness. Comedians performed burlesque German dramas that audiences enjoyed precisely because they could not understand either the language—a strange variety of German with occasional English words like "salad" and "ice cream" inserted for comic incongruity—or the reasons behind the bizarre melodrama on the stage.[47]

An obvious purpose of this linguistic play was to demean through laughter the otherness of foreign speech. Threatening foreign tongues were transformed into gibberish. Yet English also fell victim to the organs of nonsense, as can be seen in the disoriented discourse of Weber and Fields. Advertisements by agents and performers seeking vaudeville jokes gave a prominent place, among their lists of popular topics, to "bad spelling, solecisms, barbarisms, improprieties, [and] mispronunciations."[48] Vaudevillians themselves believed that an act's "coordinated tone-clashes"—its surface level of comic sound—had the power to reduce the audience to uncontrollable physical laughter.[49] Linguistic murder was a common metaphor used by vaudevillians to describe this brand of humor. To quote one late-nineteenth-century joke writer, discussing his method: "A feeble, hoary-headed idea is ruthlessly set upon, crippled, torn to pieces, put together backwards with a new head or tail on it; the King's English is deliberately murdered—all for a joke!" Brett Page, in his guide to writing for the popular stage, considered the plot of a vaudeville sketch to be trivial compared with "its murdering of the King's English and its slap-stick ways." The Cincinnati *Enquirer* in 1875 likewise considered the attraction of D. L. Morris, the "black Dutchman" of the stage, to be his ludicrous "murdering and misapplication of the Queen's English." The *Enquirer*'s point held true for much vaudeville performance: the staging of ethnic hybrids went hand in hand with an assault on American English and on the very notion of effective communication. Vaudeville seems to support Joshua Fishman's suggestion that Americans "have no particular regard for English, no particular pride in English as an exquisite instrument, no particular concern for its purity, subtlety, or correctness."[50]

Vaudeville's hostility toward spoken correctness was a means to exorcise through humor the deep linguistic insecurities of the large acculturating element of its immigrant audience. Anxieties over incoherence were exaggerated to the point of comic collapse. The deforming of standards was also a way to celebrate ethnic impact on American culture. This is one of the reasons why much vaudeville humor consisted of dialect speakers complaining about each other's bad English, why people laughed when an Irish American said to a recent Irish immigrant, "yez should spake our Unighted Shtates toong more dacently and not be givin' uz yer furren brogue."[51] This humor was not necessarily intended to confirm the correctness of conventional language; it also reveled in the destandardizing influence of ethnic culture, the power that minorities had to transform the nation's linguistic norms. Without doubt, command of "good" American English remained the ideal for many assimilating immigrants. Yet in the irresolvable situation in which immigrants were abused for "faulty" linguistic patterns that they found extremely difficult to change, the very instruments that attempted to enforce correctness became targets for resistance. The scrambling of vaudeville speech was part of a cathartic carnival of ethno-linguistic chaos in which restrictive proprieties were murdered onstage.

Nonsense also provided a way to communicate with diverse audiences, fragmented into different dialects and ethnic traditions. Vaudeville's absurd prattle was a type of noise that conformed to what Page considered a key quality of vaudeville: its ability to transcend language and appeal to members of the audience for whom English was not a first language. Much stage discourse was the linguistic equivalent to what an early student of vaudeville identified—rather disparagingly—as its most striking characteristic: the "simple stupidity" required to satisfy cosmopolitan audiences with few sentiments or ideas in common. Escaping linguistic difficulty and tension by appreciating the noise of vaudeville's verbal grotesquerie, the audience created communities of laughter that smothered the outside noise of a confusingly heterogeneous city. To paraphrase Robert Benchley's review of Weber and Fields, the disordered discourse of vaudeville was a way to shout back at the thundering cable cars, clattering hansoms, and whistling peanut stands of modern-day America.[52]

Within the Babel of the city, vaudeville dialect served a pentecostal function. Much of it could be understood by everyone because its meaning was secondary to a slapstick murdering of language. Another cohesive quality of vaudeville's ethnic language was its power to mean several things at once. Dialect acted as a multifaceted verbal mask; its popularity stemmed from a shifting capacity to satisfy a range of motivations. The Jewish singer Sophie Tucker reported how her Yiddish song "My Yiddisha Mama" appealed to Jewish members of the audience as a statement on Americanization, as well as to the audience at large for its simple sentimentality: "Mother in any language," she observed, "means the same thing." The dialects of vaudeville were part of what James Dormon calls a "semiotic code" of caricature that frequently satisfied mainstream and ethnic viewers simultaneously. "Double Dutch" comedy was doubly cathartic: its absurd accents appeased immigrants anxious over the correctness of their English while it humored the fears of mainstream Americans concerning the foreignness of urban tongues. The dialects of American vaudeville shared qualities with the "mongrelized" language that Peter Bailey has discovered in nineteenth-century English music halls—a language capable of reducing "the open social mix of the city street to some kind of territorial order" by playing off the vulgar against the pretentious.[53] In America, the mongrelization of language was based primarily on ethnicity, not class, as the compound dialects of *The Geezer* reveal. Its function, however, was the same: to form a popular consensus of pleasure by speaking a language that was various and flexible enough to contain a multitude of cultural differences.

The sudden switch between minority dialects in the typical vaudeville show, and the more radical process in which hybrid dialect created a simultaneity of ethnicities, were part of a deforming play with the very idea of ethnic identity. Vaudeville may have lacked the power to collapse ethnocentrism completely in its formation of a recreational mainstream. Yet we should not miss what was new and distinctive about vaudeville's representation of dialect: its polyvocality staged a multilayered fusion of selves that acted to destabilize essentialist categories.[54] Vaudevillians discovered that a crucial way of appealing to an ethnically fragmented audience was to burlesque the linguistic mechanisms of establishing difference. The identity of the speaking self was revealed as fluid in a culture that had tended to use dialect to stereotype ethnic traits rigidly. For this reason, stage discourse existed in an ethnically compound form: it refused to separate English into a hierarchy of dialects but instead emphasized how the wholeness of language was a hybrid mixture of different "vay[s] of shpeaking."[55]

Dialect also played a central role in the earlier tradition of blackface minstrelsy, which was largely absorbed by vaudeville at the end of the nineteenth century. The "humorous" inability of the blackface caricature to command the full meaning of conventional English suggested racial difference and deficiency; black minds were made to seem absolutely trapped in an inferior dialectal world. A debate over class was often played out within this discourse of race: Robert Toll has demonstrated how minstrel dialect allowed working-class audiences to formulate positive ideas about the level of their speech by simultaneously denigrating "high" and "low" varieties of language.[56] Toll argues that the creation of grotesque, twisted, malapropistic dialects was a means for the working-class members of the minstrel audience to learn—by inverse example—the correct use of language.[57] Recent attention to blackface minstrelsy has confirmed a similar point: the accents of minstrelsy allowed ethnic Americans—such as the Irish or, later, Jews—to construct a common sense of whiteness behind the blackface mask.[58] Blackface was not, writes Michael Rogin, "one more example of the play with group identity, that is, the supposed use of ethnic stereotypes to break those same stereotypes down." Instead, blackface moved ethnic groups like Jews into the melting pot by keeping African Americans out, thus reinforcing "the postulate of essential racial difference that justified white supremacy."[59]

As a prominent form of mass entertainment—whether in antebellum working-class saloons or 1930s Hollywood—blackface performance reinforced a binary, black-or-white sense of racial division. In late-nineteenth-century vaudeville, however, a more fluid situation of cultural and ethnic heterogeneity prevailed. Minstrelsy did not disappear entirely on the vaudeville stage—Weber and Fields began their careers as a blackface song-and-dance team, and many immigrant performers used the theatrical convention of blackface in an effort to Americanize themselves and their audiences[60]—but it became just one of many acts of ethnic masking. The minstrel show itself underwent radical transformations in the 1860s and '70s by incorporating "Irish" ballad singers and "Jewish" comedians into its acts. The minstrel star Dan Bryant switched from blackface to Irish parts in the 1860s; "Dutch," "Irish," and "Ethiopian" characters came together on the minstrel stage.[61] The new ethnic content of minstrelsy had a parallel in the humorous, dialect-speaking lecturers who became popular with middle-class audiences after the Civil War. George Washington Cable, for example, read the roles of black characters onstage, thus placing him squarely within the tradition of blackface minstrelsy, as Lott suggests.[62] Yet black dialect was only one of many ethnic dialects that Cable attempted: he read parts from his novels and stories in German-English, Irish-English, Italian-English, and most importantly, the French-English of his white Creole characters. Cable's case reveals how radically the dynamics of ethnic representation had changed by the end of the century, away from individual caricatures or black-white contrasts toward a multiethnic assortment.

To some extent, vaudeville was a confused, pluralistic medium rather than one of absolute racial boundaries. Whereas in antebellum minstrelsy the attention was on a single dialect, vaudeville contained a variety of linguistic situations. True, the polyvocality of vaudeville often had a melting-pot, "whitening" function similar to that of blackface: its fusion of dialects dissolved tensions between different ethnic groups. Yet in another sense "white" speech was being splintered into numerous parts, which registered the cracks within the idea of whiteness that arose from extensive southern and eastern European immigration—cracks not so easily glossed over in a blackface masquerade. In the black musical theater, African Americans would themselves impersonate other "dark-skinned races" like the Spanish. In addition to mimicking Chinese and Arabs, these black performers imitated newer European immigrants such as Italians and Jews, who were believed by some to be tainted with an infusion of African and "Asiatic" blood.[63] This restricted form of masquerade must not have been popular among the ethnic groups being impersonated. It illustrates the radical divisions within whiteness itself at the end of the century, a whiteness that many ethnic groups found to be far from absolute.

In the turn-of-the-century entertainment industry, African Americans were not totally excluded from playing "under the sign of their own ethnicities"—to borrow a phrase from Rogin.[64] The composers of popular postbellum "Coon Songs"—even the most offensive ones like "Coon's Salvation Army" (1884)—were often black themselves. The craze for these heavily dialectal verses was encouraged by the work of another African-American composer: Ernest Hogan's "All Coons Look Alike to Me" (1896).[65] When many white minstrels diversified their acts after the Civil War by including impersonations of white types, the more traditional blackface roles were largely taken over by black performers. As a result, the theatrical convention of minstrel dialect, issuing now from African-American mouths, was widely believed (by whites at least) to be more realistic: the fabricated came to be viewed as authentic.[66] Here, then, was the classic situation of blacks donning the white-defined mask of blackness, using the racial conventions of mainstream entertainment to gain public recognition. Many African Americans performed slow-witted black stereotypes for white audiences, wearing blackface makeup or learning versions of black English that, for some comedians like West Indian–born Bert Williams, were "as much a foreign dialect as that of the Italian."[67] Yet blacks were not solely deriding their blackness for whites: many African-American minstrels were immensely popular with black audiences too. Alongside demeaning portrayals of black speech on the popular stage were other acts in which African Americans used dialectal "Coon Songs" to comment on racist abuse, or used the ambiguity of the black vernacular to signify on the white crowd. This subtle manipulation of language, a process opposite the insensitive and oversimplistic way that "black" speech had usually appeared on the stage, could serve multiple purposes. The word *chicken*, for example, occurred in many songs as the food that the stereotypical "Coon" loved to eat. Yet, as Paul Oliver has shown, a second meaning of *chicken*—"young woman"—allowed black composers like Bob Cole to write "Coon Songs" with another, more rebellious level of meaning that appealed to a black audience.[68]

"Coon Songs" served a fragmented society in their ability to mean different things to different racial groups. The dialect of a song, for example, could be demeaning, but it could also affirm ethnic community, or act as an ambiguous form of political criticism. Moreover, certain "Coon Songs," especially those by African-American composers, had the ability to perform these functions simultaneously, and could thus appeal to a racially divided audience on different levels.[69] Black minstrelsy, and the "Coon Song" in particular, were protean genres in postbellum entertainment. They encompassed whites denigrating blacks, blacks demeaning blacks because that was what whites wanted to hear, blacks signifying on whites through dialectal double meaning, blacks protesting to blacks about racial abuse, and blacks presenting a nonoffensive version of blackness to the middle classes, both black and white.[70]

By the end of the nineteenth century, the linguistic representation of blackness had become much more complex than the blackface minstrelsy of earlier decades. Yet popular theater was hardly a "racial carnival" in which all languages were treated as masks and nobody really knew who was who. Vaudeville's racially destabilizing effects were limited. In terms of black–white relations, the subtle use of ambiguous black language had limited power in bringing racial conciliation: segregation was usually rigidly enforced in the vaudeville theater, and black performers such as George Walker and Ernest Hogan themselves fell victim to violent racist attacks. Shows that mixed both blacks and whites together in the same acts were rare.[71] Rogin's point—that the racial community of African Americans (and of other nonwhite groups) always tends to be excluded from any melting-pot attempt to dissolve ethnic barriers—remains true for much vaudeville performance. This becomes clear from analysis of Anthony Drexel Biddle's *Shantytown Sketches* (1897)—a collection of stories that, like vaudeville itself, depicts a series of dialect-speaking caricatures from Irish, German, and African-American communities. The final sketch, "At the Theatre: From the Gallery Standpoint" (57–64), represents a conversation in the "peanut gallery" of a vaudeville theater among an African American, a Jewish American, and an Irish American. The common theater audience is shown to be ethnically diverse, and each of these minorities speaks a dialect that alienates him from any mainstream standard. Yet there are key differences between the "black" and "white" sides of this ethnic composite. During the performance the African American, Mr. Lincoln, objects to "two little darkies" who let themselves be made fun of on the stage before the "w'ite trash" of the audience (63). The Irishman and the Jew immediately club together and hurl racist insults at Lincoln, asserting themselves as white against this black presence. The critical moment in the sketch comes when Lincoln attempts to raise his voice in protest, daring to assume the implicitly white status of a "gallery god" (the popular term for the heckling element of the vaudeville audience). Lincoln thinks that this is correct procedure "in de freatre, kase I'se often be'n up'n de top gallery we'n de w'ite folks in de freatre pahties talked so loud dat de people wot war actin' couldn't remember deir own elocutions" (64). This breaking of linguistic decorum, a situation in which racial dialect comes from the audience and not in stereotyped stage form, results in the black man's being expelled from the theater, leaving the Jew to exclaim to the Irishman, "I got der pest ohf der pargain dot dime!'' (64). While all these minorities are dialect speakers and are thus alienated from mainstream modes of Americanness, it is the African American whose culture is derided on the stage and whose attempt to challenge society's racial codes leads to his expulsion from public space.

Unlike earlier blackface performance, the primary aim of turn-of-the-century vaudeville was not to create an imaginative structure of whiteness by appropriating—and excluding—the voices of blacks. To some extent, vaudeville's many dialects represented conflicts in the idea of a unified white language, while African-American artists also used dialect to stage versions of their racial selves. Blacks, however, could never participate fully in vaudeville's more reconciling exploration of dialect: its mainstreaming techniques of multiethnic linguistic fusion. The African-American writer Paul Laurence Dunbar, who became famous as a performer of black dialect poems in the late 1890s, occasionally attempted to diversify his act by including verses in Irish dialect—a black impersonation of a white ethnic group to which white reviewers objected harshly.[72] The extent to which Dunbar could switch his linguistic identity was limited; he was often thrust back to a stereotypical ''black'' discourse. Like that of many of his contemporary black vaudevillians, Dunbar's dialect work trod a fine line between racial representation and the perpetration of racist conventions. The space where these African-American artists could perform was narrow, making their subtle subversions more remarkable still.

SEVEN

Paul Laurence Dunbar and the
Authentic Black Voice

"I tell you, Sadness," he said impulsively, "dancing is the poetry of motion."
"Yes," replied Sadness, "and dancing in rag-time is the dialect poetry."
The reporter did not like this. It savored of flippancy.
DUNBAR, *THE SPORT OF THE GODS* (1902), 385

Questions of authenticity have always been central to criticism of Paul
Laurence Dunbar. For William Dean Howells, whose review of Dunbar's
Majors and Minors (1896) first brought the poet to public attention, Dunbar's genuineness was a function of race. Countering the popular racist
argument that the intelligence of black writers such as Charles Chesnutt
and W. E. B. Du Bois stemmed from their white ancestry, Howells emphasized his belief that Dunbar was "of the pure African type," and he described Dunbar's racial knowledge as generating a realistic aesthetic: he
had represented, with undeniable truthfulness, the African-American
"race-life from within the race."[1] Howells's review, rewritten as the introduction to Dunbar's *Lyrics of Lowly Life* (1896), is more complex than
recent critics have recognized. True, Howells at times slips into a demeaning description of black "limits"—the "range of the race," thought
Howells, lies "between appetite and emotion"—and his introduction may
well have contributed to the judgment of Dunbar as a humorously dialectal rather than a "serious" poet, an opinion that Dunbar later believed
had done him "irrevocable harm." Yet Howells's introduction also shows
signs of a tension that would become increasingly important to debates
over race and to appreciations of African-American literature: how to transcend racist discrimination yet still recognize the essential difference of
black culture. Dunbar's literary talent was proof for Howells that a common
humanity overrode racial distinctions. Dunbar's poetic achievements undermined racist opinions of black intellectual inferiority. Having said this,
however, Howells could not ignore the "differences of temperament" that
existed between the races: there were still qualities in black culture that
set it apart from white interpretations. Howells was attempting to balance
a belief in racial equality (albeit limited) with the feeling that Dunbar's

work represented authentic difference—a difference, thought Howells, most evident in poems "of his race in its own accent of our English."[2]

Howells's introduction to *Lyrics of Lowly Life* has received sharp qualification in recent years, yet to some extent the terms of the debate have remained consistent.[3] The urge to depict an authentic black voice has been an important part of African-American literature and its criticism throughout much of the twentieth century.[4] What Howells called black dialect, and what recent linguists call African-American vernacular English—the rhetorical rituals and linguistic patterns that mark off black from white speech—are at the heart of contemporary theoretical debate.[5] Despite occasional efforts to reevaluate his achievements with dialect, however, Dunbar has fallen from critical favor. James Weldon Johnson's comments in his preface to *The Book of American Negro Poetry* (1922) have been largely responsible for this shift in critical attitude, away from the opinion—popular in black magazines at the turn of the century—that Dunbar had truthfully captured black dialect and the "real genius of the race."[6] Although admitting that Dunbar used dialect as "a medium for the true interpretation of Negro character and psychology," taking this form "to the highest point of perfection," Johnson implies that Dunbar inevitably conformed to the minstrel and plantation traditions that defined white depictions of black speech. Rather than capturing "by symbols from within" the imagery, idioms, and turns of thought that express the whole range of the "racial spirit," Dunbar resorted to a mold of convention that merely depended on the mutilation of English spelling and pronunciation, and that emphasized the "two full stops" of black life: humor and pathos. Dunbar could gain public success, in other words, only by imitating the predominantly white literary imitation of black speech. Dunbar was himself quick to recognize this problem: "I've got to write dialect poetry," Johnson once heard him say, "it's the only way I can get them to listen to me." Expanding on these comments in his preface to the revised edition of *The Book of American Negro Poetry* in 1931, Johnson confirms the passing of traditional dialect as a medium for black poets, while he clarifies the different language used by younger poets such as Langston Hughes and Sterling Brown. Theirs "is not the dialect of the comic minstrel tradition or of the sentimental plantation tradition; it is the common, racy, living, authentic speech of the Negro in certain phases of real life."[7]

Critics of African-American literature have, by and large, echoed Johnson's evaluation of Dunbar. Gayl Jones, for example, maintains to a remarkable extent the language and assumptions that mark Johnson's 1922 preface. Dunbar never moves "into the interior landscape" to discover "the true complexities of the African American voice"; it is only the writings of Brown, Hughes, and Zora Neale Hurston that reveal a true folk speech with the power to represent black life with "psychological reality."

Similarly, Henry Louis Gates judges Dunbar to have failed in the attempt "to register his authentic black voice in the tradition of Western poetry": Dunbar decided, Gates argues, to employ "the mastery of white forms to become white." Houston Baker views Dunbar's poetry as a naive and socially irresponsible failure to come to terms with the real politics of masking and minstrelsy.[8] Recent critics tend to read Dunbar as trapped within white traditions.

To rate the quality of Dunbar's poetry is to judge the relationship between literary representation and the actual patterns of black speech. Where dialect literature is concerned, however, one point becomes apparent immediately: ideas of authenticity and realism have definite limits as criteria for aesthetic evaluation. We saw in chapter two some of the technical difficulties that arise from the fundamental impossibility of depicting the human voice in the standard English alphabet, and the black vernacular poses additional problems—critics have argued—through its heightened element of tonality, its *sound*, as Baker defines it.[9] Written dialects are, at best, gestures toward a spoken reality that the reader can bring to the text from his or her recollection of heard experience (hence the emphasis on performance among students of black vernacular poetry).[10] There is, of course, a world of difference between the minstrel stereotype of "darky" dialect and Zora Neale Hurston's masterly representation of the rhythms and metaphors of African-American oral culture. Yet Hurston receives attention and praise not for her phonetic realism but because her dialect performs what late-twentieth-century critics perceive to be a sophisticated, laudable function. Gates's brilliant appreciation of *Their Eyes Were Watching God* credits Hurston's 1937 book with resolving "that implicit tension between standard English and black dialect" with a free indirect discourse that colors the narrator's literary English with the language of "a profoundly lyrical, densely metaphorical, quasi-musical, privileged black oral tradition."[11] Rather than for authenticity alone, Hurston's literary dialect is celebrated for the political tasks to which it is put.[12]

Dunbar was a black poet writing about black people in what he claims to be black dialect. Yet his dialect poetry is repeatedly lambasted, usually on the grounds that it does not capture an authentic black voice but rather perpetuates stereotypical versions of black language and life. This final chapter demonstrates that Dunbar's poetry (both in dialect and in conventional English), and to some extent his prose, constitutes a dynamic response to the historical moment in which he was writing. Rather than simply recapitulating a minstrel paradigm, Dunbar was a wily manipulator of literary conventions, a subtle overturner of racist stereotypes, and a sensitive recorder of the multiple facets of black consciousness at the turn of the twentieth century. A close analysis of Dunbar's poetry, moreover, reveals how the aesthetics of dialect writing are more complex than the single question of representational—particularly "phonetic"—realism. Dunbar may not have been groundbreaking in his formal depiction of the phonemes of African-American vernacular English, but this does not mean that Dunbar's work is thus politically retrograde or aesthetically deficient. There is much more to dialect writing, as we have seen throughout this study, than the imitation of sound.

This reevaluation of Dunbar does not detract from the revolutionary treatment of dialect by the new black writers of the 1920s and '30s. The infusion of blues energy into the poetry of Brown and Hughes, their use of a black vernacular that resisted the deforming conventions of "plantation" dialect, successfully bridged the chasm that had separated literary and black English. These radical experiments with the vernacular marked the rebellious attitudes of the 1920s and '30s, which grew in response to continued negative evaluations of African-American speech. Critics have stressed the vernacular realism of Hughes and Brown but have neglected another attitude toward literary dialect that was new with them: a fresh consciousness of dialect's conventional artificiality,[13] and moreover, a new poetic *use* of this convention as a tool of political resistance. Langston Hughes's poem "Jazz Band in a Parisian Cabaret," included in Johnson's 1931 anthology, illustrates this shift in attitude. The poem describes how the many European tongues (English, French, German, Spanish) that resound in this Parisian cabaret all move to the language of jazz that speaks in the colloquial American voice with which the poem ends:

> Play it, jazz band!
> You've got seven languages to speak in
> And then some,
> "Even if you do come from Georgia,
>   Can I go home wid yuh, sweetie?"
>   "Sure."[14]

Yet this American voice, Hughes implies, is itself multifarious: it too contains different dialects. At the lower registers of American speech there resounds a black accent that Hughes represents with the deeply dialectal "wid yuh"—a dialect reminiscent of literary depictions of Gullah, and markedly different from the black dialect that Hughes occasionally employs in his own poetry.[15] African-American dialect is not a deviation from the American language, nor merely an element to be mimicked. Instead, this dialect represents the black, southern accent underpinning the American voice, and the black creativity that sustains the international language of jazz. In the global Jazz Age, the black vernacular is at the heart of an American language that has the power to rival a host of European tongues.

However we interpret "Jazz Band in a Parisian Cabaret," one point remains clear: dialect does not function as a means of supposedly "realistic" representation, as it had, say, in the work of Joel Chandler Harris. Instead, dialect becomes a poetic device, manipulated by the poet to expose a connection between musical forms and linguistic attitudes that suggests the pervasive presence of black expression within Western culture generally and American culture specifically. Rather than being a medium of access to some purported black experience, dialect is employed to make a political point. The vacillation between voices in Hughes's poem, like the wider oscillation between vernacular and "standard" English in Johnson's *Fifty Years and Other Poems* (1917), Hughes's *The Weary Blues* (1926), and Brown's *Southern Road* (1932), was in fact a continuation of work already begun by Dunbar. His poetry resisted what Kimberly Benston describes as a "retreat into a nostalgic humanism which ignores the differences *within* black discourse(s) as well as their conflicts with other discourses."[16] Dunbar was a complex poet with many voices and many, frequently contradictory, points of view. At its finest, however, his writing achieves an effect strikingly similar to that of Hughes's "Jazz Band in a Parisian Cabaret": a playful juxtaposition of literary languages combines a variety of racial dialects. This self-conscious use of different linguistic registers, explored by Harlem poets of the 1920s, had been pioneered by Paul Laurence Dunbar.

VERNACULAR MASKING

Dunbar's short fiction contains much of the maudlin, sentimental, condescending attitude toward plantation life that has won him such condemnation in recent years. At best, in stories like "Nelse Hatton's Vengeance," Dunbar seems to be seeking the emotional conditions necessary for racial reconciliation in the black performance of superhuman acts of forgiveness. At worst, in stories like "The Strength of Gideon," Dunbar strays into the traditional territory of white writers by depicting loyal slaves who willingly relinquish their freedom and their families in the devoted service of their white masters. As with so much of his writing, Dunbar's stories are marked by severe contrasts. Amid reassuring accounts of happy "darkies" come sudden flashes of biting protest: tales that challenge the absolute racial injustice that meets young educated blacks in the workplace ("One Man's Fortunes"); that reveal the rebellious intelligence of slaves who acquire the tools of literacy through masked deceit of their masters ("The Ingrate"); that expose the corrupt political machinations repressing the organs of black protest ("A Council of State").[17] This combination of accommodation and resistance can be interpreted variously. We might say that Dunbar was an inherently insecure writer who could hardly prevent protest from assimilating to dominant modes of racist stereotype. A more sympathetic critic, however, might detect signs of the very masking always central to African-American oral literature and vernacular technique. Do the "plantation tradition" aspects of Dunbar's stories not act as an emotional smokescreen, disarming his readers, leaving them vulnerable to the sudden dagger of his moral revolt?

To credit Dunbar with this masterstroke of subtlety requires a respect for his literary intelligence—what Houston Baker would call his mastery of form—similar to that recently detected in Dunbar's contemporary, Charles Chesnutt. For example, Chesnutt's dismissive comments on the "ignorance" of black dialect, cited in chapter two, now tend to be read ironically. Baker sees them as part of Chesnutt's subversive use of dialect, as a mask behind which the sound of African spirituality operates to resist the repression of slavery and racism—an idea expanded by Eric Sundquist in *To Wake the Nations*.[18] Dunbar's representation of dialect, however, is usually seen not as a mask but as a sign of the racially compromised qualities of Dunbar's art, or, worse still, as a literal presentation of his patronizing attitude to black southern backwardness. Yet the issues surrounding the black voice in Dunbar's work are, at times, of a much more complex nature. This is clear from "The Lynching of Jube Benson" (1904), a story as remarkable as anything by Chesnutt.

The idea of language as a smokescreen is presented quite literally at the beginning of "Jube Benson." A white man, Gordon Fairfax, is both talking and smoking in his library with two other white friends, a young reporter called Handon Gay and Dr. Melville, apparently an older man: "The talk had drifted from one topic to another much as the smoke wreaths had puffed, floated, and thinned away" (232). Gay injects new life into this smoky conversation by describing a recent magazine story about a lynching. Responding to his friends' statements that they should like to see a lynching, Melville begins to narrate a tale. Lynching provides vocal and written material for this story within a story (Melville's narrative is secretly written down by the young reporter eager for material), thus suggesting how the entertainment of white society is inextricably linked—as in blackface minstrelsy—to racial injustice. Melville's is a story of two relationships: his love affair, while practicing medicine in a small rural town, with Annie Daly; and his friendship with a black servant, Jube Benson, who acts as a go-between in his relationship with Annie and comes to be truly loved by Melville.[19] One day Annie is violently raped and murdered by someone whom she incoherently describes as "That black—" (236). Jube has disappeared, and the whites immediately suspect that he is the attacker. They track him down, assume that he is lying when he denies the crime, and publicly lynch him without trial. The real murderer is then discovered—a white ruffian with his face "blackened to imitate a

Negro's" (238)—but it is too late: Jube is dead, and the words "Blood guilty!" (239) are left crying in Melville's ears.

Everyone trusted Jube Benson: he was "an apparently steady-going, grinning sort, as we used to call him" (234). It soon appears, however, that this grinning actually masks subtle rhetorical codes of deception. In his role as intermediary between Melville and Annie, Jube becomes a channel of communication, a message carrier with special linguistic skills:

> "He not only took messages to Annie, but brought sometimes little ones from her to me, and he would tell me little secret things that he had over-heard her say that made me throb with joy and swear at him for repeating his mistress's conversation. But best of all, Jube was a perfect Cerberus, and no one on earth could have been more effective in keeping away or deluding the other young fellows who visited the Dalys. He would tell me of it after-ward, chuckling softly to himself. 'An,' Doctah, I say to Mistah Hemp Stevens, "'Scuse us, Mistah Stevens, but Miss Annie, she des gone out," an' den he go outer de gate lookin' moughty lonesome. When Sam Elkins come, I say, "Sh, Mistah Elkins, Miss Annie, she done tuk down," an' he say, "What, Jube, you don' reckon hit de——" Den he stop an' look skeert, an' I say, "I feared hit is, Mistah Elkins," an' sheks my haid ez solemn. He goes outer de gate lookin' lak his bes' frien' done daid, an' all de time Miss Annie behine de cu'tain ovah de po'ch des' a laffin' fit to kill.'
>
> "Jube was a most admirable liar, but what could I do? He knew that I was a young fool of a hypocrite, and when I would rebuke him for these deceptions, he would give way and roll on the floor in an excess of delighted laughter until from very contagion I had to join him—and, well, there was no need of my preaching when there had been no beginning to his repen-tance and when there must ensue a continuance of his wrongdoing."[234]

Because "Jube Benson" has a white narrator, Gayl Jones interprets Dun-bar's representation of dialect and black character as an intentional ex-posure of superficial "minstrel parody."[20] Yet Jube's dialect is the subver-sive medium of double meaning, and Dunbar's story as a whole is a complex, politically motivated treatment of the relationship between black and white vocal cultures. The main point is not that Jube equivocates to protect himself, but that he lets white people share in his rhetorical tech-niques, just as Jube shares in his mistress's secret conversations.[21] The story depicts a merging of racial cultures particularly apparent when Jube and Melville enter into the same act of laughter, as had Annie and Jube at the time of his dissembling. The "contagion" that affects Melville is his at-traction to Jube's deceitful discourse; their laughter is a sign of a celebra-tory cross-racial exchange.

Yet this act of sharing is inevitably as dangerous as it is liberating. When suspicion falls on Jube, Melville's knowledge of the African American's skill at ambiguous discourse turns him against his friend. Sincerity, in other words, is read as the mask rather than deceit being read as truth, as had been the case when Jube duped Annie's other suitors. "Fully a dozen of the citizens had seen [Jube] hastening toward the woods and noted his skulking air," we are told after the murder, "but as he had grinned in his old good-natured way, they had, at the time, thought nothing of it. Now, however, the diabolical reason of his slyness was apparent. He had been shrewd enough to disarm suspicion, and by now was far away" (236). Melville has experienced enough of black vocal culture to realize the codes of deception at its heart, but he is not expert enough to read the African American's equally important codes of virtue and honesty—the "inner sense which neither cheats nor lies," as Dunbar expresses it elsewhere.[22] Melville is an unsubtle reader who takes a part of Jube's character for the whole; instead of seeing Jube's spoken chicanery as a rhetorical technique used in specific circumstances, he views it as defining the African American's character. Transcending their misinterpretation of Jube's words, the whites ultimately block out the black's discourse altogether—Melville strikes him a full blow on the mouth in an act of censorship—and resort instead to traditional stereotypes of the black as inherently monstrous and evil (237–38). In a story so concerned with acts of linguistic masking, the final lynching, with the simultaneous discovery of the real murderer, ironically becomes a collective act of unmasking: "No one was masked. We knew each other. Not even the culprit's face was covered" (238). The whites realize that they have taken the facts of Jube's discourse for dissimulation, and they come to face, to unmask, the deceitful racist stereotypes at the heart of their society. The fact that the real murderer is in the mask of blackface—that other bogus form of black–white "exchange"—only underscores the dangers of cultural sharing in a situation of unequal racial power. Dunbar is not "trapped" by dialect stereotypes in "The Lynching of Jube Benson," but he uses dialect with political effectiveness, emphasizing how black dialect is central to wider vernacular rituals that are partly open to the white community yet—with disastrous consequences—partly beyond full comprehension.

Dunbar gives an obvious clue to his exploration of black vernacular masking in his most famous poem, "We Wear the Mask." This work is an intense poetic concentration on what Du Bois would later attempt to capture in his image of the veil: a color line, permeable in one direction only, which facilitates the exclusion of a true image of blackness from mainstream America, thereby condemning the African American to a condition of incomplete self-consciousness.[23] Dunbar's idea of the mask relates directly to issues of black language:

> We wear the mask that grins and lies,
> It hides our cheeks and shades our eyes,—
> This debt we pay to human guile;
> With torn and bleeding hearts we smile,
> And mouth with myriad subtleties. [71]

The subtle mouthing in Dunbar's poem clearly refers to the black rhetorical masking which, as we saw in our account of George Washington
Cable in chapter four, maintains subversive meaning under conventional
or nonsensical forms. It is an ambiguous, ironic language (Dunbar's reference to "cheeks" hints at its tongue-in-cheek status), which forms the
basis of a vernacular, oral culture (Dunbar's reference to "lies" invokes
a traditional African-American word for figurative discourse or tales).[24]
The poem's subsequent references to "sighs" and "cries" signify the special language of African Americans which exists beneath the exterior expression of smiles and songs. A terse poetic image has been forged from
Dunbar's knowledge of complex rhetorical ideas.

A few critics have applied the ideas of masking in "We Wear the Mask"
to a reading of Dunbar's other poems. Marcellus Blount, for example,
argues that "An Ante-bellum Sermon"—rather than conforming to plantation stereotypes—masks a serious agenda which, like black vernacular
performance itself, calls into question "the authority of the literary conventions and racial ideologies of the dominant society." "An Ante-bellum
Sermon" does not pander to patronizing expectations: it aggressively emphasizes the ambiguous voice of black vernacular expression, thus
allowing Dunbar to console black and discerning white listeners in his
audience.[25] Such activity, I suggest, is part of Dunbar's wider manipulation
of the subversive expression beneath conventional stereotype. Rather than
a victim of racist linguistic ideology, Dunbar is the subtle mouther of
African-American rhetorical codes which in turn criticize the political
abuses of his time.

To read his poetry thus is to argue that Dunbar is *signifying*. Signifying,
explains Gates, lies at the heart of black vernacular language. Broadly
defined, it is a black rhetorical ritual of revision, a special way of meaning,
which repeats elements of "standard" (implicitly white) language while
infusing them with a black difference. Thus, signifying is a double-voiced
process that creates a level of exclusively black and deeply figurative meaning within—or rather beyond—the standard language. It is, to use a key
metaphor of Gates's, a verbal masking behind which the codes of black
culture thrive. Signifying allows us to relate vernacular practices to textual
techniques and literary relations: writers signify on one another's styles.
Signifying is, writes Gates, a "metaphor for textual revision."[26] Gates's
notion of literary revision in *The Signifying Monkey*, however, tends to priv-
ilege African-American writers who are signifying either on each other's

texts or on elements within the black tradition, to the detriment of the potentially more subversive process in which they signify on white linguistic models. Dunbar thus partially escapes from Gates's theory of the tradition because he was too concerned with explicitly white literary modes.[27] Dunbar wrote in black dialects, in white rustic dialects, and in explicitly "literary" or "standard" English. To ask whether he is signifying in his poetry is thus to engage in a variety of complex and interrelated questions. We need to address whether his use of dialect signifies on white conventions of black English to show how "the bondage of language can also be liberating," as Sundquist argues for Chesnutt. And we need to ask whether Dunbar's use of standard literary forms acts as a "shadow" to communicate meaning indirectly, as Gates describes one aspect of black signifying rituals.[28]

Dunbar was no unselfconscious, naive mocker of literary conventions; he was highly aware of the racial ramifications of any repetition of white cultural forms.[29] "The Colored Band" is sufficient to suggest Dunbar's knowledge of how African Americans reproduce white music while transfiguring it with their uniquely black rendition. The colored band is playing Sousa in ragtime, the poet tells us, yet

'T'ain't de music by itself dat meks it fine,
Hit's de walkin', step by step,
An' de keepin' time wid "Hep,"
Dat it mek a common ditty soun' divine. [179]

Sousa's "common" music is reinterpreted by black rhythmic, performative rituals—distinctly *African*-American rituals, Dunbar hints with his inclusion of "Hep," a possible Africanism that signifies the swinging, danced, jazzed style of musical improvisation. This element of dance, moreover, was emphasized by Dunbar's own performance of the poem. When the black composer Rosamond Johnson played and sang his version of Dunbar's poem, the poet "liked to give a one-man impersonation of the marching band." As Rosamond's brother, James Weldon Johnson, reported: "This impersonation was, in the main, some pretty cleverly executed cakewalk steps."[30] By performing this cakewalk—a folk custom whereby blacks burlesqued the walk and manners of aristocratic whites— Dunbar was underscoring for his friends what was implicit in his poem: his knowledge of African-American parodic rituals that reappropriate white culture by infusing it with a satirical black difference.

Yet the cakewalk was, observes Sundquist, "an equivocal trope derived from African American folk arts *and* from blackface minstrelsy."[31] Was Dunbar's cakewalk a capitulation to a blackface minstrel aesthetic, or was it a means of black resistance through an ironic repetition of white mores? As with his work as a whole, Dunbar's cakewalk performance presents us with ambiguous evidence. Dunbar often seems a black minstrel echoing white conventions and popular stereotypes. Beneath this mask, I suggest, was an inventive black poet expressing the vernacular rituals of his race.

Many poems by Dunbar exploit—quite brilliantly—the black rhetorical modes that commentators have claimed are absent from his work. "An Ante-bellum Sermon" is a clear illustration of the potential of black vernacular performance to mask subversive meaning with ambiguity. The poem depicts a black southern preacher during slavery who knowingly exploits the powerful undercurrents within the Biblical story of Moses leading the Israelites from slavery to freedom, while simultaneously claiming, with transparent irony, that "I ain't talkin' 'bout to-day. . . . I'm talkin' 'bout ouah freedom / In a Bibleistic way" (14). Rather than conforming to the "humorous" stereotypes of much dialect literature, Dunbar's poem empowers the dialect of this preaching performance as a medium of political resistance. Dunbar is operating within the conventions of dialect literature—the black sermon was a staple among white poets like Irwin Russell[32]—to reveal the black vernacular's capacity for counterdiscourse.

In "An Ante-bellum Sermon," the signifying capacities of black language are depicted with a somewhat heavy hand. "Accountability" is a less repetitious and more subtle poem that plays with the reader's expectations by using its entire structure to political effect. Again written in Dunbar's black dialect, "Accountability" at first constructs a vernacular philosophy of fatalism, a simple understanding of human differences that—typically for Dunbar, some would say—establishes the argument at a personal rather than at a racial level: "We is all constructed diff'ent, d'ain't no two of us de same; / We cain't he'p ouah likes an' dislikes, ef we'se bad we ain't to blame" (5). The poem seems to be about common human principles rather than about racial antagonism. Yet, at the end of the poem, we discover that we have been tricked all along: "Accountability" does in fact have a racially motivated meaning. The speaker's philosophy of moral determinism has been used to justify a small act of rebellion: the speaker could not help stealing "one o' mastah's chickens" (6); he is not, according to his own philosophy, accountable for his—albeit mild—subversive act. The speaker's trite observations about predestination mask deceitful purpose. The reader (often white in Dunbar's day) has been fooled, just like the master who has lost a chicken. The dialect of this poem, moreover, is not simply a condescending stereotype but contributes to the poem's overall masking effect. It is exploited *as* a convention, which acts to disarm our sense of the speaker as a threat, thus contributing to our deception. From "Accountability," there seems little reason to doubt Dunbar's sense for the structural qualities of black speech.

"When Malindy Sings" is another poem that celebrates black verbal mastery, this time of song. The poem, again in Dunbar's black dialect, juxtaposes the sublime qualities of Malindy's black vernacular voice with the artificial, "edicated" (83) music of white folk. Malindy's expression is entirely beyond "de lines an' dots" of the music book (82). It depends instead on what Houston Baker would call the soundings of African America: the culturally specific knowledge of tonal and rhythmic techniques ("tu'ns an' twistin's") that the poetic persona interprets as a function of Malindy's "nachel [natural] o'gans" (82). Gayl Jones criticizes Dunbar for never representing Malindy's voice, for never letting her speak her own story, yet the very point of the poem is that her voice inherently lies *beyond* the written medium.[33] By emphasizing the resistance of black voices to literary representation in a dialect whose purpose it was to capture this very voice, Dunbar creates a massive irony that highlights dialect as an inadequate literary convention. "When Malindy Sings" has a self-destructive logic that undermines rather than confirms the dialect stereotype.

Dunbar's dialect poems are occasionally aggressive in tone. "Discovered," for instance, reveals its black narrator to be a controlling presence, manipulating her white auditor, Miss Lucy, with the knowledge she has gained of Miss Lucy's secret love liaison while masking her aggressive intent behind the ironic statement: "Nevah min', Miss Lucy" (60). Usually, however, the best of Dunbar's black dialect poems work like "When Malindy Sings": they have a subtle duality of meaning, a subversive flip side rarely noted by critics. "Whistling Sam," for example, juxtaposes a dialectal description of the tonal magnificence of a black whistler called Sam with actual bars of musical notation that aim to represent Sam's music—a juxtaposition with a double effect.[34] On the one hand, the bars of music tend to work against the dialect, emphasizing its inadequacy: If black music can be represented in this standard notation, then why does the black voice have to be subjected to the deformities of conventional dialect? On the other hand, Dunbar predicts Du Bois's similar use of anonymous bars of music as chapter epigraphs in *The Souls of Back Folk* (1903), which, Sundquist argues, challenged their contemporary audience by demanding familiarity with a cultural language that, through its inherent tonal qualities, lay beyond their hearing.[35] While Dunbar's poem lacks the intellectual breadth of Du Bois's work, his belief that at the heart of black culture lies a dynamic convergence of musicality and meaning—a dimension of sound underpinning its expressive qualities—is clearly presented to the reader in the textual interaction of linguistic and musical modes.

A significant number of Dunbar's poems deal with the musicality of African America, and several of them repeat the equivocal pattern of "Whistling Sam." "A Banjo Song," for example, deals with a serious subject—the importance of music in maintaining cultural spirit through the troubles of slavery—and one might argue that this seriousness is inevitably spoiled by the poem's "dancing darky" dialect and caricatures. Yet read from another perspective, the "humorous" dialect actually sharpens Dunbar's political point: the dialect's nonthreatening nature disarms the reader and thus masks a bold recognition of the sustaining qualities within black creativity. Similarly ambiguous is "A Corn-Song," one of the few poems of Dunbar's to combine "standard" and "black" language in a single form. The poem presents a plantation master listening to, and being deeply moved by, the work song of his slaves. At first, the poem seems to conform to a sentimental view of harmonious plantation life: the slaves work hard but are joyous of song and contented with their lot. Yet Dunbar's larger point, underscored by rhyme, is that apparent lightheartedness masks actual sorrow: "their corn-song rises ever loud and cheery" yet "the halting steps be labored, slow, and weary" (59). Song is a means to maintain community and respect in the face of slavery's consuming labors. True, Dunbar never pushes his point, and he presents the views of both slave and master. Such balance is the remarkable quality of many poems by Dunbar: they simultaneously appeal to different ideological perspectives, upholding white sensitivity while exposing the guile of black resistance. A similar process can be glimpsed explicitly in Dunbar's fiction, where he repeats what he calls the "usual phrase" of plantation tradition literature yet qualifies it with a deeper understanding of black life.[36] Such repetition with a revisionary difference was part of Dunbar's attempt to appeal to a racially fragmented audience by combining accommodation and protest in a single poem.

THE CONVENTIONS OF DIALECT

Dunbar's "phonetic" representation of black dialect was hardly revolutionary. Close analysis shows that he used well-established, implicitly white literary conventions in his differentiation of black from white speech: more solecisms, eye dialect, elision of medial *r*, and so on.[37] Yet Dunbar's poetic exploration of other aspects of the black vernacular, especially its rituals of signifying, indirection, and ambiguity, was often structurally cunning and politically astute. Dunbar's spelling of black dialect in his short story "The Case of 'Ca'line'" might seem clichéd to modern readers, yet it masks real black vernacular values operating at a deeper level. The story describes a black servant using indirection, improvisation, and sheer verbal dexterity to trick her white mistress, turning an attempted reprimand into an increase in wages.

This argument, however, does not hold for all of Dunbar's work. Dunbar's mixed audience was mostly white, and accordingly many of his poems seem to stray into the ideological realms of white racist thought by confirming minstrel and plantation stereotypes. Too often, dialect embodies the logic of black inferiority. Slaves and former slaves are presented as chicken-stealing, 'possum-hunting victims of their appetites, who adore their loving masters and long for nothing more than the pleasures of cabin and banjo after a hard day's work in the field. Occasionally, there is a disturbing animalism to Dunbar's African Americans: dogs and "darkies" share the same frame of mind (169), and when an animal speaks—as in "Soliloquy of a Turkey"—it does so in a supposedly black voice (171). Lines like "You kin jes' tell Mistah Lincum fu' to tek his freedom back" (138) could be straight from the minstrel stage.[38] Yet there is, I suggest, a significant difference behind Dunbar's repetition of apparently racist stereotypes. The ideology of the plantation tradition worked by blurring the line between memory and reality; nostalgic stereotypes were politically powerful because they were so often taken as truths.[39] In Dunbar's poems about slave life, however, there is a radical tension between the categories of memory and reality. Rather than a natural truth, memory is presented as a convention, a retrospective construction. Dunbar's dialect, moreover, is a crucial means of emphasizing the artificiality of plantation nostalgia.

In Dunbar's poem "The Poet," the speaker famously regrets that the world has turned from his "deeper" poetry "to praise / A jingle in a broken tongue" (191). This "broken tongue" is usually taken as referring to Dunbar's dismissive opinion that the black vernacular is a downtrodden, broken language which does not measure up to the sublime potential of standard English (an idea in conflict with Dunbar's usually sympathetic statements about folk material).[40] Yet this poetic image just as readily suggests Dunbar's belief that the implicitly white literary *conventions* for representing black dialect, not the folk speech itself, are actually broken. Dunbar may be self-consciously recording his awareness of having to use imperfect literary forms—an idea that recalls Howells's out-of-place comment, in his introduction to *Lyrics of Lowly Life*, that Dunbar's poems "are really not dialect so much as delightful personal attempts and failures for the written and spoken language." Although Sterling Brown considered Dunbar's "grasp upon folk-speech" to be "generally sure," and while Dunbar was clearly conscious of the deep structures of black rhetoric in such poems as "An Ante-bellum Sermon," he never loses awareness of the artificiality of the more superficial aspects of black literary dialect—

its supposedly phonetic orthography, its clichéd vocabulary of 'possums and banjos—and he uses this artificiality to political ends.[41] Dunbar never lets his reader settle into the view that his dialect is a "natural" mode of black expression, the view that led white readers to take stereotypes for realities.

Dunbar employs several methods to emphasize literary dialect's constructed status. "A Letter" is a poem based on Dunbar's 1897 reading tour to London: the black persona is writing to his lover from England, where he is traveling, sightseeing, enjoying fine restaurant cuisine, and listening to classical music. In an actual letter Dunbar claimed to feel "entirely white" during this tour, in response to the apparently egalitarian attitudes he encountered in London's high society,[42] yet the voice of the poem is intended to be entirely black. "A Letter" is composed to a semi-literate recipient in Dunbar's typical black dialect: "I done see the Crystal Palace, an' I's hyeahd dey string-band play, / But I has n't seen no banjos layin' nowhahs roun' dis way" (152). Rather than suggesting this dialect as an integrally black means of expression, the sheer incongruity between substance (a tour of London high life) and form (plantation-flavored black speech) only emphasizes the dialect's unnatural, arbitrary status. The charade of dialect writing is blown wide open. The speaker's longing for banjos and chittlings comes to seem a little ridiculous, his "darky" idiom completely unbelievable.

Throughout his work, Dunbar highlights the conventionality of written dialect by representing very different voices in close proximity. Dunbar tends to place poems in black dialect beside poems in orthodox English—a technique he repeated in his public recitals—thus making us aware that there is no natural connection between the poet and any single language.[43] As we saw in the final section of the previous chapter, blacks were never so free to impersonate other ethnic groups as were, say, Jewish or Irish Americans; only rarely does Dunbar employ supposedly Irish dialect terms like "O chone!" (261). Within these restrictions, however, Dunbar acts to disrupt the notion of a unified linguistic standard of white English, especially in his extensive use of the rustic midwestern dialect made famous by the poetry of James Whitcomb Riley. By juxtaposing different dialects, Dunbar undercuts the reader's tendency to believe in the inevitable connection between language and mind, a connection that white writers like Joel Chandler Harris were quick to assert, a connection that fueled belief in black mental limitations. Dunbar often achieves a relativistic viewpoint to counter the absolute power of language to distort visions of reality, which he demonstrates in a lawyer's manipulation of the jury in "The Lawyers' Ways." Thus, Dunbar's most anthropological sketch, "Sister Jackson's Superstitions," illustrates how black dialect can express a range of beliefs, from the skeptical to the credulous, thereby denying any necessary identification between dialect and a superstitious mindset.[44]

Dunbar's emphasis upon language's multiple and shifting varieties reaches occasional points of intensity. In "Appreciation," to give the most explicit example, the reader is immediately confused about which dialect Dunbar is attempting to depict. The first stanza reads:

My muvver's ist the nicest one
'At ever lived wiz folks;
She lets you have ze mostes' fun,
An' laffs at all your jokes. [247]

This poem has been variously interpreted as representing the Creole (meaning French-English) dialect of New Orleans or the German-English dialect made popular by Charles G. Leland (Dunbar wrote an early poem in German dialect, called "Lager Beer," under the pseudonym of Pffenberger Deutzelheim).[45] It may well be that Dunbar is trying to depict a child's dialect from the Midwest, à la James Whitcomb Riley, who also used *ist* as a childhood form of *just*, rather than as a German word. Confusion is both the effect and the point of this poem. Dunbar places tremendous emphasis on the conventional status of language by writing in an indeterminate dialect. The reader is never allowed to rest in a cozy acceptance of the dialect's naturalness. A similar but less pronounced version of this effect is found in black dialect poems, like "Advice," which do not contain the stereotypical plantation themes of 'possum hunting and banjo playing, but concern the brand of commonsense philosophizing that marks Dunbar's white rustic dialect poems. Without the necessary signals of subject matter, it becomes much more difficult to decide whether the dialect is meant to be black or rural white. Likewise, "A Love Letter" is not obvious as black dialect until *gwine* appears over halfway through (266). By obscuring the usual relationship between substance and form, these poems emphasize how our appreciation of dialect is often a direct function of our response to obvious contextual elements, just as Dunbar's own dialect is frequently criticized—as Keeling observes—because of a negative response to Dunbar's presentation of his subject matter.[46]

Linguistic variation is typical in a volume of Dunbar poems and also occurs, to a lesser extent, within individual verses. "The Old Apple-tree," for example, oscillates between a number of different voices: mildly colloquial English defined by clipped final *g*'s; standard English with no unusual qualities; self-consciously archaic, poetic English (*passeth*); and the richer rustic dialect that Dunbar admired in Riley. "The Old Apple-tree," like so many poems by Dunbar, concerns the pleasurable recollection of a nostalgic, rural past. The dialect becomes more extreme at the moments when the speaker becomes most romantic about his youth: "I kin shet my eyes an' see it / Jest as plain as plain kin be, / That same old swing a-danglin' / To the old apple-tree" (10). The poem's persona is self-consciously aware that his nostalgia is a retrospective construct, the product of memory's adorning glow. The variations in the poem's language, moreover, make the reader aware that dialect is not an inherent way of speaking but the poetic medium of momentary nostalgic visions.[47]

The dialect in "The Old Apple-tree" illustrates a key aspect of memory in Dunbar's work. The romantic vision of a black plantation past, in which slaves are happy and master is kind, is presented as just that: a self-consciously unrealistic idea. Dunbar rarely dresses nostalgia as realism; the naked fact of memory's transformative power usually lies on the surface of his poems. In "The Old Cabin," to give the most obvious example, the speaker is overtly aware of the constructed nature of his view of plantation life:

> An' my min' fu'gits de whuppins
> Draps de feah o' block an' lash
> An' flies straight to somep'n' joyful
> In a secon's lightnin' flash. [260]

The joys of the past are clearly the product of creative recounting. In "The Party," the humorous antics of plantation festivity are again presented as the creation of an unreliable narrator rather than as events that might really have happened. The implied presence of an outside listener, whom the poem's narrator is trying to make jealous, emphasizes "the possibility of other, perhaps preferable, perspectives"—notes Keeling—which thus upsets the "stereotypical effectiveness" of the plantation tradition.[48] Even poems that dwell most outrageously on the good old days of slavery, like "The Deserted Plantation," do so from the perspective of a solitary rememberer attempting to paint a pretty history for his own psychological health.

Dunbar is more interested in how people refigure the past than in making claims about historical reality. His poems explore the creation of an ideology rather than confirming it as fact.[49] In its very creation, moreover, this potentially racist ideology is shrewdly frustrated. "To the Eastern Shore," for instance, describes a black urban dweller being called back emotionally to the purer, pastoral ways of the plantation—a classic theme of Dunbar's. The poem's final lines complicate any simple nostalgic vision:

> Fu' de ol' plantation's callin' to me, Come, oh, come.
> An' de Chesapeake's a-sayin' "Dat's de t'ing,"

W'ile my little cabin beckons, dough his mouf is closed an' dumb,
I's a-comin, an' my hea't begins to sing. [203]

The personified cabin is not a speaker of truth about the past but a censored voice. It stands as a conscious acknowledgment of all that must be
silenced in the making of an idealized picture of slavery: its mouth is
closed and dumb.

This cabin "mouf" is a symbolic equivalent to the function of black
song that Dunbar stresses throughout his poetry. Dunbar's song is always
an explicit escape from weariness: it is an intentional suppression of sorrow, ironically implying this sorrow by its very omission.[50] The "voice of
the banjo," Dunbar suggests in a poem of that name, is the voice of
honeyed memory, urging the former slave to think of pleasure and keep
a merry visage (124). Dunbar's dialect is another version of this banjo
voice. It is not, at least in its more obvious "phonetic" sense, a serious or
realistic language so much as a signal to readers that they are entering an
artificial world whose acknowledged purpose is to transmute misery into
a narrow, reassuring set of fictions.

The self-consciously fabricated nature of Dunbar's poems in the black
vernacular helps to explain a curious point about his work in general: the
dialect poems are not marked by overt sorrow, yet the "standard" English
poems are, at times, defined by little else. An absence of explicitly "black"
qualities in Dunbar's poetry, however, does not mean a lack of racial feeling: far from it. Dunbar resignifies standard forms by infusing them with
racial levels of meaning, thereby predicting a similar process detectable
in the poetry of Claude McKay and Countee Cullen.[51] Rather than ne-
glecting social issues in his conventional lyrics, Dunbar exhibits a substra-
tum of race consciousness throughout his work. And rather than aban-
doning dialect in these poems in orthodox English, Dunbar structures
several of them around the element of black vernacular expression that
is so obviously explored in "An Ante-bellum Sermon": the masking of
subversive meaning behind apparently innocent forms.

We might call this the "caged bird" effect, after Dunbar's poem "Sympathy," whose second stanza reads:

I know why the caged bird beats his wing
Till its blood is red on the cruel bars;
For he must fly back to his perch and cling
When he fain would be on the bough a-swing;
And a pain still throbs in the old, old scars
And they pulse again with a keener sting—
I know why he beats his wing! [102]

Dunbar's caged bird can be interpreted in two ways: it symbolizes the universal human feeling of entrapment that so often provokes the most sublime expressions of release; or, it is a deeply racial symbol of black cultural servitude which, from the time of slavery (here "old scars" takes a very particular meaning), has forced African Americans into physical and cultural acts of resistance. The poem turns on Dunbar's "I": Is the poem spoken in a universal, nonracial voice, or do we allow our knowledge of the poet's race to influence our reading, just as Dunbar's blackness was an integral part of the contemporary reception of his poems?[52] The answer is both. The success of many of Dunbar's "standard" poems is that they meld the nonracial and the racial, the accommodationist and the rebellious, into one ambiguous expression.

"Prometheus" seems in one sense a confession of poetic inferiority, a supplication to the master of English Romanticism:

> We have no singers like the ones whose note
> Gave challenge to the noblest warbler's song.
> We have no voice so mellow, sweet, and strong
> As that which broke from Shelley's golden throat.
>
> The measure of our songs is our desires:
> We tinkle where old poets used to storm.
> We lack their substance tho' we keep their form:
> We strum our banjo-strings and call them lyres. [117]

Yet the poem is much more than an admission of inadequacy. While "Prometheus" can be read as a general lament over the state of contemporary American poetry, the reference to banjos in the final line informs the poem with African-American significance, at least in the world of Dunbar's poems, where the banjo is a leitmotif of blackness. The final lines, moreover, treat not the inferiority but the difference of black song. African-American singers cannot "storm" but must learn to "tinkle" in significant ways. This is achieved, the poem implies, by exploiting a disparity between substance and form. Their poetry may seem like conventional lyricism at the surface, but it contains racially motivated meaning at a deeper level. And remarkably, the last line of the poem gives an example of this very technique of indirect allusion. The homophonic pun on *lyres/ liars* creates powerful ambiguity. In one sense, the black singer is bemoaning the fact that his banjo will never reach the sublime level of Shelley's lyre. In another sense, however, the black poet is quietly drawing attention to the element of deceit implicit in his own work and in the African-American lyric product in general. Banjo songs are liars because they mask alternative substance beneath conventional form. What begins as a confession of mediocrity ends as a subtle lesson in how to read the double meaning of black expression.

Dunbar wrote a great deal of mediocre poetry in conventional English, some of which repeats a dominant Anglo-Saxon ideology to an embarrassing degree.[53] Yet Dunbar also composed some exceptional nondialect poetry, the best of which is charged with racial tension. At first glance, "The Poet and His Song" seems to explore the universal theme of a poet who, despite the world's lack of sympathetic attention, gains solace from the sheer power of his song. There seems to be no racial agenda behind his regret, until we reach a striking image at the beginning of the final stanza:

> Sometimes the sun, unkindly hot,
> My garden makes a desert spot;
> Sometimes a blight upon the tree
> Takes all my fruit away from me;
> And then with throes of bitter pain
>   Rebellious passions rise and swell;
> But—life is more than fruit or grain,
>   And so I sing, and all is well. [5]

That blackness issues from "the long kiss of the loving tropic sun" is a trope employed by Dunbar in "To the South" (216); the initial line of the above quotation implicitly alludes to this popular poetic conceit. In the most subtle manner, the poet bemoans the idea, as he did in an 1892 letter to James Newton Matthews, that "the novelty of a black face associated with the power to rhyme" is the real source of attention to his work.[54] His "Rebellious passions" seem racial passions aroused by the demeaning stereotypes that limit the accepted area in which a black poet can work, thus reducing his "serious" ambitions to a "desert spot" of public recognition.

Dunbar's seemingly nonracial poetry contains another dimension, largely ignored by critics. Subversive ambiguities spring up everywhere in Dunbar's writing: many of his poems naturally contain the possibility for less accommodationist interpretation. In "The Ol' Tunes," for example, a celebration of old-fashioned, rustic white music leads the poet to conclude that "no mortal minstrel / Ever chanted sich a lay" (54). This apparent compliment, seeming to suggest that American music is superior to the ancient songs of European minstrelsy, also yields a note of protest. *Minstrel* was, of course, a loaded term to be using in an American context at the end of the nineteenth century: its allusion to blackface performance hints at how black culture, unlike its white counterpart, has fallen victim to the deforming voice of racist caricature. Similar references to what seems to be European minstrelsy in Dunbar's poems are also underscored by blackface allusions.[55] Such homonymic punning is accompanied by less obvious but more aggressively insurgent implications in "The Colored

Soldiers." What seems at first to be a fairly mild celebration of black achievement in the Civil War is transfigured in the following stanza:

> They have shared your nightly vigils,
> They have shared your daily toil;
> And their blood with yours commingling
> Has enriched the Southern soil. [51]

While the mixture of blood is, at one level, a battlefield image, the allusion to "*nightly* vigils" reinforces its secondary function as an image of miscegenation, an ultimate joining of the races that undermines the logic of post-Reconstruction segregation, and that plays explicitly on white fears.

Transcending individual images or stanzas, there are entire poems by Dunbar that lay themselves open to alternative, racially informed readings. "Ere Sleep Comes Down to Soothe the Weary Eyes," for example, seems to convey "the life of personal vision with no attention to social concerns," even for those critics who are most alert to the racial aspects of Dunbar's work.[56] Yet, on closer inspection, the poem is clearly structured around a series of ideas that naturally accommodate a distinctly African-American interpretation of its predominant tone of weariness: the forced condition of living in a world of lies; the difficulty of reconstructing the past; the need for the soul to return to strange, unspeakable lands; the spiritual damage of unremunerative labor (3–4). At their best, Dunbar's nondialect poems use such ambiguity to mask a contemplation of the problems of black consciousness. Echoing the signifying capacities of the black vernacular, they repeat conventional meanings by informing them with subversive subtexts.

FRACTURED LANGUAGES OF BLACKNESS

The linguistic complexity of Dunbar's dialect poetry, and the subtle act of masking in his nondialect poetry, represent strains within the poet's work rather than characteristics of the whole. Some poems criticize or reject the very logic of masking,[57] while in others the poet attempts to "write himself white," to imagine himself within a dominant white culture of fair-faced lovers ("The Retort," 5). This unevenness explains why Dunbar has the power to elicit such mixed responses from the most sensitive critics of African-American literature. Gates argues that Dunbar "[s]ignified upon the received white racist textual tradition and posited in its stead a black poetic diction"; turning to the poetry, however, he concludes that Dunbar was poetically renouncing his black identity. Baker describes the Dunbar who wrote *The Sport of the Gods* as a "brilliantly energetic craftsman of the vernacular" who used this novel to represent "vibrant and inversive blues energies," while the Dunbar of the poetry was "naive, politically innocent, or simply 'spoiled.'"[58]

Reading Dunbar is not a harmonious experience. Instead of a unified black self, representing folk culture in an "authentic" way, we meet a fractured consciousness, a poet fundamentally unsure about which language to use. His lament to a poetic lover, "Oh teach me the tongue that shall please thee the best" (289), might as well have been addressed to Dunbar's racially complex audience. Dunbar expressed regret that the world had followed Howells's dictum by valuing his dialect verse at the expense of what he regarded as his serious poetry. But he also declared that "my fondest love is for the Negro pieces. . . . They have grown instinctively in me." He referred to dialect as "my natural speech."[59] There has been some doubt about Dunbar's knowledge of African-American vernacular English, yet the biographical and literary evidence suggests contact with and a facility in *both* "standard" English and black vernacular.[60] Dunbar was attempting to express a situation of bidialectalism—or rather, multidialectalism—in his poetry. His confession to being a "black white man" is represented linguistically throughout his work in the juxtaposition of black dialect with white English in its several varieties. George Hutchinson argues that this simply reflects Jim Crow practices in its preservation of racial hierarchy. Yet this juxtaposition should be interpreted as Dunbar's attempt—however incomplete—to unite different racial traditions in a single work. His use of two rustic dialects, the black and the white, is an effort to establish cultural parity between two ethnic worlds: throughout these poems, blacks and whites share common concerns for the purer spirituality of the old music and the old ways. Nostalgia is shown to be transracial.[61]

In his fiction and ethnography of the 1880s, George Washington Cable exploited black–white linguistic fusion to disrupt white notions of racial separateness and supremacy. The question of linguistic and cultural interaction engaged the Jewish writer Abraham Cahan at the turn of the century. Cahan used dialect to illustrate the difficulties of establishing an integral ethnic voice amidst the intermixture of mainstream and minority groups, an intermixture that also revealed a dominant culture informed by the ethnic elements it was attempting to suppress. Perhaps the era's fullest inquiry into cultural merger was W. E. B. Du Bois's *The Souls of Black Folk* (1903), a work that highlighted the dangers of losing a coherent language of communication between blacks and whites; a work that called for America to recognize its cross-racial linguistic, cultural, and intellectual exchange in which an integral African-American element had been actively woven with "the very warp and woof of this nation." Dunbar should be seen in the context of these larger explorations of cultural and racial amalgamation.[62] To some extent, the tensions and contradictions in Dunbar illustrate the dangerous duality of DuBoisian double-consciousness. We find a writer attempting "to know and test the power of the cabalistic letters of the white man," as Du Bois phrased it, while simultaneously attempting to enter the folk materials of black culture. Poems that thematically express this double movement, like "The Paradox," leave us with a sense of ambivalence that thwarts resolution; articulation collapses into the representation of divided psychology.[63] Many would argue that the language of Dunbar's poems also expresses Du Bois's "contradiction of double aims": the vacillation between "standard" English and "black" dialect shows a poet divided between two different languages, neither of them his "natural" voice and neither of them adequate to the task of representing his racial "reality."[64]

Yet this argument fails to recognize how Dunbar goes beyond the duality in double-consciousness by acknowledging a variety of dialects, both within white and within black English—a variety of subdivisions within broad racial categories.[65] Although he never achieves—or attempts—the same kaleidoscopic switching of identity as did many vaudevillians, Dunbar frequently transcends a binary relation between black and white with his multidialectal series of shifting selves. Moreover, by seeing Dunbar only in terms of the negative aspects of DuBoisian racial psychology, we miss the degree of articulation in Dunbar's work, his creation of ambiguous, composite languages that are neither really black nor white. Like the southern white English that was indelibly transfigured by its contact with black speechways (as we saw in chapter four), and like the African-American vernacular English that was itself the "colonial interface" of African and Anglophone language cultures, Dunbar's poetic languages hover halfway between racial polarities.[66] His "black" dialect is partly an African-American way of speaking based on observations of black folk culture, and partly a white literary convention based on his reading of the plantation tradition.[67] And the language of Dunbar's nondialect poetry derives from late-Romantic England while also being infused with masked rituals of black vernacular resistance to white oppression, both racial and artistic. Stories such as "The Lynching of Jube Benson" and "The Churching of Grandma Pleasant" show Dunbar's wider interest in the interracial fusion of cultural forms.[68] Even the minstrel-like "Coon Songs" that Dunbar wrote for the black musical theater concern racial contact: "When dey hear dem ragtime tunes / White fo'ks try to pass fo' coons." And we should not forget that the character Skaggs in Dunbar's novel *The Sport of the Gods*, described by Houston Baker as a "blues detective" whose vernacular skills reveal how the literary tradition of plantation and coon-show images "can be altered through an ironic, symbolic, fictive (blues) manipulation," is *white*—a point Baker neglects to emphasize.[69] Dunbar's ideas of racial merger may not have been as fully developed as Du Bois's, yet his work contains many moments of intense concentration on black–white cultural and linguistic interaction.[70]

If vaudevillians used the versatility of the spoken voice to suggest ethnic fusion, the same was partly true for Dunbar's popular performance of his own poetry before live audiences.[71] Dunbar was faced with many problems in representing black folk, not just the fact that white writers had already appropriated black culture but also the fact that much of this culture's creativity lay at an oral, tonal level, impossible to capture in written words. We might criticize Dunbar's spelling of dialect, but the quality of his spoken rendition of the vernacular lies beyond complete recovery. By all accounts Dunbar had a musical voice, and it seems that many audiences took his dialect for an accurate rendition.[72] Yet the audiences of blackface minstrel shows seem to have taken *that* dialect for reality too. As with Dunbar's cakewalk before the Johnson brothers, considered earlier, it becomes difficult to tell whether Dunbar's work conformed to or protested its racist environment. In this respect, Jean Wagner is perhaps the most positive critic of Dunbar's performances, considering them "characteristically African" in their synthesis of poetry, music, and dance. Wagner cites Lida Keck Wiggins's account of a Dunbar reading as his example:

> His lithe form, graceful as a gazelle's, glided about the stage, with a rhythm of movement which showed that his whole being responded to the music of the orchestra and to the beauty of his own conception. Every emotion depicted in the lines came out upon his face and found expression in his wonderful eyes. The audience went wild with excitement and the wine of their applause only served to stimulate his efforts. The recital was a great success, and the southern people who had been carried back to "old plantation days" by the vivid poem-pictures and skillful acting of the wonderful negro boy, were the most enthusiastic of the audience.[73]

These apparently black folk qualities of rhythm, musicality, and pictorial imagery, however, were dedicated to an implicitly "white" poem: Wiggins is describing Dunbar reciting "The Cornstalk Fiddle," a Whitcomb Riley–like description of *white* country dancing. Rather than illustrating "characteristically African" elements, this description displays racial intermixture. When members of the audience became enthusiastic about Dunbar's depiction of old plantation days, were they responding to Dunbar's impersonation of whiteness—a type of cakewalk—or to his demonstration of "wonderful negro" dancing? Was he performing Afrocentric rituals, or perpetuating minstrel stereotypes?[74] The difficulty of answering these questions is really the point, not only to Dunbar's performances but to his poetry in general: it interfuses authentic qualities *and* white reappropriations of black folk culture, just as it reinterprets white artistic forms from an African-American perspective. Placed in the context of contemporary black poets, Dunbar reveals something of James Edwin Campbell's anthropological interest in black folk *and* Daniel Webster Davis's minstrel-style buffoonery.[75] We might view Dunbar's stage act as an example of how his performance of blackness was compromised by the incorporation of minstrel-like qualities. But it also illustrates, equally well, how Dunbar was remaking white culture in his "wonderful negro" way.

Dunbar too easily becomes a straw man in the consensus view that—apart from the spirituals—it is not until writers such as Langston Hughes and Sterling Brown that a successful poetic use of the black vernacular emerges, a form that James Weldon Johnson described as "freer and larger than dialect . . . expressing the imagery, the idioms, [and] the peculiar turns of thought" of African Americans.[76] For George Hutchinson, Dunbar "was caught in a theory of literature and an institutional matrix tragically inadequate to his poetic resources," and it is difficult not to argue that Dunbar was hemmed in by genteel literary tradition, by theories of expression that prioritized the use of dialect spelling in an attempt to capture sound, and by a predominant acceptance of racist stereotype that severely limited the portrayal of black character.[77] The often ridiculous ideological contradictions that Dunbar entertains are clear examples of protest compromised by considerations for a dominant white audience.[78] Yet to say that Dunbar was trapped in an institutional matrix is to miss the instances when Dunbar's wings beat against the cage of literary convention, the points where he cleverly redrew the limits in which he was allowed to operate. Does this forging of creativity from oppression not place Dunbar clearly within his racial tradition, not outside it in the realm of white genteel culture?

Rather than simply dismissing Dunbar on the grounds of his supposedly inauthentic portrayal of black culture, this chapter has attempted to open up some of the complexities within the idea of authenticity itself. Reading Dunbar leaves us with a profound sense of the problems involved in representing a stable racial essence of speech at a time when white Americans were themselves colored by the black culture they would publicly abuse, and when black Americans were deeply versed in the white traditions from which they were socially excluded, as well as being partially alienated from the southern black folk culture in which they were expected to work. The establishment of racial authenticity against hybrid modes and racist stereotypes became doubly difficult during Dunbar's lifetime with the entry of African Americans into "black" theatrical roles that had traditionally been played by whites in blackface, as we saw in the previous chapter. Robert Toll has described the checkered results of these blacks playing "themselves": they were able to control and resignify the portrayal of blackness, yet they also lent even more credibility to the original racist stereotypes.[79] Dunbar's use of dialect was similarly complex. Here was a black man parodying what was predominantly a white literary parody of black speech with the mixed results of both confirming racial conventions and refiguring them, from within, with his vernacular black difference.

Following the efforts of writers such as Twain, James, Cable, and Cahan, and like his contemporary ethnic performers on the vaudeville stage, Dunbar appreciated dialect not for its superficial "realism" but for its power to structure a political response to larger social, cultural, and racial issues. Critics have generally failed to recognize how Dunbar consciously plays with the linguistic tensions surrounding him in an effort to accommodate different racial motivations. Rather than being pulled apart by opposing racial voices, Dunbar manipulates their conventions, creating an acceptable space for a series of brilliant aesthetic maneuvers. True, there is much that is seemingly inauthentic in Dunbar's representation of dialect, especially his use of conventional dialect spelling and of a demeaning vocabulary of racist clichés. Yet there is also a politically subtle use of black vernacular techniques beneath this orthographic mask. And while we can accuse Dunbar of selling out to dominant literary styles, or of attempting to force black subject matter into white poetic forms, we should not miss his essays at cultural amalgamation, his fusion of white cultural models with black vernacular patterns and values.

For Paul Laurence Dunbar, as for his character Sadness in *The Sport of the Gods*, dialect poetry was the ragtime dance of American literature. To say this is to recognize the continued white dominance over the forms of American art, just as ragtime was sweeping over white America at the turn of the century. But it is also to recognize how racially mixed mainstream American culture really was.

Conclusion

I have attempted to establish the fact that dialect writing was a distinct and complex movement in late-nineteenth-century American letters. Its complexity had origins in the wider public and scholarly debate over the quality and function of American dialect. Seemingly relativistic beliefs in the normality of dialect were undercut by feelings that dialect was a degenerate force threatening the standards of civilization. And claims that the United States lacked European degrees of linguistic difference were accompanied by fears that American dialects were present everywhere, and that the forces of ethnic intermixture and social mobility were undermining the American language from within. The regional writers who turned to vernacular language in the 1870s and '80s as a major source of their subject matter betrayed similarly ambivalent opinions of dialect. Celebrations of the democratic realism and rugged raciness of subaltern speech met anxieties that dialect signaled the cultural fragmentation and deterioration of the nation. For authors such as Herman Melville and Henry James, the disruptive aspects of Gilded Age society—the growth of mass culture, for example, or the dissolution of traditional class hierarchies—were embodied in a nervous and peculiarly feminine type of linguistic disease with the power to infect the guardians of American vocal value. Their works from the 1880s explore the formal and political ramifications of a situation that had troubled regional writers: the sense of being trapped between equally problematic discourses, which arose from dialect's power to contaminate any standard against which it might be judged.

The idea of linguistic contamination dominated reactions to racial and ethnic impacts on the American language. The white writer George Washington Cable subverted attempts to establish the separateness and inferi-

ority of black language by revealing how black speech had helped to produce white southern speech while it still maintained the power to
undermine white culture with satirical techniques of ambiguous signification. Cable's use of dialectal ideas to structure a literature of political
criticism continued in the work of ethnic writers at the turn of the century.
Abraham Cahan's novels and stories about Jewish life in the New York
ghetto explored the linguistic intermixture of ethnic and mainstream languages to illustrate the complexity of immigrant culture. Stephen Crane
also turned to the unique speech of America's urban underclass, but he
did so to assault moral and literary conventions by representing how the
nation's linguistic traditions were becoming inarticulate and strange. Cahan's account of urban dialect, by contrast, was more in tune with developments on the vaudeville stage, where dialect was deployed to celebrate
the ethnic influence on mainstream values, or to register the ambivalent
conflicts in immigrant acculturation. Ethnic vaudevillians may have appealed to the diverse masses by using linguistic hybridity to collapse racial
essentialism, yet African-American artists could never fully blend their
voices into this melting pot of dialects. Attention to the black writer Paul
Laurence Dunbar, however, shows how these imposed limits could be implicitly resignified: an apparently stereotypical depiction of African-
American dialect could mask a black vernacular counterdiscourse that was
capable of overturning racist conventions.

Dialect literature rose to prominence in the Gilded Age because it was
integral to a developing cultural debate over the state of American English. Changes to the nation's language reflected central transformations
in the social, regional, and ethnic makeup of late-nineteenth-century
America; literary texts became sites in which linguistic ideologies were
created and challenged. Dialect was a slippery entity: its definition and
function shifted considerably as it was made to serve a variety of cultural
and ethical agendas. This flexibility may have been the political strength
of dialect: it was a powerful tool with which to construct hegemonic cultural languages by denigrating spoken difference. But dialect could also
act to counter or corrupt these attempts at dominance. Above all, I hope
to have convinced the reader that the politics of language in the Gilded
Age was more complex than the opposition between "nonstandard" and
"standard" that critics have tended to emphasize. Dialect could entertain
a simultaneity of different motivations, a mixture of competing functions.
As a consequence, the use of dialect to affirm ethnic identity was often
supplemented by an anxious sense of the disintegrations and compro-
mises of minority discourse. Moreover, the manipulation of language to
uphold elite values registered a fear that standards were being contaminated by a range of subaltern voices. To recognize these ironies in the
politics of language—while not implying that social hierarchies collapsed

entirely after the Civil War—is to stress dialect's counterhegemonic, disruptive potential. From the 1860s to the early 1900s, there was an overall movement away from demeaning appropriations of vernacular voices toward the use of dialect to represent the multifarious features of minority culture. This element of late-nineteenth-century dialect writing becomes particularly important in the twentieth century: the creative drawing from the vernacular language of ethnic tradition to enrich diverse depictions of a multicultural nation.

While *Strange Talk* ends with the early twentieth century, my hope is that it will provide useful background for the study of recent and current language politics (according to some linguists, aspects of social dialect variation may still be increasing in the United States).[1] African-American vernacular English, for example, is a well-established dialect so different from conventional English that some consider it a language in its own right.[2] This vernacular, moreover, has had a profound impact on the mainstream: it has influenced a range of white writers, from Mark Twain to the most radical pioneers of western modernism;[3] it has been the medium of a powerful tradition of African-American literature; it has reached an immense audience through the mass marketing of popular music and culture; and it has had a fundamental effect on white language itself. Yet despite this large cultural investment in black English, there has been strong resistance to allowing it ever to move beyond a subaltern status. Recent attempts to use the vernacular as a formal language of instruction in schools have provoked responses that echo the rhetoric of an earlier age. Black English has been described as a plague, an illness that needs to be cured, a lazy form of gibberish, an appallingly mutant strain of gutter slang signaling a "cognitive deficit" that condemns the speaker to a second-class life of immorality, crime, and economic failure.[4] More sympathetic educators have themselves changed the emphasis of their policies, away from the idea that African-American students should be partly instructed *in* their primary language of black English, toward the belief that this primary language should be used only as a bridge to move black students to a mastery of mainstream English skills.[5] Rather than freely tolerating dialectal difference within English, we continue to live with what Rosina Lippi-Green calls a Standard Language Ideology: the belief in an abstract, idealized, and supposedly unified language—based on upper-middle-class white speech—which is maintained by the institutions of the dominant class in such a way that marginalized groups become convinced of the inadequacy of their accented voices.[6]

We have seen in this book how political debates over the need to police the borders of American English have taken place in a cultural and literary sphere. Since the early 1980s, however, this informal linguistic discussion has become more explicitly political, in the form of support for an English

Language Amendment to the Constitution that would make English official once and for all. Calls for official English repeat with uncanny closeness earlier efforts to stamp out Spanish and so-called "Indian dialects" in the American West, which began to take shape in the 1870s and '80s. These two areas of debate—from the late nineteenth century and the late twentieth—share the central assumption that there is an absolute link between linguistic unity and the health of the nation-state. Civilization, cultural homogeneity, and the rightful responsibilities and privileges of citizenship are thought to be possible only within a common English tongue.[7] A case can be made for a communal language in which to maintain coherent social and political institutions, yet promotion of official English is not just about *whether* English is being spoken in the United States but about *which dialect* is acceptable—that is, which cultural variety of American English should be at the heart of the nation.[8] Critics have suggested that the Official English movement is not so much about language as about culture, just as the discussion of language as a whole can be a means to talk about other cultural or ethnic biases beyond the realms of acceptable public debate.[9] Combatting the "poly-dialectal Babel" of the United States by instituting "Ohio English"—or General American—as the nation's official tongue is less a purely linguistic measure and more a method to mask ethnic discrimination, or to impose a hegemonic standard of mainstream cultural values.[10]

It is easy to be swept into linguistic reductionism, into the romantic belief that language constitutes the very essence of cultures and selves.[11] Language is only one of several factors that help to shape ethnic, national, or personal identity. Yet language also has fundamental political and cultural functions. Dominant groups use questions of speech to form moral and intellectual judgments about cultural, regional, or ethnic minorities. The judged become victims of their language: their identity is forcibly tied to their voices. The very possibility of political representation, moreover, is often conditional not just upon mastery of a dialect of power, but upon access to prominent channels in which this dialect can be heard. Far more than an external mechanism for dealing with deeper issues, language becomes—in the words of James Baldwin—"a political instrument, means, and proof of power."[12] Internally, a speaker's dialect comes to seem hardwired into the central circuits of self; externally, issues of linguistic variety provide the framework around which the largest political decisions are structured.

Debates over language and cultural identity tend to have a double nature. Language can have a purely emblematic quality; it can act as a metaphor for other "real" political issues. Yet language also has the emotive capacity to subsume the debate, to become not merely the means to talk about an issue but the issue itself. This explains the ambivalent situation in which black dialect is embraced yet devalued by mainstream America.[13] It is only partly true to argue that the "real trouble" with black English is its indication that African Americans do not want to assimilate.[14] The antagonistic power of black English is also rooted linguistically in its creative, improvisational disruption of accepted norms, its skill in masking subversion within a seemingly common tongue, its counterhegemonic capacity to "take the oppressor's language and turn it against itself."[15] Black language does not simply stand for a wider cultural subversion. It demonstrates a point that Gilded Age writers such as Cable, Cahan, and Dunbar were beginning to explore: dialect can be an act of political resistance in itself.

NOTES

INTRODUCTION

1. *Cambridge History of American Literature*, 2: 360. The American dialect novel is "the most significant movement in American literature in our generation," wrote Edward Eggleston ("Preface to the Library Edition," *Hoosier School-Master* [1892], 6). The phrase "cult of the vernacular" was coined by Hamlin Garland ("Vernacular Poets and Novelists," 104).

2. Frederic's *Damnation of Theron Ware* follows an innocent Methodist preacher (Theron Ware) as he confronts a series of new cultural and intellectual dialects that comprise a higher world of theological debate, artistic criticism, and sexual liberation. "Talk is what tells, these days," concludes Ware at the end of the novel (344), yet it is Ware's unsuccessful attempt to understand the many ambiguous varieties of "strange talk" (296) surrounding him that leads to his verbal and mental breakdown.

3. Simpson, *Politics of American English*, 27. I agree with Simpson that the real political clash of dialects that we find in Cooper disappears—by about 1850—with the idealism of the transcendentalists (7, 230–59); it reappears, however, in an even more various and extreme way in post–Civil War literature.

4. "Use and Abuse of Dialect," 67–68; De Leon, "Day of Dialect," 680.

5. David Sewell, *Twain's Languages*, argues that the variety of language in *Huck Finn* is a moral variety that depends more upon the "purpose and moral coherence" of speech than upon its "objective form" (87). From a more literal perspective, David Carkeet, "Dialects in *Huck Finn*," argues that Twain actually uses nine and not seven dialects, but that he probably had seven in mind when he wrote the "Explanatory" and was certainly in earnest when he attempted to depict them (230–31).

6. By placing the phrase "Pike County" in quotation marks, Twain may have been referring to a multifarious, less localized understanding of this dialect, as Carkeet suggests (324–25). From the plot of *Huck Finn*, however, it would seem that Twain had a distinct regional area in mind when he used the phrase.

7. Page, *Speech in the English Novel*, 62–72.

8. Lakoff, "Favorite Writers," 244.

9. See Crowley, *Standard English*, 134, for the late-nineteenth-century philological emphasis on pronunciation as the most important factor in judging standard and nonstandard usage.

10. These regional writers include Alice French (Arkansas), Hamlin Garland (Iowa, Wisconsin), Rose Terry Cooke (Connecticut), Sarah Barnwell Elliott (Tennessee), John Fox (Kentucky), Mary Hallock Foote (California, Idaho), Richard Malcolm Johnston (Georgia), John Hay (Illinois), Kate Chopin (Louisiana), Sherwood Bonner (Michigan).

11. Cable, *Dr. Sevier*, 39, 403, 69, 127, 320, 437.

12. Brodhead, *Cultures of Letters*, 118.

13. For considerations of the upper-class market for American dialect literature, see Trachtenberg, *Incorporation of America*, 189–90, and Brodhead, 122–32.

14. "Use and Abuse of Dialect," 67.

15. Twain and Cable's lucrative lecture tour of 1884–85 played to sell-out crowds across the country. See A. Turner, *George W. Cable: A Biography*, chapter thirteen, "The Highway Robbery Business," 171–93.

16. The 1918 *Cambridge History* argues that the Civil War was itself responsible for the growth of dialect literature, as the increasing sectionalism which culminated in the War "gave place not only to an increasing sense of national solidarity but to a keener interest in how the other half lived" (2: 360).

17. See especially Krapp's "Psychology of Dialect Writing." For Krapp, there were only two types of speech in America, "the more or less formal standard and the more or less informal colloquial" (*English Language in America*, 1: 243), thus making written dialect an exaggeration of relatively minor linguistic differences.

18. In "A Theory of Literary Dialect," Sumner Ives challenged Krapp in an effort to prove the real linguistic significance of the supposedly black dialect used by Joel Chandler Harris.

19. Bridgman, 60, 9, 61. This argument leads Bridgman to make a massive jump, from the grotesque and extreme dialect misspelling of the antebellum southern humorists to the development of "colloquial normality" (51) in the work of Twain and James; he considers that only a "minority of writers were exploring the potentialities of dialect" (62) during the late nineteenth century.

20. The former point of view is that of Trachtenberg in his introduction to *Democratic Vistas* (12–13) and in *The Incorporation of America*, where he argues that dialect-speakers were subordinated to a middle-class "discourse of respectability" (189); the latter view is largely held by North and by Brodhead.

21. I am thinking here of David Sewell's *Mark Twain's Languages*, Shelley Fishkin's *Was Huck Black?*, and Elsa Nettels's *Language, Race, and Social Class in Howells's America*. Nettels provides a good introduction to the linguistic issues of the period.

22. Some of the most prominent of recent studies include Eric Sundquist's work on Charles Chesnutt in *To Wake the Nations*, Michael North's *The Dialect of Modernism*, and Henry Louis Gates's "Dis and Dat: Dialect and the Descent" and *The Signifying Monkey*.

23. Brodhead's argument is more properly about regional literature than about dialect literature, which of course tends to place dialect solely in a regional setting:

even when Brodhead talks about ethnic dialect writers like Abraham Cahan, for example, he still fits them into this regional model (118).

24. In *The Social Construction of American Realism*, Amy Kaplan has similarly argued that literary realism was more complex than is suggested by recent arguments that it represented the triumph of bourgeois mythology, the assertion of a dominant power (9–10).

25. Crawford, *Language Loyalties*, 3.

26. In his writings on language and folklore, Antonio Gramsci's main concern was with the radiations of linguistic hegemony from high-prestige to low-prestige communities, radiations that secure naturally rather than coerce a desirable reign of a unified dominant culture over a fragmented popular culture. See the editors' introduction to the section "Language, Linguistics, and Folklore" in Gramsci, *Cultural Writings*, 164–67, together with Gramsci's arguments themselves (167–95).

27. Szwed, "Race and the Embodiment of Culture," 25–29.

28. See, for example, Homi Bhabha's ideas of the hybridity and ambivalence of colonial society, which are summarized in Robert Young, *Colonial Desire*, 22–23, and "The ambivalence of Bhabha," 147–48.

29. In *Love and Theft*, Eric Lott analyzes how blackface minstrelsy was not just a technique of racial exploitation but also a means by which the dominant culture was infiltrated and transformed by its contact with the creative products of African America (Szwed's idea of cultural contamination is of key importance to Lott's argument [6–7]). In *To Wake the Nations*, Sundquist has analyzed the "complex dialectic between 'white' and 'black' cultures that has given rise to some of our most important national literature" (2), as has Fishkin in *Was Huck Black?*

30. An aim of this study is to suggest a new genre, which groups late-nineteenth-century texts under the category of dialect literature rather than the slippery, ill-defined heading of literary realism.

31. While the term *contamination* might be seen as encoding a specific moral viewpoint—the dominant culture's concern that its language is being polluted by inferior forms—it is used in this book to describe the positive power possessed by minority groups to influence and undermine hegemonic cultural ideas.

32. According to Shell, "Babel in America," the "distinctive American linkage between dialect and race" (114), an unwarranted obsession with "quirkily 'regional' literary traditions" (124), and the "still-widespread phenomenon in America of treating the politics of language mainly in terms of changes, called politically symptomatic, to the English language," have all "served to divert attention from the question of an official or national language" (112). Shell suggests that English-speaking ethnic groups offer only a "veil of cultural diversity" (119), whereas the issue of foreign language is "substantive" (127).

33. Similarly, I use the term *nonstandard language* to signify that which can antagonize, rather than simply confirm, an ideal standard of speech.

CHAPTER ONE

1. Twain, "Concerning the American Language," 265–67. This was originally written as a chapter for *A Tramp Abroad* (1880), but was excluded from the published version.

2. See Bridgman, *The Colloquial Style*, on the generalistic, often meaningless use of *democratic* when referring to the American language (3). Bridgman's own more detailed definition of linguistic democracy, however, misses the distinction that I make in this and the following chapter: the "democratic inclination" is not simply descriptive of a "mass norm" (19) but is itself divided between prescriptive and descriptive tendencies.

3. In addition to several recent works on Transcendentalism and the philosophy of language, there has been a remarkable amount of attention to the politics of language between the Revolution and the Civil War: for example David Simpson, *The Politics of American English, 1776–1850* (1986); Michael Kramer, *Imagining Language in America: From the Revolution to the Civil War* (1992); Thomas Gustafson, *Representative Words: Politics, Literature, and the American Language, 1776–1865* (1992); Kenneth Cmiel, "'A Broad Fluid Language of Democracy': Discovering the American Idiom" (1992); and Christopher Looby, *Voicing America: Language, Literary Form, and the Origins of the United States* (1996). Works that treat the antebellum period extensively but not exclusively include Dennis Baron, *Grammar and Good Taste: Reforming the American Language* (1982) and Kenneth Cmiel, *Democratic Eloquence: The Fight Over Popular Speech in Nineteenth-Century America* (1990).

4. Tanner, *Scenes of Nature, Signs of Men*, 6. For the latter point of view, see Gustafson, 21, 71, 156.

5. Irving, *History, Tales and Sketches*, 144. This line may not have been penned by Irving himself: *Salmagundi* was a collaborative effort with William Irving and James Kirke Paulding. The line is quoted in Kramer, 31; D. Simpson, 112; and Gustafson, 6, 21.

6. For the relevance of speech and eloquence to democracy, see, for example, Tocqueville, *Democracy in America*, 477; D. Simpson, 30; Gustafson, 72–76; and Cmiel, *Democratic Eloquence*, 39–40. As its title suggests, Cmiel's book is concerned throughout with the relationships among language, personality, and a "healthy democracy" (14). Gustafson places particular emphasis on the connection between political disorders like the Civil War and feelings about the omnipotence and duplicity of words (9).

7. "English Language in America," 517.

8. America's educated class, continues the *North American Review*, "allow themselves to use the language of their inferiors in culture" ("English Language in America," 528); a refined linguistic standard is degenerating into slang (519–20). See Cmiel, "'Broad Fluid Language of Democracy,'" for a summary of the problems posed by democratic theory and practice for the ideal of a standard, controlled language (914, 920).

9. For examples, see Cmiel, *Democratic Eloquence*, 81.

10. See D. Simpson, 74–92, for an account of how Webster's "essentially conservative argument" in favor of usage was grounded in the inherently rationalizing speech of the American yeomanry (74–75). "In many ways," writes Simpson, "it seems to have mattered little to [Webster's] readers that the case for the common language was a case against dialect, and against innovation, and that the American yeoman was in fact a translation of the English country squire, minus his loyal retainers" (90). For similar accounts of Webster, see Gustafson, 310–14, and Cmiel, *Democratic Eloquence*, 52–53.

11. Emerson, quoted in Cmiel, *Democratic Eloquence*, 113; Whitman, "An American Primer," 470. See Cmiel, *Democratic Eloquence*, for a description of how American Romantic philology "sanctioned folk speech, but only as a buffer against a 'rootless' popular culture" (112), and for the argument that ideas of "Saxon eloquence" often amounted to "a reformulation of the gentry ideal" (116). D. Simpson suggests that, for the Transcendentalists, "the existence of languages as functioning to connect or divide *different* selves becomes so irrelevant as to seem impertinent" (232), and he outlines in some detail how the Transcendentalists' "almost embarrassingly glib . . . loyalty to common speech" (258) masked a hegemonic, all-subsuming ideology that seems "the literary and philosophical correlative of the mythology of manifest destiny" (231).

12. Whitman, 463.

13. Lounsbury, "English Language in America," 2: 605–6. According to Lounsbury, the suffering of the Civil War developed national character and broke the sway of foreign opinion (606). R. Bailey has also shown how, by the 1870s and '80s, Americans had the confidence to suggest that British English was "the source of unwanted innovation and debasement of the common language." There developed at that time a "grudging recognition of American English as an independent, postcolonial variety" (*Images of English*, 156). Putting this recognition a few decades earlier, D. Simpson writes that "America had, by about 1850, a version of English that was recognizably its own" (3).

14. Sweet, quoted in Plotkin, *The Tenth Muse*, 16. Plotkin argues that British philologists came to see dialects as "positive, collectible, knowable data" (16).

15. "So uncritically accepted was the idea that dialects were vanishing that the [English Dialect] Society was dissolved in 1896 since it was thought, with the completion of Wright's *English Dialect Dictionary*, to have finished its task" (R. Bailey, *Nineteenth-Century English*, 71). In the United States, writes Bailey, there was a far stronger and more inclusive interest in contemporary dialects (71).

16. E. S. Sheldon, "Practical Philology," 94. The general drift of Cmiel's *Democratic Eloquence* is that, although distinctions would never be clear-cut, there was a new respect toward the end of the century for "technical, plain, and colloquial styles" (13) over refined ideas of rhetoric.

17. Whitney, "Languages and Dialects," 32; *Life and Growth of Language*, 178.

18. Some writers clearly agreed with the philological sanctioning of dialect, for example James Whitcomb Riley in "Dialect in Literature."

19. Whitney, "Evolution of Language," 413–14.

20. R. G. White, *Words and Their Uses*, 392. See Cmiel, *Democratic Eloquence*, 192, for the popularity of White's work.

21. R. G. White, *Words and Their Uses*, 60, 14.

22. W. Mathews, 61, 63. Mathews paraphrases Marsh's *Lectures on the English Language*, 224–25, where the latter records his debt to Landor. Mathews does, at least, follow Marsh in giving the Italians the benefit of the doubt: the depravity of the Italians is not hopeless; their unmanly, untruthful language is the outcome of political oppression, the end of which will see the language "burst its fetters and become once more as grand and as heroic as it is beautiful" (Marsh, 225n). There is a profound difference, argues Marsh, between words for great ideas not existing

in a language, and accidental conditions (as in Italy) that bring their disuse or misapplication (225–26).

23. W. Mathews, 13–14, 56–57.

24. Swinton, 287. This chapter from Swinton's *Rambles among Words*—"English in America"—may have been ghostwritten by Whitman.

25. Alford, 6. For this definition of *philology*, as opposed to *linguistics*, see Marsh, 222, 52. See W. Mathews, 6, for his debt to Müller.

26. Moon was the London-born son of American parents (Baron, *Grammar and Good Taste*, 190).

27. W. Mathews, 327; Cmiel, *Democratic Eloquence*, 124. Cmiel gives a detailed account of the public prominence of verbal criticism toward the end of the century (176, 191–99).

28. Cmiel, *Democratic Eloquence*, 124. I paraphrase here the main points of Cmiel's argument in chapter four of *Democratic Eloquence*. See especially 124–25 and 139–47 on the wider blurring of "the old lines between high and popular culture" (140) in the late nineteenth century. Cmiel points out the irony of the verbal critics' attempt "to withdraw from popular culture": "During the next decade . . . verbal criticism became just one more way to bring refined culture to a popular audience. By the 1880s, the books and handbooks of verbal criticism were being used by people with middling cultural credentials to assert social status. The very success of verbal criticism was undermining the original goals" (139).

29. R. G. White, *Words and Their Uses*, 43, 76, 65.

30. Marsh, 645; W. Mathews, 80.

31. Whitney, *Life and Growth of Language*, 159, 178.

32. I do not mean to imply that Cmiel, in *Democratic Eloquence*, entirely neglects the overlap between verbal critics and philologists. Occasionally, he mentions that they shared "common values" (168) and "common fears" about the "vulgarity of American life" (149–50); that critics also followed the doctrines of conventionality and usage (154); and that scholars were "interested in reconfiguring authority, not democratizing it" by asserting the strength of scholarly expertise over civil refinement (174). Yet Cmiel's stress is still on the intellectual differences between these two camps rather than their underlying moral parities, thus reinscribing the very binary he occasionally attempts to break down. My point is that the "contradictory feelings" about dialect that Cmiel describes in Whitney—his uncertainty over whether dialect was the democratic possession of everyone or the "barbaric" quality of the uncivilized (162)—were not a minor inconsistency but were at the center not just of Whitney's thought but of late-nineteenth-century American philology as a whole, especially where questions of "civilization" and national "cultivation" were concerned.

33. W. Mathews, 13–14, 73–81; Lounsbury, *Standard of Usage*, 54–57, ix, 79–80; Lounsbury, "English Language in America," 2: 608.

34. Whitney, *Life and Growth of Language*, 155; Whitney, review of White, 470.

35. This idea is present throughout Whitney's writings; see especially *Life and Growth of Language*, 18–19, 304.

36. See, for example, Whitney, "Languages and Dialects," 39–40, 61.

37. Whitney, *Life and Growth of Language*, 280. Philologists were not simply against "the Romantic assumption that style could be read to uncover the char-

acter, or soul, of individuals and nations," as Cmiel suggests (*Democratic Eloquence*, 156). The real question was about causation, not relation.

38. Whitney, *Language and the Study of Language*, 172–74; *Life and Growth of Language*, 8. B. Matthews, *Parts of Speech*, 7, 24, 9, 25, 3. In his study *Americanisms*, Maximilian Schele de Vere also praised the overwhelming power with which the English language absorbs foreign words, and the accompanying power with which the English character absorbs other nationalities (112), while he praised the way that certain regions of America have preserved the purest "English-Saxon" words, pronounced "as they were in the days of Alfred" (428).

39. "There is another great error of which those who argue this subject on the Darwinian side are sometimes guilty; namely, the assumption that the development of language has had a part in the evolution of humanity out of a lower form of animal life" (Whitney, "Darwinism and Language," 88). Darwin, *Descent of Man*, 59; Whitney, *Life and Growth of Language*, 274. For an example of Whitney's applying Darwinian ideas of "missing links" to language, see "Darwinism and Language," 87.

40. Whitney, *Life and Growth of Language*, 274, 24; "Darwinism and Language," 84.

41. See Aarsleff's introduction to Humboldt's *On Language* (x). Aarsleff also notes that "[i]nconsistencies on fundamental principle are not uncommon in Whitney," especially concerning questions of race (*From Locke to Saussure*, 324n25). One might add that such inconsistencies were endemic in late-nineteenth-century linguistic thought in the United States.

42. W. Mathews, 60. Mathews quotes a long passage from Whitney's *Language and the Study of Language*.

43. R. G. White, *Every-Day English*, 101. Attempts to reform English spelling can be traced back to the early thirteenth century; see Vallins, *Spelling*, chapter five. For Webster's earlier "democratic" attempts to reduce the gap between speech and writing, see D. Simpson, 56–63. Chapter four of Baron's *Grammar and Good Taste* charts the growing interest in spelling reform in the 1880s (especially among philologists), as well as outlining the various degrees of radicalism in the proposed reforms.

44. This latter opinion was held by Frederik A. Fernald, writing in *The Popular Science Monthly* in 1885 (638–42).

45. N. E. Dawson, quoted in Baron, *Grammar and Good Taste*, 88.

46. March, 4–5; Lounsbury, *English Spelling and Spelling Reform*, 329; Whitney, *Language and the Study of Language*, 38, 151. While he is right to stress that Whitney saw writing as a "subordinate variation" of speech, Cmiel perhaps takes the point too far when he states that Whitney "discarded literary language as a standard" (*Democratic Eloquence*, 161). As with other philologists, Whitney's support for spelling reform was part of a wish for an ideal, cultivated literary language that would hold spoken change in check.

47. Lounsbury, "English Language in America," 1: 477.

48. After the Civil War, writes J. L. Dillard, "regional characteristics, in speech as in other traits, were sufficiently pronounced to be recognizable to almost any reader and therefore usable by writers of fiction and other commercial authors," making it "reasonable to assume that regional distributions—cultural as well as

linguistic—reached some kind of high point shortly before that time" (*History of American English*, 186–87).

49. Eggleston, "Folk-Speech in America," 874. For similar recognitions, see Schele de Vere, 84; R. Bailey, *Images of English*, 152; and Garland, "Vernacular Poets and Novelists," 90.

50. Bristed, "English Language in America," 61–62; Crowley, *Standard English*, 103; Ellis, quoted in Crowley, 135. The pronunciation of this written standard was only "theoretically received," argues Crowley, because few failed to realize that the standard was itself pervaded by phonetic variations; but this did not prevent the firm belief in a standard "meta-language" (99) based on the social and educational characteristics of its speakers rather than on strictly linguistic norms (134–38).

51. Sheldon, "What is a Dialect?," 287. For similar recognitions, see Whitney, *Language and the Study of Language*, 174, and R. G. White, *Every-Day English*, 89. According to James Whitcomb Riley, the conditions of American life make its "best people" dialectal of caste (469). More recently, *Dictionary of American Regional English* (1985) makes a similar point (Hartman, xliv).

52. Whitney, *Life and Growth of Language*, 154–55; Sheldon, "What is a Dialect?," 287.

53. Whitney, *Life and Growth of Language*, 157; Tocqueville, 473, 478, 481, 479–82; Cooper, *The American Democrat*, quoted in M. M. Mathews, ed., *Beginnings of American English*, 123; Marryat, *Diary in America*, quoted in M. M. Mathews, ed., 131.

54. See Cmiel, *Democratic Eloquence*, 60–65, for a description of the new cultural styles—folksy dialects, inflated bombast, tough plain-speaking, slangy informality—that entered the public forum at mid-century.

55. Whitney, review of White, 469–70; Whitney, *Language and the Study of Language*, 151. This last passage is cited in R. G. White, *Words and Their Uses*, 4.

56. Schele de Vere, 249. See Bartlett, *Dictionary of Americanisms*, xviii, for a similar recognition that political stump-speakers take the vulgarisms of the uneducated and spread them to the colloquial language of the whole people.

57. Sheldon, "What is a Dialect?," 288.

58. Schele de Vere, 654. For some of the many observations on the problematic nature of an American standard language, see A. S. Hill, *Our English*, 203; Bartlett, xxvii; Marryat, quoted in M. M. Mathews, ed., 132; O. F. Emerson, *History of the English Language*, 109.

59. Sheldon, "What is a Dialect?," 292.

60. Howells, quoted in Nettels, *Howells's America*, 64.

61. Dawson, "American Dialect," 28; Sheldon, "What is a Dialect?," 294. See also O. F. Emerson, 110.

62. Dillard, ed., *Perspectives on Black English*, 23. The place to find American dialect, considers Dillard, is within ethnic groups contained by less rigid regional boundaries. These groups "had dialects much more extremely deviant from ordinary English than the most non-standard of the regional dialect users" (*History of American English*, 190). See Hartman, xlvi–xlviii, for a summary of the controversy over whether American dialects were formed from British regional dialects or from non-English influence.

63. Dawson, 27.

64. See Dillard, *Black English,* 171.

65. F. Hall, "Retrogressive English," 309, 327 (according to Hall, English, "being the completest mongrel of all," is thus "the most expressive of all" [327]); Bartlett, xvi; Schele de Vere, 77. See Mencken, *The American Language,* 189–97, 251–66, for some of the many foreign-language influences on American English, influences that Mencken analyzes mainly in terms of vocabulary (loan words).

66. Bridges, quoted in R. Bailey, *Images of English,* 206.

67. Molee, quoted in R. Bailey, *Images of English,* 201. Translated: it would be a union language that would reunite all Teutonic people into one language within fifty years.

68. Dodge, "Negro Patois," 161.

69. Darwin, 62; W. Mathews, 327; Campbell, "Protection for Our Language," 127; unnamed writer in *Godey's Lady's Book,* quoted in Nettels, 19; B. Matthews, 171.

70. Marsh, 218–19, 220, 222, 676, 679. The only benefit of dialect, thought Marsh, was as a conservative "means of checking the spread of popular excitements, and a too rapid movement of social changes" (678).

71. Marsh, 666–67, 676, 666.

72. W. Mathews, 327; Campbell, 127.

73. The Gilded Age was a time, writes Trachtenberg, of "new levels and forms of stratification, a segmenting of the society into professional groupings, into new distinct subcultures of vocation and gender, of race and ethnic language. The entire social world came to resemble a chart of separate categories and systems of integration" (*Incorporation of America,* 160–61).

74. Lowell, "Democracy," 8, 38. Compare this to Lowell's fear that the very idea of equality might "prove dangerous when interpreted and applied politically by millions of newcomers alien to our traditions" (quoted in Trachtenberg, *Incorporation of America,* 156).

75. Marsh, 677; B. Matthews, 49.

76. Such beliefs were sometimes qualified by a recognition that these regional dialects were so tremendously heterogeneous that they belied systematic analysis, thus rendering a "great national novel" impossible (Wauchope, "Value of Dialect," 640). According to an anonymous reviewer of George W. Cable's "Madame Delphine" in 1883, "the local peculiarities of speech are as mysterious" in the United States as they are in England (quoted in A. Turner, ed., *Critical Essays,* 47).

77. J. C. Harris, *Nights with Uncle Remus,* xxxiii. Bristed similarly notes that the peculiarity of the New England dialect comes not from new words but from "the general style of its pronunciation" (67).

78. For the ideal of colloquial English, see A. S. Hill, 190–91.

79. "English Language in America," 518.

80. For the hybrid expressions of the educated, see Bartlett, xviii, and Whitney, review of White, 471. For the spicing of novels with French and pseudo-French phrases, see A. S. Hill, 118, and "English Language in America," 524.

81. Whitney did admit, however, that there were many things in White's work for the critic to "smash." See Whitney, review of White, 476.

82. R. G. White considered that the mysterious, "grammarless" quality of English allows "that unconscious, intuitive use of idiom which gives life and strength

to the simple speech of very humble people," and he even recognized the powerful qualities of slang. See *Words and Their Uses*, 295, 45, 85.

83. Lounsbury, "English Language in America," 1: 478.

84. Cmiel shows how the early-nineteenth-century belief that regional dialects were nearer to separate languages in their capacity for difference faded out toward the middle of the century ("'Broad Fluid Language of Democracy,'" 918–19).

85. James, quoted in Trachtenberg, *Incorporation of America*, 195. For the idea that the "interchangeability of plots and characters in dime novels parallels the standardization of machine production," see Trachtenberg, *Incorporation of America*, 46. Borus makes similar points about the fragmentation of the Gilded Age readership (*Writing Realism*, 39, 101–38, 171). For discussion of Godkin's "Chromo-Civilization," again see Trachtenberg, *Incorporation of America*, 157.

CHAPTER TWO

1. D. Simpson, *Politics of American English*, 105; Dunne, quoted in Lowe, "Theories of Ethnic Humor," 448.

2. In the cruel language of Augustus Baldwin Longstreet's sketches "Georgia Theatrics" and "The Fight," argues Kenneth Lynn, we hear the Whig reaction to "the reckless spirit and childish ignorance of Jacksonian America" (*Mark Twain and Southwestern Humor*, 69). And the humorist Joseph G. Baldwin, writes Neil Schmitz, comprehended "the politics of tall talk" by linking "its monstrosities and exaggeration to the socio-economic phenomenon of Jacksonian inflation" ("Tall Tale, Tall Talk," 199).

3. Nasby was originally from Ohio, before moving to Kentucky, and his dialect represents illiteracy and ignorance rather than a particular region. Nasby's unflatteringly portrayed southern friends, however, speak in what Locke intends for a southern dialect. See Austin, *Petroleum V. Nasby*, 68, 91.

4. See Lynn, 84, and Schmitz, 196–97, for descriptions of the profound moral prevarication between vernacular and gentlemanly values and languages within much southwestern humor.

5. Longstreet, *Georgia Scenes*, iii–iv; Twain, quoted in Rickels, *George Washington Harris*, 109.

6. Mortimer Thompson (writing in 1855), quoted in Blair, *Native American Humor*, 122.

7. In his preface to *Bill Arp: So Called* (1868), Smith called attention to the "*reconstruction* of the orthography." See Austin, *Bill Arp*, 82, for these fluctuations in Smith's dialect, and for this quotation from Smith (emphasis added). See Blair, 118–19n2, for his discussion of the "misspelling bee."

8. The "eye dialect" upon which much humor depended—the respelling of words that are universally pronounced in standard and nonstandard usage (for example *duz* for *does*)—was criticized in magazine articles of the time, suggesting that people were sensitive to the difference between attempts at realism and attempts at humor in dialect (see "Use and Abuse of Dialect," 67). Blair also discusses this demise of misspelling (108–9, 118–19n2).

9. See Rourke, *American Humor*, 223–24, and Blair and Hill, *America's Humor*, 275–77, 291–92, for this new type of humor.

10. Trachtenberg, for example, describes as a defining characteristic of post-bellum dialect literature the "placement of speech in such a way that it is unmistakably recognized as 'low,' as culturally inferior to the *writing* of the narrator" (*Incorporation of America*, 189).

11. Eggleston, *Hoosier School-Master* (1871), 6.

12. Lowell, *Biglow Papers*, 38. Whitman makes a similar point about the ethics of pronunciation ("An American Primer," 463, 466).

13. Compare this to Lowell's statement that true vulgarity lies in the thought, "not in the word or the way of pronouncing it" (*Biglow Papers*, 166).

14. Lowell, quoted in Blair and Hill, 177.

15. See Lowell, *Biglow Papers*, 208, and Blair, 48n2. For the conservative side of Haliburton, see R. Bailey, *Nineteenth-Century English*, 282.

16. Howells, quoted in Blair, 115.

17. Blair, 134, 138.

18. Eggleston, preface to *Hoosier School-Master* (1892), 7–8. For Twain's claim that Harte "never did know anything about dialect," see Krapp, *English Language in America*, 1: 243.

19. J. C. Harris, *Uncle Remus*, 39; anonymous review of Harris's *Mingo*, quoted in Julia Collier Harris, *Joel Chandler Harris*, 184n6; anonymous review of "Madame Delphine," quoted in A. Turner, ed., *Critical Essays*, 26; L. B. Fletcher, "Dialect Spelling," 26; anonymous review of *Old Creole Days*, quoted in A. Turner, ed., *Critical Essays*, 6; Garland, "Vernacular Poets and Novelists," 106.

20. Francis March, for example, praised dialect writers for setting us free "from the common spelling" (*Professor March's Address*, 8).

21. J. C. Harris, *Uncle Remus*, 39–40; "Negro Folk-Lore," quoted in Bickley, ed., *Essays on Harris*, 6; Hardy, "Dialect in Novels," 688; Wauchope, "Value of Dialect," 640; J. C. Harris, *Uncle Remus*, 39–40. See Cmiel, *Democratic Eloquence*, 179, for the wider belief in the interconnectedness of language and thought in the late nineteenth century.

22. See Lakoff, "Favorite Writers," 245, for a discussion of this idea.

23. M. D. Bell, *Problem of American Realism*, 1; compare with McKay, *Narration and Discourse*, 4. "Give us the people as they actually are. Give us their talk as they actually talk it," wrote Pattee, paraphrasing the realistic spirit that had gripped America since the Civil War (*American Literature Since 1870*, 15–16).

24. Garland, *Crumbling Idols*, 74, 70, 63; Howells, quoted in Nettels, *Howells's America*, 65; Howells, *Criticism and Fiction*, 187; Marx, "Vernacular Tradition," 113; Eggleston, quoted in *Cambridge History of American Literature*, 2: 362.

25. *Cambridge History of American Literature*, 2: 361.

26. According to John Edgar Wideman, to write in black dialect was another way for white writers to say: "What we wish to hear, the way we want to hear it—that's what Negro speech is. And what we record of their speech is an accurate index to their character" ("Black Voice in American Literature," 35).

27. C. Simpson, *Local Colorists*, 10n5.

28. Sundquist, *To Wake the Nations*, 321, 323, 311–13.

29. Boas, quoted in Sundquist, *To Wake the Nations*, 6; R. G. White, *Every-Day English*, 195–96.

30. Chesnutt to Walter Hines Page, quoted in Sundquist, *To Wake the Nations*, 309 (emphasis added).

31. George Washington Cable revised the 1883 edition of *The Grandissimes*, for example, removing dialect characteristics from the speech of his more cultivated Creoles: the many deviations from standard spelling "would have given a reader the impression of much more variation in speech than was actually represented" (Evans, "Literary Dialect in *The Grandissimes*," 217).

32. R. G. White, *Every-Day English*, 139, xxiii; Krapp, "Psychology of Dialect Writing," 522–26.

33. Trachtenberg, *Incorporation of America*, 189–90; Eggleston, preface to *Hoosier School-Master* (1892), 26; Garland, *Crumbling Idols*, 74.

34. Brodhead, *Cultures of Letters*, 120; Trachtenberg, *Democratic Vistas*, 12; Brodhead, 121, 134, 137.

35. Brodhead, 137–38. Sundquist has also argued for "the portrayal in much of the period's regional fiction of a sense of crisis or loss, a breakdown in the comparatively close-knit communities of pre–Civil War America" ("Realism and Regionalism," 508).

36. Edmund Gosse, review of "Madame Delphine," quoted in A. Turner, ed., *Critical Essays*, 31; Randolphe Bourne, "From an Older Time," quoted in A. Turner, ed., *Critical Essays*, 147; "Mr. Frost's Edition of *Uncle Remus*," quoted in Bickley, ed., 25. For an account of Cable's minute efforts to transcribe dialect, see Evans. Bridgman also gives a description of the slowness of dialect writing (*The Colloquial Style*, 15).

37. See Fried, *Realism, Writing, Disfiguration*, 146, for this idea of William James's. For comment on the "hieroglyphic" nature of words, see March, 7, and Twain's 1906 sketch "Simplified Spelling." More recently, see Vallins, *Spelling*, 137–38, and Abercrombie, "Recording of Dialect Material," 88.

38. For an account of how, in the 1870s and '80s, reading was perceived to have become more rapid and less intellectual, and for an account of how this rapidity was seen as part of a wider cultural degeneration, see Hearn, "On Reading in Relation to Literature." Krapp discusses the idea of the "literary reader" becoming alienated ("Psychology of Dialect Writing," 523).

39. Leland's *Pidgin-English Sing-Song* (1876) was accompanied by a glossary of at least 500 words. Ambrose Gonzales's Gullah stories were accompanied by a glossary of over 1700 words when republished in the 1920s. See the footnotes in Eggleston's *Hoosier School-Master* (1892) for explanations of strange words like "juberous" (230–31) and "dog-on" (45), and unusual pronunciations like "aout" for *out* (39). See Liddell, "English Literature and the Vernacular," 622, for a late-nineteenth-century account of how the vernacular creates the need for translation within a single language.

40. Marsh, *Lectures on the English Language*, 677; Krapp, "Psychology of Dialect Writing," 525.

41. Fletcher, 26; Eggleston, "Folk-Speech in America," 875.

42. Howells underscored this idea in *A Hazard of New Fortunes* by having the most refined members of southern society pronounce in a distinctly nonstandard way: "'We awe from the Soath,' she said, 'and we arrived this mawning, but we got this cyahd from the brokah just befo' dinnah, and so we awe rathah late'"(99).

43. For an outline of this idea, and a demonstration of the confusion and misreading that ensues when the regional standard of pronunciation is not taken into account in the analysis of dialect literature, see Ives, "A Theory of Literary Dialect" (especially 151–73). See Howells, "Our Daily Speech," 933, for his recognition of America's lack of standards.

44. North, *Dialect of Modernism*, 22; Riley, "Dialect in Literature," 467, 469. Bakhtin has described this effect: the represented dialect is not a single language but a hybrid construction where two accents, two verbal-ideological belief systems exist simultaneously in a single utterance. In its most pervasive form, literary dialect presented the reader with what Bakhtin would call the *image* of another's language: a parodic stylization rather than a complete reproduction (*The Dialogic Imagination*, 366).

45. As Bakhtin argues: "these dialects, on entering the literary language and preserving within it their own dialectological elasticity, their other-languagedness, have the effect of deforming the literary language; it, too, ceases to be that which it had been, a closed socio-linguistic system" (294).

46. Kaplan, *Social Construction of American Realism*, 8–9; Howells, quoted in Borus, *Writing Realism*, 171. According to M. D. Bell, Howells's equation of realism with democracy was not connected to any populist political reality, but was merely a "wishful metaphoric equation," a "kind of public relations gesture" that gave the writer a "sense of 'real' social significance" (32). See Trachtenberg, *Incorporation of America*, 182–201, for the way in which the theory of realism was compromised by the "national discourses" of propriety and respectability.

47. M. D. Bell has described this belittlement of style and the aesthetic as the problem of Howellsian realism—the problem that a form of literature was denying the literary (21).

48. A. White has argued that the "sincere intention" of realism would only collapse with the new "obscurity" of writers like Joseph Conrad and Henry James (*The Uses of Obscurity*, 5).

49. Nettels, 70; Howells, *Criticism and Fiction*, 104.

50. Garland, "Vernacular Poets and Novelists," 104; Gilder, quoted in C. Simpson, 13n7; De Leon, "Day of Dialect," 682; A. S. Hill, *Our English*, 113, 139–40; Whitney, "Languages and Dialects," 64. See also B. Matthews, *Parts of Speech*, 3, for the idea that literature is traditionally that which guards against dialects.

51. Paul van Dyke, "George W. Cable and John March, Southerner," quoted in A. Turner, ed., *Critical Essays*, 96; anonymous review of *Old Creole Days*, quoted in A. Turner, ed., *Critical Essays*, 6.

52. Leland, *Hans Breitmann's Ballads*, 14–17; Schele de Vere, *Americanisms*, 140.

53. Leland, *Pidgin-English Sing-Song*, 1, 9, 2, 8.

54. Eggleston, preface to *Hoosier School-Master* (1892), 7.

55. Eggleston, preface to *Hoosier School-Master* (1892), 26, 7, 22.

56. A similar irony is recorded by the anonymous author of "Use and Abuse of Dialect": "Even the books put into our schools as models for the guidance of the young—the school 'readers' themselves—often contain examples of perverted diction that cannot fail to exert an evil influence upon the impressionable years of childhood" (68).

57. In Garland's story "A Branch Road," for example, a young man breaks off

228   NOTES TO PAGES 55–59

his romantic engagement mainly because of the vulgar talk of his friends and
colleagues (*Main-Travelled Roads*, 14), only to return and win back his former lover
with the "vast power" of his "new and thrilling words" (43).

58. See Garland, *Crumbling Idols*, 61, and Nettels, *Howells's America*, 62.

59. Fowler, quoted in Baron, *Grammar and Good Taste*, 163.

60. General Ethan Allen Hitchcock, quoted in Dillard, *History of American English*, 137. See Dillard, *History of American English*, chapter six, for an account of the
various types of pidgin English that developed in the West, from a contact between
English and many other tongues, including American Indian, Spanish, and French.
For Dillard, "[a]t least part of the general unwillingness to acknowledge the presence of Pidgin English may be associated with our general reluctance to deal with
the frontier as it actually was" (146). See the article on "South-western Slang,"
reprinted in M. M. Mathews, ed., *Beginnings of American English*, for a recognition
of words in the Texan dialect from Italian, Spanish, and German (155).

61. Schele de Vere, 162, 161, 574–75, 213, 161, 162, 576, 162; "Socrates
Hyacinth," quoted in M. M. Mathews, ed., 152.

62. By investigating fiction, journalism, letters, and diaries, Fender has described how a "double style" of writing developed in the West: not "the famous
alternative styles of American prose, the international genteel as opposed to the
regional vernacular," but a simultaneity of ambiguous feelings and styles evoked
by the strange western environment—for example, a simultaneity of the fanciful
and the scientific (*Plotting the Golden West*, 13).

63. See Krapp, *English Language in America*, 1: 365.

64. In one footnote Twain defines terms like *placer diggings* and *panning out*
because they "may be a little obscure to the general reader" (420).

65. At least, the *Oxford English Dictionary* credits Twain with the first use of this
word, in *Roughing It*.

66. At several other points the narrator similarly indicates the correct pronunciation of words, for example from the Sandwich Islands (440).

67. Mitchell, "Verbally *Roughing It*," 78, 91. Mitchell argues that in *Roughing It*
Twain undermines conventional (and implicitly eastern) accounts of and assumptions about the West by focusing not on landscape but on language, and on the
way in which language creates rather than represents the western world. According
to Mitchell, "behind the humor of *Roughing It* lies a self-conscious examination of
language itself, a serious inquiry into the process of how things happen to be put
into words. And what lends a persuasive power to the inquiry is the book's comparative structure, its use of vernacular idioms associated with the West to expose
the exhausted linguistic currency of settled eastern culture" (77).

68. Whitney, *Life and Growth of Language*, 154. Bristed also comments that, in
the West, there are "districts where it would hardly be an exaggeration to say, that
every prominent person has his own private vocabulary." He also mentions the
"infinite variety of western phraseology," "from the clumsiest vulgarity to the most
poetic metaphor; from unintelligible jargon to pregnant sententiousness" ("English Language in America," 71).

69. Bierce, "Writers of Dialect," 176, 180.

70. Language has a seductive, beguiling power, leading the narrator to echo
Mr. Ballou and use the words "Eureka" (273) and "palladium" (330) for their

seductive sound, despite his ignorance of their actual sense. Whether it be the "seductive charm" of the word "travel" (1–2), the "magic" in the name Slade (58), the irresistible sound of "Genuine Mexican Plug" (159), or the beguiling power of a "graceful and attractive" quotation (165), the narrator is repeatedly seduced by the surface level of sound. Mitchell also comments on this phenomenon (80–81).

71. Whitney, *Life and Growth of Language*, 112.

72. Twain's larger point in this episode is about linguistic appropriateness: Briggs becomes a successful parson because he can preach to "his pioneer small-fry in a language they understood!" Yet it remains impossible to tell whether the narrator is being ironic in his description of the "sacred proprieties" that this slangy language violently disrupts (317).

73. For recent readings of the inconsistent structure of *Roughing It*, see Mitchell, and Fender (chapter six). The traditional argument about *Roughing It* is that the first half of the book reveals a consistency of narrative viewpoint, while in the second half the narrator's attitudes oscillate between speaking for and burlesquing official culture (Fender, 159). Mitchell has emphasized how such narrative inconsistency is present throughout the book.

74. "Henry Nash Smith first elaborated the contrast in *Roughing It* between vernacular and ideal conventions, establishing the ways that eastern romantic conceptions are disrupted through western experience" (Mitchell, 72n6). Fender considers that Twain's inability to accommodate himself to the "savagery" of the West, or to its "unpredictable respectability" (155), resulted in the inconsistent tone and narrative ambivalence of much of Twain's western writing (130–60).

75. See M. D. Bell, *Problem of American Realism*, 48–49, for a discussion of this argument about *Huck Finn*.

76. Alongside his pioneering use of nonstandard features in *Huck Finn*, argues Janet McKay, Twain employs "a highly sophisticated, innovative literary style that uses a full range of standard English constructions and literary devices. . . . [I]n revising *Huck Finn*, Twain introduced many nonstandard features in strategic places, while regularizing the grammar at other points, so that the dialect and suggestions of illiterate usage 'might count'" (*Narration and Discourse*, 146, 148).

77. This section has been restored recently to *Huck Finn* (107–23).

78. Henry Nash Smith, quoted in McKay, 143, 190. See Sewell, *Twain's Languages*, 7, and chapter seven for Twain's increasing interest in what Sewell calls "cacophony."

79. Again, see M. D. Bell, 41–57, for the specifics of this debate. Bell considers that *Huck Finn* does not conform to the moral precepts of Howellsian realism because Huck "never takes overt *responsibility* for the moral superiority of his vernacular values" (50). From his Bakhtinian perspective, Sewell concurs with my view of Twain: he would always be caught between "lawlessness" and "obsessive obedience" when it came to the rules of English, and would always be uncertain over the respective validity of vernacular and standard speech (16, 28, 30).

80. Sewell has traced in detail Twain's deep interest in linguistic issues. He considers that Twain "moved toward an intuition of principles just beginning to appear in his day" (2).

81. For this interest in spelling reform, see Nettels, 3, 23, and A. Turner, *George W. Cable*, 344.

82. Lott has described the ambivalence—between "love" and "theft"—in white reactions to blackface minstrelsy, while North has stressed how, for white writers like Harris, black speech was "mocked as deviant and at the same time announced as the only true voice of the South" (*Dialect of Modernism*, 23).

CHAPTER THREE

1. Melville, *Billy Budd*, 53. According to the editors of *Billy Budd*, Hayford and Sealts, Melville probably began the work in early 1886 (2). It remained unpublished at Melville's death in 1891.

2. Twain, *Roughing It*, 287; *Huck Finn*, 217–18. There are many other defective speakers (and non-speakers) in Twain's work, for example Jim's deaf-mute daughter in *Huck Finn*. See also Mahl, "Everyday Speech Disturbances in *Tom Sawyer.*"

3. Sewell, *Twain's Languages*, 38; Landon, *Kings of the Platform and Pulpit*, 200.

4. The uniqueness of women's speech was recognized by philologists at the time: "Even the language of women is to a certain extent different from that of men," wrote E. S. Sheldon ("What is a Dialect?," 289).

5. Rogin, *Subversive Genealogy*, 302, 288–316. Trachtenberg sees *Billy Budd* as Melville's message concerning an American state, no longer grounded in natural reason, which represses rather than represents a "shared community of interest" (*Incorporation of America*, 201–7). Rogin compares *Billy Budd* to American folk tales in which "obstructed speech leads to frontier violence. Like the proverbial backwoodsman, Billy chokes with rage and strikes his accuser" (*Subversive Genealogy*, 306). Rogin draws on Robert Rogers's psychoanalytical study of Billy's stutter (*Psychoanalytic Study of the Double in Literature*, 150–52).

6. B. Johnson, "Melville's Fist," 94, 83, 103, 99, 101.

7. It would, of course, be difficult to argue that *Billy Budd* is not concerned with what it is explicitly about: a narrowly avoided mutiny on a British warship in the 1790s.

8. See especially Melville, 71.

9. Billy Budd is a spokesman for the masses, his language (at least when he is not stuttering) is one of absolute truth, and "like the illiterate nightingale [he] was sometimes the composer of his own song" (52).

10. Baron, *Grammar and Good Taste*, 163.

11. Schele de Vere, 575–77. Concerning this last example, Schele de Vere cites the shortening of "as well as" to "*swells*" (653), calling to mind Mrs. Touchett's inscrutable telegrams in Henry James's *Portrait of a Lady* (1881), obfuscated through the employment of the "art of condensation" as a money-saving measure (67).

12. R. G. White, *Words and Their Uses*, 85, 201. "Baseless" ideas and "worthless investment" were often described as twin manifestations of a rampant speculation, as Sewell has shown in his analysis of Mark Twain (44).

13. Whitney, in "Languages and Dialects" (1867), suggests that we are now past the "metaphysical" stage in which language is personified as "an independent existence, an organism" with its own laws and powers (31).

14. In *The Life and Growth of Language,* Whitney criticizes those who fail to see that language is simply the externalization, not the constituent, of our consciousness (304); he suggests the need to guard against the tendency to look upon language-making as a task which absorbs part of man's "nervous energy" (307).

15. A. M. Bell, 17, 225. Bell grouped together pathological conditions like stammering with defects of utterance caused by dialectal pronunciation. Indeed, Bell's phonetic studies were a direct result of his investigation into speech dysfunctions.

16. Crowley, *Standard English,* 152–53.

17. John Bechtel, quoted in Baron, *Grammar and Good Taste,* 217.

18. Holmes, quoted in B. Matthews, *Parts of Speech,* 196 (emphasis added). A similar logic informed contemporary debates over spelling reform. Images of mental disease were used to describe the threat to rationality posed by the idiosyncracy of traditional English orthography, and, on the other hand, to describe the rabid enthusiasm of the spelling reform movement. R. G. White saw the growth of spelling-book speech as a "disease," and spelling reform as an incurable "phonetic mania" (*Every-Day English,* 101, 134).

19. Crowley points to the absolute division between standard and nonstandard language in Britain during this same period (157). According to Crowley, the British preconception of vulgar language was as an "inaccurate, incorrect, ungrammatical, mispronounced, mistaken form of speech" (152). Crowley also gives British examples of dialect viewed as a diseased language in need of disinfection and purification (154).

20. R. G. White, *Words and Their Uses,* 45; Fenno, 21–22; White, *Every-Day English,* 79, 85, 40–41, 90–91.

21. M. A. Denison, "Saturated with Dialect," 2. Denison later admits that she meant her criticism of dialect as "a Goak" (joke).

22. De Leon, "Day of Dialect," 682–83; "Use and Abuse of Dialect," 67–68.

23. Cmiel, *Democratic Eloquence,* 140.

24. Is it merely coincidental that the captain shares his last name with a well-known, conservative philologist of the time, Maximilian Schele de Vere?

25. Gustafson, *Representative Words,* 70.

26. See Cmiel, *Democratic Eloquence,* 248, for the linguistic and political relevance of spellbinding. According to the *Oxford English Dictionary,* the word occurs only in the form *spell-bind* or *spell-bound* before 1888, and it has no particular reference to speechmaking. Vere represents the development that Cmiel notes in American political speechmaking in the late 1880s, whereby colloquial speech was no longer identified and dismissed as "effeminate" but was put "in the service of a tough, postgenteel masculinity" (*Democratic Eloquence,* 250).

27. By repeatedly calling Billy a *barbarian* (52, 120), and hence punning on the possible etymological root of this word in *stammering,* Melville also seems to be making a direct link between proper speech and the values of civilization.

28. In this respect I agree with Barbara Johnson's reading of the tale. According to Johnson, Billy's blow is involuntary, against his conscious intentions. When Billy strikes Claggart "it is no longer possible for knowing and doing to meet" (87).

29. Rogers, 150–52.

30. A. M. Bell, 227, 231, 228 (emphasis added), 65.

31. The image of Claggart's "mesmeristic glance" at Billy (98) further connects Billy's resulting stutter to his nervousness. As Robert Fuller has shown, there was a direct connection in the late nineteenth century between the "magnetic fluids" presupposed by mesmerism and the bodily electricity upon which nervousness depended (see Fuller, *Mesmerism*, chapter five). Earlier in the tale, we are also told that Claggart "magnetically" feels the moral phenomenon presented by Billy (78).

32. According to Tom Lutz, *American Nervousness*, neurasthenia was "imbued with the logic of the economic plot" (11); it was a means to translate a whole range of social and economic changes of the era. In an attempt to define the nature of the nervous American self and of the social, cultural, and environmental forces that might have produced it, Beard used the metaphors of bankruptcy and of Edison's recently invented lightbulb. The first metaphor revealed how an overexpenditure of nervous energy could lead to psychological bankruptcy, whereas careful reinvestment of this energy would bring spiritual peace. The image of the lightbulb, on the other hand, illustrated Beard's understanding of the finite supply of the individual's nervous energy: if the nervous system was overloaded, then one's current of energy was likely to be weak.

33. Beard, *American Nervousness*, xiv, viii, 83, 97 (emphasis added), 84. Gosling, *Before Freud*, considers that the symptoms of neurasthenia became more democratically applied toward the end of the century (50).

34. See Rosenberg, "George M. Beard," 256, and Gosling, 87.

35. Lears, *No Place of Grace*, 47; Gosling, 104. Lutz describes how neurasthenia justified Anglo-American high culture while expressing fear of decay in the gatekeepers of a delicate civilization (6–7).

36. Showalter, *The Female Malady*, 161. Showalter makes some direct comparisons between hysteria and neurasthenia (134–35).

37. Beard, *Practical Treatise on Nervous Exhaustion*, 136, 138.

38. Beard, *American Nervousness*, vi. The "American language" and "American Nervousness," owing to their vast inclusiveness as categories—the fact that they both registered virtually every effect of a changing American culture—were curiously similar. Steam-power, in particular the railroad, was frequently cited as having a terminology that differed dramatically between British and American linguistic usage (Schele de Vere, 355); the periodical press was the most noted corrupter of speech; the telegraph was a symbol of the destructive effect of economics on language; the sciences were bringing a specialized jargon into refined usage; and the mental activity of women was considered a key factor in the decay of the American tone of voice (an idea to which we will return in the following discussion of Henry James).

39. Beard, *American Nervousness*, 85–86; *Practical Treatise*, 45; *American Nervousness*, 86–87.

40. In the words of one railroad owner, concerning the nervous health of the immigrant workers he employed: "They don't suffer, they don't even speak English" (Robert Baer, quoted in Lutz, 7).

41. Beard, *Practical Treatise*, 47–48; *American Nervousness*, 87. Gosling notes that Beard added to American psychology a recognition that the subjective area could be truly diseased (137).

42. R. G. White, "Heterophemy," 697, 691–93. In *Words and Their Uses*, White also criticizes the uncultivated public speakers who use preposterous words and "do not say what they mean" (33).

43. According to Freud, "Slips of the Tongue," these slips surface in the sentence most often when purposely suppressed (78). Refuting the idea that such slips are caused by the purely phonetic relation of words (76), Freud points to the importance of influences outside the word, sentence, or context, and to the exacerbating effect of wider cultural anxieties—a time of war, for example (97).

44. Freud, 74, 85. In his 1891 work on aphasia, Freud expressed the belief that the symptom of paraphasia in examples of organic brain disorder differed little "from the incorrect use and the distortion of words which the healthy person can observe in himself in states of fatigue or divided attention or under the influence of disturbing effects" (Freud, 74n2).

45. Head, *Aphasia*, 52.

46. Brain, *Speech Disorders*, 60. *Contamination* seems to be a generally accepted term for the production of vocal nonsense (see Freud, 75, and Brain, 95). R. G. White also related his idea of heterophemy to aphasia, "that strange affection of the brain which leaves men wordless for certain thoughts and things" ("Heterophemy," 699), revealing a similar conflation of verbal slips and actual brain disease.

47. A. M. Bell, 246; Lears, 50. See Jakobson, "Two Aspects of Language," 98, for another link between aphasia and the loss of individual freedom of thought.

48. See Gosling, 15, 21, 42–44, for a discussion of the Guiteau case and the blurring of the line between madness and sanity. Guiteau was defended at his trial by a neuroanatomist called Spitzka, who argued that although "Guiteau might seem rational according to his own delusional scheme, he was still insane and hence not responsible for his actions" (Gosling, 21). Guiteau was convicted and executed, however, because his symptoms did not match those of traditional types of insanity.

49. E. C. Kinney, quoted in Gosling, 42.

50. Beard, *Practical Treatise*, 138.

51. The words "heterophemy" and "heterophemize," used by R. G. White in 1875, entered the *Oxford English Dictionary* at an early stage, suggesting the very great American input into the dictionary in the late nineteenth century.

52. Melville, 126; R. G. White, *Words and Their Uses*, 297–98. This was White's way of explaining the coherence of English despite what he saw as its grammarless condition: the "master of the English language" is he who can "transmit his freely-flowing thought" by "filling his words with a living but latent light and heat" (298).

53. Trachtenberg, *Incorporation of America*, 202.

54. According to Lutz, James manipulated his neurasthenia as a youth to gain money for his European travels, yet, when neurasthenia became popular, James stopped referring to himself in terms of it. Thereafter, neurasthenia became a symptom of American provincialism in James's work, as Lutz demonstrates in his reading of *The Ambassadors* (1903). See Lutz, *American Nervousness*, 246–61.

55. Freud, "Slips of the Tongue," 134. In fact, Wharton's comments seem to echo Freud very closely. According to Freud, a "forced and involved expression"

is often the result of insufficiently worked-out thought, or the emergence of "the stifled voice of the author's self-criticism" (134).

56. Lutz, 247, 251.

57. See Leon Edel's introduction to James, *Watch and Ward*, 5.

58. James, *Question of Our Speech*, 34, 6, 46, 20.

59. Boren, *Eurydice Reclaimed*, 91.

60. James, *Question of Our Speech*, 41–43; "Speech of American Women," 2: 1103; *Question of Our Speech*, 33, 12.

61. James, preface to "Daisy Miller [et al]," 1279.

62. James recorded these phrases on 22 August 1885, under the heading "Phrases, of the people." See James, *Complete Notebooks*, 32. Edel describes how James, following the example of Zola, spent hours in pubs and workers' meetings, recording these phrases (*Middle Years*, 172). Accordingly, in the preface to *The Princess*, James confesses his desire to show "the social ear as on occasion applied to the ground, or catch some gust of the hot breath that I had at many an hour seemed to see escape and hover" (48).

63. The equivalents to the less obvious of these dialect spellings are "Henning" (54), "shame" (163), "love" (289), and "house" (473). In his depiction of the speech of the revolutionary German, Schinkel, James follows a technique typical of the American dialect tradition represented by the southern humorists: the spelling of a mispronounced word in terms of another word from a different context, with an obvious comic intention. Thus, Schinkel's *love* becomes "loaf" and *self-love* "self-loaf" (289, 295) (this is apparently humorous in a political meeting which discusses, among other things, the cost of basic food). That there is no necessary connection between Schinkel's pronunciation and this spelling of the word becomes obvious when James later spells it "lofe" (555).

64. James, "Speech of American Women," 2: 1106.

65. Whitney, *Life and Growth of Language*, 154–55. This double nature of dialect is illustrated in the language of Hyacinth Robinson, the hero of *The Princess*: his vocabulary is peculiarized both by his highly personal experiences (the different language he uses after his experiences in France [397]) and by his allegiance to class identity (his acquisition of the vocabulary of socialism [123]).

66. Both this passage and the novel itself have many Arnoldian echoes. In *Culture and Anarchy* (1867), Matthew Arnold criticized the populace's desire—expressed here by Millicent—to "do as it likes." Arnold's dismissal of political language as "clap-trap" and self-delusion is also relevant to my discussion later of James's *The Tragic Muse* (1890). See Arnold, 81, 94–95.

67. For references to Hyacinth's nervousness, see 167, 169, 183, 231, 245, 246, 293, 306, 486. British verbal critics saw the dropping of the *h* as an "unfortunate habit" marking a man as deficient in "intelligence, self-respect and energy" (Henry Alford, quoted in Crowley, *Standard English*, 153). James is keen to represent this missing letter whenever he needs to reinforce class identity, or to emphasize the mental ineptitude of the speaker.

68. The narrator constantly reminds us of Muniment's northern pronunciation, often with little apparent purpose.

69. See *The Princess*, 144–45 and 334.

70. The "imbecility" and "insistent ignorance" that Hyacinth experiences at

the socialist meetings in the Sun and Moon lead him to the important conclusion that "one must do one's thinking for one's self" (281).

71. See Crowley, 157–61, for the sense of Britain divided at that time into different languages, based on class. Again, James's vision is Arnoldian in this respect: Arnold also saw the danger posed by "class-instinct" to the existence of an authoritative cultural center (87).

72. See *The Princess*, 197, for this new manner of pronunciation and punctuation. The difference in lexical capacity between classes emerges throughout Hyacinth's intercourse with the aristocracy: he also finds Captain Sholto "altogether incomprehensible" (224).

73. Although Mr. Vetch's unintelligible words are what Amanda Pynsent finds most remarkable about him, "What that was she would have been unable to say" (72). Her lexical deficiency signals mental ineptitude—an inability to think.

74. This interaction of blood and language is of central importance to Hyacinth's construction of class and national identity. Concerning class, the fine aristocratic talk Hyacinth hears at Medley forms a spirit which was "passing into his own blood" (317); and concerning nationality, the "universal light and the many-voiced sound" Hyacinth experiences in Paris form a "kind of pleasant terror" which also "entered into his blood" (393). Hyacinth's blood becomes a receptacle for the languages of identity.

75. The masses both disgust and fascinate Hyacinth (160), yet when it comes to their language we are given more examples of Hyacinth's often excessive disgust than examples of his fascination (218). Hyacinth is particularly nervous about Millicent's speech: "There were two or three little recurrent irregularities that aggravated him to a degree quite out of proportion to their importance" (385).

76. For Hyacinth's faltering voice at the end of the novel, see 538 and 546; for his developing nervous breakdown, see 528, 530, and 582.

77. Tony Tanner also discusses the role of the human voice in *The Bostonians*: he sees it as part of an ontological, sexual, and political battle—endemic to every society—between public and private spheres (*Scenes of Nature, Signs of Men*, 148).

78. James, *Complete Notebooks*, 20.

79. James, "Speech of American Women," 2: 1104, 2: 1105; *Question of Our Speech*, 25, 16; "Speech of American Women," 3: 21, 4: 113, 3: 18.

80. Cmiel, *Democratic Eloquence*, 129–30, 195; Trachtenberg, *Incorporation of America*, 145–46, 141. Fears were also developing that American literature "was being emasculated because its determining readers were women" (Budd, "The American Background," 37). See Borus, *Writing Realism*, 110–11, for a similar point.

81. See Cmiel, *Democratic Eloquence*, 136.

82. Beard, *Practical Treatise*, 46; Schele de Vere, *Americanisms*, 574; R. G. White, *Every-Day English*, 94, 77; Howells, "Our Daily Speech," 930; White, *Every-Day English*, 93–94.

83. James, *Complete Notebooks*, 20. The climax of *The Europeans* (1878) is the point at which the hyperbole and flattery of Madame Münster's European speech strikes a false note in the purity and strictness of New England culture: "The Baroness . . . instantly felt that she had been observed to be fibbing. She had struck

a false note. But who were these people to whom such fibbing was not pleasing?" (75).

84. For other comments on the defective language and pronunciation of women, see *The Bostonians*, 93, 100, 247.

85. *The Bostonians*, 307, 322–25.

86. Jamieson, *Eloquence in an Electronic Age*, 76.

87. In a similar fashion, while thinking the age too talkative, Ransom himself rather likes to talk (181).

88. Most criticism of *The Bostonians*, since the work of Philip Rahv, Lionel Trilling, and Irving Howe in the 1940s and '50s, has revolved around the question of James's politics in the novel, which in turn depends on whether or not we should see James as siding with Ransom's opinions. Alfred Habegger, for example, attacks the novel because James supposedly declares within it that Ransom's antidemocratic and sexist notions are "right" (*Henry James and the "Woman Business*," 191). Habegger criticizes scholars who consider James's novel to be a truthful representation of the facts about American life in the Gilded Age: it is "gravely and insidiously wrong," especially in its presentation of American culture as feminized at that time (225). Rather than an accurate historical document, however, *The Bostonians* seems more a construction of a particular point of view, common among members of "Anglo-Saxon" culture (as Lears and Trachtenberg have shown), concerning the state of American cultural health.

89. Compare this with Hélène Cixous's idea of hysteria, described by Showalter as "a kind of female language that opposes the rigid structures of male discourse and thought" (*The Female Malady*, 160). For a survey of recent feminist ideas of female language as a disruptive force, see Furman, "The politics of language," 72–75.

90. James plays with the "local color" tradition at another point, in his apparently purposeless description of a Dutch bakery, not important for "any particular influence it may have had on the life or thoughts of Basil Ransom, but for old acquaintance sake and that of local colour" (177).

91. James, "Novel of Dialect," 17–18.

92. Chesnutt, 6. I return to the literary significance of this possible African influence on southern speech in the following chapter.

93. There are many moments in which James establishes his distance from Ransom's opinions: he is described as being very provincial (8), with ideas 300 years out of date (180). There seems to be a direct link between Ransom's southern accent and conservative political ideology: we are told that his accent becomes more pronounced when he says anything gallant (189).

94. James did make one more attempt at a novel with an American setting, *The Ivory Tower*, but it remained unfinished at his death.

95. Edel describes James's disastrous flirtation with the theater, which ended in James's public humiliation in front of the dissatisfied audience of his final play, *Guy Domville* (*A Life*, part 5). James's rejection of public opinion for the "private religion" of his art is recorded in a letter to William James (July 1890; quoted in Gard, ed., *Henry James: The Critical Heritage*, 194).

96. For example, Nick Dormer becomes "more and more conscious" that he and Julia "spoke a different language" (369), and he has problems communicat-

ing with the elderly Mr. Carteret, who "had almost a vocabulary of his own, made up of old-fashioned political phrases and quite untainted with the new terms, mostly borrowed from America" (199). There are many examples of conversations based on semantic debate: take the following interchange between Julia and Nick: "'I shall expect you on Tuesday, and I hope you'll come by a decent train.' / 'What do you mean by a decent train?' / 'I mean I hope you'll not leave it till the last thing before dinner, so that we can have a little walk or something.' / 'What's a little walk or something?'" (253).

97. The possibility of the magical access to another's mind, with which Sharon Cameron, *Thinking in Henry James*, shows James to be concerned in his late work, is not entirely absent from his earlier novels. Thus, *The Princess* also suggests the possibility of a "mystic language," a "reciprocal divination" in which people "understand each other with half a word" (283). Yet, significantly, this type of communication in *The Princess* is not so much mystical as political: it is a secret language of the socially disinherited.

98. This point of view is expressed early in the novel by the Wildean character, Gabriel Nash: style is a private terminology; "from the moment it's the convenience of others, the signs have to be grosser, the shades begin to go" (28).

99. *The Tragic Muse* never sets up a realistic alternative to the problems of public discourse: virtually every example of transcendent communication in the novel is couched in a romantic lexicon of mystic divinations, suggesting the fabulous nature of any perfect intersubjective communication. The problem of representing character is demonstrated vividly by Gabriel Nash's mysterious disappearance from the surface of Nick Dormer's canvas, and from the novel itself (511–12).

100. See Cameron, 83–121. Cameron argues that *The Golden Bowl* displaces the attempt of characters to speak for one another by retreating from "the possibility of speaking 'meaningfully' at all," a retreat which marks a shift in attention from speech to thought. Yet the novel also displaces the characters' resulting supposition that they can transcend speech by accessing directly each other's minds because "what is visible, or audible, when a character engages in such scrutiny looks, or sounds, like thought's impenetrability" (85). Compare this with Yeazell's description of Jamesian dialogue as "a peculiarly solipsistic communing of self with self" (*Language and Knowledge in the Late Novels*, 71). For James's comments on the subservience of speech to consciousness, see "Speech of American Women," 4: 114.

101. Yeazell, 75; see also Todorov, "The Verbal Age."

102. James, *Awkward Age*, xxxvii; "Speech of American Women," 4: 115 (emphasis added).

103. Todorov, 369; Beard, *Practical Treatise*, 47. *The Awkward Age* reflects the sociolinguistic concerns of an unsigned contemporary article titled "The Philosophy of Slang" (1899), which discussed the problems of interpreting the rampant slang—"a kind of private language"—used by the "higher classes" (325–26).

CHAPTER FOUR

1. *Cambridge History of American Literature*, 2: 358–59; North, *Dialect of Modernism*, 22 (emphasis added).

2. I take my definition of *creolization* from Edward Kamau Brathwaite's notion, described by Robert Young as "the imperceptible process whereby two or more cultures merge into a new mode" (*Colonial Desire*, 21).

3. Many of the essays in Mufwene, ed., *Africanisms in Afro-American Language Varieties*, return to the elusiveness and complexity of creole genesis, especially in situations in which the component African and European languages were not themselves "homogeneous units" (12).

4. Sundquist, *To Wake the Nations*, 308.

5. Elizabeth Robbins Pennell, quoted in Tregle, "Creoles and Americans," 131. For another account of Cable's relations with the white-Creole population of New Orleans, see Ekström, *George Washington Cable*, chapters thirteen and fourteen.

6. Herskovits, *The Myth of the Negro Past*, 246. Except for scant references to his political essays, Sundquist virtually ignores Cable in *To Wake the Nations*.

7. Fishkin, 143. Fishkin's and my arguments depend on many of the same sources, and I agree with her account of the impact of black English on white southern speech and with the idea that the American mainstream has a mixed racial heritage. At least in *Was Huck Black?* Fishkin seems unaware of the relevance of her argument to *The Grandissimes* and to Cable's ethnographic work.

8. Similarly, Allen believes many of these spirituals to be the equal possession of white singers while also stating that the "voices of the colored people have a peculiar quality that nothing can imitate" (iv).

9. Dillard has detected this logic in accounts of black speech that de-emphasize African survivals ("Creoles, Cajuns, and Cable," 89).

10. Montgomery, "Africanisms in the American South," 444.

11. There is no doubt that Gullah is a creole language, yet there is some debate over how African it is. Recent discussions have emphasized Gullah's "complex genesis," its consolidation of "features selected, partly under the influence of universal principles, from African and English sources" (Mufwene and Gilman, "How African is Gullah, and why?", 133, 134). We should not lose sight of the fact that Gullah in the nineteenth century was less decreolized than the Gullah of today, and may well have contained a greater African element. Ironically, Gullah may have been most African at a time when observers were least able to recognize it.

12. L. Turner, quoted in Herskovits, 276. For his rejection of conventional beliefs about Gullah's origin, see L. Turner, v.

13. However, Turner does not consider Gullah to have "significant tone"— the use of tone or pitch to "convey meaning and to show grammatical relationships"—as do many West African languages (29–30).

14. See L. Turner, 223–31, for a discussion of Gullah grammar.

15. Other examples given by Allen include *all-two* (both), *one* (alone), *draw* (receiving in any way), *meet* (find), *gang* (for any large number), *mash* (crush), *stantion* (substantial) (xxvii).

16. There are many other observations of Allen's that reverberate throughout subsequent accounts of black vocal products: the endless variations in black music and speech (iv); the fragmentation of the black linguistic community into different localities (xi) and into different "grades" of speaker in the same community (xxiv); the strong degree of spontaneity and improvisation (xxi); the working of contemporary event into song (xviii).

17. Montgomery, 442–43; Bennett, quoted in Montgomery, 443. According to Montgomery, Bennett was able to confirm African sources for the words *yam, voodoo, banjo, duppy, mumbo-jumbo, okra, pinder, goober, coonjure, cootah,* and others (442).

18. For an account of Gullah influence on the "cultivated" speech of whites in South Carolina, see McDavid and McDavid, "The Relationship of the Speech of American Negroes to the Speech of Whites," 13–17.

19. Harrison, "Negro English," 143; Payne, "A Word-List from East Alabama," 196; Elam, "Lingo in Literature," 286.

20. Dillard, *Black English*, 191. Compare this to the recognition from 1908 that "the Negro uses in many instances a kind of pigeon [*sic*] English or dialect. The whites heard this jargon on southern plantations and copied it, and thus the language of the whites and blacks on southern plantations had a strange similarity" (Giles Jackson and G. Webster Davis, *The Industrial History of the Negro Race in the United States* [1908], quoted in Montgomery, 445).

21. Payne, 196; Elam, 287; Harrison, "Negro English," 144–45, 175.

22. Schele de Vere, 148–50.

23. See North, 21, for Harris's account of Uncle Remus's English. For discussions of—and reactions to—the notion that black English is an archaic form of British English, see McDavid and McDavid. According to Dillard, the idea of black linguistic archaism is extremely racist as it suggests innate mental deficiency and a natural tendency to imitate (*Black English*, 190).

24. See Dunn, "The Black–Southern White Dialect Controversy," and Dillard, *Black English*, 211–12, for the link between language and politics in the postbellum South.

25. Elam, 286; Du Bois, *The Souls of Black Folk*, 8.

26. See Young's discussion of linguistic hybridity, which he derives mainly from M. M. Bakhtin and Homi Bhabha (*Colonial Desire*, 20–26).

27. Young quotes Bakhtin on this double-voiced discourse: "the same word will belong simultaneously to two languages, two belief systems that intersect in a hybrid construction—and, consequently, the word has two contradictory meanings, two accents" (Bakhtin, *The Dialogic Imagination*, 305; quoted in Young, *Colonial Desire*, 21–22).

28. Harrison, "Negro English," 144–45; Reisman, "Cultural and Linguistic Ambiguity in a West Indian Village," 132; for "signifying" see Gates's argument in *The Signifying Monkey*.

29. I draw the terms "double-consciousness," "veil," and "two-ness" from Du Bois, 4–5.

30. See Homi Bhabha's discussion of minority discourse, in "DissemiNation," 306–7.

31. Morrison, quoted in Fishkin, *Was Huck Black?*, 95; Frances Kemble, writing in the 1830s, quoted in Dillard, *Black English*, 26.

32. Dodge, 161–62.

33. The traditional "proof" of the impossibility of slaves maintaining African languages—the fact that the mixing of slaves from mutually unintelligible linguistic communities would preclude African retentions—is thus contradicted by Gonzales. Furthermore, he observes that the Gullahs of the coastal regions "retained more

of the habits and traditions of their African ancestry" (11), and he is aware of native Africans still living on the Carolina coast after the Civil War (17–18).

34. *'Dafa*, continues L. Turner, is in fact the Gullah word for "fat," *'dafa fat* being therefore a repetition (14). Beneath Gonzales's word *swonguh*, which he considers to mean "swank" (from the English "swagger"), Turner reveals the Mende word *suwango*, which signifies "to be proud." And beneath the word *lilly*, supposedly an abbreviated form of the English *little*, is in fact the Wolof *lir*, which means "small" (Turner, quoted in Herskovits, 277). The knowledge gained from Turner shows how the aspect of Gullah explicitly denied by Gonzales—it is a creole language that combines African and English elements—is implicitly represented.

35. The climax of the piece arrives when a local doctor cannot "exceed" in curing the granddaughter of a former slave, despite throwing "one dollar en' sebenty-fi' cent' wut' uh med'sin een de gal" (244).

36. J. C. Harris refers to two works: G. M. Theal's *Kaffir Folk-Lore; or, A Selection from the Traditional Tales current among the People living on the Eastern Border of the Cape Colony* (London, 1882), and W. H. I. Bleek's *Reynard, the Fox, in South Africa; or, Hottentot Fables and Tales* (London, 1864).

37. North, 22.

38. Kathleen Light suggests that the stories in *Nights with Uncle Remus* that revolve around Daddy Jack involve an unusual "probing into comparative folklore." By moving toward an earlier black experience, these stories lead the reader "to expect a concurrent movement toward more authentic and primitive stories whose modifications and variations will furnish insight into the cultural evolution of the Negro," an ethnological movement that Harris inevitably rejects by "reaffirming his belief that the stories are a conscious artistic representation of the black experience" ("Uncle Remus and the Folklorists," 150–51).

39. Dillard considers Harris, Gonzales, and Jones to be "outstanding" dialect writers (*Black English*, 193).

40. Levine, *Black Culture and Black Consciousness*, xv.

41. C. C. Jones, 130. The last few tales in Jones's collection, however, are told in "standard" English.

42. Translations from Mercier are mine. Mercier was a native Louisianian, educated in Paris, a practicing doctor as well as novelist and essayist, and—toward the end of his life—the leader of efforts to preserve French literature and language in the state. His novels criticized slavery in Louisiana and suggested its corrupting influence on the former slave owners (Reinecke, "Alfred Mercier," 160).

43. Mercier, 1–3. "The negro patois, the creole, as we say, is still widespread in Louisiana; there is a complete quarter of New Orleans where we use it, in intimacy, while addressing domestics and children" (2). See Dillard, ed., *Perspectives on Black English*, for the influence of the creole on the "standard" French of Louisiana and the Caribbean (18).

44. Harrison, "Creole Patois of Louisiana," 286, 285, 287. At the time, *creole French* was also known as "Creole patois" or "African-Creole dialect."

45. In antebellum Louisiana, argues Joseph Tregle, the fact that nonwhites did not vie for social and political positions meant that *creole* could signify "native born" without reference to color ("Creoles and Americans," 137, 139). The term

only gained its resonance of racial exclusiveness with the "menace of black domination" (173) after the Civil War.

46. Gayarré, quoted in Ekström, *George Washington Cable*, 112.

47. The etymology of *creole* is similar to the Latin etymology of *vernaculus:* both signify, roughly, a slave born in his master's house.

48. Harrison, "Creole Patois," 286, quoted in Cable, *Creoles of Louisiana*, 41n (emphasis added). It seems here (and it is certainly Cable's reading) that the word was created by blacks to designate whites born in the Americas. Tregle cites a more extreme position from the early 1600s: "The name was invented by the Negroes. . . . They use it to mean a Negro born in the Indies" (137).

49. Cable, *Creoles of Louisiana*, 41 (emphasis added). While Tregle argues that neither slaves nor free persons of color could control language in this way (139), this chapter—without going so far as to suggest that people of color could "mandate" white usage—reveals the various hidden ways in which African Americans were indeed influencing the language and habits of white people. Cable's assertion is prefigured by Lafcadio Hearn's essay "Los Criollos" (1877). Although concurring with the idea that *creole* can refer to people of color only through a misapplication of its original meaning, Hearn describes how this error is a common one—even in New Orleans itself—because the "colored element . . . call themselves Creoles, and desire to be so called" (196). Again, in "The Dance in Place Congo," Cable talks of the "ever-growing number of negroes who proudly called themselves Creole negroes, that is, born in America" (522).

50. Tregle reads *The Creoles of Louisiana* as an "endorsement of the all-white definition of creole" (175). To some extent, however, Cable undermines his own definition of Creoles as "the French-speaking, native portion of the ruling class" (42) with his assertion of the black creation and resignification of this word.

51. Herskovits, 246.

52. In "Creole Slave Songs," Cable refers to work on creole languages by J. J. Thomas, M. Marbot, Père Gaux, M. Turiault, Alfred Mercier, James A. Harrison, and John Bigelow (807).

53. Cable does describe the formation of the "Creole *patois*" in the conventional terms of a "savage people" taking up the language of a "highly refined civilization" ("Creole," 807); he is capable of making reference to "the thick negro tongue" ("Dance," 525) and of hinting that the dialect was formed from the active input of "French tongues" that were misheard by "so many more African ears" ("Creole," 807). Yet the great number of Africanisms observed by Cable in his essays undercuts this negation of the African sources for the linguistic and cultural situation of Louisiana. It remains implicit in Cable's observations that the master caste, rather than simply giving away "Gallic archaisms" ("Creole," 807), was in fact receiving Africanisms.

54. Sundquist, *To Wake the Nations*, 479. Cable's call for "some one who has studied African tongues" ("Creole," 822) had to wait to be answered.

55. G. M. Hall, *Africans in Colonial Louisiana*, 157. Strong cases for a thoroughly Africanized early Louisiana slave culture, which led to the significant and early contribution of African elements to Louisiana creole, are made by Hall (159–88) and John Holm (*Pidgins and Creoles*, 387–91).

56. Cable makes Congo Square in New Orleans an important motif of cultural

mixing and of the cultural dominance of African-American forms. In this space, originally between the city walls and the wilderness of the swamp—a space where all races of the lower classes meet ("the butcher and baker, the raftsman, the sailor, the quadroon, the painted girl, and the negro slave" ["Dance," 518])— African-American song and dance play a central role.

57. The type of interaction between white-Creole and African-Creole culture observed by Cable is similar to the ambivalence and the attractive intermingling of "racial cultures" detected by Eric Lott within the American tradition of black-face minstrelsy (*Love and Theft*, 6). Lott makes passing reference to Cable's lecture tour with Mark Twain, in which both authors read the roles of black characters, with "Cable even singing songs" (31). Lott uses this lecture tour to strengthen his point concerning the contradictions inherent in white reactions to black culture: political agitation on behalf of African Americans (Lott mentions that Cable's essay "The Freedman's Case in Equity" was published during the lecture tour) coexisted with the "hierarchical assumptions of the minstrel tradition" (32). Although minstrelsy surely informed the context in which Cable's songs were received, Cable's interaction with black culture suggests that he was highly conscious of the processes of cultural intermixture and influence assigned by Lott to the white "social unconscious." When Cable sang slave songs, he was at least partly mimicking the white-Creole tradition through which these songs were filtered.

58. Krehbiel, *Afro-American Folksongs*, 144. Krehbiel's work contains in its final chapter perhaps the first scholarly treatment of the satirical songs of the African Creoles. Cable's essays feature heavily in Krehbiel's work; in fact, these essays were originally projected as a joint work between Cable and Krehbiel, until the latter withdrew owing to "the many prior claims of the journalist's profession" ("Dance," 529). In 1886, Lafcadio Hearn also recognized that "the once celebrated art of our French-speaking negroes in improvising satire may be traced to a Griot tradition" ("Some Notes on Creole Literature," 158).

59. Fortier, "French Language in Louisiana," 98; "Bits of Louisiana Folk-Lore," 168.

60. According to Cable, the number of stanzas in this song "has never been counted" ("Dance," 528), implying that it became a general song of satire that might be improvised to fit various circumstances.

61. Together with "Dé Zab," which supposedly translates as "Out from under the trees our boat moves into the open water—bring us large game and small game" ("Creole," 823), Cable prints two other African-language songs together with their accompanying musical notation: "Annoqué, Annobia," which Cable heard sung in the cane field ("Dance," 523), and "Héron mandé," a "genuine Voodoo song, given me by Lafcadio Hearn" ("Creole," 820–21). Cable also includes a voodoo chant, without musical notation ("Creole," 819), and suggests that voodoo practices "have not always in view ... good order and public tranquility" ("Creole," 818), thereby confirming his knowledge of the insurgent element of the "African-Creole lyric product" ("Creole," 809–10).

62. Like Cable, William Piersen describes the various ways in which both Africans and African Americans sought to mask this satire by making use of unintel-

ligible native language ("Puttin' Down Ole Massa," 26), apparent foolishness and self-parody (28), or by alternating their satire with songs of praise and flattery (20).

63. Piersen, 22; Morgan, "The Africanness of Counterlanguage," 423.

64. As a whole, Cable's essays contradict Morgan's statement that, in the United States, satirical songs functioned in secrecy and went largely unnoticed by whites, while confirming her observation that, owing to the ambiguity and irony inherent in "counterlanguage," "it was not always possible to know when a song was satirical" (428).

65. See Hearn, *Two Years in the French West Indies*, 268–69, and Krehbiel, 135–38.

66. Tregle, 175. According to Cable, it was the mixing of the "wild," "striking" music of Congo Square with French taste that gave these African-Creole songs a "great tenderness of sentiment" ("Dance," 522). Krehbiel would make much of this idea, calling African-Creole songs a "hybrid art" (ix), a basic mixture of Latin melody with African rhythm (135). Cable considered that the "Creole music" of whites had also developed from the situation in which African-American songs entered the white-Creole drawing room through the "master's growing child of musical ear" ("Creole," 809).

67. Thomas, 113. Thomas includes a list of sixty nouns "peculiar to the dialect," with the suggestion that three-quarters of them may well have African origins (19–21), and he records many idiomatic expressions that he considers "most difficult of interpretation" (116). Like Cable, Thomas also notices the effects of African-Creole French upon English: "the nullifying effects of the *patois* on English instruction among us" (iv).

68. Lafcadio Hearn, Hjalmar Boyesen, and Edward Eggleston, quoted in A. Turner, ed., *Critical Essays*, 9, 12, 5.

69. Anonymous review of *Old Creole Days*, quoted in A. Turner, ed., *Critical Essays*, 6.

70. De Menil, 217–18; Gayarré, quoted in Ekström, 176.

71. Cable, quoted in Tregle, 176.

72. Another example is the ambiguous statement, again from Cable's 1884 *Encyclopaedia Britannica* entry, that the name *Creole* "does not necessarily imply any more than it excludes, a departure from a double line of Latin descent" (quoted in Tregle, 175). *The Grandissimes* dwells on the irony that Agricola Fusilier, a white supremacist, descends directly from an Indian queen (15, 18).

73. Gayarré, quoted in Ekström, 176n11. Ekström considers it "evident that Cable made no attempt to reconstruct the English of the Creoles of the early nineteenth century but took the artistic liberty of putting into their mouths the English of contemporary Creoles" (177).

74. Evans, "Literary Dialect in *The Grandissimes*," 210. Evans notices that the loss of the preconsonantal *r* and the copula are common in black English and in black French, but not in "conventional" French, therefore making them possible influences on the French-English dialect of white Creoles in the novel (212). Evans observes, however, that resemblance between French English and black English "is not necessarily influence" (219n13), that much white southern English is itself

"*r*-less" and lacking in the copula. Evans's suggestion of white influence fails to take into account the possibility that African influence was already present in this "prestige speech," and—in his belief in a conscious control over speech acquisition—Evans fails to leave room for surreptitious linguistic influence. Cable seems to have intentionally suggested the possibility of "africanized" influence. See "Creole Slave Songs" for his observation of the missing final syllables in black French (807).

75. Evans, 213–17.

76. For this unclear use of "Creole dialect," see *Grandissimes,* 58. There was much confusion at the time over whether the "Creole dialect" was "broken" English or creole French. W. S. Kennedy was so confused that he considered "Gumbo French" to be "the broken English of Cable's books" ("The New Orleans of George Cable," quoted in A. Turner, ed., *Critical Essays,* 72). Cable tried to sort out this confusion in "The Dance in Place Congo": "The Creole 'dialect' is the broken English *of the Creoles,* while the Creole *patois* is the corrupt French, not of the Creoles, but rather of the former slave race in the country of the Creoles" (522).

77. See the response to Cable's novella "Madame Delphine" (1881), quoted in A. Turner, *George W. Cable,* 107.

78. In "Creole Slave Songs," Cable records that *courri* ("to run") is the African-Creole equivalent of *aller* ("to go") (808).

79. Hearn, "Creole Patois," 146.

80. Rouquette, 9, 4, 23–24.

81. Krehbiel traces this African-American satirical tradition to the professional minstrels, or mountebanks, of African tribes, who use their powers of improvisation and their sharp wit to get money from those who fear them (142–43). These griots (as they are called in Senegambia, the homeland of many early Afro-Louisianians and a significant influence on their early culture) were masters of the art of satire. Piersen, expanding on Krehbiel's comments, describes how these songs—both in African and African-American societies—were used as a mechanism of social control, a manner of political criticism, an empowerment of the weak (20).

82. Lott, 20, 6. A similar type of exchange in *The Grandissimes* is also discovered in the white characters' belief in and use of voodoo. See *Grandissimes,* 55, 74, 98, 184, for some of the many examples of this.

83. We know from "Creole Slave Songs" that Cable possessed a translation of this song—"Dé Zab"—but he does not refer in *The Grandissimes* to the lyrics' African origin. See also the cane-cutting song, "Anoqué, Anobia" (*Grandissimes,* 188), which also appears in "Dance" (523).

84. Ladd, "'An Atmosphere of Hints and Allusions,'" 75n6. Ladd also suggests that Bras-Coupé's wedding song "may contain some veiled references to West Indian traditions of marronage" (74n6). Importations from the West Indies were viewed with suspicion by whites in Louisiana, mainly owing to the San Domingo slave revolution of 1791 and to the fact that most slaves imported from the French Caribbean were the "bad and vicious" individuals who were considered uncontrollable by their masters (G. M. Hall, 181). According to Cable, Congo Plains "drew all inspirations" from the West Indies ("Dance," 519), and the Calinda

dance was a particular area of continuity between Louisianian and West Indian culture ("Dance," 527).

85. G. M. Hall, 345.

86. Ladd, 69–71.

87. G. M. Hall, 166.

88. See *The Grandissimes*, 134, for another word "all in African b's and k's."

89. George Parsons Lathrop and Richard Watson Gilder, quoted in Ladd, 63. Ladd believes that Cable was forced to displace the context of insurrection into the romantic love plot of the novel (72). It is therefore "beneath the surface" of *The Grandissimes* (74)—namely, within Cable's many allusions—that we must look for the highly charged politics of slave rebellion.

90. Cable, quoted in Tregle, 176.

91. See G. M. Hall, 344–45. According to Hall, the Pointe Coupee slave rebellion became "the cornerstone of an ideology justifying racist violence and oppression of Afro-Louisianians and of whites who opposed slavery and racism" (344). The "coup," as it was referred to at the time (Hall, 358), was seen as part of the spread of revolutionary fever from San Domingo. Bras-Coupé's name, like the date that Cable ascribes to his insurrection, implicitly refers to this slave conspiracy.

92. G. P. Lathrop, "Mr. Cable's History of the Creoles," quoted in A. Turner, ed., *Critical Essays*, 67.

93. For an account of how white Creoles used this dialect as a satirical response to what they described—with pointed irony—as the "abject slavery" of the carpetbagger regime, see Tinker, "French Newspapers of Louisiana," 268–71.

94. Referring to the *Code Noir* according to which Bras-Coupé is savagely punished after his rebellion, the narrator states that "we have a *Code Noir* now, but the new one is a mental reservation, not an enactment" (181). See *Grandissimes*, 315, for another example of historical parallelism.

95. "My Politics," in Cable, *Negro Question*, 14. Cable's essays on the "Negro Question" in the South were among the few contributions of the period from a "Southern white man" (as Cable occasionally signed himself) against the racism and the growing civil distinctions of the era. "My Politics" remained unpublished in Cable's lifetime.

96. In "The Negro Question," Cable states that those people of mixed blood find "the race line not a race line at all" because "no proportion of white men's blood in their own veins, unless it washes out the very memory of their African tincture, can get them abatement of those deprivations decreed for a dull, vicious, and unclean race" (*Negro Question*, 131). See also "The Freedman's Case in Equity" (*Negro Question*, 54–55, 72) for Cable's use of the idea of racial hybridity to undermine the notion of race instinct.

97. Cable, *Negro Question*, 143, 118, 43–46, 65, 62, 47–48.

98. According to Tregle, illiteracy was rampant among French Creoles (142–43).

99. Du Bois, 5.

100. This is a quotation from *le Carillon* (1869), cited in Tregle, 170.

CHAPTER FIVE

1. Howells, *Hazard of New Fortunes*, 57.

2. "Low life" is Howells's term for the socially disadvantaged of the city (see Howells, "New York Low Life in Fiction" [1896], 18).

3. Trachtenberg, *Incorporation of America*, 88. John Higham argues that, although the mass immigration of the period did not necessarily create the American city, it supplied America with a working class possessing an urban frame of mind, which enabled the development of mass industrial production (*Send These to Me*, 22–23).

4. Many historians have pointed out that Italians, Jews, Poles, Russians, and Slavs began to outnumber the British, Irish, Scandinavians, and Germans toward the end of the nineteenth century (see Higham, 21; and Lubove, *The Progressives and the Slums*, 53). Higham stresses the diversity of these groups (15).

5. For discussions of this new journalism, see Park, "The Natural History of the Newspaper," Trachtenberg, *Incorporation of America*, 124–26, and Trachtenberg, "Experiments in Another Country."

6. Thomas De Witt Talmage's *The Abominations of Modern Society* (1872), for example, took readers into a sordid world of urban sin: "I open to you a door, through which you see . . . [t]he victims, strewn over the floor, writhe and twist among each other in contortions indescribable" (16).

7. See Fine, *The City, the Immigrant, and American Fiction*, 43–46, 74, 100, for discussion of these aspects of tenement fiction and the immigrant novel.

8. Hutchins Hapgood described his *The Spirit of the Ghetto* (1902) as "an attempt made by a 'Gentile' to report sympathetically on the character, lives, and pursuits of certain east-side Jews with whom he has been in relations of considerable intimacy" (5). See Ziff, *The American 1890s*, 120–65, for an account of how newspapers in the 1890s began to emphasize the daily life of the "humble" (147).

9. See Trachtenberg, *Incorporation of America*, 101–39, for a detailed analysis of this popular idea of entry into a menacing urban space.

10. Aldrich, *Poems*, 276; Hapgood, 25. See Higginson, "New York as a Literary Centre," for one of many references to the Babel of New York (230).

11. Kaplan, *Social Construction of American Realism*, 8–9, 23; Borus, *Writing Realism*, 101, 108–9. Between a "New York novelist, who wishes to deal with proletarian types, and his subject"—noted an 1899 article on New York fiction—"there is usually the barrier of race" (Maurice, "New York in Fiction," 35).

12. Howells, *Hazard of New Fortunes*, 162, 165, 162.

13. Howells, "New York Low Life," 18.

14. See Fine, 38–54, for an account of Crane's and Cahan's similar reactions to the conventional accounts of urban and immigrant life that were firmly established by the 1890s.

15. J. Riis, 3, 15–16.

16. Although admitting that "our mixed races, not being yet consolidated, are wanting in that unity of thought and character that forms and harmonizes public sentiment" (59), J. W. Gerard—in an 1890 article on New York City—expresses his belief that the Anglo-Saxon still "dominates while the new [race] is forming"

("The Impress of Nationalities on New York City," 58). See Clark, "The Chinese of New York," for another account of this reverse "colonization" (104).

17. *Harper's Weekly* cited Ward School Number 23 as an example of linguistic assimilation. Although the school contains children speaking twenty-six different languages, their ability to learn English has the crucial effect of Americanization. After six months, with your eyes closed "you will not be able to distinguish Chinese child or Arab child or Tunisian child from the few pure-blooded Americans who form the curiosities of the school" (Phillips, "Ward School No. 23," 535).

18. Mawson, "Hot Wave among the Poor," 814; E. Emerson, "The New Ghetto," 44.

19. J. Riis, 38, 101, 87; Howells, *Hazard of New Fortunes*, 165. Although Riis was not born in America (he was a Danish immigrant), he tended to echo dominant opinions about foreign immigration—part of an effort, one imagines, to become more American himself.

20. J. Riis, 91, 100.

21. An article in the first issue of the journal *Dialect Notes* considered the "English of the lower classes in New York City and vicinity" to be worthy of notice (quoted in R. Bailey, *Nineteenth-Century English*, 72).

22. R. G. White, *Words and Their Uses*, 56.

23. In Alger's first novel, *Ragged Dick; Or, Street Life in New York* (1867), Dick's social progress is marked by the loss of his "peculiar way of speaking and use of slang terms" (207).

24. Thomas Lounsbury, quoted in B. Matthews, *Parts of Speech*, 194; B. Matthews, 195–96, 197. For *growler*, see B. Matthews, 197; for *cheese it*, see Ralph, "The Language of the Tenement-folk," 90.

25. R. G. White, *Words and Their Uses*, 85. Writing in 1891, F. K. Wischnewetzky regarded the period 1879–89 as a "decade of retrogression."

26. Sherman, "A Study in Current Slanguage," 153. Sherman considers that "[s]lang, in sooth, is a whiskey-distillation of language. It is so strong that it may be taken only very rarely with impunity"; and that a "careful study of the qualities of men and women who habitually interlard their remarks with slang will furnish anybody with a world of convincing conclusions in favor of pure English" (153).

27. Miscommunication in Alger's *Ragged Dick* is based on occasional mispronunciations: for example, the glazier's cry of "glass put in" is heard by a visitor from the country as "glass puddin'" [91]). See Trachtenberg, *Incorporation of America*, 105–7, for a discussion of this example and of Alger's novel as a whole. R. G. White used a similar example of "parrot wheezers" (pair of tweezers) to illustrate the same urban phenomenon (*Every-Day English*, 119).

28. Talmage, *Abominations of Modern Society*, 243–44.

29. Frederick Pierce explained in 1895 that Scottish, Welsh, English, Scandinavian, and Canadian immigrants were "perhaps less foreign than the others" ("The Tenement-House Committee Maps," 62).

30. Ralph, 90 (emphasis added). Trachtenberg discusses the "foreign culture" of labor (*Incorporation of America*, 88).

31. Ralph, 90; James, *American Scene*, 525.

32. James, *American Scene*, 456, 470, 471, 454–55. See Park, 81–82; Ziff 121–22; and Cmiel, *Democratic Eloquence*, 246–47, for the importance of this new, less

"literary," language. The urban newspaper had a self-proclaimed mission to Americanize the immigrant (Ziff, 148).

33. James, *American Scene*, 453; Howells, "New York Low Life," 18. See James, *Question of Our Speech*, 45, for the opinion that immigrants have as much property in speech as do "native" Americans.

34. Garland, "An Ambitious French Novel and a Modest American Story," quoted in Wertheim, ed., *Merrill Studies*, 6. Crane was not a native of New York City, as Garland suggests; he was born in New Jersey and began to write about the city before really experiencing it (Benfry, *Life of Stephen Crane*, 56; Ziff, 187).

35. Bergon, *Stephen Crane's Artistry*, 75. Bergon's view of Crane's "inside" perspective is unusual because it seems to work against his own argument that Crane constantly undermines this type of literary convention and seeks to test "the authenticity of this strange world" (149).

36. Trachtenberg, "Experiments in Another Country," 68, 69, 73. There have been notable dissenters from this view of Crane. Frank Norris suggested that Crane "does not seem to . . . have gotten *into*" the life of his characters (quoted in Stallman, "Crane's *Maggie* in Review," 22). Ziff argues that *Maggie* is an exaggeration, a "vision of what typically happens rather than a report of what actually happens" (191).

37. The original version of "An Experiment in Misery" ends with the young man's doubt that he has discovered the tramp's point of view (42).

38. This emphasis on strangeness in Crane's work transcends some of the parameters of my discussion: the life of a millionaire presented in "An Experiment in Luxury," for example, is just as alien, inaccessible, and inhuman as that of a Bowery tramp (Bergon, 34).

39. For opinions endorsing the reality of Crane's dialect, see the various reviewers quoted in Stallman (16, 21, 23). Crane himself insisted to Howells that "that is the way they *talk*" (quoted in Howells, "From 'Frank Norris,'" 12). The epigraph to this section quotes a typical genteel reader, who did not know for sure what language was like in a Bowery bar.

40. See Beer, "From *Stephen Crane*," 26, for details of Gilder's refusal to publish Crane in *The Century*. Howells, quoted in Cady, "From *Stephen Crane*," 53; *Home Journal*, quoted in Stallman, 20. Crane printed *Maggie* privately under the pseudonym Johnston Smith; it met with little success.

41. Stallman, 16. Although Ziff points to journalistic moves to attract a less "cultivated" public, he still considers that the American literary establishment exhibited a suppressive purism in the last years of the century (128–29). Readers were "guarded not only from the offensive but from the potentially offensive" (124).

42. Howells, "New York Low Life," 18 (emphasis added).

43. Townsend, 5–6, 12.

44. *Godey's Magazine*, quoted in Stallman, 14. The phrase "dangerous classes" is taken from the title of Charles Loring Brace's *The Dangerous Classes of New York* (1872).

45. Crane altered both of these phrases in the 1896 *Maggie*: the first became "almost kicked the breath out of," and the second became "I'll stamp yer faces tru d' floor" (see the "Historical Collation" to *Maggie*, 93, 95).

46. According to James Colvert, Crane "had a strong feeling for the effect of the contrast between the colloquial and the elevated 'literary' style, a device commonly used in *Maggie*" ("Introduction to *Maggie*," xlvi). There are other instances of this narrational borrowing of clichéd slum-talk: "she shook him until he rattled," for example (12).

47. Ziff describes the strict line between the literary and the nonliterary in the 1890s. There was a great difference between writing about the realities of life that appeared in cheap magazines and newspapers, and writing about these elements in a work of literature—such was the moral control of the literary establishment (128).

48. Crane, quoted in Katz, "The *Maggie* Nobody Knows," 97, and in Colvert, xlii.

49. See the "Historical Collation" to *Maggie* for these details. Also, see Bowers's textual introduction to this edition for another account of Crane's revision of the 1893 text, especially concerning the removal of blasphemy and the maintenance of "tamn" in dialect (lxix). Bowers considers that there is "some difficulty" (lxvii) in the fact that certain examples of cursing are maintained by Crane; his strictly textual approach disregards Crane's decision to retain blasphemy at key moments in the novel, which act to emphasize its portrayal of a world in which conventional moral and religious sentiment have become meaningless. Katz stresses the importance of Crane's blasphemy to the novel's religious theme and to the inarticulate quality of the characters (101).

50. In fact, Crane's spelling was so unreliable that it is occasionally difficult to say for sure whether certain "misspellings" are dialectal at all. The spelling of "doctor" as "docter" in *George's Mother* (153) may not be dialect, because Crane frequently misspelled the word this way.

51. "Above all things he despised obvious Christians and ciphers with the chrysanthemums of aristocracy in their button-holes. He considered himself above both of these classes. He was afraid of nothing" (*Maggie*, 21).

52. Talmage, 14. See Ellison, "Stephen Crane and the Mainstream of American Fiction," 60, for details of Crane's religious upbringing.

53. New York *Town Topics* and anonymous English critic, quoted in Stallman, 15, 19.

54. Howells, "From 'Frank Norris,'" 13.

55. John Berryman wrote that "in Pete's jawing . . . we hear a rhythm of the artist" ("From *Stephen Crane*," quoted in Wertheim, ed., 28). Bergon reads Crane's Bowery dialect as the epitome of Bridgman's idea of a stylized colloquial prose that stresses individual words and uses repetition to bind and unify (6).

56. For Howells's exhortation, see Crane, "Howells Fears Realists Must Wait," 172.

57. Bridgman, *The Colloquial Style*, 52.

58. Frank Bergon has pointed to a similar undermining of moral opposites throughout Crane's work, which forces the reader to question a culture that collapses at all levels and a language that seems unable to express, communicate, or make coherent (71, 27–29).

59. M. D. Bell, *Problem of American Realism*, 137. Bell argues that Crane undermines the "authority naturalist texts usually invest in the outside narrator's per-

spective" (139), together with the naturalist promise that language is able to give "a direct transmission of 'real' life in which style remains transparent" (133).

60. See Ziff, 192, and M. D. Bell, 139–40, for this argument.

61. According to Nagel, the "tragedy of *Maggie* is not the result of inexorable doom or impersonal forces but the more poignant result of numerous choices freely made on the basis of naiveté, confusion, and self-deluding pride" (*Stephen Crane and Literary Impressionism*, 111).

62. Dreiser, 7; Norris, 230.

63. Ziff notices this breakdown of communication in *Maggie*: "Crane's characters, gabbling on in a lingo which is, like their setting, chosen only for being extreme, communicate not at all when they talk to one another." This is part of Ziff's claim that there is "no literal level of social reality" in the novel (191).

64. Although M. D. Bell suggests that "Crane apparently recognized that if environment shapes lives it does so, above all, by predetermining perception, by granting so much authority to the styles in which others' perceptions have been expressed" (139), he still considers that *Maggie*'s characters are not so much trapped by these styles as willing to indulge in them (140). To say that characters are self-deluded in *Maggie* is to suggest that there are preferable ways of seeing, of which the characters are unaware. But what choice do "low life" characters have when the moral discourse of the "high life" alternative is equally corrupt?

65. See especially the comments of Garland ("An Ambitious French Novel and a Modest American Story," quoted in Wertheim, ed., 6), and Howells, "From 'Frank Norris,'" 13.

66. In fact, according to Benfry, *Maggie* "was apparently sketched *before* Crane had any direct experience of the metropolis" (56). See also Ziff, 187.

67. Cahan published another English-language novel, *The White Terror and the Red: A Tale of Revolutionary Russia* (1905), together with several uncollected short stories (see the bibliography in Fine, *The City, the Immigrant, and American Fiction*, 167).

68. Howells, "New York Low Life," 18. Howells also noted that Cahan was "strictly of the great and true Russian principle in literary art" (18). According to John Higham, Cahan's third culture—Russia and its literary models—supplied a detachment that broke the traditional "double vision" of "hyphenated" ethnicity (*Send These to Me*, 89).

69. For the often negative reaction of American-born, German Jews to Cahan's work, see Fine, 22. Cahan's audience was more various—in terms of ethnicity and social class—than Crane's. Hutchins Hapgood admired Cahan's ability to translate, which gave "the pleasure of easily understanding what is unfamiliar" (*The Spirit of the Ghetto*, 237).

70. According to Moses Rischin, while Dunne's immensely popular "Mr. Dooley" column in the Chicago press was pioneering the Irish brogue as an acceptable literary form, marking the acceptance of the Irish American as a hyphenated ethnic group within the nation, the "green Yiddish idiom was as yet ill equipped to blend and resonate in familiar counterpoint with American speech, too undomesticated to insinuate its way onto the printed page" (Introduction to Cahan, *Grandma Never Lived in America*, xviii).

71. The studious character Bernstein, observing Yekl's demonstration of the

rules of American boxing, comments that "America is an educated country, so they won't even break bones without grammar. They tear each other's sides according to 'right and left,' you know," referring to a "term relating to the Hebrew equivalent of the letter *s*, whose pronunciation depends upon the right or left position of a mark over it" (7).

72. Cahan had first-hand experience of teaching English to immigrants (Rischin, xxv).

73. Rischin, xli. Again in the words of Rischin: "Writing in a newly fashioned American English that mixed at least three English dialects—those of the street and shop, the school, and the study—with German, Italian, Russian, Yiddish, and old Hebrew words, Cahan forced brilliant advantage out of seemingly insuperable obstacles to communication" (xl).

74. Susan K. Harris argues that Cahan was forced to use dominant forms that were "inherently biased against sympathetic representations of the Other" (135). Thus, in "The Imported Bridegroom," Cahan uses representations of language to mock and denigrate his Jewish characters in a superficial way ("Problems of Representation," 138). Although Werner Sollors more subtly suggests that Cahan uses language to signal the immigrant's divided self (*Beyond Ethnicity*, 163–64), he still considers Jake's "bastardized language," in *Yekl*, to be rendered "quite derogatorily" (164).

75. In his language, writes David M. Fine, "Glass exploits the stereotyped Jewish penchant for hyperbole or exaggeration and such supposedly Yiddish-derived syntactical peculiarities as placing verbs at the end of sentences and misplacing modifiers" (71).

76. For example, *satisfied* appears variously as "*saresfied*" and "*salesfiet*" (*Yekl*, 180).

77. J. Riis, *How the Other Half Lives*, 16.

78. See *Yekl*, 3, 40, and 105, for examples of these various linguistic differences.

79. For a detailed discussion of Cahan's concern with characters trapped between Old World and New World values, see Fine, 121–38. Fine interprets this as Cahan's reply to the glibness in immigrant novels that celebrated unproblematic acculturation (121).

80. Shaya's intended bride, Flora, speaks Yiddish that "sounded at once like his native tongue and the language of the Gentiles" (53). See "Imported Bridegroom," 119, for an observation of how Hebrew "gesticulations" are imported into English.

81. For this common theme of the Jewish misfit, see Fine, 23–24, 32.

82. See *Rise of David Levinsky* for a similar point about the "meaningless words" of Hebrew prayer (12).

83. Shell, "Babel in America," 120.

84. See *Rise of David Levinsky*, 130–31, for the observation of what Rosina Lippi-Green describes as the "breakthrough of native language phonology into the target language" (*English with an Accent*, 43). Many individuals, argues Lippi-Green, find this accent impossible to change (45).

85. See *Rise of David Levinsky*, 327–28, 139, 176, 154, and 133–34, for Levinsky's ambivalent attitude toward English. Ironically, his hatred of English words makes them easier to memorize (133–34).

86. Gitl, Jake's wife in *Yekl*, also has a lisp: it becomes the focus of Jake's disgust at her Old World ways (94). At one point Levinsky even boasts of his "affected Yankee twang" (323).

87. Hapgood makes a similar point about Americanization: the question "Why don't you say your evening prayer" is met with the slangy reply "Ah, what yer givin' us!" (27).

88. Levinsky's assimilation of American ways leads him to acquire brutal, exploitative business practices (270–71). As with Levinsky's lessons in English, the entire novel is based on a desire to assimilate what is already recognized to be a civilization honeycombed with conventional lies, a "sham" culture of "sham ecstasy, sham sympathy, sham smiles, sham laughter" (380).

89. In the words of Catherine Metcalf Roof: "We aren't Americanizing them. *They* are de-Americanizing the country" (quoted in Fine, 14).

90. Fine, 103, 119.

91. Cahan clearly conforms with what Werner Sollors describes as a process— developing in the late nineteenth century—in which "the very assertion of the ethnic dimensions of American culture can be understood as part of the rites and rituals of this land" (15).

92. See Fishkin, *Was Huck Black?*, 199n58, for Howells's realization in 1895 that the general reader "has got tired of dialect"; see Nettels, *Howells's America*, 66, for the wider reaction against dialect in the 1890s.

CHAPTER SIX

1. Crane, *Maggie*, 32–33.

2. John Corbin gives this example: "Ich danke dir, dear, dear Mr. Blumenfeld. Tankaiou [thank you]. . . . Oh du, my swittest. Oh du, meine lufly goil" ("How the Other Half Laughs," 40).

3. See Mark Slobin's analysis of the 1895 Jewish playlet *Among the Indians* (*Tenement Songs*, 109).

4. Albert McLean discusses how typical vaudeville shows were not prepared to initiate foreigners directly (*American Vaudeville as Ritual*, 41). For details of the attempt of vaudevillians to form a consensus of mass entertainment, see McLean, 33–34, and Robert Snyder, *The Voice of the City*, xiii, 4, 20.

5. See Snyder, 42–43, and McLean, 121, for discussion of the ethnic origins of many vaudeville performers.

6. McLean, 120.

7. Robert Toll, *Blacking Up*, 161–62.

8. Several film critics have suggested this point (see Charles Musser, "Ethnicity, Role-playing, and American Film Comedy," 60–61).

9. John W. Ransome, quoted in Carl Wittke, "The Immigrant Theme on the American Stage," 225.

10. Lott, *Love and Theft*, 6, 63.

11. Brandes, "Jewish-American Dialect Jokes," 234–35.

12. Welch, quoted in Paul Antonie Distler, "Rise and Fall of the Racial Comics," 164. In his guidebook, *Writing for Vaudeville* (1915), Brett Page urged playlet

writers to take their language directly from the hard-hitting slang of the street (258–59).

13. Bernard, quoted in Distler, 65.

14. Landon, *Kings of the Platform and Pulpit*, 194–98.

15. Charles S. O'Brien, "Ma Angeline" (1896), quoted in James H. Dormon, "Shaping the Image," 460. Dormon gives a thorough account of this "Coon Song" phenomenon.

16. Gilbert, *American Vaudeville*, 61. Compare Lott's observation on minstrelsy (20) with what Dormon has called an "astonishing act of psycho-social prestidigitation" that made vaudeville audiences believe in caricatures ("American Popular Culture," 187).

17. Maureen Murphy makes the point that early appearances of Irish caricatures on the stage contrasted them with a mainstream persona, whereas later, in the plays of Edward Harrigan in particular, the Irish were contrasted with other ethnic groups ("Irish-American Theatre," 223, 226).

18. The Russell Brothers, known for their offensive Irish servant girls act, feared for their lives after intimidation from Irish societies and were finally driven from the vaudeville stage (DiMeglio, *Vaudeville U.S.A.*, 44). See McLean, 23, 68, 121, on the softening of ethnic humor in the early 1900s. Much vaudeville censorship was at the level of language: profane and ambiguous words were forbidden in an effort to protect genteel norms (Snyder, 29).

19. Distler notes that "there was little, if any, negative criticism of the racial comics by the immigrants upon whom the burlesques were based" (93).

20. McLean, 120. Also see Snyder, 110, and Toll, 169, for discussions of this positive side of stereotypes.

21. Dormon, "American Popular Culture," 192–93.

22. Snyder, 109.

23. Harrigan, quoted in Slobin, 61. Caricatures of the Irish as drunken menials with a predisposition to go on strike were often accompanied by more positive celebrations of Irish labor and nationalism (Gilbert, 64–65).

24. Although his depiction of the Irish-American community was by no means negative, Finley Peter Dunne was criticized by fellow Irish Americans for using the "devil of dialectism" in his newspaper columns (John Finerty, quoted in Fanning, *Mr. Dooley and the Chicago Irish*, xix). See Snyder, 110, for reactions to Jewish performers lampooning their own ethnic group.

25. See Dormon, "American Popular Culture," 190, for an example of the popularity of "stage Hebrews" among Jews themselves. Distler reads this phenomenon as a form of deflection through appropriation (160).

26. "In its very format," writes McLean, "vaudeville reflected the pluralism and fluidity of social thought during its time and, as a ritual, had to accommodate itself to the most contradictory and ambiguous influences" (67). Snyder also discusses the adaptability of vaudeville performance (50, 107).

27. Benchley, 195–96.

28. On humor's role in "oiling the psychic wheels of an industrial democracy," see McLean, 110.

29. Snyder discusses the linguistic reasons behind the Jewish impersonation of "Dutch" personae (117).

30. Musser, 66.

31. Most of the pool room act is cited in Felix Isman, *Weber and Fields*, 166–70.

32. Weber and Fields, quoted in Isman, 83–85.

33. Brandes, 237–39; McLean, 56.

34. The vaudeville manager E. F. Albee recognized the power of vaudeville to appeal through infinite diversity (Jenkins, *What Made Pistachio Nuts?*, 63).

35. For example, *The Emigrant Train, or Go West*, which was performed at Tony Pastor's theater in 1879 (Wittke, 225).

36. Sollors, *Beyond Ethnicity*, 137; Isman quotes Weber and Fields's attempts at Gaelic (51); Barth, quoted in Snyder, 111; Baker, quoted in Snyder, 112. Not all "racial comics" claimed to reproduce an actual speech type: John T. Kelley confessed that he had constructed his baffling dialect out of "every kind of Irish brogue that ever was imported" (quoted in Distler, 116).

37. Jenkins, 61, 70.

38. Unnamed *Post* critic, quoted in Dormon, "American Popular Culture," 184; B. Page, 117; Weber and Fields, quoted in Isman, 51.

39. See Gilbert, 73–77, and Wittke, 213, 226, 230, for these strange ethnic hybrids.

40. T. S. Denison, *Patsy O'Wang*, 84, 93.

41. Herbert, in the introductory notes to *The Geezer* (no page).

42. These lines are quoted in Isman, 204. In the typescript of the play that I consulted, the speech of the Chinese characters is in "Chinese" dialect rather than Irish brogue or Dutch-Chinese composite, suggesting that the ethnic fusions were created on the stage by the German and Irish comedians themselves.

43. Jenkins, 71; B. Page, 254.

44. Edward Harrigan, *The Mulligans*, 137.

45. See Distler, 76, for *gesproken*.

46. Herbert, 5, 16; Claude T. Martin, quoted in Wittke, 224n51.

47. Gilbert quotes an example of this mock German: "Hat Ich ein thaler Ich bin kartoffel salad essen. Hat Ich ein thousand thaler Ich bin ice cream feressen till bauer fa blatz" (74).

48. Quoted in McLean, 117. Slobin cites a similar rule, used by "Tin Pan Alley" composers of popular songs: "The mispronunciation of words and other evidences of deficient mentality should always be accepted as the height of wit" (121).

49. Vaudeville stars Cohan and Nathan, quoted in Jenkins, 73. Jenkins describes how this "new humor" at the turn of the century—with its uncontrollable laughter and incongruous crudity—was believed to arise from the cultural impact of foreign immigrants (47). McLean makes a similar point (106, 109).

50. Tom P. Morgan, quoted in Jenkins, 40; B. Page, 146; Cincinnati *Enquirer,* quoted in Wittke, 213; Fishman, *Language Loyalty in the United States*, 30. Jenkins cites Raymond Durguat on a similar point about the Marx Brothers: the real aim of their tearing of language was "to devastate social custom" (8). Snyder stresses the anarchic inversion of standards and genteel norms in Weber and Fields (138).

51. Landon, 197.

52. B. Page, 247–48; Davis, *The Exploitation of Pleasure*, 32. See Jenkins, 45, on how the new humor was seen as a way to relieve the stress caused by the harsh quarreling and mechanical roar of a noisy city.

53. Tucker, quoted in Snyder, 119; Dormon, "American Popular Culture," 191; P. Bailey, "Victorian Music Hall," 199–201.

54. This fusion of languages did not end with the demise of vaudeville but continued in Hollywood comedies of the 1930s, which occasionally feature Yiddish-speaking "Indians," Chinese characters who suddenly switch into German, and others who speak a "mixed European" composite: "Yah-yah and Ou-la-la, I will get zem for you, Señor, Yowsah" (Jenkins, 203–4).

55. *Choice Dialect*, 22.

56. The typical show would juxtapose an over-dignified, pompously speaking "interlocutor" with the raucous comedy of the "endmen": "When the endmen mocked [the interlocutor's] pomposity, audiences could indulge their anti-intellectualism and antielitism by laughing at him. But when [the interlocutor] patiently corrected the ignorant comedians with their malaprop-laden dialects, audiences could feel superior to stupid 'niggers' and laugh with him" (Toll, 53).

57. Toll, 272. It is not difficult to find "black" stage dialect after the Civil War that mocks stupidity and intellectualism simultaneously (see T. Riis, *Just Before Jazz*, 131, for an example).

58. While David Roediger has hinted that, even in its antebellum manifestations, blackface minstrelsy was not always so black-or-white—it also mocked rural whites, German speech, and Irish "thickness"—he emphasizes that whites could usually participate easily in an "increasingly smug whiteness" under the blackface makeup (*The Wages of Whiteness*, 118). Eric Lott's *Love and Theft* offers perhaps the most complex of recent arguments: Lott emphasizes how minstrelsy was a sign of white anxiety over and attraction toward black culture—at times even a form of cross-racial interaction—as well as a form of white racist domination. Michael Paul Rogin has criticized this element of Lott's argument, pointing out that the color line was only ever permeable in one direction (*Blackface, White Noise*, 36–37).

59. Rogin, *Blackface, White Noise*, 35, 23. Rogin admits, however, that attention to vaudeville and Broadway "would offer a rawer, more variegated picture of Jewish blackface" than the Hollywood films that he discusses (13).

60. See Snyder, 120–21, for this use of blackface.

61. See McLean, 25, and Wittke, 212–13, for these transformations in minstrelsy.

62. Lott, 31–32.

63. In a 1900 review of the African-American musical *A Trip to Coontown*, a Boston reviewer was astonished at how easily the "African face" could be made to represent these other ethnic groups (T. Riis, 77). See Musser, 62, on the ambiguous racial status of many new immigrants. Roediger also discusses the difficulties of establishing an unambiguous whiteness after the Civil War (175–80).

64. Rogin, *Blackface, White Noise*, 6

65. Dormon, "Shaping the Image," 452. On Hogan, see Dormon, "Shaping the Image," 459, and T. Riis, 37.

66. See Toll, 201–9, for the ways that blacks were exploited to lend "authenticity" to stereotypes of culture and language.

67. Williams, quoted in Rogin, *Blackface, White Noise*, 43.

68. Oliver, quoted in T. Riis, 52.

69. See Toll, 246–62, and T. Riis, 187, on the ability of black minstrels to

appeal in different ways to different racial sections of the audience. Toll considers that some black performers refashioned white stereotypes, creating an implicit level of black protest beneath a seemingly demeaning mask (248, 261–62).

70. This last case is what Thomas Riis suggests happened in the early twentieth century, as vicious and violent stereotypes of blacks disappeared from the "Coon Song" owing to the influence of black writers and critics (53–54).

71. Toll mentions the fact that some theaters allowed blacks into the main body of the audience to watch black minstrels (227), yet segregation—both on the stage and in the auditorium—seems to have been the norm (T. Riis, 105, 151). Snyder also argues that vaudeville did not unify through homogenization: there were always theaters that appealed to different social groups (83–84). See DiMeglio, 115–16, on the racial abuse of Hogan and Walker.

72. A reviewer for the New York Sun objected to Dunbar's use of Irish English (Cunningham, Paul Laurence Dunbar, 154).

CHAPTER SEVEN

1. Howells, review of Majors and Minors, quoted in Cunningham, Paul Laurence Dunbar, 145, 147. On first seeing Dunbar, his friend Dr. Henry A. Tobey exclaimed: "Thank God, he's black! . . . Whatever genius he may have cannot be attributed to the white blood he may have in him" (quoted in Wiggins, Life and Works of Dunbar, 48).

2. Howells, introduction to Lyrics of Lowly Life, ix. Dunbar wrote to a friend in March 1897: "I see now very clearly that Mr. Howells has done me irrevocable harm in the dictum he laid down regarding my dialect verse" (quoted in Wagner, Black Poets of the United States, 109).

3. Critics like John Edgar Wideman tend to cite the more obviously racist elements in Howells's review of Dunbar without giving full credit to the range of Howells's argument ("Black Voice in American Literature," 35).

4. See Gates, Signifying Monkey, 172–80, for an account of the debate between 1895 and 1935 over how an authentic black voice should be represented in literature.

5. Houston Baker's belief that analysis of black literature must begin at a vernacular level, with black folk language (Blues, Ideology, 103), is shared by a host of recent critics.

6. Mary Church Terrell, quoted in Bruce, "On Dunbar's 'Jingles in a Broken Tongue,'" 96.

7. J. W. Johnson, Book of American Negro Poetry, 35, 41–42, 35–36, 3, 4. In his prefaces, Johnson expresses his clear belief that there are two kinds of dialect, and although he emphasizes his view that black poets could do more than write in dialect, he wishes only to dismiss the conventional dialect of the "plantation tradition" rather than the new dialect voices of Hughes and Brown. Gates suggests that Johnson's opinion explains a neglect of dialect in the Harlem Renaissance, and that "with the passage of dialect went, in the main, the potential for the expression of that which was hermetic and singular about the black in America. With the passage of dialect went a peculiar sensitivity to black speech as music,

poetry, and a distinct means of artistic discourse on the printed page" ("Dis and Dat," 181).

8. Gayl Jones, *Liberating Voices*, 22, 64; Gates, *Signifying Monkey*, 115, 117; Baker, *Modernism and the Harlem Renaissance*, 39–40. Gates's and Baker's responses to Dunbar are more complex than summarized here, as we shall see later in the chapter. There have been notable exceptions to this negative evaluation of Dunbar, especially the recent essays by John Keeling ("Paul Dunbar and the Mask of Dialect") and Marcellus Blount ("The Preacherly Text").

9. See Baker's preface to *Modernism and the Harlem Renaissance*. "The problem with any close reading of black poetry, particularly in dialect," writes Gates, "is that of translation of the music itself into meaningful language. The music is the poetry of the rhythmic word; the printed word cannot be fully understood as 'meaning' if treated alone" ("Dis and Dat," 187). In *To Wake the Nations*, Sundquist reaches similar conclusions about the tonal aspects of black language, as we saw in chapter two.

10. Kimberly Benston has outlined the importance of performance to an appreciation of the "ever-widening activity and ever-deepening complexity" of black poetry ("Performing Blackness," 165). See also Baker, *Blues, Ideology*, 104.

11. Gates, *Signifying Monkey*, 192, 174.

12. Wideman makes a similar point about representation: "Once a convention for dramatizing black speech appears in fiction, the literary critic should be concerned not with matters of phonetic accuracy, but with the evolution of a written code and how that code refers to the spoken language in suggestive, artful, creative ways" (36).

13. J. W. Johnson emphasized the "conventionalized" form of much literary dialect in his 1931 preface to *Book of American Negro Poetry* (4).

14. Reprinted in J. W. Johnson, *Book of American Negro Poetry*, 239–40. In the version of this poem published in *The Collected Poems of Langston Hughes*, the last three lines are not given in quotation marks (60).

15. Hughes's dialect poems included in J. W. Johnson's 1931 anthology do not spell "wid yuh" in this way; Hughes maintains the conventional spelling of these words (237–38).

16. Benston, 183. For a comparison between Dunbar and these later volumes of poetry, see Myron Simon, "Dunbar and Dialect Poetry," 118.

17. All of these stories appear in Dunbar, *Paul Laurence Dunbar Reader*. See Bruce, *Black American Writing*, chapter two, for a sensitive account of the iconoclasm and militant protest that defines much of Dunbar's work.

18. Baker, *Modernism and the Harlem Renaissance*, 44–46. In *To Wake the Nations*, Sundquist sees Chesnutt as a deliberate signifier on stereotypes (304). Chesnutt uses black dialect as "an assault on the authoritative diction of the master's language and a means of generating a secret language in which linguistic and musical traces of African heritage survive" (323).

19. Presumably, the story is about a postbellum lynching, although it is never made entirely clear whether Jube is a servant or a slave.

20. Gayl Jones, 61. Dunbar's depiction of dialect in stories with racially neutral or implicitly black narrators is not substantially different from that represented by the white Dr. Melville.

21. The story as a whole depicts various acts of interracial contact and feeling: Melville practices medicine to both blacks and whites; Annie has a spell of beauty that makes both blacks and whites her slaves (233).

22. "Ere Sleep Comes Down to Soothe the Weary Eyes," 4. All quotations from Dunbar's poetry are from his *Complete Poems*.

23. Du Bois, *Souls of Black Folk* (1903), 4–5.

24. Gates, *Signifying Monkey*, 56n.

25. Blount, 583, 587–90. Keeling also suggests that Dunbar's dialect becomes a "powerful active force" when we pay attention to the element of masking in his poetry (29).

26. Gates, *Signifying Monkey*, 88.

27. Gates uses Dunbar briefly to explain the idea of "tertiary revision"—the threefold process whereby black writers revise specific texts simultaneously with "white" models of form and "black" models of substance (*Signifying Monkey*, 122).

28. Sundquist, *To Wake the Nations*, 306; Gates, *Signifying Monkey*, 68.

29. Dunbar's many poetic references to mocking-birds (see, for example, "The Lesson," 8) suggest some degree of self-awareness in his literary echoes.

30. J. W. Johnson, *Along This Way*, 161–62.

31. Sundquist, *To Wake the Nations*, 273. Sundquist gives a thorough account of the cultural and literary implications of the cakewalk (271–94).

32. Wagner, 55.

33. Gayl Jones, 21–22. If this were a poem by Chesnutt then the argument would be that it expresses the impossibility of capturing the tonal qualities of black language on the printed page (see Sundquist's discussion of Chesnutt in *To Wake the Nations*, especially 300, 312–13, 323).

34. According to Dunbar's wife, Alice, these bars of music were attempts to transcribe Sam's whistle accurately (Wagner, 115n153).

35. Sundquist, *To Wake the Nations*, 470. "Whistling Sam" was first collected in *Lyrics of the Hearthside* (1899).

36. In "Nelse Hatton's Vengeance," the narrator repeats the "usual phrase" about the gaudy pretentiousness of black interior decoration while remotivating it by suggesting the existence of alternative black tastes (*Paul Laurence Dunbar Reader*, 88). Baker detects a similar procedure in the first sentence of *Sport of the Gods* (*Blues, Ideology*, 130).

37. See Simon, 126, for this linguistic analysis of Dunbar's dialect.

38. Dunbar was capable of using minstrel-like, pseudodialectal exaggeration; he occasionally depicted blacks using words like *dictionumgary* (Wagner, 108).

39. On the taking of minstrel caricatures for truths, see Wagner, 47, Wideman, 34, and Lott, *Love and Theft*, 20.

40. For Dunbar's comments on the need to preserve "those quaint old tales and songs of our fathers," see his letters to James Newton Matthews (Feb. 7, 1893), Alice Ruth Moore (April 17, 1895), and Henry A. Tobey (July 13, 1895), quoted in *Paul Laurence Dunbar Reader*, 417, 428, 431. Keeling suggests that "The Poet" can be read as *only* referring to the dialect poems. It thus laments the misapprehension of the deeper aspects of dialect, and regrets the trivialization of its masking techniques (25).

41. Howells, introduction to *Lyrics of Lowly Life*, ix; Brown, *Negro Poetry*, 35. It is

also possible to find similar statements from Dunbar himself: "I am sorry to find among intelligent people those who are unable to differentiate dialect as a philological branch from the burlesque of Negro minstrelsy" (quoted in Bruce, *Black American Writing*, 60).

42. Dunbar, letter to Matilda Dunbar (Feb. 28, 1897), quoted in *Paul Laurence Dunbar Reader*, 439.

43. Dunbar mentions his juxtaposition of dialect and orthodox English during public recitals in a letter to James Newton Matthews (July 17, 1893), quoted in *Paul Laurence Dunbar Reader*, 423. Simon points out that *Majors and Minors* and *Lyrics of the Hearthside* are the only volumes of Dunbar's poetry to place dialect compositions in separate sections (115). Gates describes this example of black language use as the "self-conscious switch of linguistic codes . . . from standard English to the black vernacular" ("Dis and Dat," 171).

44. Harris, *Uncle Remus*, 39–40; Dunbar, "Sister Jackson's Superstitions," reprinted in *Paul Laurence Dunbar Reader*, 103–6.

45. See Wagner, 107n118, for these interpretations of "Appreciation." See Cunningham, 50, for Dunbar's use of German dialect.

46. Keeling, 38. See Bierce, "Writers of Dialect," 183, for some acerbic comments on Riley's use of *ist*.

47. A similar effect is reached in the poem "James Whitcomb Riley," Dunbar's tribute to the Hoosier poet. The celebration of Riley's dialect as a natural and truthful means of expression is undercut by a variation between standard English and dialect which emphasizes the latter as a conventional rather than a natural language (287).

48. Keeling, 34.

49. See the poems "A Cabin Tale" (153–55), "Long Ago" (192–93), and "The Veteran" (256–57) for other contemplations of the problem of constructing a black past.

50. See "Lover's Lane" (132–33) and "Hope" (247) for expressions of this idea.

51. Baker argues that McKay and Cullen "blacken" standard poetic forms by using them as masks (*Modernism and the Harlem Renaissance*, 85).

52. Dunbar's *Majors and Minors* was published with a photograph of the poet as its frontispiece (Cunningham, 154), and Howells's review of this volume made Dunbar's race well known thereafter.

53. "Columbian Ode," for example, supports the idea of manifest destiny, whereby the native savages are replaced by "men of Nature's noblest types" (48).

54. Dunbar to Matthews (Oct. 19, 1892), quoted in *Paul Laurence Dunbar Reader*, 412.

55. For example, "The Unsung Heroes" juxtaposes a reference to minstrels with a reference to "the pride of face and the hate of race" (197).

56. This is the opinion of Jay Martin and Gossie Hudson, editors of *The Paul Laurence Dunbar Reader* (262).

57. See, for example, "A Choice" (125), "Philosophy" (212–13), and "Limitations" (250–51).

58. Gates, *Signifying Monkey*, 176; Baker, *Blues, Ideology*, 115, 121; *Modernism and the Harlem Renaissance*, 40.

59. Dunbar, quoted in *Paul Laurence Dunbar Reader*, 262.

60. Debate over Dunbar's knowledge of dialect centers on whether Dunbar's mother, from whom he gained much of his knowledge of the slave South, spoke in dialect (see Wagner, 109–10n137). To say that Dunbar's "natural" speech was not dialect, or to say that Dunbar made explicit efforts to record the dialect of his mother's friends (Cunningham, 71–72), does not necessarily mean that he was otherwise unversed in black English. It seems incredible, as Addison Gayle suggests, that a black man growing up in a large industrial town at the end of the nineteenth century "had never heard dialect spoken" (*Oak and Ivy*, 78).

61. Dunbar, quoted in Wiggins, 81 (Dunbar considered this to be an "unfortunate" position); Hutchinson, *Harlem Renaissance in Black and White*, 113. In "Deacon Jones' Grievance" (39) and "The Ol' Tunes" (53–54), Dunbar celebrates old-fashioned white music, thus paralleling similar celebrations of black music.

62. Du Bois, 215. Sundquist writes that *Souls of Black Folk* was "an act of cultural transfiguration that melded African and white American traditions into a distinctly African American cultural form, as had the spirituals themselves" (*To Wake the Nations*, 481). Dunbar tended to follow the assertive ideas of Du Bois rather than the accommodationist stance of Booker T. Washington, as is clear from his letter to Alice Dunbar (Sept. 3, 1898; quoted in *Paul Laurence Dunbar Reader*, 453). Many of his poems, however, seem Washingtonian in logic—for example, "Limitations" (250–51).

63. Du Bois, 8. "The Paradox" never seeks to resolve its racial conflict, but simply states it in paradoxical terms: "Dark is my frown as the midnight, / Fair is my brow as the day" (89). "To A Lady Playing the Harp" also fails to resolve the tension between "black" and "white" identity (116).

64. Du Bois, 6. See Simon, 114–17, for this argument.

65. Dunbar scorned those who criticized him for using various kinds of "negro dialect" in a single volume. "Just think of it!" said Dunbar, "a literary critic and yet doesn't know that there are as many variations of the negro dialect as there are states in the Union!" (quoted in Wiggins, 109). Dunbar also explores the different registers of language and styles of speaking among blacks in stories such as "Old Abe's Conversion."

66. Wideman, 35. See Gates, "Dis and Dat," 172, for a parallel point about the dialectic within black English.

67. Dunbar was a keen recorder of different dialects from an early age, *and* a keen follower of dialect poetry in *The Century* (see Cunningham, 57–58, and Wagner, 106, 75). In a poem like "A Cabin Tale," which records the story of a weasel tricking a bear, it is difficult to tell whether Dunbar is writing in a black folk tradition or in the literary tradition of Joel Chandler Harris et al.

68. The short story "The Churching of Grandma Pleasant" describes how a puritanical, white northern community finally comes to accept Grandma Pleasant's singing of old plantation songs, which she remembers from her days in the antebellum South (*Paul Laurence Dunbar Reader*, 253–58).

69. Dunbar, "On Emancipation Day," from the musical *In Dahomey* (109); Baker, *Blues, Ideology*, 137.

70. Bruce suggests that Dunbar was ultimately skeptical that the effort of blacks

to present their Americanness would have any effect on white Americans (*Black American Writing*, 98); hence the difference from Du Bois in *Souls*.

71. So popular were Dunbar's live performances that he could boast in 1901 that he had become a teacher of "elocution," educating eager Dunbareans in how to recite his work properly (Dunbar to Alice Dunbar, April 8, 1901; quoted in *Paul Laurence Dunbar Reader*, 455).

72. "His voice was a perfect musical instrument, and he knew how to use it with extreme effect" (J. W. Johnson, *Along This Way*, 159–60).

73. Wagner, 112; Wiggins, 65, quoted in Wagner, 115.

74. Dunbar was highly aware of the blackface implications of his poetry performances, especially when they occurred between dancing girl acts and clowns. See Dunbar's letter to William Dean Howells (April 26, 1897), quoted in *Paul Laurence Dunbar Reader*, 444.

75. See Wagner, 127–45, for a discussion of Dunbar's black contemporaries.

76. J. W. Johnson, *Book of American Negro Poetry*, 41.

77. Hutchinson, 113. See Wagner, 72, on the wide acceptance of stereotype at the end of the century, which made it difficult to suggest that African Americans were otherwise than their caricatures.

78. For example, "To the South: On Its New Slavery" has a deeply flawed logic. The poet appeals to the noble, honorable southern past in his plea to end racism, overlooking the fact that this past was itself the time of slavery (218).

79. See Toll, *Blacking Up*, chapter seven.

CONCLUSION

1. See Ferguson and Heath, *Language in the USA*, xxviii, xxxvii.

2. For many scholars, to call African-American vernacular English a *dialect* is to uphold the Eurocentric view that it is a nonstandard variety of English; to call it a *language* is to take the Afrocentric view that it has a distinctly African grammatical base and is thus fundamentally separate from English. For different views on these issues, see Ernie Smith (quoted in Perry and Delpit, eds., *The Real Ebonics Debate*, 14–15), and Rickford, "Suite for Ebony and Phonics."

3. Compare Fishkin's account of Twain in *Was Huck Black?* with North's argument that modernists such as Gertrude Stein, T. S. Eliot, and Ezra Pound needed the "linguistic mimicry and racial masquerade" of dialect writing to develop an "entirely new literature" (*Dialect of Modernism*, i, 99); it seems a stretch, however, for North to suggest that English literary modernism "could not have arisen without the example of dialect" (195).

4. This medley of negative responses to African-American vernacular English (or Ebonics) is drawn from Perry and Delpit, eds., 2, 5, 10; *Ebonics: Hearing*, 68; and Nunberg, "Topic . . . Comment," 671. On "cognitive deficit" theories of black English, see Smitherman, *Talkin and Testifyin*, 205. Wayne O'Neil gives an overview of media reaction to Ebonics, quoted in Perry and Delpit, eds., 10.

5. The Oakland, California, School Board—to give a recent example—reflected this change of emphasis in rewording its initial resolution on the classroom teaching of Ebonics (see Perry and Delpit, eds., 25).

6. Lippi-Green considers this ideology to be an implicit infringement of civil liberties because many people find their accent impossible to change (*English with an Accent*, 64, 45).

7. Compare J. D. C. Atkins, "Barbarous Dialects Should Be Blotted Out" (1887), 48–51, with the ideas behind the recent English Only movement, which—according to Dennis Baron—presuppose the belief that language embodies the moral, cultural, and political essence of the nation (*English-Only*, xiv, 7). Such absolute language–nation, language–culture equations have been questioned by critics of official English, who argue that national identity can be forged from a condition of linguistic pluralism, while ethnic difference and conflict can thrive quite happily in a situation of linguistic sameness.

8. "[I]t is not enough for Spanish speakers to become bilingual," writes Lippi-Green: "they must learn the *right* English—and following from that, the right US culture, into which they must assimilate completely" (234). The Virginia General Assembly has recently changed the official language of the state from "English" to "Standard English," which it vaguely defines as the language "accepted by generally recognized authorities as grammatically correct in the United States [that] shall not include any dialect, patois, or jargon based on the English language" (quoted in Nunberg, "Topic . . . Comment," 674).

9. Nunberg, "Official English Movement," 483, 485. Similar points about language being a way to talk about other things are made by O'Neil (quoted in Perry and Delpit, eds., 10), Lippi-Green, 215, and Crawford, *Language Loyalties*, 3. Nunberg has suggested that certain advocates of official English preserve a type of pluralism by arguing that a common language enables a cohesive society without imposing a strict homogeneity ("Official English Movement," 489).

10. See Shuy, "Ohio English," 129–31, for an ironic account of these efforts to make "Ohio English" the official dialect of the United States, against the countermoves of "ethnic blocs" like the Minnesota Language Institute. Lippi-Green points out that not all foreign accents are discriminated against in the United States, only those that are "linked to skin that isn't white, or which [signal] a third-world homeland" (238).

11. Members of American ethnic groups have themselves made this point, criticizing the idea that—in the words of Paula Gunn Allen—"language is culture and that without a separate language a culture is defunct" (quoted in Ammons, "Expanding the Canon of American Realism," 102).

12. Baldwin, quoted in Perry and Delpit, eds., 16. Compare this with Michel Foucault's idea of *discourse:* "discourse is not simply that which translates struggles or systems of domination, but is the thing for which and by which there is struggle, discourse is the power which is to be seized" ("The Order of Discourse," 110).

13. See Orlando Taylor, quoted in *Ebonics: Hearing*, 70–71, and Homi Bhabha, "Queen's English." Taylor describes well how Ebonics returns us to "one of the quintessential issues in American contemporary life": "how do we accommodate, indeed, celebrate cultural and linguistic diversity on the one hand, and on the other hand teach all of our students a language system, in this case standard English, that will facilitate academic achievement and career opportunities as well as cohesion and harmony within our Nation?" (69).

14. Lippi-Green considers that the "real trouble" with black English is its "tangible and irrefutable evidence that there is a distinct, healthy, functioning African American culture which is not white, and which does not want to be white" (178).

15. bell hooks, quoted in Perry and Delpit, eds., 23.

WORKS CITED

Aarsleff, Hans. *From Locke to Saussure: Essays on the Study of Language and Intellectual History*. Minneapolis: University of Minnesota Press, 1982.

———. Introduction. *On Language: The Diversity of Human Language-Structure and Its Influence on the Mental Development of Mankind*. By Wilhelm von Humboldt. Cambridge: Cambridge University Press, 1988. vii–lxv.

Abercrombie, David. "The Recording of Dialect Material." *Studies in Phonetics and Linguistics*. London: Oxford University Press, 1965.

Aldrich, Thomas Bailey. *The Poems*. Boston: Houghton, Mifflin, 1904.

Alford, Henry. *A Plea for the Queen's English: Stray Notes on Speaking and Spelling*. New York: Dick & Fitzgerald, 1864.

Alger, Horatio. *Ragged Dick and Mark the Match Boy*. 1867. New York: Collier, 1972.

Allen, William Francis, et al., eds. *Slave Songs of the United States*. 1867. New York: Peter Smith, 1951.

Ammons, Elizabeth. "Expanding the Canon of American Realism." *The Cambridge Companion to American Realism and Naturalism*. Ed. Donald Pizer. Cambridge: Cambridge University Press, 1995. 95–114.

Arnold, Matthew. *Culture and Anarchy: An Essay in Political and Social Criticism*. 1867. New York: Macmillan, 1912.

Atkins, J. D. C. "Barbarous Dialects Should Be Blotted Out . . ." 1887. *Language Loyalties: A Source Book on the Official English Controversy*. Ed. James Crawford. Chicago: University of Chicago Press, 1992. 47–51.

Austin, James C. *Bill Arp*. New York: Twayne, 1969.

———. *Petroleum V. Nasby (David Ross Locke)*. New York: Twayne, 1965.

Bailey, Peter. "Custom, Capital and Culture in the Victorian Music Hall." *Popular Culture and Custom in Nineteenth-Century England*. Ed. Robert D. Storch. London: Croom Helm, 1982. 180–208.

Bailey, Richard. *Images of English: A Cultural History of the Language*. Ann Arbor: University of Michigan Press, 1991.

———. *Nineteenth-Century English*. Ann Arbor: University of Michigan Press, 1996.

Baker, Houston A., Jr. *Blues, Ideology, and Afro-American Literature: A Vernacular Theory.* Chicago: University of Chicago Press, 1984.

———. *Modernism and the Harlem Renaissance.* Chicago: University of Chicago Press, 1987.

Bakhtin, M. M. *The Dialogic Imagination: Four Essays.* Ed. Michael Holquist. Trans. Caryl Emerson and Michael Holquist. Austin: University of Texas Press, 1981.

Baron, Dennis E. *Grammar and Good Taste: Reforming the American Language.* New Haven: Yale University Press, 1982.

———. *The English-Only Question: An Official Language for Americans?* New Haven: Yale University Press, 1990.

Bartlett, John Russell. *The Dictionary of Americanisms.* 1849. New York: Crescent, 1989.

Beard, George M. *American Nervousness: Its Causes and Consequences.* New York: G. P. Putnam's Sons, 1881.

———. *A Practical Treatise on Nervous Exhaustion (Neurasthenia), Its Symptoms, Nature, Sequences, Treatment.* 1880. New York: E. B. Treat, 1888.

Beer, Thomas. "From *Stephen Crane: A Study in American Letters.*" *The Merrill Studies in "Maggie" and "George's Mother."* Ed. Stanley Wertheim. Columbus, Ohio: Bell and Howell, 1970. 25–26.

Bell, Alexander Melville. *Principles of Speech and Dictionary of Sounds: Directions and Exercises for the Cure of Stammering and Correction of All Faults of Articulation.* Boston: James P. Burbank, 1886.

Bell, Michael Davitt. *The Problem of American Realism: Studies in the Cultural History of a Literary Idea.* Chicago: University of Chicago Press, 1993.

Benchley, Robert. Untitled Review. *Life.* 7 Oct. 1926: 9. Reprinted in Anthony Slide, ed. *Selected Vaudeville Criticism.* Metuchen, N.J.: Scarecrow Press, 1988. 195–96.

Benfry, Christopher. *The Double Life of Stephen Crane: A Biography.* New York: Knopf, 1992.

Bennett, John. "Gullah: A Negro Patois." 2 Parts. *South Atlantic Quarterly* 7 (1908): 322–47; 8 (1909): 39–52.

Benston, Kimberly W. "Performing Blackness: Re/Placing Afro-American Poetry." *Afro-American Literary Study in the 1990s.* Eds. Houston A. Baker, Jr., and Patricia Redmond. 164–85.

Bergon, Frank. *Stephen Crane's Artistry.* New York: Columbia University Press, 1975.

Bhabha, Homi K. "DissemiNation: time, narrative, and the margins of the modern nation." *Nation and Narration.* Ed. Homi K. Bhabha. New York: Routledge, 1990. 291–322.

———. "Queen's English." *Artforum* 35.7 (1997): 25–26, 107.

Bickley, R. Bruce, ed. *Critical Essays on Joel Chandler Harris.* Boston: G. K. Hall, 1981.

Biddle, Anthony Drexel. *Shantytown Sketches.* Philadelphia: Drexel Biddle, 1897.

Bierce, Ambrose. "Writers of Dialect." 1892. *The Collected Works of Ambrose Bierce.* Vol. 11. New York: Neale Publishing, 1912. 173–86.

Blair, Walter. *Native American Humor (1800–1900).* New York: American Book Co., 1937.

Blair, Walter, and Hill, Hamlin. *America's Humor: From Poor Richard to Doonesbury.* New York: Oxford University Press, 1978.

Blount, Marcellus. "The Preacherly Text: African American Poetry and Vernacular Performance." *PMLA* 107.3 (May 1992): 582–93.

Boren, Lynda S. *Eurydice Reclaimed: Language, Gender, and Voice in Henry James.* Ann Arbor, Mich.: UMI Research Press, 1989.

Borus, Daniel H. *Writing Realism: Howells, James, and Norris in the Mass Market.* Chapel Hill: University of North Carolina Press, 1989.

Brain, Russell. *Speech Disorders: Aphasia, Apraxia and Agnosia.* Washington, D.C.: Butterworth, 1961.

Brandes, Stanley. "Jewish-American Dialect Jokes and Jewish-American Identity." *Jewish Social Studies* 45.3–4 (Summer–Fall 1983): 233–40.

Bridgman, Richard. *The Colloquial Style in America.* Oxford: Oxford University Press, 1966.

Bristed, Charles Astor. "The English Language in America." *Cambridge Essays, Contributed by Members of the University.* London: J. W. Parker, 1855. 57–78.

Brodhead, Richard H. *Cultures of Letters: Scenes of Reading and Writing in Nineteenth-Century America.* Chicago: University of Chicago Press, 1993.

Brown, Sterling A. *Negro Poetry and Drama, and the Negro in American Fiction.* 1937. New York: Atheneum, 1969.

Bruce, Dickson D., Jr. *Black American Writing from the Nadir: The Evolution of a Literary Tradition, 1877–1915.* Baton Rouge: Louisiana State University Press, 1989.

———. "On Dunbar's 'Jingles in a Broken Tongue': Dunbar's Dialect Poetry and the Afro-American Folk Tradition." *A Singer in the Dawn: Reinterpretations of Paul Laurence Dunbar.* Ed. Jay Martin. New York: Dodd, Mead, 1975. 94–113.

Budd, Louis J. "The American Background." *The Cambridge Companion to American Realism and Naturalism.* Ed. Donald Pizer. Cambridge: Cambridge University Press, 1995. 21–46.

Cable, George Washington. *The Creoles of Louisiana.* New York: Charles Scribner's Sons, 1884.

———. "Creole Slave Songs." *The Century Magazine* 31 (1885–86): 807–28.

———. "The Dance in Place Congo." *The Century Magazine* 31 (1885–86): 517–32.

———. *Dr. Sevier.* 1885. Upper Saddle River, N.J.: Gregg Press, 1970.

———. *The Grandissimes: A Story of Creole Life.* 1880. Harmondsworth, England: Penguin, 1988.

———. *The Negro Question: A Selection of Writings on Civil Rights in the South.* Ed. Arlin Turner. Garden City, N.Y.: Doubleday, 1958.

Cady, Edwin H. "From *Stephen Crane.*" *The Merrill Studies in "Maggie" and "George's Mother."* Ed. Stanley Wertheim. Columbus, Ohio: Bell and Howell, 1970. 50–53.

Cahan, Abraham. *The Imported Bridegroom and Other Tales of the New York Ghetto.* Boston: Houghton, Mifflin, 1898.

———. *The Rise of David Levinsky.* 1917. Harmondsworth, England: Penguin, 1993.

———. *Yekl: A Tale of the New York Ghetto.* New York: D. Appleton, 1896.

Cambridge History of American Literature. Vol. 2. Ed. W. P. Trent et al. New York: G. P. Putnam's Sons, 1918.

Cameron, Sharon. *Thinking in Henry James.* Chicago: University of Chicago Press, 1989.

Campbell, N. A. "Protection for Our Language." *North American Review* 149 (1889): 127–28.

Carkeet, David. "The Dialects in *Huckleberry Finn.*" *American Literature* 51 (1979): 315–32.

Chesnutt, Charles. *The House Behind the Cedars.* 1900. Harmondsworth, England: Penguin, 1993.

Choice Dialect and Vaudeville Stage Jokes. Chicago: Frederick J. Drake, 1902.

Clark, Helen F. "The Chinese of New York." *The Century,* n.s. 31 (1896–97): 104–13.

Cmiel, Kenneth. "'A Broad Fluid Language of Democracy': Discovering the American Idiom." *Journal of American History* 79 (Dec. 1992): 913–36.

———. *Democratic Eloquence: The Fight over Popular Speech in Nineteenth-Century America.* New York: William Morrow, 1990.

Colvert, James. Introduction to *Maggie. Bowery Tales. The University of Virginia Edition of the Works of Stephen Crane.* Ed. Fredson Bowers. Vol. 1. Charlottesville: University of Virginia Press, 1969. xxxiii–lii.

Corbin, John. "How the Other Half Laughs." *Harper's New Monthly Magazine* 98 (Dec. 1898): 30–48.

Crane, Stephen. "An Experiment in Misery." 1894. *Stephen Crane: An Omnibus.* Ed. Robert Wooster Stallman. New York: Alfred A. Knopf, 1968. 31–42.

———. *George's Mother.* 1896. *Bowery Tales. The University of Virginia Edition of the Works of Stephen Crane.* Ed. Fredson Bowers. Vol. 1. Charlottesville: University of Virginia Press, 1969.

———. "Howells Fears Realists Must Wait." 1894. *Stephen Crane: An Omnibus.* Ed. Robert Wooster Stallman. New York: Alfred A. Knopf, 1968. 169–72.

———. *Maggie: A Girl of the Streets.* 1893. *Bowery Tales. The University of Virginia Edition of the Works of Stephen Crane.* Ed. Fredson Bowers. Vol. 1. Charlottesville: University of Virginia Press, 1969.

———. "The Men in the Storm." 1894. *Stephen Crane: An Omnibus.* Ed. Robert Wooster Stallman. New York: Alfred A. Knopf, 1968. 23–30.

Crawford, James. Editor's Introduction. *Language Loyalties: A Source Book on the Official English Controversy.* Ed. James Crawford. Chicago: University of Chicago Press, 1992. 1–8.

Crowley, Tony. *Standard English and the Politics of Language.* Urbana: University of Illinois Press, 1989.

Cunningham, Virginia. *Paul Laurence Dunbar and His Song.* New York: Dodd, Mead, 1947.

Darwin, Charles. *The Descent of Man, and Selection in Relation to Sex.* 1871. Princeton, N.J.: Princeton University Press, 1981.

Davis, Michael M. *The Exploitation of Pleasure: A Study of Commercial Recreations in New York City.* New York: Department of Child Hygiene of the Russell Sage Foundation, 1911.

Dawson, Richard L. "American Dialect." *The Writer* 4 (1890): 27–29.

De Leon, T. C. "The Day of Dialect." *Lippincott's Magazine* 60 (Nov. 1897): 679–83.

De Menil, Alexander Nicolas. *The Literature of the Louisiana Territory.* St. Louis: St. Louis News, 1904.

Denison, Mary A. "Saturated with Dialect." *The Writer* 7 (1894): 2–3.

Denison, T. S. *Hans von Smash: A Farce.* Chicago: T. S. Denison, 1878.

———. *Patsy O'Wang: An Irish Farce with a Chinese Mix-Up.* Chicago: T. S. Denison, 1895.

Dillard, J. L. *Black English: Its History and Usage in the United States.* New York: Random House, 1972.

———. "Creoles, Cajuns, and Cable with some Hearn and a few assorted babies." *Caribbean Studies* 3 (1963): 84–89.

———. *A History of American English.* London: Longman, 1992.

———, ed. *Perspectives on Black English.* The Hague: Mouton, 1975.

DiMeglio, John E. *Vaudeville U.S.A.* Bowling Green, Kentucky: Bowling Green University Popular Press, 1973.

Distler, Paul Antonie. "The Rise and Fall of the Racial Comics in American Vaudeville." Diss. Tulane University, 1963.

Dodge, N. S. "Negro Patois and Its Humor." *Appleton's Journal of Popular Literature, Science, and Art* 3 (1870): 161–62.

Dormon, James H. "American Popular Culture and the New Immigration Ethnics: The Vaudeville Stage and the Process of Ethnic Ascription." *Amerikastudien* 36.2 (1991): 179–93.

———. "Shaping the Popular Image of Post-Reconstruction American Blacks: The 'Coon Song' Phenomenon of the Gilded Age." *American Quarterly* 40.4 (Dec. 1988): 450–71.

Dreiser, Theodore. *Sister Carrie.* 1900. Oxford: Oxford University Press, 1991.

Du Bois, W. E. B. *The Souls of Black Folk.* 1903. Harmondsworth, England: Penguin, 1989.

Dunbar, Paul Laurence. "The Case of 'Ca'line'." *The Strength of Gideon.* By Paul Laurence Dunbar. New York: Arno Press and the New York Times, 1969. 107–12.

———. *Complete Poems.* New York: Dodd, Mead, 1913.

———. "The Lynching of Jube Benson." *Paul Laurence Dunbar Reader.* Eds. Jay Martin and Gossie H. Hudson. New York: Dodd, Mead, 1975. 232–39.

———. "Old Abe's Conversion." *The Heart of Happy Hollow.* New York: Dodd, Mead, 1904. 105–21.

———. "On Emancipation Day." *In Dahomey.* Music by Will Marion Cook. Book by J. A. Shipp. Lyrics by Paul Laurence Dunbar & Others. London: Keith, Prowse, 1902. 100–109.

———. *Paul Laurence Dunbar Reader.* Eds. Jay Martin and Gossie H. Hudson. New York: Dodd, Mead, 1975.

———. *The Sport of the Gods.* 1902. *Paul Laurence Dunbar Reader.* Eds. Jay Martin and Gossie H. Hudson. New York: Dodd, Mead, 1975. 343–404.

Dunn, Ernest F. "The Black–Southern White Dialect Controversy: Who Did What to Whom?" *Black English: A Seminar.* Eds. Deborah Sears Harrison and Tom Trabasso. Hillsdale, N.J.: Lawrence Erlbaum, 1976. 105–22.

Dunne, Finley Peter. *Mr. Dooley on Ivrything and Ivrybody.* New York: Dover, 1963.

Ebonics: Hearing Before a Subcommittee of the Committee on Appropriations. United States Senate. 105th Cong., 1st sess. Washington, D.C.: GPO, 1997.

Edel, Leon. *Henry James: A Life.* New York: Harper & Row, 1985.

————. *Henry James, The Middle Years.* Philadelphia: J. B. Lippincott, 1962.

Eggleston, Edward. "Folk-Speech in America." *Century Illustrated Monthly* n.s. 26 (Oct. 1894): 867–75.

————. *The Hoosier School-Master.* 1871. Bloomington: Indiana University Press, 1984.

————. *The Hoosier School-Master.* New York: Orange Judd, 1892.

Ekström, Kjell. *George Washington Cable: His Early Life and Work.* Cambridge, Mass.: Harvard University Press, 1950.

Elam, William Cecil. "Lingo in Literature." *Lippincott's Magazine* 55 (1895): 286–88.

Ellison, Ralph. "Stephen Crane and the Mainstream of American Fiction." *Shadow and Act.* New York: Vintage, 1972. 60–76.

Emerson, Edwin. "The New Ghetto." *Harper's Weekly* 41 (1897): 44.

Emerson, Oliver Farrar. *The History of the English Language.* 1894. New York: Macmillan, 1897.

"English Language in America." *North American Review* 91 (1860): 507–28.

Evans, William. "French-English Literary Dialect in *The Grandissimes.*" *Critical Essays on George W. Cable.* Ed. Arlin Turner. Boston: G. K. Hall, 1980. 209–20.

Fanning, Charles. Introduction. *Mr. Dooley and the Chicago Irish: The Autobiography of a Nineteenth-Century Ethnic Group.* Ed. Charles Fanning. Washington, D.C.: Catholic University of America Press, 1987.

Fender, Stephen. *Plotting the Golden West: American literature and the rhetoric of the California Trail.* Cambridge: Cambridge University Press, 1981.

Fenno, Frank H. *The Science and Art of Elocution, Or, How to Read and Speak.* Philadelphia: John E. Potter, 1878.

Ferguson, Charles A., and Heath, Shirley Brice. Introduction. *Language in the USA.* Eds. Charles A. Ferguson and Shirley Brice Heath. Cambridge: Cambridge University Press, 1981. xxv–xxxviii.

Fernald, Frederik A. "How Spelling Damages the Mind." *The Popular Science Monthly* 27 (1885): 638–42.

Fine, David M. *The City, The Immigrant, and American Fiction.* Metuchen, N.J.: Scarecrow Press, 1977.

Fishkin, Shelley Fisher. *Was Huck Black?: Mark Twain and African-American Voices.* Oxford: Oxford University Press, 1993.

Fishman, Joshua A., et al. *Language Loyalty in the United States: The Maintenance and Perpetuation of Non-English Mother Tongues by American Ethnic and Religious Groups.* The Hague: Mouton, 1966.

Fletcher, L. B. "Dialect Spelling." *The Writer* 4 (1890): 26–27.

Fortier, Alcée. "Bits of Louisiana Folk-Lore." *Transactions of the Modern Language Association of America* 3 (1887): 100–168.

————. "The French Language in Louisiana and the Negro-French Dialect." *Transactions of the Modern Language Association of America* 1 (1884–85): 96–111.

Foucault, Michel. "The Order of Discourse." *Language and Politics.* Ed. Michael J. Shapiro. Oxford: Blackwell, 1984. 108–38.

Frederic, Harold. *The Damnation of Theron Ware, or Illumination.* Harmondsworth, England: Penguin, 1986.

Freud, Sigmund. "Slips of the Tongue." *The Psychopathology of Everyday Life.* 1901. Trans. and Ed. James Strachey. New York: W. W. Norton, 1989. 74–139.

Fried, Michael. *Realism, Writing, Disfiguration: On Thomas Eakins and Stephen Crane.* Chicago: University of Chicago Press, 1987.

Fuller, Robert C. *Mesmerism and the American Cure of Souls.* Philadelphia: University of Pennsylvania Press, 1982.

Furman, Nelly. "The politics of language: beyond the gender principle?" *Making a Difference: Feminist Literary Criticism.* Eds. Gayle Greene and Coppélia Kahn. London: Routledge, 1985. 59–79.

Gard, Roger, ed. *Henry James: The Critical Heritage.* London: Routledge & Kegan Paul, 1968.

Garland, Hamlin. *Crumbling Idols: Twelve Essays on Art and Literature.* 1894. Gainesville, Florida: Scholars' Facsimiles & Reprints, 1952.

———. *Main-Travelled Roads.* 1891. Lincoln: University of Nebraska Press, 1995.

———. "Vernacular Poets and Novelists." *Roadside Meetings.* New York: Macmillan, 1930. 90–108.

Gates, Henry Louis, Jr. "Dis and Dat: Dialect and the Descent." *Figures in Black: Words, Signs, and the "Racial" Self.* Oxford: Oxford University Press, 1987. 167–89.

———. *The Signifying Monkey: A Theory of African-American Literary Criticism.* Oxford: Oxford University Press, 1988.

Gayle, Addison. *Oak and Ivy: A Biography of Paul Laurence Dunbar.* Garden City, N.Y.: Doubleday, 1971.

Gerard, J. W. "The Impress of Nationalities on New York City." *Magazine of American History* 23 (1890): 40–59.

Gilbert, Douglas. *American Vaudeville: Its Life and Times.* New York: McGraw-Hill, 1940.

Gonzales, Ambrose E. *The Black Border: Gullah Stories of the Carolina Coast.* Columbia, S.C.: The State, 1922.

Gosling, F. G. *Before Freud: Neurasthenia and the American Medical Community.* Urbana: University of Illinois Press, 1987.

Gramsci, Antonio. *Selections from Cultural Writings.* Eds. David Forgacs and Geoffrey Nowell-Smith. Trans. William Boelhower. Cambridge, Mass.: Harvard University Press, 1985.

Gustafson, Thomas. *Representative Words: Politics, Literature, and the American Language, 1776–1865.* Cambridge: Cambridge University Press, 1992.

Habegger, Alfred. *Henry James and the "Woman Business."* Cambridge: Cambridge University Press, 1989.

Hall, Fitzedward. "Retrogressive English." *North American Review* 119 (1874): 308–31.

Hall, Gwendolyn Midlo. *Africans in Colonial Louisiana: The Development of Afro-Creole Culture in the Eighteenth Century.* Baton Rouge: Louisiana State University Press, 1992.

Hapgood, Hutchins. *The Spirit of the Ghetto.* 1902. Cambridge, Mass.: Harvard University Press, 1967.

Hardy, Thomas. "Dialect in Novels." *The Athenaeum* 30 (1878): 688.

Harrigan, Edward. *The Mulligans.* New York: G. W. Dillingham, 1901.

Harris, Joel Chandler. *Uncle Remus: His Songs and Sayings.* 1880. Harmondsworth, England: Penguin, 1986.

———. *Nights with Uncle Remus.* Boston: Houghton, Mifflin, 1883.

Harris, Julia Collier, ed. *Joel Chandler Harris: Editor and Essayist.* Chapel Hill: University of North Carolina Press, 1931.

Harris, Susan K. "Problems of Representation in Turn-of-the-Century Immigrant Fiction." *American Realism and the Canon.* Eds. Tom Quirk and Gary Scharnhorst. Newark: University of Delaware Press, 1994. 127–42.

Harrison, James A. "The Creole Patois of Louisiana." *American Journal of Philology* 3 (1882): 285–96.

———. "Negro English." 1884. *Perspectives on Black English.* Ed. J. L. Dillard. The Hague: Mouton, 1975. 143–95.

Hartman, James W. "Guide to Pronunciation." *Dictionary of American Regional English.* Ed. Frederic G. Cassidy. Vol. 1. Cambridge, Mass.: Belknap Press of Harvard University Press, 1985. xli-lxi.

Head, Henry. *Aphasia and Kindred Disorders of Speech.* Vol. 1. Cambridge: Cambridge University Press, 1961.

Hearn, Lafcadio. "The Creole Patois." 1885. *An American Miscellany.* Vol. 2. New York: Dodd, Mead, 1924. 144–53.

———. "Los Criollos." 1877. *Occidental Gleanings.* Vol. 1. New York: Dodd, Mead, 1925. 195–207.

———. "On Reading in Relation to Literature." *Life and Literature.* New York: Dodd, Mead, 1919. 1–20.

———. "Some Notes on Creole Literature." 1886. *An American Miscellany.* Vol. 2. New York: Dodd, Mead, 1924. 154–58.

———. *Two Years in the French West Indies.* Boston: Houghton, Mifflin, 1923.

Herbert, Joseph. *The Geezer.* TS. 1895. Harvard University Theatre Collection.

Herskovits, Melville J. *The Myth of the Negro Past.* New York: Harper & Bros., 1941.

Higginson, Thomas Wentworth. "New York as a Literary Centre." *The Critic,* n.s. 15 (1891): 229–30.

Higham, John. *Send These to Me: Immigrants in Urban America.* Revised Edition. Baltimore: Johns Hopkins University Press, 1984.

Hill, Adams Sherman. *Our English.* New York: Harper & Bros., 1889.

Holm, John. *Pidgins and Creoles.* Vol. 2: Reference Survey. Cambridge: Cambridge University Press, 1989.

Howells, William Dean. *Criticism and Fiction.* New York: Harper & Bros., 1891.

———. "From 'Frank Norris.'" *The Merrill Studies in "Maggie" and "George's Mother."* Ed. Stanley Wertheim. Columbus, Ohio: Bell and Howell, 1970. 12–13.

———. *A Hazard of New Fortunes.* 1890. Oxford: Oxford University Press, 1990.

———. Introduction to *Lyrics of Lowly Life* by Paul Laurence Dunbar. 1896. Reprinted in *Complete Poems.* By Paul Laurence Dunbar. New York: Dodd, Mead, 1931. vii–x.

———. "New York Low Life in Fiction." *New York World.* 26 July 1896: 18.

———. "Our Daily Speech." *Harper's Bazar* 40.10 (Oct. 1906): 930–34.

Hughes, Langston. *The Collected Poems of Langston Hughes.* Ed. Arnold Rampersad. Assoc. ed. David Roessel. New York: Vintage, 1995.

Hutchinson, George. *The Harlem Renaissance in Black and White.* Cambridge, Mass.: Belknap Press of Harvard University Press, 1995.

Irving, Washington. *History, Tales and Sketches.* New York: Library of America, 1983.

Isman, Felix. *Weber and Fields: Their Tribulations, Triumphs and Their Associations.* New York: Boni & Liveright, 1924.

Ives, Sumner. "A Theory of Literary Dialect." *Tulane Studies in English* 2 (1950): 137–82.

Jakobson, Roman. "Two Aspects of Language and Two Types of Aphasic Disturbances." *Language and Literature.* Ed. K. Pomorska and S. Rudy. Cambridge, Mass.: Harvard University Press, 1987. 95–114.

James, Henry. *The American Scene.* 1907. *Collected Travel Writings: Great Britain and America.* New York: Library of America, 1993. 351–736.

———. *The Awkward Age.* 1899. Oxford: Oxford University Press, 1984.

———. *The Bostonians.* 1886. Oxford: Oxford University Press, 1990.

———. *The Complete Notebooks.* Eds. Leon Edel and Lyall H. Powers. Oxford: Oxford University Press, 1987.

———. *The Europeans.* 1878. Oxford: Oxford University Press, 1992.

———. "The Novel of Dialect." *Literature* 3 (1898): 17–18.

———. *The Portrait of a Lady.* 1881. Harmondsworth, England: Penguin, 1984.

———. Preface to "Daisy Miller [et al.]" *Literary Criticism.* By Henry James. New York: Library of America, 1984. 1269–86.

———. *The Princess Casamassima.* 1886. Harmondsworth, England: Penguin, 1987.

———. *The Question of Our Speech.* Boston: Houghton, Mifflin, 1905.

———. "The Speech of American Women." 4 Parts. *Harper's Bazar* 40 (1906): 980–82, 1103–6; 41 (1907): 17–21, 113–17.

———. *The Tragic Muse.* 1890. Harmondsworth, England: Penguin, 1978.

———. *Watch and Ward.* 1871. New York: Grove Press, 1979.

Jamieson, Kathleen Hall. *Eloquence in an Electronic Age: The Transformation of Political Speechmaking.* Oxford: Oxford University Press, 1988.

Jenkins, Henry. *What Made Pistachio Nuts? Early Sound Comedy and the Vaudeville Aesthetic.* New York: Columbia University Press, 1992.

Johnson, Barbara. "Melville's Fist: The Execution of *Billy Budd.*" *The Critical Difference: Essays in the Contemporary Rhetoric of Reading.* Baltimore: Johns Hopkins University Press, 1983. 79–109.

Johnson, James Weldon. *Along This Way: The Autobiography of James Weldon Johnson.* New York: Viking Press, 1968.

———, ed. *The Book of American Negro Poetry.* 1922. Revised Edition 1931. New York: Harcourt, Brace & World, 1958.

Jones, Charles Colcock, Jr. *Negro Myths from the Georgia Coast, Told in the Vernacular.* 1888. Columbia, S.C.: The State, 1925.

Jones, Gayl. *Liberating Voices: Oral Tradition in African American Literature.* Harmondsworth, England: Penguin, 1992.

Kaplan, Amy. *The Social Construction of American Realism.* Chicago: University of Chicago Press, 1988.

Katz, Joseph. "The *Maggie* Nobody Knows." *The Merrill Studies in "Maggie" and "George's Mother."* Ed. Stanley Wertheim. Columbus, Ohio: Bell and Howell, 1970. 93–107.

Keeling, John. "Paul Dunbar and the Mask of Dialect." *Southern Literary Journal* 25.2 (Spring 1993): 24–38.

Kramer, Michael P. *Imagining Language in America: From the Revolution to the Civil War*. Princeton, N.J.: Princeton University Press, 1992.

Krapp, George Philip. *The English Language in America*. 2 Vols. New York: The Century, 1925.

———. "The Psychology of Dialect Writing." *The Bookman* [New York] 63 (1926): 522–27.

Krehbiel, Henry Edward. *Afro-American Folksongs: A Study of Racial and National Music*. 1914. New York: Frederick Ungar, 1975.

Ladd, Barbara. "'An Atmosphere of Hints and Allusions': Bras-Coupé and the Context of Black Insurrection in *The Grandissimes*." *The Southern Quarterly* 29.3 (Spring 1991): 63–76.

Lakoff, Robin Tolmach. "Some of my Favorite Writers are Literate: The Mingling of Oral and Literate Strategies in Written Communication." *Spoken and Written Language: Exploring Orality and Literacy*. Ed. Deborah Tannen. Norwood, N.J.: Ablex, 1982. 239–60.

Landon, Melville D. *Wise, Witty, Eloquent Kings of the Platform and Pulpit*. Chicago: F. C. Smedley, 1890.

Lears, T. J. Jackson. *No Place of Grace: Antimodernism and the Transformation of American Culture, 1880–1920*. Chicago: University of Chicago Press, 1994.

Leland, Charles G. *Hans Breitmann's Ballads*. Philadelphia: T. B. Peterson & Bros., 1884.

———. *Pidgin-English Sing-Song, or Songs and Stories in the China-English Dialect*. London: Trübner, 1887.

Levine, Lawrence W. *Black Culture and Black Consciousness: Afro-American Folk Thought from Freedom to Slavery*. New York: Oxford University Press, 1977.

Liddell, Mark H. "English Literature and the Vernacular." *Atlantic Monthly* 81 (1898): 614–22.

Light, Kathleen. "Uncle Remus and the Folklorists." *Critical Essays on Joel Chandler Harris*. Ed. R. Bruce Bickley. Boston: G. K. Hall, 1981. 146–57.

Lippi-Green, Rosina. *English with an Accent: Language, ideology, and discrimination in the United States*. London: Routledge, 1997.

Longstreet, Augustus Baldwin. *Georgia Scenes, Characters, Incidents, &c., in the First Half of the Republic*. New York: Harper & Bros., 1851.

Looby, Christopher. *Voicing America: Language, Literary Form, and the Origins of the United States*. Chicago: University of Chicago Press, 1996.

Lott, Eric. *Love and Theft: Blackface Minstrelsy and the American Working Class*. Oxford: Oxford University Press, 1993.

Lounsbury, Thomas R. "The English Language in America." 2 Parts. *The International Review* 8 (1880): 472–82, 596–608.

———. *English Spelling and Spelling Reform*. New York: Harper & Bros., 1909.

———. *The Standard of Usage in English*. New York: Harper & Bros., 1908.

Lowe, John. "Theories of Ethnic Humor: How to Enter, Laughing." *American Quarterly* 38.3 (1986): 439–60.

Lowell, James Russell. *The Biglow Papers*. *The Writings of James Russell Lowell in Ten Volumes. Poems II*. Vol. 8. Boston: Houghton, Mifflin, 1890.

———. "Democracy." 1884. *Democracy and Other Addresses*. Boston: Houghton, Mifflin, 1887. 3–42.

Lubove, Roy. *The Progressives and the Slums: Tenement House Reform in New York City, 1890–1917*. Pittsburgh: University of Pittsburgh Press, 1962.

Lutz, Tom. *American Nervousness, 1903: An Anecdotal History*. Ithaca: Cornell University Press, 1991.

Lynn, Kenneth. *Mark Twain and Southwestern Humor*. Boston: Little, Brown, 1959.

Mahl, George F. "Everyday Speech Disturbances in *Tom Sawyer*." *Explorations in Nonverbal and Vocal Behavior*. Hillsdale, N.J.: Lawrence Erlbaum, 1987. 286–309.

March, Francis A. *Professor March's Address Before the International Convention for the Amendment of English Orthography, Philadelphia, August 15, 1876*. New York: n.p., n.d.

Marsh, George Perkins. *Lectures on the English Language*. New York: Charles Scribner, 1860.

Marx, Leo. "The Vernacular Tradition in American Literature." *Studies in American Culture: Dominant Ideas and Images*. Eds. Joseph J. Kwiat and Mary C. Turpie. Minneapolis: University of Minnesota Press, 1960. 109–22.

Mathews, M. M., ed. *The Beginnings of American English: Essays and Comments*. Chicago: University of Chicago Press, 1931.

Mathews, William. *Words; Their Use and Abuse*. 1876. Chicago: S. C. Griggs, 1882.

Matthews, Brander. *Parts of Speech: Essays on English*. 1901. Freeport, Maine: Books for Libraries Press, 1968.

Maurice, Arthur Bartlett. "New York in Fiction." Part 1. *The Bookman* 10 (1899–1900): 33–49.

Mawson, Harry P. "A Hot Wave among the Poor." *Harper's Weekly* 36 (1892): 814.

McDavid, Raven I., Jr., and McDavid, Virginia Glenn. "The Relationship of the Speech of American Negroes to the Speech of Whites." *American Speech* 26 (1951): 3–17.

McKay, Janet. *Narration and Discourse in American Realistic Fiction*. Philadelphia: University of Pennsylvania Press, 1982.

McLean, Albert F. *American Vaudeville as Ritual*. Lexington: University of Kentucky Press, 1965.

Melville, Herman. *Billy Budd, Sailor (An Inside Narrative)*. Eds. Harrison Hayford and Merton M. Sealts. Chicago: University of Chicago Press, 1962.

Mencken, H. L. *The American Language: An Inquiry into the Development of English in the United States*. The Fourth Edition and the Two Supplements, abridged, with annotations and new material, by Raven I. McDavid, Jr. New York: Alfred A. Knopf, 1989.

Mercier, Alfred. *Étude sur la langue créole en Louisiane*. New Orleans: n.p., 1880.

Mitchell, Lee Clark. "Verbally *Roughing It*: The West of Words." *Nineteenth-Century Literature* 44 (1989): 67–92.

Montgomery, Michael. "Africanisms in the American South." *Africanisms in Afro-American Language Varieties*. Ed. Salikoko S. Mufwene. Athens: University of Georgia Press, 1993. 439–57.

Morgan, Marcyliena. "The Africanness of Counterlanguage among Afro-Americans." *Africanisms in Afro-American Language Varieties*. Ed. Salikoko S. Mufwene. Athens: University of Georgia Press, 1993. 423–35.

Mufwene, Salikoko S. Introduction. *Africanisms in Afro-American Language Varieties.* Ed. S. S. Mufwene. Athens: University of Georgia Press, 1993.

Mufwene, Salikoko S., and Gilman, Charles. "How African is Gullah, and why?" *American Speech* 62 (1987): 120–39.

Murfree, Mary Noailles (Charles Egbert Craddock). *In the Tennessee Mountains.* 1884. Boston: Houghton, Mifflin, 1897.

Murphy, Maureen. "Irish-American Theatre." *Ethnic Theatre in the United States.* Ed. Maxine Schwartz Seller. Westport, Conn.: Greenwood Press, 1983. 221–35.

Musser, Charles. "Ethnicity, Role-playing, and American Film Comedy: From *Chinese Laundry Scene* to *Whoopee* (1894–1930)." *Unspeakable Images: Ethnicity and the American Cinema.* Ed. Lester D. Friedman. Urbana: University of Illinois Press, 1991. 39–81.

Nagel, James. *Stephen Crane and Literary Impressionism.* University Park: Pennsylvania State University Press, 1980.

Nettels, Elsa. *Language, Race, and Social Class in Howells's America.* Lexington: University Press of Kentucky, 1988.

Norris, Frank. *Vandover and the Brute.* 1914. Lincoln: University of Nebraska Press, 1978.

North, Michael. *The Dialect of Modernism: Race, Language, and Twentieth-Century Literature.* Oxford: Oxford University Press, 1994.

Nowell-Smith, Simon, ed. *The Legend of the Master.* Oxford: Oxford University Press, 1985.

Nunberg, Geoffrey. "The Official English Movement: Reimagining America." *Language Loyalties: A Source Book on the Official English Controversy.* Ed. James Crawford. Chicago: University of Chicago Press, 1992. 479–94.

———. "Topic . . . Comment: Double Standards." *Natural Language and Linguistic Theory* 15 (1997): 667–75.

Page, Brett. *Writing for Vaudeville.* Springfield, Mass.: Home Correspondence School, 1915.

Page, Norman. *Speech in the English Novel.* London: Longman, 1973.

Park, Robert E. "The Natural History of the Newspaper." *The City.* By R. E. Park et al. Chicago: University of Chicago Press, 1925. 80–98.

Pattee, Fred Lewis. *A History of American Literature Since 1870.* New York: The Century, 1915.

Payne, L. W., Jr. "A Word-List from East Alabama (Excerpts)." 1903. *Perspectives on Black English.* Ed. J. L. Dillard. The Hague: Mouton, 1975. 196–201.

Perry, Theresa, and Delpit, Lisa, eds. *The Real Ebonics Debate: Power, Language, and the Education of African-American Children. Rethinking Schools* 12.1 (Fall 1997).

Phillips, David Graham. "Ward School No. 23." *Harper's Weekly* 36 (1892): 535.

"Philosophy of Slang." Reprinted from *The Saturday Review. The Living Age,* 7th Series, Vol. 5 (Oct.–Nov.–Dec. 1899): 324–26.

Pierce, Frederick E. "The Tenement-House Committee Maps." *Harper's Weekly* 39 (1895): 60–62.

Piersen, William. "Puttin' Down Ole Massa: African Satire in the New World." *African Folklore in the New World.* Ed. Daniel J. Crowley. Austin: University of Texas Press, 1977. 20–34.

Plotkin, Cary H. *The Tenth Muse: Victorian Philology and the Genesis of the Poetic Lan-*

guage of Gerard Manley Hopkins. Carbondale: Southern Illinois University Press, 1989.

Ralph, Julian. "The Language of the Tenement-folk." *Harper's Weekly* 41 (1897): 90.

Reinecke, George. "Alfred Mercier, French Novelist of Louisiana." *In Old New Orleans.* Ed. W. Kenneth Holditch. Jackson: University of Mississippi Press, 1983. 145–76.

Reisman, Karl. "Cultural and Linguistic Ambiguity in a West Indian Village." *Afro-American Anthropology: Contemporary Perspectives.* Ed. Norman E. Whitten, Jr., and John F. Szwed. New York: The Free Press, 1970. 129–44.

Rickels, Milton. *George Washington Harris.* New York: Twayne, 1965.

Rickford, John R. "Suite for Ebony and Phonics." *Discover* (Dec. 1997): 82–87.

Riis, Jacob. *How the Other Half Lives: Studies among the tenements of New York.* 1890. New York: Hill & Wang, 1969.

Riis, Thomas L. *Just before Jazz: Black Musical Theater in New York, 1890–1915.* Washington, D.C.: Smithsonian Institute, 1989.

Riley, James Whitcomb. "Dialect in Literature." *Forum* 14 (1892–93): 465–73.

Rischin, Moses. Introduction. *Grandma Never Lived in America: The New Journalism of Abraham Cahan.* By Abraham Cahan. Bloomington: Indiana University Press, 1985. xvii–xliv.

Roediger, David R. *The Wages of Whiteness: Race and the Making of the American Working Class.* London: Verso, 1991.

Rogers, Robert. *A Psychoanalytic Study of the Double in Literature.* Detroit: Wayne State University Press, 1970.

Rogin, Michael Paul. *Blackface, White Noise: Jewish Immigrants in the Hollywood Melting Pot.* Berkeley: University of California Press, 1996.

———. *Subversive Genealogy: The Politics and Art of Herman Melville.* New York: Alfred A. Knopf, 1983.

Rosenberg, Charles E. "The Place of George M. Beard in Nineteenth-Century Psychiatry." *Bulletin of the History of Medicine* 36 (1962): 245–59.

Rouquette, Adrien Emmanuel. *Critical Dialogue Between Aboo and Caboo on a New Book, or a Grandissime Ascension.* New Orleans: Mingo City, 1880.

Rourke, Constance. *American Humor: A Study of the National Character.* New York: Harcourt, Brace, 1931.

Schele de Vere, Maximilian. *Americanisms: The English of the New World.* New York: Charles Scribner, 1872.

Schmitz, Neil. "Tall Tale, Tall Talk: Pursuing the Lie in Jacksonian Literature." *On Humor: The Best from "American Literature."* Eds. Louis J. Budd and Edwin H. Cady. Durham, N.C.: Duke University Press, 1992. 190–210.

Sewell, David R. *Mark Twain's Languages: Discourse, Dialogue, and Linguistic Variety.* Berkeley: University of California Press, 1987.

Sheldon, E. S. "Practical Philology." *PMLA* 17 (1902): 91–104.

———. "What is a Dialect?" *Dialect Notes* 1 (1896): 286–97.

Shell, Marc. "Babel in America; or, The Politics of Language Diversity in the United States." *Critical Inquiry* 20.1 (Autumn 1993): 103–27.

Sherman, Ellen Burns. "A Study in Current Slanguage." *The Critic,* n.s. 28 (1897): 153.

Showalter, Elaine. *The Female Malady: Women, Madness, and English Culture, 1830–1980.* New York: Pantheon, 1985.

Shuy, Roger. "'Ohio English': A Modest But More Specific and Patriotic Proposal Than the One Offered Recently by U.S. English." *Language Loyalties: A Source Book on the Official English Controversy.* Ed. James Crawford. Chicago: University of Chicago Press, 1992. 129–31.

Simon, Myron. "Dunbar and Dialect Poetry." *A Singer in the Dawn: Reinterpretations of Paul Laurence Dunbar.* Ed. Jay Martin. New York: Dodd, Mead, 1975. 114–34.

Simpson, Claude M. Introduction. *The Local Colorists: American Short Stories, 1857–1900.* Ed. Claude M. Simpson. New York: Harper & Bros., 1960. 1–20.

Simpson, David. *The Politics of American English, 1776–1850.* Oxford: Oxford University Press, 1986.

Slobin, Mark. *Tenement Songs: The Popular Music of the Jewish Immigrants.* Urbana: University of Illinois Press, 1982.

Smitherman, Geneva. *Talkin and Testifyin: The Language of Black America.* Detroit: Wayne State University Press, 1986.

Snyder, Robert W. *The Voice of the City: Vaudeville and Popular Culture in New York.* New York: Oxford University Press, 1989.

Sollors, Werner. *Beyond Ethnicity: Consent and Descent in American Culture.* Oxford: Oxford University Press, 1986.

Stallman, Robert Wooster. "Crane's *Maggie* in Review." *The Merrill Studies in "Maggie" and "George's Mother."* Ed. Stanley Wertheim. Columbus, Ohio: Bell and Howell, 1970. 14–26.

Sundquist, Eric J. "Realism and Regionalism." *Columbia Literary History of the United States.* Ed. Emory Elliott. New York: Columbia University Press, 1988. 501–24.

———. *To Wake the Nations: Race in the Making of American Literature.* Cambridge, Mass.: Belknap Press of Harvard University Press, 1993.

Swinton, William. "English in America." *Rambles Among Words: Their Poetry, History and Wisdom.* New York: Charles Scribner, 1859. 286–91.

Szwed, John F. "Race and the Embodiment of Culture." *Ethnicity* 2 (1975): 19–33.

Talmage, Thomas De Witt. *The Abominations of Modern Society.* New York: Adams, Victor, 1872.

Tanner, Tony. *Scenes of Nature, Signs of Men.* Cambridge: Cambridge University Press, 1987.

Thomas, J. J. *The Theory and Practice of Creole Grammar.* 1869. London: New Beacon Books, 1969.

Tinker, Edward Larocque. "French Newspapers of Louisiana." *Proceedings of the American Antiquarian Society* 42 (1932): 247–370.

Tocqueville, Alexis de. *Democracy in America.* Trans. George Lawrence. Ed. J. P. Mayer. New York: Harper & Row, 1988.

Todorov, Tzvetan. "The Verbal Age." Trans. Patricia Martin Gibby. *Critical Inquiry* 4 (1977): 351–71.

Toll, Robert C. *Blacking Up: The Minstrel Show in Nineteenth-Century America.* New York: Oxford University Press, 1974.

Townsend, Edward W. *"Chimmie Fadden," Major Max, and Other Stories.* New York: Lovell, Coryell, 1895.

Trachtenberg, Alan, ed. *Democratic Vistas, 1860–1880*. New York: George Braziller, 1970.

———. "Experiments in Another Country: Stephen Crane's City Sketches." *Modern Critical Views: Stephen Crane*. Ed. Harold Bloom. New York: Chelsea House, 1987. 65–79.

———. *The Incorporation of America: Culture and Society in the Gilded Age*. New York: Hill & Wang, 1982.

Tregle, Joseph G., Jr. "Creoles and Americans." *Creole New Orleans: Race and Americanization*. Eds. Arnold R. Hirsh and Joseph Logsdon. Baton Rouge: Louisiana State University Press, 1992. 131–85.

Turner, Arlin, ed. *Critical Essays on George W. Cable*. Boston: G. K. Hall, 1980.

———. *George W. Cable: A Biography*. Durham: Duke University Press, 1956.

Turner, Lorenzo D. *Africanisms in the Gullah Dialect*. 1949. New York: Arno Press, 1969.

Twain, Mark (Samuel L. Clemens). *Adventures of Huckleberry Finn*. 1884. Eds. Walter Blair and Victor Fischer. Berkeley: University of California Press, 1988.

———. "Concerning the American Language." *The Stolen White Elephant*. New York: Charles L. Webster, 1888. 265–69.

———. *Roughing It*. 1872. Eds. Harriet Elinor Smith, Edgar Marquess Branch, Lin Salamo, and Robert Pack Browning. Berkeley: University of California Press, 1993.

———. "Simplified Spelling." 1906. *Letters from the Earth*. Ed. Bernard DeVoto. New York: Harper & Row, 1974. 130–34.

"Use and Abuse of Dialect." *The Dial* 18 (1895): 67–69.

Vallins, G. H. *Spelling*. Revised Edition. London: Andre Deutsch, 1973.

Wagner, Jean. *Black Poets of the United States: From Paul Laurence Dunbar to Langston Hughes*. Trans. Kenneth Douglas. Urbana: University of Illinois Press, 1973.

Wauchope, Armstrong. "The Value of Dialect." *North American Review* 158 (1894): 640

Wertheim, Stanley, ed. *The Merrill Studies in "Maggie" and "George's Mother."* Columbus, Ohio: Bell and Howell, 1970.

White, Allon. *The Uses of Obscurity: The Fiction of Early Modernism*. London: Routledge & Kegan Paul, 1981.

White, Richard Grant. *Every-Day English*. Boston: Houghton, Mifflin, 1880.

———. "Heterophemy: The World's Blunder." *The Galaxy* 20 (1875): 691–99.

———. *Words and Their Uses*. New York: Sheldon, 1870.

Whitman, Walt. "An American Primer." Ed. Horace Traubel. *Atlantic Monthly* 93 (1904): 460–70.

Whitney, William Dwight. "Darwinism and Language." *North American Review* 119 (1874): 61–88.

———. "The Evolution of Language." *North American Review* 97 (1863): 411–50.

———. *Language and the Study of Language: Twelve Lectures on the Principles of Linguistic Science*. New York: Charles Scribner, 1867.

———. "Languages and Dialects." *North American Review* 104 (1867): 30–64.

———. *The Life and Growth of Language: An Outline of Linguistic Science*. 1875. New York: Dover, 1979.

————. Review of *Words and Their Uses* by Richard Grant White. *North American Review* 112 (1871): 469–76.

Wideman, John Edgar. "Frame and Dialect: The Evolution of the Black Voice in American Literature." *American Poetry Review* (Sept.–Oct. 1976): 34–37.

Wiggins, Lida Keck. *Life and Works of Paul Laurence Dunbar.* New York: Dodd, Mead, 1907.

Wischnewetzky, Florence Kelley. "A Decade of Retrogression." *Arena* 4 (1891): 365–72.

Wittke, Carl. "The Immigrant Theme on the American Stage." *Mississippi Valley Historical Review* 39.2 (Sept. 1952): 211–32.

Yeazell, Ruth Bernard. *Language and Knowledge in the Late Novels of Henry James.* Chicago: University of Chicago Press, 1976.

Young, Robert J. C. "The ambivalence of Bhabha." *White Mythologies: Writing History and the West.* Chapter 8. London: Routledge, 1990. 141–56.

————. *Colonial Desire: Hybridity in Theory, Culture and Race.* London: Routledge, 1995.

Ziff, Larzer. *The American 1890s: Life and Times of a Lost Generation.* New York: Viking, 1968.

INDEX

Text: 10/12 Baskerville
Display: Baskerville
Composition: Binghamton Valley Composition
Printing and binding: Maple-Vail